STUDIES IN MODERN JEWISH LITERATURE

Arnold J. Band

דור דור JPS
ודורשיו SCHOLAR
OF DISTINCTION
SERIES

ARNOLD J. BAND

STUDIES IN MODERN JEWISH LITERATURE

THE JEWISH PUBLICATION SOCIETY

Philadelphia   *2003 • 5764*

The Jewish Publication Society
2100 Arch Street, 2nd floor
Philadelphia, PA 19103

Composition by Book Design Studio

Manufactured in the United States of America

03 04 05 06 07 08 09 10   10 9 8 7 6 5 4 3 2 1

Publisher's Note:
With few exceptions, the articles in this anthology are as they appeared in their original. As a result, there are variations in spelling and language style from piece to piece.

Library of Congress Cataloging-in-Publication Data
Band, Arnold J.
  Studies in modern Jewish literature / Arnold J. Band—1st ed.
  p. cm.
  ISBN 0-8276-0762-8
  1. Jewish literature—History and criticism. 2. Hebrew
literature—History and criticism. 3. Rabbinical literature—History
and criticism. 4. Jewish authors. 5. Agnon, Shmuel Yosef,
1888-1970—Criticism and interpretation. 6. Band, Arnold J. 7.
Jews—Identity. I. Title.
  PN6067.B35 2003
  809'.88924—dc22

Publication of this volume
was made possible by generous gifts from
The Joseph H. and Belle R. Braun Chair in Modern Hebrew
Literature at Brandeis University

and

Emanuel and Nancy Abrams
Ashley Family Fund
Dr. Oded Bahat
David, Debbie, Zvi and Gabriel Band
Sylvia and Harold M. Band
Jonathan Band and Leesa Fields, Jeremy and Jessica Band
Rabbi Elliot and Marlynn Dorff
Jacqueline Koch Ellenson and David Ellenson
Helene and Robert Feingold
Rabbi and Mrs. Samuel Fishman
Jean and Dr. Jerry Friedman
Mr. and Mrs. Abner D. Goldstine
Drs. David and Felice Gordis
Dr. and Mrs. Harry L. Green
Sheila and Milton Hyman Foundation
Dr. and Mrs. Robert Kinstlinger
Peachy and Mark Levy
Judith and Morton Margolis
Dan and Ruth Merritt
Carl and Ilana Rappaport
Herman and Lucille Schoen Family Fund
Rabbi Harold M. Schulweis
Dr. Jason and Rabbi Barbara Sachs Speyer
Fran and Arnold Stengel
Edith and Arthur Stern
Barbi and Larry Weinberg
Harold Weinstock
Drs. Irving and Joan White
Joseph H. Zernick, DMD

To Ora
Who Illuminates
My Maps

Contents

Foreword

The twenty-six essays in this volume, *Studies in Modern Jewish Literature*, speak for themselves, each in its particular clarity and each with its own argument. Their author is bold and often unequivocal, so that commentary may not seem necessary. But the appearance of this important Jewish Publication Society collection is a good occasion to cast Arnold Band's work in a broader context than the author would permit of himself. He has always made his arguments on the basis of historical and cultural contexts, and so a bit of context is warranted on his behalf.

Arnold Band is a product of the lush intellectual environment of Boston, with its pre-World War II intensity for immigrants, (Jews as well as others) whose ambitions to become "Americans" and to excel on these shores resulted in remarkable contributions to science, business and letters. Band's essay on an aspect of that world, ("Confluent Myths," the first essay in this volume) was composed originally for a book honoring a beloved friend, Walter Ackerman, who shared in that confluence and who joined with Band in a variety of tough-minded intellectual predispositions. Both David Ellenson and I (in the Band Festschrift, *History and Literature*) have suggested that Band's "Confluent Myths" has emerged as even more telling than its author anticipated. It is a statement about those Boston Jews who were part of a special kind of cerebral ambition and blending of American thinking, a respect for Greek and Latin classics, and a commitment to Judaic-Hebraic studies. The outward reach of Band's intellectual life and the harmonies he sought to establish are suggested in that opening essay, and represent a kind of psycho-sociological echo of the author's wide interests and talent for synthesis. I imagine Arnold Band now saying two contrary things about that essay: *davar vehipukho,* a phrase I might have learned from him ("You can't understand Arnold Band without that essay!"), and "Don't think you can ever understand a person based on a single essay." This is no true contradiction, as one comes to understand that Band's studies of other people's texts are actually texts in themselves, with their own surprises and secrets, and only apparent contradictions. In those articles and essays he demonstrated time and again that opposing worlds meet and find their synthesis through dominant and contending imageries. "Confluent Myths" is now available as a document of informal sociology, and is surely one of the great controlling metaphors of Arnold Band's work.

An additional central metaphor of Band's career has to do with his teaching and the legacy of protégés, as I cited in the Festschrift that over forty of his colleagues and former students devoted to him on the occasion of his seventieth birthday. When the *UCLA Bruin* newspaper honored Band as one of the century's important teachers, he was pictured alongside the legendary UCLA basketball coach, John Wooden, known most for the great athletic heirs he produced—stars who counted Wooden as their mentor generations after having learned from him. Band's legacy has been similarly illustrious, even if there is less celebrity attached to it.

Band's devotion to his students and to other young scholars who have sought his help is certainly legendary. For some of us, his challenges of discipline and his peculiar way of surprising us with details of historical context were a lot to deal with. In another regard, he discouraged young graduate students from beginning with theoretical points of view before learning the text that was being examined. In some ways he fought against instructors in the various doctoral programs as well as many of the dominant theories that captured us, even as he was studying them himself. But I like to think that his wide-ranging expectations and his resistance to fads and ephemeral methods made me a better scholar and teacher. In my case, he was occasionally tolerant—only tolerant—of the "new age" thinking to which I was exposed in the extra-academic aspects of my life. But he was always benevolent about my interests, and I think he may even have learned something from them. I see traces of that benevolence in his work from time to time. In a recent review of a book on the tales of Rabbi Nachman of Bratslav, (the review—of Ora Wiskind-Elper's *Tradition and Fantasy in the Tales of Reb Nahman of Bratslav*—is not included in this collection), Band demonstrated his appreciation for young scholars, his contempt for stylish phrases, and his awareness of critical theory with just the fatherly tone he has been capable of showing to those he trusts (*AJS Review*, 2001). On almost all occasions his interlocking concerns and his persistent pedagogical impulses have become the signature of Arnold Band's remarkable essays: tightly constructed, well researched and provocative. But his argument or the case he was making never got in the way of his basic appreciation for the thoughtful work of younger scholars.

✿   ✿   ✿

I turn my attention now to his major essays that are so well represented by the present volume. We read Arnold Band's essays not only with an awareness of the contemporaneity that they represent, but also with a sense of the history they reflect. His essays usually are surprising examinations of well-known and well-documented materials, which may not have been scrutinized or contextualized adequately. At times they may be surprising because they run against the grain of the reader's expectations, at other times because they aren't afraid to foreground the obvious. Following a narrative principle that he himself has taught his many students, they tell a story whose outcome is often contrary to our expectations. Band has been able to join disparate concerns and universes within the same essay, so that his synthetic interests often foster synthetic competence in his readers. His writing may create better writing in its readers because of an implied dialogue between him and his audience.

Band's career spans the remarkable last half of the twentieth century in American Jewish letters and in the development of modern Hebrew literature. I will concentrate on the Hebrew literary tradition in the paragraphs that follow, for he has tracked that small literature from its function as an affirmation of nationalist aspirations to the point where it has become an important literature of the Western industrial world. Hebrew prose and poetry is more widely translated and read now than even its most messianic enthusiasts could have imagined.

When Arnold Band began teaching modern Hebrew literature, new techniques of criticism and scholarship were being applied to the grand classics of Hebrew letters. Band, along with colleagues like Robert Alter and a handful of other Americans, exposed that tradition to a kind of American intellectual scrutiny. He came on the scene at a turning away from the essays and feuilletons of early Hebrew "critics" and historians of literature like Steinberg and Fichman, Lachower and Kurzweil. The

New Criticism dominated critical thinking during Band's early work in literature, and that fact continued to be vital for Hebrew literary study in the university long after it was the dominant critical hegemony. His work—as an American—added richly to the achievements of the Israeli giants of criticism in his generation: Shaked and Miron. During the early days of his scholarly career, he was continuing to explore works of the founding greats like Bialik and Tschernichowski, Brenner, Berdyczewski, Gnessin and Uri Tsvi Greenberg. By that time the artists of the next generation had already begun to define Hebrew literature in the period before the War of Independence: Avraham Shlonsky, Natan Alterman, Lea Goldberg, and Yocheved Bat Miriam. But as Band began to attract graduate students, Israeli literature was to make yet another new turn, and names appeared suddenly whom we take for granted today: Amichai, Carmi, Pagis and Ravikovitch and their occasional theoretical spokesperson, Natan Zach. Amos Oz and Alef Bet Yehoshua were just appearing. Arnold Band was there to greet these new figures, with his unusual critical intelligence and his timely application of critical method combined with his appreciation of the historical situation that fostered each of them.

His students also "met" these figures. Band required on occasion that his students meet those literary celebrities who came through Los Angeles, and during the 1960s I, as his graduate student, was able to spend time with A. B. Yehoshua, Amalia Kahana Carmon, Amos Oz, Dan Pagis, T. Carmi, Aharon Appelfeld, and Yehuda Amichai. Dissertations written under his guidance broke ground in understanding some of the earliest developments in modern Hebrew literature. Some of the dissertations dealt with the classicists of the early twentieth century, like Brenner, Shoham, Tschernichowski and Bialik; but theses under Band later treated younger luminaries like Pagis and new ideas such as folkloric influence and critical interest in Hasidic literature (which was just coming into fashion).

Looming behind his wide-ranging familiarity with the entire field of Hebrew literature, and to some extent leading the way into Band's neverending curiosity, lay his comprehensive interest in the prose creations of Nobel laureate S. Y. Agnon. Agnon's world-wide recognition in 1967 coincided more or less with the appearance of Band's large study of Agnon. The writing of *Nostalgia and Nightmare* also coincided with the flourishing of Jewish Studies in the American university, and thus Arnold Band became a major figure on two fronts. The editors of this JPS volume have set off an entire section for four essays on the subject of Jewish Studies, and another section for four of Band's essays on the Nobel laureate. Two of those essays on Agnon serve to expose readers to Agnon's literary study and interest, and two of them situate him in relation to seminal figures of the era, Franz Kafka and Sigmund Freud. Those men were both children of complex Jewish provenance and the latter was especially alluring because of his relationship to Buczacz, Agnon's birthplace. Freud figures in other ways in Band's work when, late in the 90s, he delves into Freud's relationship to Judaism. ("Back to Moses: Reflections on Reflections on Freud's Reflections on Jewish History"). Band's interest in Freud is emblematic of his way with things: beginning with Freud's relationship to a parochial localized concern and then writing a second essay that expands outward into a more general treatment of his subject.

∘   ∘   ∘

Band's career and the collection before us reveal a scholar whose training and theoretical interests have taken him into areas far beyond the limited range of modern Hebrew literature. The section on "traditional" texts represents only a hint of his interest in Bible and classic Jewish thought. But always, he has written as a man of aesthetic cultural interest, with a deep background in comparative literature.

Band's active personal involvement and his intellectual interest in the condition of Jewish Studies within the American university is particularly noteworthy. He has, of course, played an important role in the practical aspects of developing the organizations that dominate the general field. His essays in this current volume have aspects of subjectivity about them, since he is one of the people who has created the field he is discussing. Of course a kind of subjectivity exists in all essay writing, if we are to take post-modern criticism seriously, but Band would be skeptical of the deep running establishment of that principle within a literary or philosophical movement. Reading these essays adds to our impression of Arnold Band's broad intellectual preoccupations, but one cannot deduce from his writing the extent to which he effected the practice of Jewish studies in his private way through affiliations and organizational leadership. While he has been bold in his intellectual claims, he has actually preserved a kind of modesty when writing about Jewish Studies as a field. Band, who has consistently disavowed membership in any critical or theoretical movement, draws upon theory in article after article, and demonstrates his ability to create his own ideas from theory—even when he criticizes those who rush too swiftly to use it themselves.

He has carried his influence into the more quotidian realm of public pre-college Hebrew education, and has worked along with his wife, Ora, herself a prominent and imposing educator. Few of our scholars have so self-consciously engaged the community in their day-to-day intellectual lives, although Band would argue (and I would agree) that scholarship and intellectual activity are automatically and fundamentally important to communal and even organizational progress.

I conclude my essay with a "trope" that Band invoked for his consideration of Moses, Ahad HaAm, Freud, and Yosef Hayim Yerushalmi: My short introduction to the JPS volume is a reflection on his reflection on the reflections of some of the great narrators of Jewish life. This reflectiveness, which itself is too stylish for Band's taste, is only possible when one makes knowledge come alive. In the words of David Weiss HaLivni (*Textual Readings*, p. 144): "a text is true to itself only when it is more than itself." That is true of the texts that Arnold Band has studied for us, and it is no less true of the texts he has given us here from his own hand.

William Cutter
Professor of Hebrew Literature and
Steinberg Professor of Human Relations
Hebrew Union College-Jewish Institute of Religion, Los Angeles
August, 2003

BIBLIOGRAPHY

History and Literature: New Readings of Jewish Texts in Honor of Arnold J. Band. Ed. William Cutter and David C. Jacobson, Brown Judaic Studies, Providence, 2002.

Judaism and Education: Essays in Honor of Walter I. Ackerman. Ed. Haim Marantz, Ben-Gurion University of the Negev Press.

Arnold Band, *Nostalgia and Nightmare*, University of California Press, 1968.

Preface

A map is not a place and a book is not a life, but both a map and a book are texts that represent real places or persons. Maps, in fact, have always intrigued me precisely because they strive to encompass in their flatness, lines on a sheet of paper, the richly textured earth and the fullness thereof. Since they invite skilled reading to capture their meaning they have become, for me, the metaphor for the mystery of representation and the challenge of interpretation. Maps, furthermore, invoke the desire for travel, for journeys of discovery.

The maps I read in the essays in this volume are not maps found in an atlas, but rather literary texts, more specifically, Jewish literary texts, largely written in the modern period. Most are the work of a variety of Jewish writers who have something special to say about the condition of being Jewish in the modern world. Since these texts are often complex, reading them cannot be simple. My ambition to arrive at a defensible interpretation of these writings has led me in three directions at the same time. First, because all serious Jewish texts emerge out of centuries of intellectual activity, I had to read bifocally, simultaneously scrutinizing both the text at hand and allusions to previous texts: primarily to the Bible, rabbinic, and hasidic works. In these essays, we find many connections between these modern writers and the Bible (as in the Book of Jonah); Midrash, especially in the writings of Agnon, Bialik, or Berdiczewski; and the hasidic tale. Second, since all the authors I study were deeply involved in the events of their times, I always seek to situate each work within its historical context, thus bringing me into a relentless preoccupation with Jewish history. Third, the intricacies of interpretive problems have generated a keen interest in literary theory, a perspective that is always present, but deliberately hidden within these articles so as not to overwhelm the central focus on the writer and his work.

The essays in this volume cover a wide range of topics and employ a variety of approaches from the essay to the scholarly article, from text analysis to historical discourse. While they are a representative selection of my intellectual preoccupations, they are by no means the totality of my production. Another volume of English essays could be assembled from articles that were not included in this volume, and my many Hebrew essays, often more detailed analyses of Hebrew texts, await collection. With two exceptions, all articles included in this volume are published as they originally appeared, with but minor adjustments for the passage of time.

As I was preparing this preface, word reached me from Jerusalem of the passing of my friend of many years, Walter Ackerman. He shares the stage with me in the first article of this volume, "Confluent Myths," which, as William Cutter suggests in his splendid foreword, is essential for understanding my intellectual world. "Confluent Myths," originally written for a Festschrift in Walter Ackerman's honor, now becomes part of his eulogy.

For a volume of essays representing a life's work, the expression of gratitude is complicated and, to be accurate, would have to be unbearably long. First, there are the institutions of financial support: the Council for Research of the UCLA Academic Senate, the American Council for Learned Societies, the National Endowment for the Humanities, and the Guggenheim Foundation. Special mention, of course should be made of those who have contributed to the publication expenses of this volume. Then there are the many colleagues and students with whom I have carried on a dialogue over the years, on or around the topics of my interest. These dialogues might have been fully stated, merely suggested, or not even articulated, but they provided the stimulus every intellectual needs. Both Ellen Frankel and Janet Liss of the Jewish Publication Society have been exceedingly helpful in preparing this volume—the former for shaping it, the latter for keeping the text clear and consistent. The volume is dedicated to my wife Ora, my navigator of many years, who has seen all these essays grow line by line, draft after draft. In a long voyage with many tacks, she has been a steady and reliable mate.

Arnold J. Band

Acknowledgments

We are grateful to the following publishers for their kind permission to reprint the articles included here.

"Confluent Myths." Reprinted from *Judaism and Education: Essays in Honor of Walter I. Ackerman*, edited by Haim Marantz. (Beer Sheva: Ben-Gurion University, 1998).

"Back to Moses: Reflections on Reflections on Freud's Reflections on Jewish History." Reprinted from *The Jerusalem Review*, Vol. 1, 1997.

"Kafka and the Beilis Trial." Reprinted from *Comparative Literature*, XXXII/2, Spring 1980.

"Kafka: The Margins of Assimilation." Reprinted from *Modern Judaism*, Summer 1988.

"Swallowing Jonah: The Eclipse of Parody." Reprinted from *Prooftexts*, Vol. X. No 2., May 1990.

"The Politics of Scripture: The Hasidic Tale." Reprinted from *Michigan Quarterly Review*, Summer 1983.

"Folklore and Literature." Reprinted from *Studies in Studies in Jewish Folklore*, edited by Frank Talmage. *Association for Jewish Studies*, 1980.

"The New Diasporism and the Old Disapora." Reprinted from *Israel Studies*, I, 1, 1996.

"Adumbrations of the Israeli 'Identity Crisis' in Hebrew Literature of the 1960s." Reprinted from *Israeli and Palestinian Identities in History and Literature*, edited by Kamal Abdel-Malek and David C. Jacobson. (New York: St. Martin's Press, 1999).

"The Impact of Statehood on the Israeli Literary Imagination: Hayyim Hazaz and the Zionist Narrative," Reprinted from *Divergent*

Jewish Cultures: Israel and America, edited by Deborah Dash Moore and S. Ilan Troen (New Haven: Yale University Press, 2001).

"A Jewish Existentialist Hero." Reprinted from *Judaism*, Vol. 10, No. 3, (Summer 1961).

"The Evolving Masks of S. J. Agnon." Reprinted from *Judaism*, Vol. 12, No. 3 (Summer 1964).

"Negotiating Jewish History: The Author, His Code, and his Reader." Reprinted from *Tradition and Trauma: Studies in the Fiction of S. J. Agnon*, edited by David Patterson and Glenda Abramson. (Oxford: Westview Press, 1994).

"Perspectives on Modernity: The Beginnings of Modern Hebrew Literature." Reprinted from *Association for Jewish Studies Review*. Vol. XIII, No. 2 (Summer 1989).

"The Ahad Ha-Am and Berdyczewski Controversy." Reprinted from *At the Crossroads: Essays on Ahad Ha-Am*, edited by Jacques Kornberg. (Edison, N.Y.: State University of New York Press, 1983).

"The Archaeology of Self Deception: A. B. Yehoshua's *Mar Mani*." Reprinted from *Prooftexts* 12 (1992).

"Refractions of the Blood Libel in Modern Literature." Reprinted from *The Uses and Misuses of History*, edited by Michael Signer. (Notre Dame: University of Notre Dame Press, 2001).

"Scholarship as Lamentation: Shalom Spiegel on 'The Binding of Isaac.'" Reprinted from *Jewish Social Studies*, Vol. 5, Nos. 1 and 2 (Fall 1998/Winter 1999).

"Our 'She'ela Nikhbada': Whose Hebrew is It?" Reprinted from *Shofar: An Interdisciplinary Journal of Jewish Studies*, Vol. 9, No. 3/ Spring 1991. (University of Nebraska Press, 1991).

"Jewish Literature in the University." Reprinted from *Judaism*, Vol. 11, No. 4 (Fall 1962).

"Jewish Studies in American Liberal Arts Colleges and Universities." Reprinted from the *American Jewish Yearbook*, Vol. LXVII (Philadelphia, 1966).

"Popular Fiction and the Shaping of Jewish Identity." Reprinted from *Jewish Identity in America*, edited by David M. Gordis and Yoav ben-Horin. (Los Angeles: University of Judaism, 1991).

INTRODUCTION

❧ Confluent Myths: Two Lives

If we have learned anything from a generation of post-modern discourse which it has become so fashionable to dismiss together with all *post-isms*, it is the freedom and sensitivity to analyze the myths or narratives we have grown up on, to trace their constructions, their attenuations, and transformations. We now strive to situate these intimate processes in a set of historical matrices. Were the term not so ugly, I would say that we try to historicize the mythicized. Fundamentally, this is an autobiographical project, tempered and controlled, perhaps, by reference to provable fact, but still fundamentally autobiographical. The first person singular or plural is thus the proper voice since I make no pretense at objective, scientific statement. This voice is certainly the right one to adopt when one sits down to write an essay in honor of a friend and colleague with whom one has shared so many significant experiences over a half century.

What I intend to write is rare for jubilee volumes which normally are an assemblage of disparate articles written in honor of a colleague. What I am writing is a joint intellectual biography of two friends who were educated at the same moment in history at the same institutions. I shall focus on their elementary and secondary schools since these were the most formative; subsequently, they moved into broader historical contexts and each went his own way. Though the following narrative concentrates on the early education of Walter Ackerman and Arnold Band, it is written against the backdrop of one of the most crucial periods in Jewish history, 1935-1950. Focusing on their schooling rather than on the historical background was intentional, since full integration of both education and historical contexts would merit book-length treatment. The world has changed so much since then—after the Shoah, the establishment of

Israel, and the maturation of American Jewry—that it is at times difficult to imagine the world that existed then, only two generations ago and therefore all the more imperative to do so. I hope that this piece may serve as the opening to a deeper understanding of a significant phase of modern Jewish intellectual history, one usually eclipsed by the portentous events of the times. I call this a "joint biography" though it has only one author for both subjects. The second subject, Walter Ackerman, whose voice—for once—will not be heard, will simply have to suffer my analysis in silence. Though we have discussed these issues many times, the responsibility for specific perceptions and formulations is mine.

Walter Ackerman and I grew up in the Jewish part of Dorchester, an inner suburb of Boston, Massachusetts. Today a slum inhabited mostly by African-Americans and recent immigrants to the United States, Dorchester had in our childhood a thriving Jewish community with all the traditional institutions: synagogues, schools, shopping streets with kosher butchers, Jewish bakeries, small grocery stores catering to the tastes of East European Jews. The neighborhood had been built mostly in the last decades of the nineteenth century and was comprised of a range of houses from substantial, but far from palatial, one-family homes, to two comfortable family dwellings, to crowded three-decker tenement-style wood-frame apartment houses deliberately built for working class immigrants. Growing up in Dorchester, you knew hundreds of Jews of all ages and types and developed a true sense of urban community. We all knew, however, that our richer relatives lived elsewhere, mostly on the west side of Boston, in communities such as Brookline and Newton. Though Dorchester and the adjacent, densely Jewish districts of Roxbury and Mattapan constituted a secure, self-assured Jewish world, the dream to earn more money and move to Brookline was ever-present even before World War II. This dream dimmed considerably during our childhood which coincided with the Great Depression of the 1930s with its high unemployment and economic stagnation. While Dorchester was probably similar to dozens of other communities of first and second generation American Jews in the cities of the eastern seaboard, it was different in that it was a part of the City of Boston.

Boston looms large in the map of our biographies since it is one of the more distinctive cities in America. The peculiarity of the city touched our lives even when we were children growing up in one of its less prosperous, declining districts some six miles from the historical center of the city. For it was, even then, a city of stark contrasts. Boston in the 1930s and 1940s, the period of our story, was proud of its colonial and revolutionary past, its famed educational institutions, museums, and hospitals. You could not escape this presence since it was frequently hailed in the schools and in the newspapers. We were told that our city was "the cradle of liberty," and "the hub of the universe." And yet, the city was sinking in a steady economic decline after World War I: it had lost much of its trade to New York and its manufacturing to the south and midwest of the country where labor was cheaper. The Boston skyline, in fact, had changed little between 1910 and 1960 when a period of renewal began thus creating the Boston one visits today.

In our personal lives we were affected more by the mundane Boston of the streets, the tension between its various ethnic groups: the long entrenched white Protestant elite, the *Wasps;* the well organized masses of Irish Catholics who had wrested political, but not financial power from the Wasp establishment by the latter decades of the nineteenth century; the Sicilian laborers and peddlers concentrated in the North End and East Boston; and, of course, our Jews, scattered in many areas, but centered in our parts of Mattapan, Dorchester, and Roxbury. The strains of the economic depression fueled much popular animosity. Antisemitism, inspired by the church and national demagogues like Father Coghlan was a fact of life and occasionally broke out in violence at the peak of World War II.

Ackie and I are both second generation American Jews, the children of immigrant parents who came from Eastern Europe, his after World War I, mine some two decades earlier. My mother actually was brought as a child as early as the mid-1890's, and already knew little Yiddish. We were both educated in roughly the same public schools: the local elementary school, then the Boston Latin School from the seventh through the twelfth grades, and Harvard University for all our academic degrees. Our Jewish education was almost identical: the Beth El Hebrew school, a six year elementary school where classes were held in the afternoon and Sunday mornings; the High School (Prozdor) and College (Bet-Midrash) divisions of the Boston Hebrew Teachers College, then situated in Roxbury, another district of Boston adjacent to Dorchester. We both belonged to a variety of Jewish youth groups at various periods of our childhood: HaShomer HaTzair, HaBonim, Young Judea, even to Young Israel. Until you reached adolescence, you could shift back and forth from one group to another depending upon your friends of the year. We both spent a year in Israel at the Hebrew University after our graduation from the Hebrew Teachers College, I in 1949–1950, he in 1950–1951. In the 1950s we both worked at Camp Yavneh, a Hebrew-speaking camp associated with the Boston Hebrew Teachers College. Ackie was its Head Counselor, then its Director; I was a teacher. The major difference in our backgrounds—apart from obvious family influences—stems from the difference in our ages: three years older than I, Ackie was drafted into the American Army in World War II and saw action in Europe. I was too young for military service at that time.

Significantly, neither of us came from families of any intellectual distinction or economic achievement; there was no impressive cultural traditions in our homes, no financial stability or social position. The public schools we attended, therefore, were crucial in our education and our aspirations to rise above the often fragile economic conditions of our families. Like most first generation immigrants, our parents had brought with them from Europe no great traditions of Jewish learning. For that, the Hebrew schools, though not legally mandatory, were crucial for our knowledge of *Hebrew* and everything that that nebulous, yet significant term implied. The centrality of educational institutions in our lives makes the present essay the logical vehicle to celebrate the career of one who has contributed so much to education as a field of social change, professional enterprise, and research both in America and in Israel.

From childhood through graduate school we were usually involved in two educational systems: the general American public school and, later, a private or public university—in our case, Harvard; the voluntary, supplementary Hebrew school and Hebrew College. While significant numbers of young Jews at that period also attended both school systems in their first years of school experience, relatively few continued with their Jewish education through high school and the numbers at the college level were paltry. Those of us who did continue with this double track were repeatedly told that we were special because we were studying in two schools at the same time, carrying a double burden, to be praised for being part of an elite that transcended the pedestrian life of American Jews in the 1930s and 1940s, and by transcending it, might perhaps save it from itself. We were infused with this elitist myth and should examine it more closely. The description of this myth was always institutional: two schools, but there was little if any further analysis or penetration into what this really implied. Nor did one ever challenge the validity of its claims; we never asked if this was a sensible way to educate children or, if those who dropped out—and they were the majority—really were less worthy as alleged because they had less interest or perseverance. (Perhaps they had more imagination and ambition?) The two schools, furthermore, represented and espoused two radically different cultures. The public school represented American culture as understood between the wars: roughly speaking, it was still Jeffersonian in its privileging the individual over the society, though I doubt if anyone in the school administration would articulate this distinction. In its secondary level, in the Boston Latin School we attended, it aspired to emulate the English *public school*. The Hebrew schools were shaped by an ideology generated by the needs of Polish or Lithuanian Jewry after World War I. Among other matters, it privileged the society over the individual. Each culture had its set of myths. At times these myths clashed, but in our childhood we hardly perceived these tensions, probably because we were, in effect, the product of these very tensions. For us they were simply facts of life, a confluence of myths that we rarely questioned.

Obviously, the two schools were different: one, the public school attended in the morning and early afternoon, the other, the *Hebrew School*, (never the *Jewish* or the *religious school*) in the late afternoon or early evening. Most pronounced, in addition to the difference in institution and place, there was a difference in language. The English schooling reflected the general culture in which we lived; the Hebrew schooling reflected the aspirations of our parents, on the one hand, and our teachers, on the other. Our parents had some general notion that Jewish children should know something about the tradition of their ancestors, some *ivri* which meant the ability to follow synagogue services, some knowledge of books Jews are supposed to study, primarily the Chumash, and some ability to participate in holiday celebration, especially the Passover Seder.

Our teachers, often the products of the Tarbut schools in Poland, had a different, clearly articulated agenda. While not really rejecting the desires of our parents, they saw themselves as agents in the Jewish national cultural revival associated with Zionism which most of our parents might have supported as something vaguely good for the Jews, but not an ideal to be discussed or cultivated seriously. In childhood, we were not instilled with any desires for halutziut, or settling in Palestine in any other capacity, though we knew that such an ideal existed. For most of our parents, the prime concern in the period of our childhood was more mundane, though no less noble: they had to support their families in difficult times and steer their children in the direction of a better living than the one they themselves enjoyed. Here there was an existential conflict: the path to that better living led through the general, English school, not the Hebrew school. We lived simultaneously in two different, though at times merging worlds, one oriented towards English, the other towards Hebrew.

Behind or beyond that difference was some vague sort of cultural difference: the morning was Gentile, Christian, the evening, Jewish; the morning a bit foreign, formal, a segment of the public culture; the evening familiar, nurturing, closer to home. The morning was official, legal, mandatory; the evening, somewhat voluntary—at least on the part of the parents who would usually follow social norms and keep their male children in Hebrew school at least until Bar Mitzvah, unless other, more compelling pressures intervened: a recalcitrant child, or competing interests like sports or piano lessons. You could not drop out of the morning school without severe penalty, whereas dropping out of the evening school was the norm. Many began; few finished. Two schools, separate, and clearly unequal, each with its own inherent mythic system.

The public school years through high school graduation were clearly divided into two parts: there was the general neighborhood elementary school which took you from the kindergarten through the sixth grade, and after that, from the seventh through the twelfth, the Boston Latin School, situated in the Back Bay district, about a forty-five minute ride by public transportation from our neighborhood. Though we did not live far apart, Ackie lived in one elementary school district and I, in another. There was little difference, however, between the quality or ambience of these elementary schools. In describing first my elementary school and then the Hebrew School, we can provide a picture of the institutional education I shared with Ackie.

My elementary school, named after one long forgotten Sarah Greenwood, was an imposing—to a child—three story brick structure surrounded by much more modest two story frame residential dwellings sheathed in painted overlapping shingles or boards. The brick school with its brick schoolyard imparted a sense of solidity and authority: this was the local embodiment of the government, an integral part of our community, respected but not feared. Though the neighborhood was far from wealthy and a few houses were not well cared for, probably because of the financial straits of their owners, the school was not defaced by graffiti, broken windows, or piles of trash. That building and the Hebrew School building several blocks away were, in fact, in fine condition in our childhood. Both rose above the neighborhood and though several blocks apart, they actually faced the same major street, Glenway Street. The world of my childhood was circumscribed by an ellipse focusing upon these two buildings which represented permanence, community, home.

Today, that neighborhood is a black ghetto resembling other similar depressed neighborhoods in American cities and none of us ever revisit it. In this sense the physical neighborhood of our childhood has been destroyed: quite literally, we "cannot go home again," and the loss of our childhood neighborhoods, however humble they may have been, is unsettling.

The student population of the school was almost entirely Jewish, as was the neighborhood while the teachers were almost all Irish Catholic spinsters (married women were not hired to teach in Boston elementary schools in those days). The administrators were naturally men, again Irish Catholics. It is hard to imagine that there was no subtle dissonance between these two groups, the Jewish children and their Irish Catholic teachers, but as a child I was not aware of it. The Jews, for instance, were absent during the High Holy Days, the first and last days of Succoth and Pesah, and the absence was allowed upon a presentation of a note from one's parents. The rooms, on the other hand, were decorated in December for the Christmas season as a matter of course, and though the cross and Christ were not prominent features, the presence of these decorations signaled some degree of foreignness to the world of our homes.

The school, like most urban public schools, taught us the basics: reading, writing, and arithmetic, and trained us to the discipline of school-life. Much time was devoted to phonics, to learning to write cursively by the Palmer Method, to multiplication tables, and spelling lists. In retrospect I would imagine that the school was well-run, certainly orderly and disciplined, the classes not too crowded, and the teachers probably all had credentials. (Steady employment in the public school system was treasured in those days of high unemployment and economic instability.) Even at the primary level, some vague sense of American patriotism was inculcated by the stories of the Pilgrim Fathers, Plymouth Rock, the heroism of Paul Revere, and the Battle of Concord and Lexington. These were the foundational myths of the primary schools and it was obviously assumed that these myths were relevant to these children of immigrants who were to be worthy successors of these brave founding fathers. In a fifth grade Civics class we learned the rudiments of democratic government institutions: the courts, city administrations, the states and their capitals, the Federal government and its branches. No specific political ideology was imparted; we were taught to be law-abiding, to give elderly people our seats on the street car, but little more than that. The American dream was presented in its pristine form since there was no reference to the severe economic problems besetting the country which had raised many doubts in intellectual circles about the viability of American liberal democracy. Nor was there any mention of contemporary foreign wars, of Ethiopia, of Nanking, of the rise of fascism, of Hitler. Perhaps it was felt that we were too young to handle these issues, or that they did not belong in a public school whose purpose was to take the children of mostly first generation Americans and prepare them for life in an open society.

The elementary Hebrew School or *Talmud Torah* was also a six year institution, but you entered it at about the age of seven, roughly two or three years after your initiation into public school education. Supplemental, and voluntary, it had to be relegated to the late afternoon or early evening hours, four to six or six to eight, Monday through Thursday, and two hours on Sunday morning, for an average total of ten class hours. In addition, there were *Saturday services* which one had to attend, where one learned to participate in the traditional prayers. The teachers were not pious Jews and probably regarded the Saturday services not as acts of worship, but as part of the cultural repertoire of a properly trained Jewish child.

In most cases, the Hebrew School was a natural source of resentment: after all, one had to go there after a long day at public school and be deprived of play time; and though our parents earnestly wanted their children to have a Jewish education, it was inevitable that the basic preparation for life in America would take priority in their desires, articulated or not. Given this unavoidable handicap, it is remarkable that these Hebrew Schools accomplished what they did. For if you did persist through the six year course of studies—skipping perhaps a grade here or there—you were graduated with a fair knowledge of Hebrew, still pronounced in the Ashkenazic dialect (really an amalgam of Ashkenazic vocalic pronunciation with an ultimate accent), much of the Pentateuch, and the Early Prophetic Books, and a familiarity with the Jewish holiday cycle. It was the only formal type of traditional Jewish training available in Boston in those days since there were no Jewish Day-Schools in our childhood.

Though the school was supported by private donations and the meager tuition our parents were asked to pay, the Beth El Hebrew School was in an impressive building, looming above the neighborhood, and had an entire floor of real classrooms with all the required equipment. The staff had both men and women, both American and European born teachers. At that time we thought these teachers were ancient; in retrospect they were probably in their thirties or forties. Those born and trained in Europe set the tone of the school. Born in Eastern Europe in the first decade of the century, they had been taught in the newly founded Tarbut schools after World War I and brought with them their idealism and their myths which we did not appreciate then. None of them was a pious, religious Jew, but we did not know this since they spoke English with a Yiddish accent which we associated with the *Old Country* and its folkways. They did, however, exude a fierce love for the Hebrew language the logical expression of the Jewish national revival, of Zionism. While Zionism as such was not discussed—we were, after all, children—we were exposed to all the appurtenances of a Zionist education: the map of Eretz Yisrael on the wall, the picture of Herzl, the Jewish National Fund tree with the stamps we pasted on it, the songs, stories of Trumpeldor and Tel Hai, of Bar Kokhba and Rabbi Akiva, occasional crude movies of halutzim making the desert bloom. We were also told of Hitler and antisemitism in Europe. In many ways, our Jewish education, however attenuated, paralleled that of school children in Tel Aviv. Ironically, the Hebrew School was much more in touch with current events and realities than was the elementary public school down the street.

One of the more memorable, emblematic figures of our childhood was, indeed, one of our European born Hebrew teachers, Mrs. Rivkah Babin, the subject of numerous stories and the source of enduring anxiety. Stocky and of middle height, she dominated a classroom with an extraordinary, raw energy. Though not a religious woman, she trained her pupils with devotion and zeal to master the Holy Tongue and the texts written in it. There were no compromises in her attitude: if you learned the Chumash lesson to perfection, you were treated fairly well, with an occasional smile and restrained praise; if not, you earned a hail of prophetic invective which you never forgot. A superb drill master for the gifted and motivated students, she left behind her the many casualties of her wrath. Her cutting sarcasm was classic, remembered for generations by the survivors of her instruction. Her impact, when tolerable, was profound, because you sensed that she was really a true believer in the sacred, though secular, role of Hebrew in the revival or survival of the Jewish people. Her passion for Hebrew was palpable. In that sense, she represented the best in the Hebrew culture of European Jewry that the school was supposed to impart to us.

Since we started our public elementary school a year or two before our Hebrew elementary school, we finished the first at about the age of eleven and the second some two years later. In both cases, the completion of the course of studies signaled a decided break since at that point we had to leave our familiar, sheltered neighborhood for further schooling and this involved traveling, often by public transportation, to a different area and a different world, a radical jump in maturity and responsibility. The secondary school we entered in the seventh grade, the renowned Boston Latin School, was in the then elegant Back Bay area of the city. In the map of our parents dreams, the royal road to success in America led from Dorchester through the Latin School to a good university, hopefully Harvard, and out to the land of the Wizard of Oz which beckoned at the end of the rainbow. For us, it was street cars, buses, and subways. While our daily trip there took less than an hour, it was a voyage to a new continent, alluring and forbidding at the same time. Situated among some of the major cultural institutions of the city— the Boston Museum of Fine Arts, the Harvard Medical School, the Gardner Museum, the Beth Israel Hospital—the Latin School prided itself in its long history (founded in 1635) and in its concentration of gifted, eager students selected from the entire city of Boston. The trip from our Jewish Dorchester to the Back Bay with its aura of Waspish culture always evoked a buzz of emotions. Carrying our green cloth book bags and our brown paper (kosher) lunch bags, we shuttled back and forth daily for six years between these two worlds. Even the superficial differences were striking. While our elementary school was almost entirely Jewish, the Boston Latin school was only about 40 per cent Jewish in those days. And since there was a Boys Latin School and a Girls Latin School nearby, one never studied with persons of the opposite sex until one left the Boston School System for college. It was a totally masculine world, by no means monkish, but utterly unlike anything we experienced at home. It was, on the contrary, anything but home, designed to take you out of your immigrant home into a wider, often hostile world of opportunity. Far beyond the experience of your parents, it was attractive, yet quintessentially "goyish."

The High School Department of the Boston Hebrew Teachers College, called the Prozdor, was significantly closer to home, still in the predominantly Jewish residential district of Roxbury. Today, like our Dorchester, it is a black slum. The Prozdor, too, attracted a select group of students, both boys and girls, from the entire Greater Boston area, but its selectivity was different from that of the Latin School. Entrance to the latter was by high scholastic achievement and the recommendation of the elementary school staff. Probably following the example of the Latin School, the Prozdor also insisted upon entrance examinations, but the possibility of failing the examinations was slight since those who took the examination were the relatively few students who had survived the six years of their local Hebrew elementary school and whose parents were still eager to have them continue their Jewish education past the graduation from elementary school or, in the case of boys, their Bar Mitzvahs. Here, too, since attendance at the Jewish school was not mandated by law but by parental desire or nascent student interest, and one attended classes there in the late afternoon or early evening hours, the disparity between the public and Jewish school begun in the elementary years was maintained and reinforced in the secondary years of schooling. Again, two schools, two myths, separate but unequal.

Much has been written about the Boston Latin School since it has been the secondary school of generations of talented young men who later went on to prestige universities and professional careers. Most accounts are uncritically hagiographical and nostalgic. The curriculum, fashioned after that of the better New England private college preparatory schools which, in turn, emulated the English public schools, was designed to prepare young men for elitist careers in professions and business. Since most of the teaching staff was Irish, there was, in retrospect, a certain irony in having these men train us in the model of the elite schools of England which they were all brought up to detest for its colonialist suppression of their ancestors. If you entered the school in the seventh grade—you could also enter in the ninth grade—you had six years of Latin, English and History, five years of mathematics, four of French, three of German or Greek, and an assortment of subjects of lesser prominence. The demands and the attrition rate were high, but those who finished—probably less than of a third of those who entered— were well prepared to excel in the College Entrance Examinations and be accepted to the better universities. Precisely because those six years were so trying, those who survived the rigors of the academic curriculum readily accepted its self-styled myth. Criticism of the institution is rarely sounded.

And yet, the Boston Latin School fell, in reality, far from its purported ideals. While it was impossible to graduate without an immense store of knowledge and a well exercised discipline of study, and we were occasionally exposed to inspired *masters*, some with Harvard educations, even Ph.D.s, the goal of turning out cultured gentlemen had died at least a generation before our days there. The population of the school was primarily the children of middle to lower class immigrants: Irish, Jews,

Italians, Slavs. The children of the Protestant aristocracy were sent to study at such private schools as Andover, Exeter, and Groton and only the penurious among them would be found in the Boston Latin School. For most of us, the school was not a preparatory academy for a life of high culture, or even the training field for leadership, but rather a vaguely chartered road to the university, and, more important, out of the immigrant neighborhoods from which we came, for us from Dorchester and Roxbury. Yes, we studied Shakespeare and Virgil, but the real goal was high grades and the ticket to a better life than the one enjoyed by our parents. Later romanticizations of the school miss this point, as do subsequent studies of the disintegration of our Jewish neighborhoods in the 1960s. The goal was to succeed, to move out to better neighborhoods. This was the subtext of the master narrative of your childhood.

As students we were not that aware of the enormous cognitive gap between the avowed aspirations and ideals of the school and the real needs and ambitions of its students. We were impressed, to be sure, by the august names of alumni emblazoned on the frieze of the spacious auditorium with its New England Congregationalist aura: the Mathers, Emerson, Santayana, etc. Many of our textbooks had been written by Oxford dons or Harvard professors. In retrospect, however, the curriculum of the school was challenging, not because of its imaginative sweep or intellectual vision but rather the amount of work assigned nightly and the talents and aspirations of our peers, the other children of immigrant parents.

The curriculum, in fact, had not been changed much since the turn of the century. While one might expect the Latin or Greek curricula to be similar to what they were in the beginning of the nineteenth century, one would expect the English curriculum to recognize some English literature after Dickens and George Eliot, or American literature other than Emerson and Longfellow. The same was true for French and German literatures which barely recognized the twentieth century. We studied Ancient History, English History, some European History, but even the courses in American History rarely reached World War I even while we were being told to "Remember Pearl Harbor" and were instructed in self-protection during potential German air raids. The mathematics curriculum was classical, traditional and the sciences were barely taught, at most a year of physics or a year of chemistry, and no biology. One would never know that we were living through the great period of High Modernism in art or the dynamic advances in modern physics. The classes stressed more rote memory than intriguing problem solving. I recall one instructor who prepared us for the reading of each Shakespearean play, not by a presentation of the play's moral issues, but rather by assigning the footnotes in the Kittredge edition for memory each night for a week: five acts, five nightly assignments. Given the superb, motivated student body, so much more could have been done, but neither we nor our parents could conceive that our *masters* (for so we called our teachers) were far behind the times. The myth of the Latin School was so overwhelming that our parents did not know what there was to criticize, how to criticize, or even that criticism was conceivable. The Latin School was, in a sense, foreign territory. I can't imagine that our parents knew or cared much about Macbeth, or Cicero's "Catalinian Orations," or quadratic equations, but they clearly understood that good grades paved the way towards a higher standard of living.

If the Latin School was foreign territory, the Boston Hebrew Teachers College was familiar country, not exactly home, but perhaps a surrogate home. The Dean of the College, Louis Hurwich, instilled a familial atmosphere and constantly fretted about the physical welfare of his students. The social situation was crucial, for you spent several hours five days a week for six to eight years with a relatively small group of Jewish friends, more or less of similar backgrounds to yours. You often spent more time with them than with your own family and your relationships with them were far less troubled than that with your siblings or your parents as you progressed through adolescence. Since the school was small and electives few, you studied with the same group of friends in all your classes, ten or twelve hours each week. If the tenor of the Latin School was determined by the students' need to prepare for the American marketplace, the goals of the Hebrew College were mediated through this social nexus.

The goals of the institution were very clear. In the Prozdor years, your Hebrew was improved by reading stories; your knowledge of traditional Jewish texts, Bible and Talmud, greatly enriched. In the Bet Midrash, the Teachers' College, you were ostensibly trained to become a Hebrew teacher in one of the many Hebrew Schools in the Greater Boston area. While the Hebrew College did, indeed, provide teachers for the Hebrew Schools for several decades, the teacher-training function of the school was secondary to the dissemination of the ideals and achievements of modern Hebrew culture. As such, the Hebrew College was a logical continuation of the Hebrew elementary schools and was staffed by instructors who had the same post-World War I East European training and ideology as our earlier teachers, though at a much more advanced degree. The ideology was secular, Ahad HaAmic: the Hebrew College, like other institutions of its type in America, Europe, and the Yishuv, were designed to be bastions of cultural or spiritual Zionism. Since Bible, Talmud, and modern Hebrew literature were all expressions of the national culture, and were in Hebrew (or Aramaic), they were all integrated into the curriculum. Hebrew was naturally the language of instruction. Identifying with the norms of the Yishuv, our Hebrew pronunciation was converted from what we called Ashkenazic, to the Sephardic which attempted to escape the European, Ashkenazic tones and accents. Yiddish, of course, was never studied or used; Yiddish literature, such as Shalom Aleichem or Peretz, was read only in Hebrew translation. Most of our parents, of course, were native Yiddish speakers, but it was never apparent to us that there was a contradiction or, even more, an ideological tension between the language world of our Hebrew school and the language world of our parents. There were Yiddish schools in the neighborhood, but they were never prominent and I never knew anyone who studied there. Similarly, when we joined various youth groups in our early adolescence, they were usually Zionist youth groups like HaBonim, HaShomer HaTzair, or Young Judaea, each with varying emphases on halutziyut. When we began to work in summer camps, they were usually Jewish camps with some sort of mild Zionist orientation. At Louis Hurwich's initiative, the Hebrew College opened its own Hebrew-speaking camp, Yavneh, in 1945 which attempted to fuse traditional religious practices with the Hebrew nationalist ethos that was more prominent at the Hebrew College itself. It was at Yavneh, for instance, that many of us participated in Birkat HaMazon or Havdalah for the first time, or met friends from Orthodox, observant homes, mostly in New York. While our homes, with their dense texture of East European customs and practices could never be defined as secular, the practice of strict halakhic Jewry was rare. Many of our fathers, for instance, did work on Saturdays.

The faculty of The Boston Hebrew Teachers College, though small, was extremely varied. All the instructors were men, all were born in Europe, and their intellectual interests and achievements usually surpassed by far those of our Latin School masters. Most of our Hebrew instructors had advanced degrees and were active scholars and writers, some of renown. For instance, in my first few years in the Prozdor, as a teen-ager, I had as my instructors Nahum Glatzer for Talmud, Eisig Silberschlag for Bible, and Yohanan Twersky for Hebrew Language and Literature. All three were born in the early years of the century in Eastern

Europe, but made their way to the United States before World War II. The basic facts of their biographies form a fascinating cultural tapestry. Nahum Glatzer, born in Lemberg, moved to Frankfort where he did his university studies and was close to Franz Rosenzweig. After teaching at the University of Frankfort in the early 1930s, he moved to Haifa where he taught at the Reali School in Haifa from 1933 to 1937. When he came to America he taught at various Hebrew Colleges, first in Chicago, then in Boston, then at Yeshivah College. Finally, he was invited to teach at Brandeis University where he was central in the development of its Department of Near Eastern and Jewish Studies. For years he edited many Judaica volumes for the Schocken Press in New York. Eisig Silberschlag, a Hebrew poet and translator, received his gymnasium training in classics and Hebrew in Galicia, studied in New York, but completed his doctorate in European History at the University of Vienna. Before coming to Boston, he had taught in higher institutions in New York. In addition to writing his poetry and articles, he edited *HaTekufah* and translated all of Aristophanes into Hebrew verse. He became the Dean of the Hebrew College upon the retirement of his predecessor, Louis Hurwich in 1948. When Josef Klausner retired from his post in Hebrew Literature at the Hebrew University, Silberschlag was one of the serious candidates for the position. Yohanan Twersky, a scion of Ukrainian Hasidic Tzadikim, had studied psychology in Berlin; more a novelist than a scholar, he left the Hebrew College for Israel in 1948 to assume an editorial post for Devir. While these three examples differed vastly in interest and personality, they fused Jewish learning with a broad European erudition, and each in his own way was an exemplar of the higher aspirations of the Hebrew cultural revival. Again, while each was a native Yiddish speaker, we never heard them utter a word in Yiddish, and rarely in English.

All three of these instructors were closely allied with cultural enterprises in Europe and Israel and resembled to a remarkable degree their contemporaries who taught in Tel Aviv. It is no coincidence that many of our textbooks were published in either Warsaw or Tel Aviv. In many ways unknown to us, we were part of a broad international educational network with a specific ideology. We were exposed to the same world of ideas and sentiments as our Israeli contemporaries: its emphasis on Hebrew, its Ahad HaAmic emphasis on culture and the primacy of the group over the individual, its indirect evocation of the self-sacrificing ideals of practical halutziut.

What probably mitigated this emphasis on the group was our American schooling, Jeffersonian by implication, which privileged the

individual and regarded society or the state as the vehicle for the realization of the individual's aspirations. The confluence of these two myths
shaped the attitudes that determined our subsequent life careers. I
believe that the different emphases in this fusion characterizes some of
the differences in our interests. While personality differences should not
be neglected—I am a much more private person than Ackie who thrives
in a variety of social situations—it is undeniable that his work usually
encompasses the group, the institution, while mine focuses upon individuals. These varying valences in the fusion are easily discernible even
though his studies or philosophy of education rarely neglect the individual student, and my critical approaches to literature always insist upon
historical contextualization. Ackie studies schools, even school systems;
I study individual authors (Agnon, Kafka, Nahman of Bratslav), or specific literary works. For me, institutions are a necessary evil whose justification is the protection and fostering of individual talents and
aspirations; for him, they are the natural organ through which individuals grow. Briefly, Ackie likes committee meetings and I don't. Despite
these diverse tendencies, we both were shaped by these confluent myths;
and though we can recognize them as myths, they are still powerful
forces in our lives. They led Ackie to Jewish Education and finally to
Beer Sheva, and me to Jewish Studies and to Los Angeles. They attuned
us to life in both Israel and America to such an extent that we, like others of our background, can shuttle back and forth without much cultural
or psychological displacement.

Since the two myths were confluent and fused in the imagination of
each person, it would be foolhardy to attempt to isolate the various
strains. External events, however, did actually mobilize various attitudes
inculcated by one culture or the other. Such an event was provided by
the bombing of Pearl Harbor, the signal mobilizing historical incident of
our youth, our entrance to real history. The signal impact of this event
deserves special mention especially because in most accounts of modern
Jewish history, December 7, 1941 is a marginal date, not as important as
September 1, 1939, or June 22, 1941. In the Jewish history and memory
of World War II, the narrative of the war in the Pacific attributes importance only to the refugee community in Shanghai. Yet for us, born and
raised in America, Pearl Harbor and the war in the Pacific are integral
parts of our memories of World War II. If you came from a home with
newspapers and a radio, or if you went to the movies weekly where you
saw the Fox Movietone News of the Week, you could not escape the
"March of Time," the historical events as they unfolded vividly and often

menacingly. I can remember "The Rape of Nanking," the *Anschluss*, Munich, *Kristallnacht*, and the German invasion of Poland. I knew that our Jews were being persecuted in Nazi Germany, that Germans were bad, but so were the Japanese. All this was distant, across two broad oceans. Pearl Harbor brought it all close and immediate, for by the next day we were officially at war and many things changed: military conscription, the beginning of rationing, even the visible dimming of street lights since Boston was a port city and there were actually German U-Boats off the coast. For me, the possible date of conscription was years away, never a real threat, but for Ackie and my brother, his contemporary, the possibility of conscription and military duty was close. Ackie was indeed drafted in 1943, sent to fight in Germany, and, had the war not ended by July, 1945, would have been transferred to fight in the Pacific theatre, too.

How did our schools react to these momentous events? In the Latin School, several homeroom teachers inscribed "Remember Pearl Harbor" on the blackboard, in English or even in Latin, but the events of the war were not closely watched, especially in the first disastrous months. When the war was discussed, it always involved the two theatres, the European and the Pacific; it was a *world war*. It was certainly not a *war against the Jews*. We did receive Civil Defense instructions in school, but not much more. Our training in military drill was a custom going back at least a century and had as little to do with the contemporary war as our Latin lessons. In the Hebrew College, there was constant reference to the suffering of Jews in Europe at the hands of the Germans; we knew Jews were being killed, but had no information about *Einsatzgruppen* or death camps. Of course, until late 1942 even the best informed Jews in America were unaware of what was happening to the Jews of Europe. I do recall a commemorative assembly for the fall of the Warsaw Ghetto, but little more specific information than that was forthcoming until the camps were liberated in 1945. With information so sketchy and *beyond belief,* I imagine that an institution like the Hebrew College, still foreign to the American scene, was incapable of shaping any consciousness of the import of these events for its students. I never heard of any protest meetings demanding the admission of more Jewish immigrants to the United States during the war. In general, it was the youth movements and the summer camps which were more attuned to respond to the events of the times be it the Shoah or the struggle for Israeli Independence.

Two generations have passed since the period described above and much has changed. The Boston school system caters to an even more motley population than it did in our time, including many blacks, Hispanics, and Asians. There are hardly any Jews in the city and the Jewish neighborhoods that were our home no longer exist. The Latin school reflects this population change and even admits women. The curriculum has finally been updated to accommodate these new populations. The Hebrew Schools have long ceased to offer the intensive Hebrew training we were given; the faculty of the elementary schools are mostly Israelis, while many Americans teach at the Hebrew College. The Boston area, after decades of stagnation, rebuilt its economic base through the development of its universities and a host of high technology laboratories. The existence of a viable Hebrew speaking state has changed the entire situation we knew in our childhood as did the destruction of European Jewry. Both Ackie and I have traveled many miles from Boston, he to the east and I to the west. With the advantage of the perspectives created by this considerable distance in time and space, we can look back upon the conjunction of historical forces that shaped the institutions which, in turn, shaped us. I would like to think that as we summarize the educational achievements of the past century since the First Zionist Congress, the "joint biography" I have sketched above might constitute more than a footnote.

LITERATURE IN ITS HISTORICAL CONTEXTS

Back to Moses: Reflections on Reflections on Freud's Reflections on Jewish History

The apparently coincidental publication of two books, one by Y. H. Yerushalmi (*Freud's Moses*), and the other by Emanuel Rice (*Freud and Moses*) on the role of Moses in the life and writings of Sigmund Freud, has inspired renewed interest in the Jewishness of this seemingly uncharacteristic Jew. I say "seemingly uncharacteristic Jew" for good reasons: I believe Freud interests many of us precisely because we find in him the paradigm of the problematics of Jewish identity. The shape and allure of this paradigm is not hard to find: Freud, after all, is one of the defining figures in modern intellectual thought; his Jewishness, though never denied, was problematic and defied definition. He repeatedly rejected all religion and nationalism, yet was repeatedly attracted to many manifestations of what we today would call Jewish ethnicity. He saw himself as a victim of anti-Semitism, yet never became a Zionist or a Socialist; he opted for emigration from Vienna, the locale of very palpable threats to his security, only after the Anschluss. He was obviously puzzled by the very nature of his Jewish identity and *Moses and Monotheism* was apparently his final, massive attempt to investigate this problem.

Freud's obsession with Moses, the most defining of all figures in Jewish history might not have been as pervasive as his obsession with Oedipus, but then Oedipus was a fictional character and not a Jew. If the *historical Moses* might defy scientific definition and might therefore be open to widely divergent interpretations—including that of Freud himself—the cardinal, inescapable fact is that throughout history, the Jews and their enemies considered Moses to be a historical figure, or at least, a figure whose legacy was so pronounced and enduring that denying his existence, or the existence of a similar leader with a different name, was unthinkable. Here, the comparison with Abraham, who never intrigued Freud that much, is instructive, since one can relegate Abraham to the realm of patriarchal mythology and still construct a coherent history of the Jews. But if you are to construct a coherent history of the Jews, the figure of Moses as formative, originary leader is unavoidable.

Freud, of course, was not the first Jew to be obsessed by Moses. The history is complex and long, goes back as far as the Deuteronomist historians in the seventh century B.C.E., and there is no need to rehearse it here. Suffice to say that in the Biblical texts themselves, Moses has at least three cardinal roles. First, he is the chosen leader of God's chosen people, the man who took them out of Egypt and to Sinai. As such, he is the founder and leader of a new religion. Second, he is the first and greatest of the prophets, the one man who actually had an intimate encounter with God, and as such, the model of all subsequent yearning for spiritual inspiration. And third, he is the lawgiver, the historical source of authority for all subsequent Jewish law that clearly defined how a Jew must live and thus, who he was. These features, known to anyone with a rudimentary knowledge of Bible—and Freud's knowledge of Bible was far from rudimentary—become options of identification for subsequent generations.

Let me take two relevant examples from the eighteenth century, from the very threshold of modernity. The name of Moses Mendelssohn readily leaps to mind, since he was the dominant figure of the Jewish Enlightenment movement (the Haskalah) that emanated from Berlin to points east: to Freud's Vienna, to Kafka's Prague, to the Galicia of Jakob Freud, and further east to the Pale of Settlement. The accident of his name, Moses, allowed his admirers to sloganize his relationship to the medieval Moses Maimonides and the Biblical Moses. More important, of course, was the notion that this man introduced a new period in Jewish life based on Western European criteria of rationalism. His great *Mosaic* work, certainly the most influential for Jewish intellectuals, was his translation of the Pentateuch into German and his modernizing Hebrew commentary upon it. The Philippson Bible which Freud possessed and apparently studied was certainly influenced by it. (It is curious that Yerushalmi gives scant reference to Mendelssohn, but devotes an entire paragraph to Naftali Hertz Wessely, the author of a Hebrew epic on Moses and the Exodus. In connecting Wessely with Freud, he states: "That the figure of Moses should confront us at both the bright beginning and the dark end of the Jewish romance with German civilization is emblematic of our theme." [p. 9]

The other eighteenth century figure may seem to be distant from our interests today, Freud's fascination with Moses, but I think that the relevance will become clear in a moment. I refer to Nahman of Bratslav (1772–1811), one of the most enigmatic of the early Hasidic Rabbis, a grandson of the Baal Shem Tov, the titular founder of the Hasidic movement. Though he never attracted many followers, Nahman is widely known for his artfully constructed tales, his sermons, and his rich dream life that was recorded by his closest disciples. He lived a generation after Moses Mendelssohn, but probably never heard of him or his writings, even his Bible translation, since the world of the Hasidim of the Ukraine, and even of Galicia where Nahman spent several years, was only slightly affected by the ferment in Berlin or Hamburg or Prague during the years of Nahman's maturity.(Arthur Green's *Tormented Master* admirably analyzes the life and work of Nahman of Bratslav.)

Jakob Freud was born in 1815, several years after Nahman's death, and the distance he traveled between the Hasidism of his childhood town, Tysmenitz, and the bourgeoisie Vienna of his adulthood is an example of the great saga of modernization, shared by so many other Jews. And though Nahman of Bratslav might be an extreme case of religiosity, his world view might serve to signal the parameters of the culture in which Sigmund Freud's father, Jakob, was reared. Here, too, I must be brief: I offer for your consideration only three items. First, Nahman's great erudition was restricted to Rabbinic and Kabbalistic texts and his behavior was marked by an oscillation between depressive ascetic piety an exultive identification with Moses ("Tzadik behinat Moshe"). Second, Nahman, perhaps more than other Hasidic Rabbis, believed that this experiential world is only an illusion behind which lies the world of truth, hence his reliance on fantastic tales and dreams. Finally, Nahman identified a fascinating list of the five great paragons of virtue in Jewish history, a list which is instructive since it distinguishes not great leaders or jurists, but mystics. These are: Moses, for him the paradigm of all mystical inspiration; Shimon bar Yohai, whom he believed was the author of the Zohar; the Ari (Rabbi Isaac Luria Ashkenazi) the founder of Lurianic mysticism in sixteenth century Safed; Israel B. Eliezer, the Baal Shem Tov, his grandfather; and characteristically, himself, Nahman of Bratslav. Note: such intellectual giants as Rashi or Maimonides don't make the list, but Moses does. This Moses, of course, is not the Moses of Sigmund

Freud. (For Nahman, history, or rather tradition, was Jewish history or tradition; non-Jewish history was irrelevant.) Note, for comparison, the list of great men to which Freud adds his name as innovator: Copernicus, Darwin, Freud—all subverters of previously held views of human nature.

Leaping forward one century, I must mention, briefly again, another Moses-obsessed Jew who was Freud's contemporary, actually born in the same year, 1856, but whose life was so suggestively different that a Plutarchian contrastive study of the two lives would constitute a wonderful seminar of the varieties of modern Jewish historical typology. I refer, of course, to Ahad Ha'Am (Asher Ginsburg), the great Zionist essayist and politician, the founder of what is known as cultural Zionism. (Steven Zipperstein's study of Ahad Ha'Am, *Elusive Prophet*, presents this central figure fully and suggestively.)

In the early 1890s, while living in Odessa, Ahad Ha'Am inspired a select group of Zionist intellectuals living throughout Russia called B'nei Moshe, (The Sons of Moses). This elite group of intellectuals was committed to the spiritual renaissance of the Jewish people in preparation for their return to their ancestral homeland. Ahad Ha'Am, appointed its leader, outlined its purpose in his essay, "Derekh ha-Hayim" (The way of life) (1892) where he stated that the name Moshe (Moses) was to serve as a "sign to all members ever to keep in mind this chosen son of his people, a symbol of humility and morality." In this Mosaic mode, the organization was to "broaden the scope of nationalism, elevating it to an ethical ideal based on the love of Israel, embracing moral values." The personal identification of Ahad Ha'Am with the historic personage of Moses is inescapable. Secular, Hebraist, strangely secretive, the movement had a significant impact on pre-Herzlean Zionist circles, but was superseded by the first Zionist Congress, 1897.

In a subsequent essay, called "Moshe"(Moses), Ahad Ha'Am developed a characterology of the Biblical Moses as prophetic leader, dedicated to the highest ethical ideals, struggling to guide his recalcitrant people out of bondage to a higher plane of ethical existence. The emphasis on the qualities and travails of Moses, the national leader, are patently autobiographical; by the time this essay was written (1902–1904), its author had been shunted aside by more astute and aggressive Zionist politicians, such as Herzl, Nordau, Ussishkin, and Weizman. His Moses is, indirectly, a critique of those leaders who had usurped what he thought was his legitimate role: the modern Moses who would lead the Jews out of the Egyptian bondage of modern life, forge a new nation of high ethical purpose during a sojourn in the desert of political agitation, and bring them to the Promised Land of national spiritual renewal free of anti-Semitism and endowed with new cultural energies.

Ahad Ha'Am's vision of Moses was collective and redemptive as was that of Sigmund Freud. Before turning to Freud's Moses, or rather to Freud's Moses as seen by Yerushalmi and Rice, I am compelled to mention one more Moses, that of Martin Buber published in 1946 (completed in 1944). Though Buber claims that his study is a response to Eduard Meyer's assertion in 1906 that it is impossible to "depict Moses as a concrete historical figure, or to produce anything which he could have created or which could be his historical work," and though Buber can refer to his many previous Biblical studies, some in collaboration with Franz Rosenzweig, we cannot escape the notion that this book is in some sense a response to Freud's *Moses and Monotheism* (Der Mann Moses and die monotheisthische Religion) fully published in 1939. Buber was among the more prominent critics of Freud's book that horrified, upon its publication, so many Jewish readers who regarded it as an act of political betrayal in a difficult period of Jewish history. We should not forget the context: the Nuremberg Laws and Kristallnacht. Freud, who had been an intellectual hero somewhat like Einstein, for many educated Jews, lost significant part of his popular following upon the publication of this book. (It is illuminating to investigate here the work of Yael Feldman who traces the rejection of Freudianism by certain central Zionist leaders after the early 1920s.)

If the Freud book on Moses was the foil for Buber's Moses, the foil of the Yerushalmi and Rice books was Peter Gay's three books on Freud, beginning with *Freud, Jews, and Germans* published in 1977. Throughout these articles and books, Gay repeatedly argued that Freud's Jewishness was minimal and had little impact upon his life work. For all their differences in method and scope, both Yerushalmi and Rice make the same basic argument (as does Robert Wistrich in his fine essay on Freud's Jewish identity in his *The Jews of Vienna in the Age of Franz Joseph*). Freud's Jewish background was much richer than Peter Gay or Ernest Jones would have us believe; Freud's Jewishness was problematic and ambiguous; and, in some sense, psychoanalysis was, indeed, a *Jewish science* or a *Jewish national affair*—however Freud might have feared it be considered so. In each book (Yerushalmi's and Rice's) the author conducts his basic argument in three stages: first, he assembles a body of evidence, some circumstantial, regarding Freud's Jewish upbringing in order to counter Freud's own statements that his Jewish education was almost non-existent, that he knew neither Hebrew nor Yiddish; second, he adduces as a prime document the 1891 dedication in Hebrew to the Philippson Bible in which Jakob Freud urges his son, in flowery, complicated Maskilic Hebrew, to return to his Bible studies and all they entailed after having abandoned them for so many years; and third, he finds in *Moses and Monotheism* evidence of Freud's belated return to the Bible, to his father's request or admonition of 1891.

The notion of return is found in both books, most emphatically in Rice's *Freud and Moses* which has as its subtitle: *The Long Journey Home*. Even the convoluted, enigmatic—and ultimately misleading—Yerushalmi subtitle: "Judaism Terminable and Interminable" conveys a similar notion: Jewishness (rather than Judaism, see Yerushalmi p. 90) is transmitted through successive phases of forgetfulness and remembering, both in history and the life of individuals, Freud in particular. For both authors, *Moses and Monotheism* is Freud's affirmation of his Jewishness. (One cannot escape the notion that both writers are affected in some way by the strange *Baal Teshuvah* phenomenon of the past twenty years in which we see, running parallel to the unprecedented efflorescence of Jewish Orthodoxy and Hasidism, the *return* of thousands of Jews to a more traditionally observant way of life.)

Though these two books agree on many basic points, they differ widely in their approach to the investigation of Freud's Jewishness and its implication. Each scholar predictably follows the dictates of his discipline: Yerushalmi is ever the historian and Rice, the psychoanalyst. Consequently, when Rice examines *Moses and Monotheism*, he concentrates upon the Family Romance and regards the book as Freud's resolution of his problematic relationship with his father's wishes; Yerushalmi, avowedly rejects a psychoanalytic approach to the book and investigates Freud's *conscious intentions* in writing the book. These intentions are articulated in Freud's oft-quoted letter to Arnold Zweig of September 30, 1934: "Faced with the renewed persecution, one asks oneself again how the Jew came to be what he is and why he has drawn upon himself this undying hatred." In his own way, Freud was investigating the two interrelated issues that are often conflated under the rubric of The Jewish Question: first, How did the nature of Jewishness get to be what it is, or persist in being what it is in the modern period without the original religious forms? Second, Why are Jews so persecuted, even in the post-emancipation era?

While this double question and Freud's answer to it are central for Yerushalmi, Rice is clearly more interested in Freud's Jewishness, its repression throughout his life, and its final resolution in *Moses and*

Monotheism. Rice examines all the available material to argue for a depth of Jewish background which Freud denied throughout his adult life: the Jewish backgrounds of his parents, both from Galicia; the curriculum of his religious education; his admiration for his Judaics instructor, Samuel Hammerschlag; the family Bible and its Hebrew dedication written by Jakob Freud; and his lifelong obsession with the figure of Moses as seen in both his essay of Michelangelo's Moses (1914) and in *Moses and Monotheism* (1939). (Neither Yerushalmi nor Rice mention Freud's friendship in his adolescence with Nathan Weiss, the despondent son of Rabbi Isaac Hirsch Weiss, one of the greatest Talmudic scholars of the nineteenth century. The young Weiss was treated brutally by his father and committed suicide.)

Of particular interest is Rice's analysis of Freud's relationship to the burgeoning Jewish population of Vienna. Here, a clearer statement of residential space, like that presented by Wistrich, would have been helpful. Freud grew up as did most new arrivals from Galicia in the capital in Leopoldstadt, east of the Danube canal, the area of the old ghetto where the population in Freud's gymanasium was 73% Jewish and where one could readily see pious Jews of all sorts. Only in his early twenties does he move out of his parental home across the canal to the heart of the city and all that such residence implies. Rice traces Freud's ambivalence towards his Jewishness to his attitude to two types of Jews: those who have already been acculturated in Viennese society; and the more recent immigrants from Galicia who lived in Leopoldstadt. In *Moses and Monotheism*, according to Rice, Freud identifies the Israelite tribes which had been in Egypt where they learned monotheism from Moses, an Egyptian prince, with the acculturated Jews of Vienna; the uncouth, pagan tribes which had been sojourning in Midian where they worship the volcano God, Yahweh, he identifies with the Galician Jews of Leopoldstadt. Rice thus anchors the book not only in Freud's Family Romance, his ambivalent feelings for his father, but in the social realities of Viennese Jewry. Prophetic Judaism, which Freud greatly admired since it nurtured the ethos of ethical monotheism that had been submerged by Yahwism, sounds very much like the concept of essentialist ethical Judaism described by Reform Rabbis. Note the following passage from *Moses and Monotheism*:

> We reserve for discussion in later pages how the special peculiarities of the monotheist religion borrowed from Egypt affected the Jewish people and how it was bound to leave a permanent imprint on their character through its rejection of magic and mysticism, its invitation to advance in intellectu-

ality and its encouragement of sublimations; how the people, enraptured by the possession of the truth, overwhelmed by the consciousness of being chosen, came to have a high opinion of what is intellectual and to lay stress on what is moral; and how their melancholy destinies and their disappointments in reality served only to intensify all these trends. (S.E. XXIII: 85–86)

This description certainly could not be appropriate for "the savage Semites" from Midian, the "immigrant foreigners at a backward level of civilization." Rice's most valuable contribution to our understanding of Freud's Jewishness, specifically as it is manifested in *Moses and Monotheism*, derives from his contextualization of the Jewishness in the Family Romance and in the social situation. As such, Rice, though an analyst, thinks in the categories of the historian.

Somewhat the opposite happens to Yerushalmi. For me, the most insightful and personally revelatory passage of his book is not the final, confessional "Monologue With Freud," but the last few pages of the Second Chapter, called "Sigmund Freud, Jewish Historian." By the end of that chapter you realize that this study is really a sequel to Yerushalmi's book *Zakhor* (1982) subtitled "Jewish History and Jewish Memory" in whose last chapter called "Historiography and Its Discontents" (certainly a Freudian echo), he calls into question the entire project of modern Jewish historiography. Yerushalmi begins the second chapter of *Freud's Moses* with a brief comparison between historicism and psychoanalysis:

> That Freud should have turned to history to solve his Jewish riddles comes as no surprise. Historicism of one kind or another has been a dominant characteristic of modern Jewish thought since the early nineteenth century, while the "historical" bent of psychoanalysis itself is, theoretically and therapeutically, part of its very essence. (22)

In trying to understand the nature of Jewishness as he experienced it, Freud applied the same historical method he would apply to the analysis of the neurosis of a patient: the analyst returns to the childhood of the nation, to its origins, hence to Moses. Noting that Freud's concept of inherited characteristics is Lamarckian, Yerushalmi contrasts the traditional Jewish notion of tradition which emphasizes the unbroken chain of transmission with the Freudian concept that insists upon repression of historical memory, its lingering in the unconscious, and its eruptive return at a later date. Freud wrote: "A tradition that was based only on [direct] communication could not lead to the compulsive character that attaches to religious phenomena. It would be listened to, judged, and perhaps dismissed, like any other piece of information from the outside."

When Yerushalmi begins to speculate on Freud's anachronistic Lamarckism (after all, it had been discredited as biological theory in his day, and as psychology, it evoked Jung's *collective unconscious*) he becomes bold—and revelatory. The moves he makes, often based on daring speculation, deserve to be followed carefully, because the conclusion of the argument is utterly fascinating. Yerushalmi: "Yet I find myself wondering whether, beyond the reasons that have been proposed, Freud's Jewishness may not also have played a role in his Lamarckian predilections" (31). By this, he means that because of Freud's vexed consciousness, he could not escape the feeling of Jewishness that led him to believe that there are inescapable inherited characteristics. (Clearly, this justifies the Jewish pride of Yerushalmi the historian, a pride admirably obvious throughout, but with which he is a bit uncomfortable.) Further on, Yerushalmi sums up:

> Thus as a historical essay, *Moses and Monotheism* offers a singular vision of history as essentially a story of remembering and forgetting. To be sure, this is analogous to Freud's conception of the life history of the individual. What has been overlooked is how strangely analogous it is also to the biblical conception of history, where the continual oscillation of memory and forgetting is a major theme through all the narratives of historical events. (34)

Relying on a statement in an article by Martin Bregmann, Yerushalmi deftly substitutes terms to arrive at the astounding assertion: "...the return of the repressed is the Freudian counterpart to biblical revelation, both equally momentous and unfathomable, each ultimately dependent, not on historical evidence, but on a certain kind of faith, in order to be credible." [If this is so,] "*Moses and Monotheism* is not merely history, but a countertheology of history in which the Chain of Tradition is replaced by the chain of unconscious repetition." Yerushalmi is intrigued by the notion that he has identified Freud as the greatest of modern Jewish heretics— greater even than Spinoza—for in his book "Moses is, in effect, apotheosized and takes the place of God." As such, Freud has not merely done away with the Torah but has produced a new one.

What Yerushalmi does not say is that Freud, in this book, has produced a new Torah only if we assume that Freud identifies with Moses. In fact, returning to the Ahad Ha'Am model, I would argue that Freud identifies with Moses precisely because he believes that he, Sigmund Freud, has produced a new redemptive Torah: psychoanalysis. I would go one step further and argue that we find here another intriguing identification: that of the troubled historian, Yosef Hayim Yerushalmi, with Sigmund Freud, the paradigm of the modern problematic Jew. And Yerushalmi is not the only one to make this identification.

This identification is actually admitted at the very beginning of Yerushalmi's *Freud's Moses* (2) which picks up where his book *Zakhor* left off:

> My own preoccupation with *Moses and Monotheism* arises out of a profound interest in the various modalities of modern Jewish historicism, of that quest for the meaning of Judaism and Jewish identity through an unprecedented reexamination of the Jewish past which is itself the consequence of a radical break with that past, a phenomenon of which Freud's book is at once an exemplary and idiosyncratic instance. (2)

An attentive reading of this book must convince the reader that Yerushalmi's preoccupation with Freud is not merely the ordinary interest of a professional historian in the life and works of a central figure in modern intellectual history. Could it be, I wonder, that in making Sigmund Freud a Jewish Historian, Yerushalmi is conjuring up a model of the new type of Jewish historian for the post-Freudian age. This historian could be like Freud, a *Godless Jew*, whose Jewish memory is not nourished by celebratory ritual, and the matrix of whose Jewishness is not the Revelation at Sinai, but rather "the return of the repressed" which always defies easy definition yet requires an act of faith which modern man seems willing to make. This historian could comprehend and perhaps transcend his own fractured subjectivity by controlling his own memories and thus recreate the past with new understanding. For this historian, *interminable Jewishness* would be not a curse, but a blessing.

In conclusion, I would like to call attention to a feature of Freud's lifelong enterprise which neither Yerushalmi nor Rice mention. Freud produced a corpus of texts which have become a new scripture, eliciting countless commentaries from many schools of hermeneutics. One would be hard pressed to find any other twentieth-century corpus of texts which has attracted such ingenious exegetical activity. And yet, there is an irony in the scripturality of the Freudian text: Jakob Freud, in the now famous dedication to the Philippson Bible that he presented to his son on the latter's thirty-fifth birthday, bid him to return to the study of the Torah, "the well the sages dug" (*be'er hafru hakhamim*). Little did he know that this son, Shlomo/Sigmund, would write a new Torah that would inspire the exegetical energies of generations of sages.

➥ The Beilis Trial in Literature:
Notes on History and Fiction

Few years in Franz Kafka's life have attracted as much attention as 1912, the year his art advanced from uncertain groping to structured composition. In the fall of 1912, he wrote "Das Urteil," "Die Verwandlung," and the initial chapters of the novel *Der Verschollene* (later called *Amerika*), whose first chapter was for years considered a separate story under the name "Der Heizer." Even though Max Brod maintained in 1907 that Kafka was one of the great German writers of his generation, it is doubtful whether we would remember him today if he had ceased writing before 1912. A series of accomplished works such as these indicates a substantial turn in Kafka's life and presents critics with a tempting opportunity to solve some mysteries in his fiction. It is common knowledge that Kafka's style manipulates realistic conventions and approaches parable, thus raising many problems of hermeneutics. When a work abounds with polysemous statements, *erlebte Rede,* and flagrant narrative unreliability, interpretive possibilities multiply and it is difficult to determine the range of legitimate readings. It is logical that critics are attracted to these stories of fall 1912 in the hope of finding within them, or in the events of that year, keys to the author's works in general. Intrinsic criticism by itself yields, however, so many varied meanings that we must search for any information which might contribute to the stabilization of the text, the object of our hermeneutic endeavors. At times, carefully sifted shards might yield information of great heuristic value.

Klaus Wagenbach's first biographical book on Kafka (1958),[1] the publication of Kafka's letters to his first fiancée Felice Bauer (1964) and to his sister Ottla,[2] and Evelyn Torton Beck's book on Kafka and the Yiddish theater (1971)[3] all aspire to discover thematic parallels between events in Kafka's life and his works. Unlike Max Brod, who relied primarily on his memory and private archives, Wagenbach collected data from various sources and verified them, and his work is consequently more reliable. Though in his first book Wagenbach mentions the Yiddish theater troupe which visited Prague in 1911–1912, he has yet to discover the identity of the initials F. B. In the second, however, Wagenbach declares that F. B. is Felice Bauer and attributes great importance both to the engagement and to the appearance of the Yiddish theater troupe in Prague for the formation of Kafka's literary imagination during 1912–1913.[4]

About two years after the first appearance of the *Briefe an Felice*, a book on these letters by Elias Canetti reinforced the opinion, long held by critics, that this first love affair, involving two formal betrothals and their dissolution, had a crucial effect on Kafka, spurred his writing, and nourished his imagination.[5] Heinz Politzer, for instance, associates "Das Urteil" with Kafka's first meeting with Felice in August 1912.[6] His reasons are twofold. Kafka stated in a letter to Felice that this story was hers but added no explanation, and Kafka made use of the word *Urteil* both when he made entries about Felice in his diary, and when he titled the story (the parallel will be developed below). Canetti went even further and called his book *Kafka's Other Trial*, the first trial being the novel *The Trial* and the second the stormy love affair with Felice. Canetti relies partly on philological evidence, pointing out that Kafka called the meeting place with the Bauer family in 1914 *Der Gerichtshof* ("the courthouse").[7] Before that meeting, Kafka had broken his formal engagement to Felice for the second time. It is convenient, therefore, for critics to connect this intensive correspondence with his prolific writing during this period. And yet, despite the undeniable fact that Felice played a central role in Kafka's life during these years, it does not necessarily follow that his obsession with such dominant themes as guilt, defendants, trials, the accused, judges, verdicts, and the like is a direct result of the Felice affair. Since the philological evidence is rather shaky and the internal analogies unconvincing, the relationship between Felice and the works of this period is not sufficient to explain the overwhelming obsession with trials.

Evelyn Beck develops, in greater detail, an argument presented by Wagenbach in 1958 and Binder in 1966.[8] Between October 1911 and February 1912, the Yiddish theater troupe under the direction of Isaac Löwy presented in Prague a complete repertoire of Yiddish plays. Kafka saw most, if not all, of the performances, accompanied by his friend Max Brod, befriended the actors (especially Löwy), and entered in his diary more than a hundred pages of detailed comments about these productions. As a result of this encounter with the Judaism of Eastern Europe, which seemed to him more natural than that of his own immediate surroundings in Prague, Kafka began to reacquaint himself with Jewish problems after a long period of estrangement. Evidence of this change appears in his diary and letters and in statements by his friends, especially Max Brod. Beck, going further than Wagenbach or Binder, maintains that this encounter stimulated him to write and shaped the development of his art. Beck collected and analyzed almost all the plays mentioned in the diaries, but the analogies she draws between the plays and the stories are often forced. Just as it is not possible to attribute Kafka's literary development specifically to the Felice affair, it is unlikely that exposure to the Yiddish theater was its only cause. The two experiences made a deep impression on Kafka, but they do not explain the obsession with guilt and trials in so many of his stories written between 1912 and 1915.

To move beyond these suggestions, it suffices to ask a rather obvious question: Was there during this period a trial in Kafka's world which could have deeply impressed a sensitive writer of Jewish origin, himself a lawyer by profession? The answer is readily available, though I have yet to see it mentioned among Kafka scholars, even Wagenbach and Binder. It is the famous trial of Mendel Beilis, who was imprisoned in Kiev on March 20, 1911, and finally brought to trial after two years on October 25–28, 1913. The Beilis affair was a traditional blood libel: Beilis was accused of killing a Christian child before Passover in order to use his blood in the preparation of unleavened bread for the holiday. Associated in the mind of the Christian populace with the passion of Christ, the blood libel inevitably led to anti-Jewish riots. This particular blood libel shook the entire Jewish world because the Czar's government supported the prosecution and took advantage of the incident to fan the flames of anti-Semitism in Russia, resulting in familiar consequences, from scurrilous accusations to pogroms. As in the Dreyfus affair some fifteen years earlier, echoes of the trial reached all corners of the world. Besides threatening the security of Jewish communities, the Beilis affair implanted in the mind of the observer, a basic structure: a powerless man, innocent of any crime, stands alone before an awesome state tribunal whose sole aim is to convict him. Justice is perverted and subordinated to political or private interests which have nothing to do with the defendant and which he cannot comprehend. The cynical perversion of the truth, the mass hysteria, the eruption of the repressed primitive instincts and fears, all called into question the validity of rational consciousness, particularly as it manifested itself in language. The threat to the ideological assumptions and physical well-being of the Jewish bourgeoisie, to which Kafka and all his friends belonged, evoked both feelings of insecurity and demands by the militant Jewish leadership upon the loyalty of every Jew. A young Jewish writer with Flaubertian artistic ideals would find his moral position severely challenged. A sensitive artist whose relationship with his father was one of conflict might suffer a radical exacerbation of these personal tensions.

Was Kafka aware of the Beilis affair or trial *(der Beilis Prozess)*? If so, why have critics overlooked this connection? Both direct and indirect evidence attests to Kafka's awareness. Max Brod testified that Dora Dymant, Kafka's last love, burned, at his request and before his very eyes, several notebooks of works that were never published, and that among these was a story on Mendel Beilis. This testimony has eluded scholars because it first appeared in the expanded 1954 edition of Brod's biography.[9] (It is mentioned elsewhere that Dora Dymant burned these notebooks, but their content is not described.)[10] Brod learned this either from Dora Dymant herself, when she visited Israel in the early 1950s, or from Felix Weltsch, who interviewed her. There is no reason to doubt the authenticity of this testimony since Dora Dymant was the daughter of the sexton of the Rebbe of Ger, knew Hebrew well, and was fully acquainted with the customs of East European Jews. She must have been familiar with the name Mendel Beilis. It is well known that Kafka lived with her during the last year of his life (1923–1924) and wanted to marry her, but on the Rebbe's advice her father dissuaded her from doing so.

Kafka, it is true, makes no mention of the Beilis affair either in literary works (in which Jewish matters occupy no explicit place) or in his diaries and letters (in which Jewish matters are constantly mentioned). Still, Kafka leaves unmentioned many significant things discovered by Brod, Gustav Janouch,[11] and Wagenbach. A master of alienation whose narrative technique is energized, according to Sokel, by what the protagonist's consciousness hides from itself,[12] Kafka masked much in his letters and diaries and above all in his literary works.

Even if Brod's biography did not establish that Kafka wrote a story about Mendel Beilis, we could show that Kafka was aware of the trial. Several facts indicate that Kafka was aware of Jewish problems:[13]

1. In Prague, one of the major cities of the Austro-Hungarian Empire during the latter part of the nineteenth century, each national minority was aware of its status. The majority of the population was Czech, and the small German minority consisted of Austrian officials, Sudeten farmers who had migrated to the city, and Jews. The Jews, therefore, were a minority within a minority and belonged to the middle class. Most of Kafka's friends in elementary and high school and at the university were German-speaking Jews. Anyone whose friends included Max Brod, Felix Weltsch, Oskar Pollack, and Hugo Bergmann could not have been radically alienated from the Jewish community in Prague (considered as a social class rather than as an official institution).

2. Kafka's parents were among the many Jews who migrated from provincial towns to urban areas at the end of the nineteenth century. They settled in Prague, a city whose population quadrupled between the years 1850 and 1900. Many Jews felt that their status in the towns was disintegrating with the rise of Czech nationalist aspirations and German or Russian anti-Semitism. Hermann Kafka, Franz's father, had been a Jewish peddler in Bohemian towns. He arrived in Prague in 1881; within ten years he achieved middle-class status and all that pertained to it: pride in his achievements, fear of bankruptcy, and a great desire to see his eldest child become a rich merchant or high official.

3. Kafka was close to his family and knew its history. He knew that his grandfather had been prohibited by anti-Jewish legislation from marrying because he was not the eldest son, and had married only in 1848 when that prohibition was repealed. He could relate that his mother's maternal grandfather, after whom he was named (Amschel), was a learned rabbi who conducted circumcisions. His mother (about whom he wrote very little) also told him about various Jewish customs.

4. Kafka lived most of his life in the central district of the city, where most of the population was Jewish. Moreover, in his youth during the 1890s, the ghetto which had for a long time been deteriorating into a slum was razed, and in its place rose new apartment houses. The disappearance of the ghetto was, therefore, a fact of life for Kafka, not merely a metaphor for the fate of Western Jewry.

5. His religious education was like that of other members of his class: routine visits to the synagogue, usually during the High Holy Days; a certain preparation for the Bar Mitzvah in a modern temple; and

instruction in religion for two hours every week in the German *Gymnasium* where most of the students were Jewish. During these hours Kafka read from a translation of the Old Testament and passages from rabbinic literature and Jewish history, the history of the Jews in Prague, in particular. According to Wagenbach, the strongest personality among those teaching these sessions was Nathan Grün, the Jewish community librarian, who was well versed in the history of the community.[14] Despite the fact that Kafka always belittled this aspect of his education, it cannot be assumed that he reached adulthood totally devoid of Jewish consciousness.

6. As stated earlier, Kafka frequented performances of the Yiddish theater. Furthermore, he volunteered his services to Isaac Löwy, its director, distributed advertising for its performances, and sold tickets. He even organized a concert of dramatic readings in 1912, at which he lectured in German about the history of the Yiddish language.[15] During that year he began reading Grätz's history of the Jews and (in French) M. A. Pines's history of Jewish literature, and participated in debates with Hugo Bergmann at meetings of the local Zionist organization, Bar Kochba. In September 1913 he visited the Eleventh Zionist Congress in Vienna and wrote an account of his disappointment with it. After 1917 he began to take private lessons in Hebrew.

7. With the exception of Milena Jesenská (who was married to a Jew and was killed during the Holocaust), all of Kafka's intimate women friends we know of were Jewish and aware of their Jewish background: Felice Bauer (active in welfare programs for Jews during World War I), Grete Bloch (Felice's friend and as active as she), Julie Wohryzek (a synagogue sexton's daughter), and Dora Dymant (the daughter of the synagogue sexton of the Rebbe of Ger).

8. The summer resorts in which Kafka spent his vacations were, generally speaking, typical of those frequented by Prague Jews: Schelessen, Zürau, Marienbad, Muritz on the Baltic seashore.

9. Kafka read two Prague newspapers. The first, *Das Prager Tagblatt*, was a liberal newspaper whose editors were Jews, most of whom Kafka knew from meetings in the city. Many of its readers were well-to-do Jewish merchants like those in the families of Kafka's friends. Jewish concerns were mentioned, if only indirectly, in the paper. More important for our discussion is the national Jewish

weekly of Bohemian Jewry, *Selbstwehr*,[16] which became the formal organ of the Zionist organization after 1912. According to Binder, in all of Kafka's writing, no book or newspaper is mentioned as often as this one. The paper's editors were among Kafka's friends; he often participated in their meetings, requested that the newspaper be sent to his summer residence at various resorts, and even contributed some stories to it. Each week the newspaper related all that occurred in the Jewish world, both in Prague (the performances of the Yiddish theater troupe, for example)[17] and elsewhere (settlements in Israel, the Zionist Congress, Jewish suffrage in Russia, and the Beilis affair).

10. The blood libel against Mendel Beilis was not the only one which affected Jews in Europe during Kafka's lifetime. It is worth mentioning those which might have had an impact on the consciousness of the Jewish community in Prague:

   a. *The blood libel at Tisza Eszlar* (1882). An entire Jewish congregation in Hungary was accused of murdering a young Christian woman as a result of false testimony the sons of its sexton were forced to give. The prosecution relied primarily on the fantastic story of Moritz Schwartz, the sexton's son, who claimed he saw his father and three butchers slicing the girl's flesh and pouring her blood into a vessel. When the corpse, bearing no signs of ritual murder, was eventually found in the river, witnesses were bribed to deny its identity. During the entire summer of 1882 newspapers gave extensive coverage to this affair; the riots which erupted in Hungary in its wake caused the government to declare a state of emergency. Only after a lengthy appeal was the corpse examined: no signs of ritual homicide were found and the corpse was identified as the body of the missing girl. Though the accused Jews were acquitted, the entire affair and the distorted court proceedings, especially the false testimony given by the boy Moritz, generated deep anxiety among Jews of the Austrian empire who were also acutely aware of the pogroms across the border in southern Russia. During these years Hermann Kafka first arrived in Prague, married Julie Löwy, and begat his son Franz.[18]

   b. *The Dreyfus Affair* (1894–1899). During Kafka's childhood years, the news concerning the Dreyfus affair reached Prague as well as Vienna, where Theodor Herzl resided. And though this plot did not involve the assassination of a Christian child, the accusation of spying and subversion of the law sufficed to provoke anti-Semitic reaction and undermine the security of the Jewish community. Once again a relatively unimportant, innocent Jew became the pawn in a political struggle. Dreyfus spent many years imprisoned on an isolated island (see "In der Strafkolonie," [The Penal Colony] written by Kafka in 1914) and was partially acquitted only after a widely publicized protest. During this prolonged affair Franz Kafka was a high school and university student.

c. *The blood libel at Polna, or the Hilsner Prozess* (1899–1900). In 1899 Leopold Hilsner, a Jew, was convicted of murdering a young Christian woman in Polna, Bohemia, and sentenced to be hanged. Even before the verdict was brought in, rumors were spread by the country's anti-Semitic newspapers that the murder was a ritual one, despite the fact that the prosecutor's dossier contained no mention of such a crime. The Hilsner trial became the Austro-Hungarian Dreyfus affair. Thomas G. Masaryk, as is well known, composed a pamphlet against this subversion of justice, and its circulation was forbidden by the authorities. Czech students attacked Jews; in Vienna, Prague, and other cities, Jews held rallies protesting the anti-Semitic provocation. In the Reichsrat in Vienna, several anti-Semitic speeches were delivered on December 12, 1899. Hilsner was acquitted after the faculty of medicine in Prague determined that the original medical testimony was erroneous. Hilsner was convicted again and sentenced to death in a second trial, though his sentence was commuted by Franz Joseph in 1901 to life imprisonment. This affair, which lasted about a year and a half, undoubtedly caused the most bitter anti-Semitic repercussions to which the Jews of Prague were exposed during Kafka's youth.

d. *The trial of David Blondes* (1900–1902). Even before the Hilsner affair was over, a Vilna barber, David Blondes, was accused on December 2, 1900, of plotting to kill his Christian maid. He won his case after extensive and complicated court proceedings in the court of appeals. Oskar Gruzenberg, defense counsel, was the same attorney who defended Beilis in Kiev in 1913.

e. When the Beilis affair erupted, it revitalized all the blood libel experiences of Kafka's youth. Though its reverberations in the

Jewish world have been well documented, the impression it made on Prague Jewry is worth mentioning here. *Selbstwehr* was obsessed with the affair from its very inception. It reported, for example, that on December 21, 1911, as a result of riots in Kiev, 1800 Jewish students were prevented from attending their occupational high schools. In 1912 alone, twenty-two articles were devoted to the Beilis trial, and by the end of the summer of 1913, the trial had become so notorious that the name of the accused, Mendel Beilis, was often deleted and the trial was simply called "Der Prozess," a generic term with all the cosmic power of Kafka's generic titles of his stories.

No article in *Selbstwehr* sums up the emotions of the period as pointedly and passionately as the editorial of April 12, 1912, entitled "Kiev." The reader familiar with Kafka's vocabulary will recognize here some of the terms that haunted his early stories:

KIEV

It's like it once was, when Dreyfus' name was in all mouths and Jews everywhere believed they were in the accused's dock. This time he is named Beilis and is accused by the Kiev state attorney, that he murdered the youth Justezynski "in a torturous manner." In a torturous manner! This accusation is inscribed cunningly and maliciously in everyone's imagination so that the ring of the word "ritual-murder" should be evoked. And Russian justice cynically and recklessly arranges that the conviction of the accused Jew should be achieved. As the countless witnesses presented by the defense were rejected, it was impossible for the defense to fulfill its task. The anti-Semitic Russian press teemed with instigating inflammatory articles, all brutal instincts were incited to drown out all the better voices: The Jew Beilis must be condemned.

So far he has not yet been condemned. The trial is still under way, the judgement has not yet been consummated, some events can still intervene to ward off the evil.

For what will happen if Beilis the Jew of "the torturous murder" of the Christian youth will be pronounced guilty—this even the experts in Russian relations can hardly know today. But they certainly know that this condemnation will be a signal for a legalized storm against the Jews. They also know that from Kiev there will again fly a bloody message throughout the Czarist empire.

And while what is feared has not yet become an event, it should be asked in the final hour: Has everything been done to strengthen the voices of justice in Russia? Have the Jews—even among us—summoned up their strength, exerted all influence, to oppose the menaces of the wild mobs?

We should not and cannot investigate this today. We can only offer the frightening impression, that influential circles have not let themselves be terrified out of their comfort, because the entire situation affects not only Russian Jewry with whom educated West-Europeans have nothing to do. Each person, who reads about the Kiev ritual murder trial, should test himself, how strong his sense of solidarity is. And whoever feels his heart shudder at the unspeakable insult against which no successful defense is afforded us, whoever fears from inescapable threats, he will do his duty so that our people will enjoy a freer fate, not only for today and tomorrow, as long as the judgment has not been announced, in which the Kiev Jew will be thought to condemn our entire people. We should strive so that our entire people will finally for once awaken to freedom from the painful sorrows of the thousands of years of Galut.

A close analysis of this impassioned plea, which Kafka certainly read, reveals much more than the model of an innocent man falsely accused by a malicious government. From the initial reference to the Dreyfus affair to the closing mention of Galut, the framework is that of Jewish alienation in a hostile Gentile world; the assumptions and much of the language are those of classical Zionism, as befits such a newspaper. Just as Jewish history is viewed as a continuum, the Jewish people are assumed to be an indivisible whole with a common destiny and thus with obligations of solidarity. When Dreyfus or Beilis is accused, all Jews are in the prisoner's dock and, though some might resist this conclusion, the facts are inescapable. The author calls attention to the perversion of language in the cunning and malicious accusation and to the concomitant threat to all Jews. When primitive instincts are unleashed, the truth is subverted in the name of truth. The words *verurteilt*, *Urteil*, and *Prozess*, which appear together in the second paragraph are key terms in Kafka's vocabulary, and many of the basic notions of the editorial are familiar to any reader of his fiction. Absent from the editorial, however, is the preoccupation with the ruminations of the protagonist, his adoption of the guilt laid upon him, his struggle to present a portrait of reality which masks his own consciousness, which are found in rudimentary form in Kafka's work before 1912. (These motifs, we should remember, were also evident before Kafka met Felice Bauer or Isaac Löwy.)

While it would be rash to argue that Kafka would not have written his trial and guilt-ridden stories of 1912–1914 if the Beilis affair had not occurred, it is highly improbable that he was unaffected by the claims the trial made upon his allegiance or the moral lesson it suggested. It is also possible that the prolonged pressures of the Beilis affair enabled him to universalize and objectify certain emotions which had hitherto seemed private, even solipsistic. Even though the reader might claim that my argument is ex silentio, hence speculative, since no direct reference has yet been found to the Beilis affair in Kafka's extant diaries or letters, it must be granted that Kafka's silence is both characteristic and revelatory. Perhaps his silence on this particular topic is related to the almost total absence of Jewish motifs in his fiction, since his diaries and letters often mention Jewish events. As for speculation per se, Kafka criticism is perforce so speculative that my speculations are no more flagrant than most. Avowedly pragmatic, my speculation attempts to answer two questions: (1) Are elements of the Beilis affair reflected in Kafka's stories? (2) How might these elements fuse with other concerns which obsessed Kafka during this period? Since they overlap, both questions will be answered jointly.

Strong support for my contention that the Beilis trial made a definite impression on Kafka can be found in the short story "Das Urteil," written in a single night (September 22–23, 1912); in it, Kafka broke away from the norms of the fragmentary sketch. The story begins with the hero, Georg Bendemann, ruminating about his upcoming marriage to Frieda Brandenfeld, and his hesitation to write about it to his friend who works in St. Petersburg. In the course of the story there is a clash between father and son, and after a violent quarrel the father condemns his son to death by drowning. Bound by this injunction, Georg jumps off the bridge near their apartment.

The story has been subjected to various interpretations: psychoanalytic, sociological, and metaphysical, and sometimes a combination of all three. The threatening father is compared to Hermann Kafka (Franz's father) and perhaps to God. Frieda Brandenfeld represents, in the view of most critics, Felice Bauer, with whom Kafka began to exchange letters only days before the story was written. The hero's love for his bride is construed by the father as a betrayal, either of the mother who had recently died, or of the family in general. The friend in St. Petersburg represents a character who mediates between the father and the son, or an alter ego of the hero, or even (according to Evelyn Beck) Isaac Löwy, an archetype of the East European Jew. Many critics argue that the story deals with the guilt feelings the hero harbors for having committed some crime against himself or his family and with the punishment he voluntarily suffers by carrying out the brutal sentence imposed upon him by his father.

Despite the various illuminating interpretations of the story, several mysteries remain. Why, for instance, does the friend wander about in Russia, a land described as foreign and hostile? Why was the son

sentenced to such an unnatural death by drowning? And what is the
implication of the apparently unspecific title "Das Urteil"?

In reference to the friend in Russia, it is worth citing a paragraph
from the story itself. Georg Bendemann quarrels with his father over several things, but especially over the friend in Russia. At one point the
father doubts the very existence of the friend. Georg protests by saying
that the friend paid them a visit and in fact recounted several bizarre stories which interested the father.

> "He used to tell us the most incredible stories of the Russian Revolution.
> For instance, when he was on a business trip to Kiev and ran into a riot, and
> saw a priest on a balcony who cut a broad cross on the palm of his hand and
> held it up and appealed to the mob. You've told that story yourself once or
> twice." (p. 83)[19]

On various occasions in the story the friend is referred to as the friend
from St. Petersburg since that is where he resides. However, in the passage just quoted, the priest's appeal to the mob occurs in Kiev, the city
where Beilis was tried. The reference to the revolution (apparently that
of 1905) could be a convenient ploy.

A page later, the father changes his line of argument and shouts: "Of
course I know your friend. He would have been a son after my own heart.
That's why you have been playing him false all these years." (84–85) And
in that horrendous moment, when Georg's very personality is challenged,
he reflects on his friend in Russia. "Georg stared at the bogey conjured
up by his father. His friend in St. Petersburg, whom his father suddenly
knew too well, touched his imagination as never before. Lost in the vastness of Russia he saw him. At the door of an empty, plundered warehouse
he saw him. Among the wreckage of his showcases, their slashed remnants of his wares, the falling gas brackets, he was just standing up. Why
did he have to go so far away!"(85) Evelyn Beck is correct in comparing
this description with the accounts of pogroms which Kafka encountered
in *Selbstwehr;* however, she does not connect them with the Beilis trial.[20]

Though these two passages are among the most dramatic in the story,
their position in a plot dealing with the relationship between a father and
his son is not patently motivated. The motivation becomes clear when
Georg's orderly and rational world falls apart, and he is beset by images
associated with disintegration and terror: Kiev, blatant religious provocations, pogroms, and the like. Though it is impossible to establish that
the friend in Russia is Mendel Beilis or Isaac Löwy or for that matter
any other personage, it is plausible that the image of Beilis, the wretched

accused, played a role in the formation of the character of the friend in Russia, as well as in the various passages cited above. Since this friend is linked psychologically to the hero, the reference to a barbaric environment across the border cannot be without significance.

The hero's death by drowning prompted Erwin Steinberg to connect this short story with "Who by water" of the "Netaneh Tokef" prayer of the Jewish High Holy Days.[21] Steinberg's original suggestion tying death by drowning to "Who by water" is both interesting and plausible; however, he fails to support and develop it. He checked the date on which Yom Kippur fell in the year 1912 and concluded that it must have been September 22 (actually, it was September 21), and consequently conjectures that the story "Das Urteil" was written at the end of the day of Yom Kippur and expresses Kafka's guilt for having alienated himself from the synagogue. Steinberg assumes that since the diaries tell about Kafka's visiting the synagogue on Yom Kippur in 1911, but not about the days that follow, Kafka must have regretted his behavior. This is the reason, according to Steinberg, that the story says Georg Bendemann "had not entered his father's room for several months."

This inference, like Steinberg's other inferences, is without foundation. Kafka did not frequent a synagogue, not even after 1917 when he was studying among Jews who kept the commandments, such as Friedrich Thieberger and Georg Langer, or when he lived with Dora Dymant, the daughter of a Hasid.

Had Steinberg been more careful, he would have been more convincing, and would have discovered more. Overtones of "Netaneh Tokef," for example, are not proof of a visit to the synagogue on Yom Kippur since the prayer is also said on Rosh Hashanah; and since it was well known and characterized the mood of the High Holy Days, it was printed in many newspapers and textbooks. Kafka might have learned it in his religion classes in high school. In his article, Steinberg relied on the English translation of an American mahzor (*High Holy Day Prayerbook*) published fifteen years after Kafka's death. The mahzor customarily used in Prague in 1911 was either in Hebrew alone or in Hebrew with German translation. It is impossible to determine with certainty in which mahzor Kafka read the translation of the prayer, or which mahzor was the source for the translation he used (Kafka knew little Hebrew during this period). However, since he did not visit the synagogue often and was acquainted primarily with upper middle-class Jews, it may be assumed that he examined the liberal mahzor which was published in Hamburg and translated in a free, psychological style.

In the 1904 edition of the *Gebetbuch* of the Jewish Reform Temple of Hamburg, we find the following free paraphrase:[22]

> *Unetaneh.* Thus we wish to offer you our homage and praise you as king of the world. Let us know the day's might and its sacred meaning. Your call to awaken shakes our hearts and makes them tremble, and our souls tremble in the knowledge of their guilt, in the thought of your universal judgment. You are the omniscient judge, before you no deed is hidden, no thought concealed. What we long yearn to forget, stands inscribed in flaming letters before your all-seeing eyes. And though the voice of conscience rings in vain in the noise of daily activity, today it speaks and we must listen, today the memory of sins torments us, and we acknowledge and confess that we have transgressed; the divine voice accuses us and we tremble; awaiting your pardon, we stand before you. Who is guiltless in your presence? Even angels blush before your holiness on the Day of Judgment! Now all men born of dust draw near your judgement-throne, and you in your divine wisdom inflict upon each his judgment.

This passage is comprised of the same notions which inform Kafka's "Das Urteil": the trembling of the soul; the consciousness of guilt; the recognition of God's eternal judgment (or the father's judgment); an omniscient judge; man's inability to hide from him, though he might attempt to do so; the begging for forgiveness; every man's sinfulness; and above all, the final sentence containing the translation of the Hebrew expression *Gezar Hadin* as *Urteil* (and not as *Geschick* or *Verhängnis*, which appear in other mahzorim).

The noun *Urteil* and the verbs derived from it *(beurteilen, verurteilen)* with all the sundry implications deriving therefrom (such as the sentence, a trial, the judge's relationship to the accused and that of the accused to the judge) comprise the focus of Kafka's thoughts during the decisive years 1912–1915, during which he wrote "Das Urteil," "Die Verwandlung," "Der Heizer," "In der Strafkolonie," and *Der Prozess.* These terms occur in many contexts in all of these works and should be subjected to intensive investigation. Toward the end of "Das Urteil," the father pronounces the following sentence in a loud voice: "So now you know what else there was in the world besides yourself, till now you've only known about yourself! An innocent child, yes, that you were, truly, but still more truly have you been a devilish human being!—And therefore take note: I sentence you now to death by drowning!" (p. 87). In this passage, the father's sentence appears to be closely associated with man's basic sense of identity and his self-perception. In the eyes of the judging father, the son is a demonic human being—a perception of himself which the son might have banished from his consciousness until forced to accept it because of his father's indictment.

Years later when Kafka wrote the "Brief an den Vater" (1919), he was still under the influence of this complex of terms and ideas. "But for me as a child everything you called out at me was positively a heavenly commandment, I never forgot it, it remained for me the most important means of forming a judgment of the world, above all of forming a judgment of you yourself, and there you failed entirely."[23] (p. 27) The father stands for God, His reprimands and commandments; by these commandments the son assessed the world and by this assessment the father failed abjectly.

Likewise with family relationships in general:

...this terrible trial that is pending between us and you, to examine it in all its details, from all sides, on all occasions, from far and from near—a trial in which you keep on claiming to be the judge, whereas, at least in the main (here I leave a margin for all the mistakes I may naturally make) you are a party too, just as weak and deluded as we are. (p. 69)

The similarities in terminology and ambience among the four items I have adduced—-the Beilis affair, "Das Urteil," the "Nethaneh Tokef" prayer of the Day of Atonement, and Kafka's description of his relations with his father, yield a structural pattern worth noting:

Protagonist	the citizen	man	the son
Nexus	Urteil	Urteil	Urteil
Foil	society	God	the father

In all these cases, the relationship between the protagonist and the foil (a term justified by Kafka's unremitting concentration on the protagonist) is not one of mutuality and fulfillment, but of contention, of *Urteil*. The figures are adversaries in the legal sense. This structure, like all structures, is obviously reductionist and simplistic, but it helps us uncover Kafka's unique linguistic and situational strategies.

A court scene, for instance, is a staple of narrative fiction, particularly the detective story, since it allows for economical, dramatic concentration of conflict, manipulation, and evasion. Though we find court scenes in *Der Prozess*, we are less interested here in actual court scenes than in the courtroom atmosphere where there are set rules which often defy commonsense logic, where every word is meaningful and must be recorded, where one constantly resorts to situational and linguistic strategies to make a point, where one's motives are constantly probed and one's identity repeatedly called into question. Kafka's use of the trial atmosphere is the opposite of that in the standard detective story. In the latter, the trial scene is convergent and centripetal, pulling things together and thus arriving at a plausible solution. In Kafka, the trial atmosphere is divergent and centrifugal, tearing the fabric of normal existence asunder and thus arriving at a solution which is either ambiguous or puzzling. For Kafka, the structural energy of *Urteil* both unifies his fiction and tears it apart.

While it would be foolish to attribute the peculiarity of Kafka's artistic obsessions and strategies to any specific personality trait or experience, it would be no less foolish to eliminate from our consideration of his fiction either his immediate family background or so central an event in the life of Prague Jewry as the Beilis affair. Identification with Mendel Beilis, or even a more remote, though prolonged, observation of his plight, could have provided Kafka with the necessary validation of his own feelings of insecurity and loneliness, an expansion and objectification of his Oedipal torment, corroboration of his doubts about the validity and viability of language, and a moral justification for the bewildering dialectic between self-corrosive guilt and subtle imposture which marks so many of his protagonists.

NOTES

1. *Franz Kafka: Eine Biographie seiner Jugend, 1883–1912* (Bern, 1958).

2. *Briefe an Felice und andere Korrespondenz aus Verlobungszeit* (Frankfurt, 1967); *Briefe an Ottla und die Familie*, ed. Hartmut Binder and Klaus Wagenbach (Frankfurt, 1974). The collection, *Letters to Friends, Family, and Editors*, trans. Richard and Clara Winston (New York, 1977), is an expansion of *Briefe, 1902–1924*, ed. Max Brod (New York, 1958).

3. *Kafka and the Yiddish Theater* (Madison, 1971).

4. *Franz Kafka in Selbstzeugnissen und Bilddokumenten* (Hamburg, 1964) also, see n. 1.

5. *Der andere Prozess: Kafkas Briefe an Felice* (Munich, 1969).

6. *Franz Kafka: Parable and Paradox* (Ithaca, 1962), 48–49.

7. Franz Kafka, *Tagebucher, 1910–1923*, ed. Max Brod (New York, 1949), 407.

8. Hartmut Binder, *Motiv und Gestaltung bei Franz Kafka* (Bonn, 1966).

9. Max Brod, *Franz Kafka: Eine Biographie* (Frankfurt, 1954): "Among the burnt writings there was, according to Dora's statement, also a story of Kafka's, that had as its subject the Odessa ritual murder trial of Beilis, in addition to a drama of unknown content." 248.

10. See J. P. Hodin, "Memories of Franz Kafka," *Horizon,* 17 (1948), 39, and "Erinnerungen an Franz Kafka," *Der Monat, 1,* Nos. 8–9 (1949), 89–96. In his letter to

Buber on January 25, 1927, Brod wrote that the notebooks had been burned but that he did not know what was in them: "Do you know that in the last year of his life he had 20 thick notebooks thrown in the oven by his girlfriend (Dora Dymant)? He lay in the bed and saw how his manuscripts burned," in Martin Buber, *Brief wechsel aus sieben Jahrzehnten,* II, (Heidelberg, 1973), 278. Only Chris Bezzel refers to a play and a story in his *Kafka-Chronik: Daten zu Leben und Werk* (Munich, 1975).

11. Gustav Janouch, *Gespräche mit Kafka: Erinnerungen und Aufzeichnungen* (Frankfurt, 1951).

12. Walter H. Sokel, From *Kafka-Tragik und Ironic: Zur Struktur seiner Kunst* (Munich, 1964) and *Franz Kafka* (New York, 1966). The paradoxes inherent in Kafka's style and characterization have also been dealt with at length by Binder, Emrich, and Politzer, among others. Binder's *Kafka in neue Sicht: Mimik, Gestik und Personengefüge als Darstellungsformen des Autobiographischen* (Stuttgart, 1976) and *Kafka-Kommentar zu samtlichen Erzählungen* (Munich, 1975) are particularly helpful.

13. In this survey I rely on the following: Beck, *Kafka and the Yiddish Theater;* Bezzel, *Kafka-Chronik;* Hartmut Binder, "Franz Kafka und die Wochenschrift 'Selbstwehr,'" *DVLG,* 41 (1967), 283–304, abridged as "Franz Kafka and the Weekly Paper 'Selbstwehr,'" in *Publications of the Leo Baeck Institute: Year Book XII* (London, 1967), 135–148; Hartmut Binder, "Kafkas Hebräischstudien: Ein Biographisch-interpretatorischer Versuch," *IDSG, 11* (1967), 527–556, and *Motiv und Gestaltung;* Jurgen Born, "Vom 'Urteil' zum 'Prozess': Zu Kafkas Leben und Schaffen in den Jahren 1912–1914," *ZDP,* 86 (1967), 186-196; Brod, *Franz Kafka;* Janouch, *Gespräche mit Kafka; The Jews of Czechoslovakia: Historical Studies and Surveys* (Philadelphia, 1968); Kafka, *Tagebücher, 1910–1923,* ed. Brod; Paul Eisner, Franz Kafka and Prague, trans. Lowry Nelson and René Wellek (New York, 1950); Wilhelm Emrich, *Franz Kafka* (Bonn, 1958); Rita Falke, "*Biographisch-literarische Hintergründe von Kafkas 'Urteil,'"* GRM, NS 10 (1960), 164-180; Hodin, "Memories of Kafka" and "Erinnerungen an Franz Kafka"; Politzer, *Franz Kafka: Parable and Paradox;* Marthe Robert, "Dora Dymants Erinnerungen an Kafka," *Merkur, 7,* No. 9 (1953), 848–851; *Selbstwehr: Unabhängige judische Wochenschrift (Prague; 1907–1939)* ; Sokel, *Franz Kafka Tragik und Ironie;* Hans Tramer, "Prague-City of Three Peoples," in *Publications of the Leo Baeck Institute: Year Book IX* (1964), 305–339; Wagenbach, *Franz Kafka: Eine Biographie* and *Franz Kafka in Selbstzeugnissen;* Felix Weltsch, "The Rise and Fall of the Jewish-German Symbiosis: The Case of Franz Kafka," in *Publications of the Leo Baeck Institute: Year Book* I (1956), 255–276.

14. Wagenbach, *Franz Kafka: Eine Biographie,* 40–41.

15. Franz Kafka, *Hochzeitsvorbereitunge auf dem Lande und andere Prosa aus dens Nachlass* (1953; rpt. New York, 1966): 421–426; hereafter cited in the text.

16. See note 13.

17. Several articles on the theater have been noted by Beck and Binder. In the appendix of her book, on pages 224–226, Beck provides an English translation of these articles.

18. Referring to this affair, Arnold Zweig wrote his play *Die Sendung Semaels,* whose original name was, however, *Ritualmord in Ungarn* (Leipzig, 1918).

19. References to "Das Urteil" (The Judgment) are from *Franz Kafka: The Complete Stories* ed. Nahum N. Glatzer (New York, 1971); hereafter cited in the text.

20. Beck, p. 118, n. 121.

21. Erwin R. Steinberg, "The Judgment in Kafka's 'The Judgment,'" *MFS*, 8 (1962), 23–30.

22. *Gebetbuch,* ed. Israelitischer Tempelverband (Hamburg, 1904), 354-355.

23. References are Franz Kafka, *Letter to his Father*, trans. by Ernst Kaiser and Eithne Wilkins (New York, 1954).

A Crusades Triptych in Modern Hebrew Literature

In his oft-cited lament on the "discontents of historiography," Yosef Hayim Yerushalmi states:

> Only in the modern era do we really find, for the first time, a Jewish historiography divorced from Jewish collective memory and, in crucial respects, thoroughly at odds with it.[1]

He is dismayed by the thought that modern Jewish historiography, "the single most sustained Jewish intellectual effort in modern times…has impinged so little upon modern Jewish thinking and perception generally"(96). In his historiographer's discontent, he concedes that "literature and ideology" have been far more decisive in shaping modern Jewish conceptions of the past. (Some historiographers have offered remedies for this malady.)[2]

Leaving this discontent to the historians, I would like to claim that this laudatory description: "the single most sustained Jewish intellectual effort in modern times" belongs more properly to modern Hebrew literature and not to historiography. Even Yerushalmi seems to sense this when he states, only one page later:

> The deep ambivalence of modern Jews to the past is perhaps best discerned in modern Hebrew literature, which,…reflects the widest spectrum of modern Jewish sensibility.[3]

He does not elaborate on this fully, but suffices to say that in modern Hebrew literature one does find both "the fiercest antagonism to the Jewish past" and "an aching nostalgia for a vanished Jewish past." I would refine this contention by saying that modern Hebrew writers, in their relentless efforts to revitalize the Hebrew language as a mode of contemporary cultural expression, constantly confronted the past by appropriating the languages of Hebrew texts of all periods. They appropriated the past word by word, revitalized, and reshaped it, always with a full consciousness of the personal and communal struggle involved in this effort. They believed deeply—and perhaps naively—that they were contributing to the construction of a new Hebrew society. They understood their mission, and they won in their wrestle with the angel of history. Historians and critics of Hebrew literature may feel underpaid, but they should have no sense of disciplinary discontent. On the contrary: the story they can tell is one of heroism and triumph.

Now let me turn from this prefatory provocation to three prooftexts of my argument. I am going to deal with three modern Hebrew texts in which the Crusades figure significantly:

1. Avraham Shalom Friedberg's "HaMa'akhelet" (The slaughterer's knife) 1893ff.
2. Saul Tchernichowski's "Baruch miMagentza" (Baruch of Mainz) 1902.
3. Amos Oz's *Ad mavet* (Until death) 1971.

I select three texts, not in deference to the trinity, but rather because these are the most significant texts in modern Hebrew Literature that focus upon the Crusades. There are, to be sure, many passing references elsewhere to martyrs, to Kiddush HaShem, but these are fragmentary allusions that could have been appropriated from the liturgy and do not refer specifically to the Crusades. The martyrs of the Hadrianic persecutions, *Aseret haruge malkhut*, and the Chmielnitzki pogroms were a significant presence in the minds and texts of the period, certainly more than the Crusades. In fact, in the first century of modern Hebrew literary creativity, from the end of the eighteenth to about the end of the nineteenth century, there is no story or poem about the Crusades, though we do have the popular Biblical novels of Mapu or the poems of Y. L. Gordon dealing with Hebrew slaves in Rome after 70 C.E. or exiles from Spain.[4] At first surprising, this lacuna may, indeed, reflect the relative lack of information available. I will focus on these three substantive works rather than a range of significant, but lesser pieces such as Shneour's, "Yeme habenayim mitkarvim," (The Middle Ages are approaching) (1913) or passages in U. Z. Grinberg's poetry, or Y. L. Baruch's "Birkat HaMazon" (Grace after meals) (1944), or Dalia Rabikovitch's poem "Karne Hitim"(The horns of Hitim) (1966).[5]

❖   ❖   ❖

It is not at all coincidental that the first sustained literary work in modern Hebrew dealing with the Crusades is a lengthy story by Avraham Shalom Friedberg (1838–1902), called "HaMa'akhelet" (The slaughterer's knife), first published in the mid 1890s, perhaps in 1893, and republished many times—as recently as 1958.[6] Friedberg was the ideal person to do so since, almost entirely forgotten today, he was, in many senses, the paradigmatic maskil. A writer of boundless energy, keen sensitivity to the trends of Jewish life, and some talent, he worked as translator, editor, and journalist-commentator for forty years in many of the centers of Eastern European Hebrew culture. He served as an editor on *HaMelitz*, *HaTzefira* and the first Hebrew encyclopedia, *HaEshkol*. He was one of the main propagators of knowledge about the Jewish Middle Ages, and as such, shaped the historical consciousness of generations of Jews. As a young man in the Pale, he fell under the spell of Mapu's historical novels and corresponded with him intensively in the 1850s and 1860s. As early as 1876 he reworked into Hebrew (apparently from the German) Grace Aguilar's *Vale of Cedars* (1850), the famous idealized portrait of Marrano life. After the pogroms of 1881–1882, he divided his time among three projects: articles espousing the ideals of Hibbat Tzion and commenting upon the contemporary situation of Jews; translations from significant works about the Jewish Middle Ages: Samter, Lewanda, Kayserling, and Güdemann; and his multivolume collection of stories on focal episodes in Jewish history, *Zikhronot levet David* (1893 ff.) which educated several generations of Hebrew readers about Jewish history. In a sense, Friedberg was one of the foremost creators of the modern Jewish historical consciousness, specifically dealing with the Middle Ages.

The Middle Ages were, of course, rediscovered for the Jews—as they were for many other peoples—in the nineteenth century. After the pogroms of 1881, attention was turned towards the Chmielnitzki massacres and the Crusades, both pre-modern, hence medieval. Here is where we can see how historiography began to impinge upon the Jewish historical consciousness. Hayyim Yonah Gurland's collection and annotation of documents from 1648–1649, published between 1887 and 1889, added measurably to the available source literature on that period. The publication of the Crusade chronicles by A. Neubauer and M. Stern in

1892, *Hebräische Berichte über die Judenverfolgungen während der Kreuzzug* (Hebrew reports about the persecution of Jews during the Crusades), were followed by the more connected narrative of Shimon Bernfeld, *Toldot masa'ey hatzlav* (History of the Crusades) in 1899 ff. The availability of these texts, and Shmuel Pinhas Rabinovitz' Hebrew translation of Graetz's monumental history of the Jews in the 1890s, made available for the Hebrew reader and writer a rich source of detailed accounts of events, many ghastly, that inspired the imagination. The *publitsistika* (journalism) of the period begins to absorb this information; the readers imbibe it and it becomes part of their collective consciousness. Note that two of the three major Crusades works we will discuss were written within ten years after the Neubauer-Stern publication of the texts. And while it is highly unlikely that masses of readers read the texts published by the scholarly philologists, generations of readers have read Friedberg and Tchernichowski.

Read today as a literary artifact, Friedberg's "HaMa'akhelet" is fairly dismal: its Biblicized style is stilted; its plotting and dialogue are predictably melodramatic; its ideological tendencies are patently and simplistically those of Hibbat Tzion. But as a historical document it is fascinating. This eighty page story, half straightforward history of the Jewish Middle Ages, purports to be a *te'uda*—a document or even an ethical will, written in 1130 by one Abraham ben Elyakim, for his son Shelomo, to inform him of the tribulations of the Jews, which exceeded by far the persecutions in the time of Antiochus and Hadrian. The family descended from the Chazar nobility which settled in Cordova, but, after the Berber invasions, moved to Christian Spain, then to the Rhineland. The plot of the story actually begins after twelve pages of historical background which seems to interest Friedberg more than the plot itself. In 1096, at a pastoral Pesah seder scene in the home of the rabbi of Worms, we learn of the slaughter of the Jews of Metz from a seven year old girl who had escaped from there. The Jews of Worms are next attacked by the Crusaders, and the rabbi encourages all his congregation to commit suicide rather than agree to conversion. As the rabbi is about to slaughter his five year old son, he faints. The son tries to commit suicide by jumping out the window, but he is caught by a wealthy Christian who converts him and brings him up as his son.

Note that Friedberg actually subverts the martyrological theme here since he uses two conventional melodramatic devices—the opportune faint and the surprising safe landing of the jump from a window or precipice—to avoid the violent, irreversible slaughter of the son by the father, or the father's own suicide, which one expects in a martyrological document. These acts, intended to prevent the forced conversion to Christianity, were the passion of the Jewish Crusades chronicles. To subvert them as did Friedberg and later Tchernichowski was truly daring.

Twenty years pass during which we learn—in a lengthy historical digression—that Jerusalem had been conquered and the Muslims had amassed formidable armies to drive them out. (The background echoes Lessing's *Nathan der Weise,* one of the great favorites of Jewish readers.) In a mighty battle somewhere to the northeast of Jerusalem, the carnage is horrendous. At this point, the second plot is introduced: a rabbi Elyakim of the neighboring city of Helbon, walks with his daughter, Sarah, through the field after the battle and finds a young Christian knight still alive, though severely wounded. They take him home, tend to his wounds, and discover that he was once a Jew. After a series of pastoral family scenes, a Shabbat meal where they sing a zemira of twenty stanzas written in typical Hibbat Tzion style, and then a poem of Shlomo Ibn Gabirol, we discover that Rabbi Elyakim was the former rabbi of Worms who had escaped and fled to the Muslim Middle East and the young Christian knight was—no surprise—his son who had jumped out the window in Worms in the first plot.

The son is restored to Judaism and given a new name, Avraham, since his old name had been given to the rabbi's son from his second wife. It is this rediscovered son who writes the document that comprises the story called "HaMa'akhelet." The author of this document, now called Avraham ben Elyakim (shortened as Abrabanel), ends the document with instructions to preserve and cherish this *te'udah* and the *ma'akhelet* which he retrieved in some unexplained way from the bishop of Worms.

"HaMa'akhelet," frequently republished and anthologized, embodies a fictive world of recognizable didactic situations and attitudes: the matrix, the melodramatic plots with the "surprising" discoveries, is characteristic of popular Hebrew fiction of the 1890s; the matrical plots are embedded in a meaningful and authenticated historical setting; the Hibbat Tzion ideology emphasizing Zion and the perennial hatred of Christians for Jews is concretized in the Crusade milieu, its perfect ideological fit; the knight who turns out to be a Jew is an adumbration of the machismo of the new Jew soon to be extolled by Berdyczewski and Tchernichowski; traditional Jewish life is portrayed in sentimental genre scenes such as the Passover seder, the Shabbat meal, the learned father discussing Torah lessons with his sons—all demonstrably sentimental and pastoral as are the idylls of Tchernichowski dealing with Jewish home life. One senses in them as in the pastoral, a nostalgic yearning—perhaps unconscious—for a form of life rapidly disappearing. Above all, one cannot neglect the daring subversion of martyrology which, we shall see, Tchernichowski carries a step further.

✿   ✿   ✿

When one mentions the Crusades in connection with modern Hebrew literature, the one literary work that immediately comes to mind is Tchernichowski's "Baruch miMagentza" (Baruch of Mainz).[7] Generations of readers, schooled in Hebrew, have learned this poem since its publication in 1902. Scores of thousands could retell the story of Baruch who narrates at the grave of his wife who had been killed by Crusaders, the woeful, frenetic tale of his own conversion, his slaughter of his daughters, his wrathful curse of the Christians who had tortured him and his people, and his setting the monastery and the whole city on fire in an act of justifiable revenge. In fact, for many people, this is the major source of knowledge of the Crusades; this is the one Crusade chronicle they have read.

And yet, this is a most problematic poem: complex, ambivalent, open to a variety of interpretations. In the most recent monograph on Tchernichowski (1992), Hillel Barzel informs us that the normative reading still focuses on Baruch as a symbol of true heroism.[8] Readers thrill to his explosive curse of the Gentiles. Barzel, on his part, finds Baruch a fallen hero, like other heroes of Tchernichowski, King Saul and Bar Kokhba. The most nuanced reading to date is that of Alan Mintz who confronts the ambiguities in the portrayal of the hero: Baruch, after all, did convert, and his contorted narrative is our only source of information.[9] Mintz wrestles with Baruch's febrile confession to his wife, his agonized guilt over his conversion, his slaughter of his daughters, his identification with the vampire-bats. Mintz considers these as markers of the poem's "subversion of the martyrological ideal" of the Crusader chronicles; for him "Baruch emerges as the new figure with its own prototypical force: the tainted survivor of modern literature" (129). While this formulation betrays Mintz' preoccupation with the "responses to catastrophe" theme of his book and with the Holocaust survivor, his analysis, shifting our attention to Tchernichowski's attempt to project the psyche of the outraged yet guilt-ridden victim, has much to recommend it.

To avoid the anachronistic Holocaust reference, yet take advantage of Mintz' insights, I suggest that we identify the genre of the poem and contextualize it. The poem, 730 lines in length, is usually referred to as a *poema* which means nothing more than a long poem. If we examine the poem more closely, we notice that it is a ballad and a Gothic ballad, at that. It is mostly written in trochee tetrameter, it has a consistent narrative which is preoccupied with violence, mystery, lust for revenge. The sequence in which the narrative voice, that of Baruch, invites his dead wife to join him as a vampire to suck the blood of the enemies of the Jews after he has already set the town on fire, is the epitome of the Gothic ballad. Blood and fire are the two elements of destruction and revenge. Goethe, who, together with Homer, was one of Tchernichowski's two literary idols at that period, wrote in 1797 a popular Gothic ballad "Die Braut von Korinth," (The bride from Corinth) in which the Christian women lover becomes a vampire and sucks the blood of her pagan lover whom she cannot betroth since they are of different religions.

As for the historical context, "Baruch miMagentza" was written mostly between 1899 and 1901, during Tchernichowski's early Heidelberg days when he was studying medicine and, more important, writing much of his most innovative poetry. There is nothing in this early poetry that suggests any kind of *response to catastrophe*. The poems of this period earned him his reputation with their confident, youthful voice, their variety of themes and metaphors, and, most notably, their incorporation of things Nietzschean, specifically the world of ancient Greece. Among these poems we find such popular signature poems as "Dianeira," "Lenokhah pesel Apollo," (Before the statue of Apollo) and "Sirtutim."(Sketches)[10] These three poems already present a range of perceptions of ancient Greece, much of which he inherited from Goethe.

"Dianeira" embodies the story of the violent revenge Dianeira wreaked upon Heracles when he betrayed her for another women: she induced him to wrap himself in the poisoned robe that burned and tore off his skin. In "Lenokhah pesel Apollo," the speaker, a Jew, comes to worship the Greek god of youth and vitality who embodies for him the ideals the ancient God of Israel had before he was trammeled by Rabbinic laws. And in "Sirtutim," a long apostrophe to the wonders of Greek civilization, he describes his Heidelberg study with its bookshelf holding the works of Homer and Goethe, his sun-bathed desk above which hung a picture of Herzl with his glowing eyes. An ardent Zionist since his schooldays in Odessa, Tchernichowski saw in this political activism the revitalization of the heroic ethos of ancient Israel which paralleled the dynamism and grace of ancient Athens.

As for the utilization of the Crusades motif, I would suggest, furthermore, that Tchernichowski is reacting less to the political events of his period than to the texts of the Crusade chronicles which he, a voracious reader, probably read in Shimon Bernfeld's recently published rendition.[11] By the late 1890s, the Crusades, as we have noted, had become an integral part of the historical consciousness of Tchernichowski's potential Hebrew audience, most of whom were as taken, as he was, by the charismatic figure of Theodore Herzl. While Herzl did not represent the Greek gods, his dynamic activism induced a young Zionist to fuse his political dreams with broader ideological notions concerning the rejection of the passivity in Jewish history.

The poet's receptivity of these ideas is entirely plausible once we assemble the information about Tchernichowski's milieu and activities in that period. A few items should suffice to demonstrate the rich possibilities of emotional and ideational sources—in addition to the abundant material we now have about his early years, 1875–1890 in Mikhaelovka.[12] First, the *ideological* positions—specifically, the disgust with Jewish passivity—which informs his poetry are not so different from those of the young men who grew up in the 1890s in Odessa, the center of Hibbat Tzion.[13] During this period, Herzl published *Judenstaat* (The Jewish state) and convened the First Zionist Congress. Zionist interest was intense in those circles. Note the adulation of Herzl in the poem "Sirtutim." Second, he began working on this long poem after 1896, the 800th anniversary of the First Crusade which was covered in the Hebrew press. The poet could assume that his readers knew stories conveyed by the texts of the chronicles. Third, between 1896 and 1899, Tchernichowski invested major energies in learning Greek and Latin. He had read the Greek epics in abridged Russian prose translations years before in Mikhaelovka. They were thus texts he assimilated at a very early age, not later additions to his literary repertoire. Fourth, in his first Heidelberg year, 1899–1900, when he wrote most of the poem, he apparently took a seminar in Goethe's *Faust*, in addition to his medical studies. The impact of Goethe was considerable, particularly Goethe's use of Greek sources to forge a modern, non-religious humanism. Goethe's "Die Braut von Korinth," in addition, was a standard item in many student's anthologies.

The better criticism written on "Baruch miMagentza" does connect this poem with Tchernichowski's disgust with traditional passivity. In *Hebrew Reborn* (1930), for instance, Shalom Spiegel (who is a valuable critical source since he knew both the literary criticism of the period in

Tel Aviv and the medieval sources) calls attention to the fact that in alter-
ing the historical facts of the chronicle account of Isaac ben David of
Mainz, Tchernichowski expressed his outrage at traditional Jewish passivity which he would replace with rage and revenge, "pagan joys."[14] In
writing this poem, the poet faced a serious compositional problem: if he
wanted to write a lengthy, highly subjective poem like "Baruch
miMagentza," but deliberately chose to eliminate from the Crusade narrative the traditional matrix, Kiddush Hashem—and that is precisely
what he is doing: he is "secularizing" the Crusade narrative—he had to
find some motivational substitute for Baruch's behavior and speech. He
had to concentrate on the psychology of manic rage and revenge. Where
would he find such a norm-shattering precedent? There certainly does
not seem to be a Jewish precedent: King Saul, or Elisha ben Avuyah, or
even Bar Kokhba do not fit the bill.

If, however, in a speculative mood we seek among the texts that
Tchernichowski admired most at this period, we might find a logical candidate in Homer's Iliad, particularly those passages towards the end of
the epic, books 21–24, dealing with the rage/wrath of Achilles and his
relentless passion for revenge. Baruch of Mainz is no Achilles, but the
famous *rage* (menis) of Achilles and his desire for revenge (nemesis)
might very well have served as the model for Baruch's speech and behavior. Here, too, the dominant images of revenge are blood and fire.
Achilles was also portrayed as an ambiguous character, a heroic warrior
whose behavior and motivation often run against the heroic grain.
Achilles, for instance, in his desire to take revenge for the death of
Patroclus, slaughters on his funeral pyre twelve young Trojan prisoners
and burns them with his dead comrade-in-arms. The Homeric warrior
like Achilles curses his enemy then sets out to destroy him. So does
Baruch; unlike the traditional Jew who usually sublimated his anger in
curses, Baruch actually does something. And after conjuring up the
lengthy image of vampire-bats—lengthy like a classic Homeric simile—
he invites his dead wife to rise from her grave and join him in preying
upon their enemies. In the Tchernichowski poem, we encounter lengthy
digressions which seem to interrupt the rush of the poem: the description of the Bar Mitzvah; the pastoral evocations of home life before the
Crusades, the scene at the swallow's nest. Together these comprise about
one quarter of the poem (of 730 lines!) and have confounded readers for
generations. And yet, these digressions are typical and calculated in the
Homeric poems. In sum, the literary strategies which add so much to
the poem, give it its distinctive voice and power, are very familiar to

anyone who has been immersed in the Homeric—or Vergilian—epics from childhood, as was Tchernichowski.[15]

In both "Baruch miMagentza" and "Lenokhah pesel Apollo," both Heidelberg poems, the narrator speaks from a clearly designated spot. In the first, the imaginary speaker, Baruch, recites his confessional narrative at the grave of his murdered wife. In the second, the poet comes to worship before the statue of Apollo who represents everything opposed to traditional Judaism envisaged by the poet: abundance of light, life, joy, strength, youth, heroism. The antinomies there are simplistically binary. In "Baruch miMagentza," though classified as a poema, and not a lyrical poem (in the now standard 1966 edition they are, unfortunately, in separate volumes), the cultural and emotional attitudes are far more complex. Here the poet speaks through the mask of an agonized, guilt-ridden Jew, who had converted to Christianity under duress, had killed his daughters, despite their protestations, who had set the monastery and the city on fire, and cries for further revenge at his wife's grave. The author of this poem cannot accept the simple dichotomy of "Lenokhah pesel Apollo"; and the poem is far more than an outraged malediction of the Christians for what they had done to the Jews. The probing of the complexities of Baruch's mind transforms the poem into a brooding meditation on Jewish history and Jewish identity. Broadly speaking, "Lenokhah pesel Apollo" is a belated paean to Enlightenment value, while "Baruch miMagentza" reflects all the complexities of Jewish identity at the turn of the century.

There is further proof that this is not a "response to catastrophe." A later (1937) and shorter (250 lines) Crusade *poema* that Tchernichowski wrote proves this point. In his "Haruge Termunia" (The murdered of Dortmund), Tchernichowski tells the story of a Rabbi Eliyahu who was killed during the Crusades, actually buried twice. In retelling—deliberately and admittedly—the Crusade chronicle story, Tchernichowski is reacting to the events in Germany in the middle 1930's with the rise of Nazism. There is no subtlety or complication in this poem; it is rather a straightforward response to the events of the time which were taking place in the same Rhineland of the Crusades of the eleventh and twelfth century.

✿   ✿   ✿

The third major text that features the Crusades theme is Amos Oz's *Ad mavet* (Unto Death) first published in 1971, certainly the most challenging text we have to confront, for though the narrative is clear, the reader is left with the problem of the referent.[16] The novella tells the story of a group of Crusaders led by one Count Guillaume de Toumon who set out from France on his way to Jerusalem in the fall of 1096. He is accompanied by a small group of retainers, most notably by a strange adoptive heir named Claude Crookback (ʿakum-katef) whose chronicle seems to be the main source of our information concerning what happened. Briefly, this group never reaches Jerusalem, but after a variety of adventures and mishaps, wanders aimlessly through Italy and apparently the Balkans, and finally reaches a broken-down, abandoned monastery where they waste away during a harsh winter. After weeks of starvation, indolence, and feverish fantasies, the group disintegrates, the men begin to savage one another, and the account ends enigmatically as the survivors seem to pass into another realm of existence:

> Not turning homeward—they had given up all thought of human habitation. Not even toward Jerusalem, which is not a place but disembodied love. Shedding their bodies, they made their way, growing ever purer, into the heart of the music of the bells and beyond to the choirs of angels and yet farther, leaving behind their loathsome flesh and streaming onward, a jet of whiteness on a white canvas, an abstract purpose, a fleeting vapor, perhaps peace. (81)

This is clearly the realm of magic realism where the determinacy of what transpired is called into question. Throughout the novella, Oz creates many scenes which fuse the characters' thoughts with the scenery, or their religious aspirations with concrete situations. Nurit Gertz, in her trenchant analysis of the book, demonstrates that there are frequent confusions of narrative perspectives.[17] While there is a narrative voice, apparently looking back upon the historical events viewed both broadly and narrowly, and he does quote verbatim, as it were, from the chronicles of Claude, there are many instances of perspectival confusion—or merging. The reader, for instance, does not know how the narrator knows the inner thoughts of the characters or many other things he narrates outside the cited chronicle; there are, furthermore, many shifts from chronicle to narrator.

The use of the chronicle as a narrative device evokes associations with the Crusade Chronicles we have discussed above with which the literate Hebrew reader has some familiarity. Probably unwittingly, Oz is following in the footsteps of Friedberg. Jews appear throughout, usually as victims of casual brutal massacres or as the source of a mysterious, polluting terror. The atmosphere of deep religiosity and sinfulness are vivid vehicles for the polluting Jews. Much authorial care is devoted to generating both the self-contained spirituality and the pagan inclinations of both the Count Guillaume de Tournon and Claude, the Chronicler, yet the reader is invited to ask: Is this merely an artful evocation of a failed Crusade? Or is there an allegorical referent to this evocation?

What possibilities have we encountered so far in our review? In Friedberg's story, we have the Crusades presented as the paradigm of persecution of Jews, with reference to—but no realization of—the Jewish heroic response: Kiddush HaShem, accompanied by sentimental descriptions of traditional Jewish life. In Tchernichowski, we find the rejection of Kiddush HaShem and a thirst for bloody revenge, of *Shefokh hamatkha* (Pour out they wrath) actually affected by the hero, Baruch. But in *Ad mavet* the focus is not upon the Jews who are no more than tangential victims, but on the Crusaders themselves. We might conjecture that the Crusaders in the story are fictional surrogates for the Jews, a trope we find in Uri Avneri's *Sedot Pleshet* (The fields of Philistia) (1951) and in A. B. Yehoshua's *Mul haya'arot* (Opposite the forests) (1963). In those narratives, the Zionist incursion into Arab Palestine is analogous to the Crusader incursion into Muslim Palestine of the Middle Ages. In both cases, the foreign power is ultimately thrown out by the indigenous resident. This is a common theme of Palestinian poetry and propaganda. But this paradigm does not fit here, since the Crusaders never reach Jerusalem but seem to disintegrate and consume themselves somewhere in the Balkans in the winter of 1096–1097.

The most we can say is that this failed Crusade could represent the failure of any human venture intensely energized by a variety of complicated motives, some religious or ideological, and some personal. It has been suggested that Oz, here, is obsessed with one of his favorite themes, the disintegration of the Zionist dream, a subject we see in one way or another in many of his works, especially in *Menuha nekhonah* (Proper rest) (1982). While there are no specific details that would produce a clear identification of this story as an allegory of the destiny of Zionism, expressing the author's concern about the dissipation of the Zionist dream and the brutalization of the Arabs, one could make a case for this interpretation. If this is an allegory, the author has struggled mightily to erase any traces of allegoresis, a struggle which might explain the opacity of parts of the story.

◦   ◦   ◦

Each of the three writers we have examined *uses* the Crusades material for specific purposes, wittingly or unwittingly. Friedberg's Hibbat Tzion ideology is transparent and not problematic: no contemporary reader would find serious objection to the coupling of anti-Semitism seen as a perennial phenomenon with a romantic Zionism and sentimental admiration of traditional Jewish customs and ideals. The Tchernichowski *poema* is more daring since it represents a more personal, idiosyncratic perspective that subverted expected admiration for Kiddush HaShem. And yet, most readers had little difficulty accepting the vitalism and vengeance of the poem. The Oz novella is the most problematic since it frustrates all expectations by focusing on the Crusaders not on the Jews who are, nonetheless, present as victims. On the simplest level, it can be read as an allegory on the failure of the Zionist dream; but a more complex reading would discover many other departures of the author from the expectations of his readers, thus producing a rich and complex work. No one interpretation will exhaust the narrative's possibilities. What strikes me most is the amazing progress in sophistication we see from Friedberg's story of 1893 to Oz's of 1971. This explosive growth in sophistication, in the potentiality of the Hebrew language, is one of the great success stories in Jewish history—a deliberate Crusade which did, indeed, reach Jerusalem.

NOTES

1. Yosef Hayim Yerushalmi, *Zakhor* (Seattle: University of Washington Press, 1982), 93.

2. Yerushalmi's dichotomy between historiography and collective memory has been criticized and modified by the late Amos Funkenstein several times, most recently in his *Perceptions of Jewish History* (Berkeley and Los Angeles: University of California, 1993) 10–11 and passim, for being simplistic and vague. Funkenstein injects a third, medial mode, "historical consciousness," which he argues would resolve this bifurcation.

3. Yerushalmi, 97.

4. Dan Miron discusses a genre of translated or paraphrased Hebrew prose historical/fictional works which was relatively popular from the 1860s to the 1890s , but these did not generate any original Hebrew compositions. Dan Miron in *Bodedim bemo'adam* (Tel Aviv: Am Oved, 1987), 62–65.

5. Zalman Shneour, *Shire Zalman Shneour* (Tel Aviv: Am Oved, 1952) Vol I, 163–169; U.Z. Grinberg, *Kol ketavav* (Jerusalem: Mosad Bialik, 1990–1995) Vols I-X; Y.L. Baruch, *Ashdot harim.Shirim* (Tel Aviv, 1960) I, 78-79; Dalia Rabikovitch, *Kol hashirim ad ko* (Tel Aviv: HaKibbutz Hameuhad, 1995), 133.

6. Abraham Shalom Friedberg, *Zikhronot levet David* (Warsaw, 1893 ff.) Part II, 348–427.

7. In *Otzar Hasifrut,* ed. Moshe Margal (Krakow, 1902)VI/1, 54–65.

8. Hillel Barzel, *Shirat hatehiya: Sha'ul Tchernichowski* (Tel Aviv: Sifriyat Poalim, 1992), 104–111.

9. Alan Mintz, *Hurban* (New York: Columbia University;1984) 123–129.

10. These three poems appeared in 1901 in *Manginot vehezyonot. Part Two* (Warsaw, 1901).

11. For proof of this familiarity see Shlomo Eidelberg in "Hayesod hahistori beshirat Tchernichowski," *HaDoar*, January 4, 1963, 162–163. 1962. Eidelberg demonstrates Tchernichowski's familiarity with Neubauer. I suggest that in addition to Neubauer, he was reading Bernfeld.

12. The two main autobiographical sources for this early period are: "Avtobiographia," *HaShiloah* (1918)XXXV/2, 97–103. (Originally written in Lausanne, 1904); "Me'en Avtobiographia," ed. B. Arpali and A. Wilenski in *Sha'ul Tchernichowski: Mehkarim ute'udot* (Jerusalem: Mosad Bialik, 1994).

13. Our standard source of information on Tchernichowski in this period is Yosef Klausner, who also entertained radical anti-passivity notions. Yosef Klausner, *Sha'ul Tchernichowski, ha'adam vehameshorer* (Jerusalem: Hebrew University Press, 1947). Klausner reports that when he first met Tchernichowski in 1890, he asked him what he had read of Hebrew authors. The latter mentioned Avraham Mapu, Mikha'l (Micha Yosef Lebensohn), Riba'l (Yithak Ber Levinsohn) and A.S. Friedberg. For a tentative reevaluation of this period in Odessa see Steven J. Zipperstein, "Remapping Odessa, Rewriting Cultural History," *Jewish Social Studies* II/2, Winter 1996, 21–36.

14. Shalom Spiegel, *Hebrew Reborn* (New York: MacMillan, 1930), 317–329, 423–435.

15. One could add to the repertoire of possible sources Goethe's "Braut von Messina" or Berdyczewski's early stories that were published in several volumes in 1901.

16. Amos Oz, *Ad mavet* (Merhavia: Sifryat Poalim), 1971. Citations from English translation *Unto Death* by Nicholas de Lange (Harcourt, Brace, Jovanovich, N.Y., 1975).

17. Nurit Gertz, *Amos Oz* (Merhavia: Sifriyat Poalim, 1980). Also see Abraham Balaban, *Ben el lehaya* (Tel Aviv: Am Oved, 1986).

❧ Kafka: The Margins of Assimilation

The more we advance into the post-modern age, the more Kafka's writing seems to move from the margins of our literary canon to its center. Whatever post-modernism may mean—the collapsing of categories of thought and form, heightened, articulated self-consciousness, the blurring of distinctions between subject and object, or between life and literature—Kafka is referred to as a prooftext. He has become, however paradoxically, one of the scriptural texts of post-modernism. At the same time, the historical research of the past decade has given us a firmer grasp on the writer's biography; the trend towards demystification has been enlightening.

We now begin to see Kafka's Jewishness in a new light, not as a vague allusion to the Golem legend or to the Talmudic intricacies of his thought patterns, but rather as the concrete context of his existence in Prague between 1883 and 1924, the years of his life. To be a young Jew in Prague at the turn of the century meant to be aware of the precarious social and political situation of the community with which you were identified. For Kafka and most of his friends, it meant to be the child of newly middle-class parents with all their anxieties. If, finally, one was not committed to a traditional religious style of life and was yet deeply interested in a variety of Jewish concerns—as Kafka was—being Jewish was a nagging identification problem. Your friends, your work, your language, all implied who you were. You knew you were categorized as an *assimilated* Jew, that you lived on the margins of several societies, but at the heart of none. What that assimilation meant varied from person to person, and was thus never clear.

Kafka dealt with all these problems, often obliquely, in his fiction, his diaries, and his letters. In the fiction, the specifics of the problems are usually repressed or decentered, thus hardly recognizable. Reading Kafka today we should realize that behind the non-specific text, there lies a world of very specific items and events, which have been suppressed in the process of composition. While I would not argue that a knowledge of the historical context is indispensable for the understanding of any text, or the *oeuvre* as a whole, I maintain that the historical information, used cautiously, can shed light on our interpretation. The following pages are therefore an exercise in reading Kafka in this newly historicist way.

                          ✿   ✿   ✿

> As the explorer prepared to leave the Penal Colony, he approached the tea house which made on him "the impression of a historic tradition of some kind," and he "felt the power of past days." Led by the soldier who had just been saved from a horrible death in the machine, he discovered, covered by some tables in the tea house, the grave of the old Commandant of the Penal Colony, the man who had given it its shape and purpose. On a simple stone, there was an inscription in small letters:
>
> Here rests the old Commandant. His adherents, who now must be nameless, have dug this grave and set up this stone. There is a prophecy that after a number of years the Commandant will rise again and lead his adherents from this house to recover the colony. Have faith and wait.[1]

Kafka's narrator attributes an ambiguous, indirect reaction to the explorer who ignores the smiles of the bystanders in the tea house, which might reflect his amusement at the "ridiculous" inscription.

The present inhabitants of the colony apparently scorn and ridicule the inscription, but should we, the readers—and, as such, explorers—do likewise? Are we the ones who are advised to "have faith and wait" for the old Commandant who will "rise again" and lead his adherents from the tea house to recover the colony? Are we, the readers, the adherents "who now must be nameless," adherents since we have experienced the powerful effect of Kafka's fiction, have shared his insights, and are therefore redeemable?

Cardinal among these insights is the pained realization that in the present there is no meaningful authority, no old Commandant, and consequently all commandments are meaningless; justice is meted automatically by a machine that breaks down in the process. In the days of the old Commandant, punishment, though harsh, was intelligible and inspired enlightenment; in the present, we have breakdown, boredom, and confusion. "In the Penal Colony" is a narrative dramatization of the central penal ritual, the execution of a prisoner, here a soldier, for insubordination to the rules or laws of his society. The lack of popular interest in the execution, the disintegration of the machine, the suicide of the officiating executioner who substitutes his own body for that of the prisoner in the penal contraption, are all concrete examples of the author's awareness of the chaos of his times. The old order exists only as a hollow ritual, devoid of meaning or authority; acts, statements, even gestures, never have one agreed-upon interpretation; people and places are nameless; justice is indeterminate and guilt, unmotivated. This is the fictional world we properly characterize as *Kafkaesque*.

Precisely because "In the Penal Colony" is so quintessentially Kafka, both in theme and technique, and also firmly established as part of the canon of modern fiction—and, more specifically, of post-modern fiction—we should address the question of Kafka's canonicity at this point. Considerations of the literary canon, surely one of the cardinal preoccupations of modern critical theory, inevitably raise a host of intriguing questions. Apart from the obvious concerns related to authority, who, for instance, has the power or the right to determine what is properly to be included in a certain literary canon or tradition? We are often troubled by the criteria for determining canonicity. The appeal to tradition is no longer enough. Once this line is broken, we are more often than not led into a vicious circle, cycling back and forth between authority and the criteria for inclusion. Furthermore, whether or not we place a specific work in a certain canon, may very well suggest how we should read it, since a canon implies historical contexts, linguistic and literary conventions, a world of concrete conventions and assumed values.

Contemplating Kafka's works from the point of view of canonicity—the general strategy of this essay—one is led directly into the problematics of interpretation which, we believe, can be given coherent direction with reference to their canonicity. While it is obvious that these stories and novels are now part of the international canon of modern literature, hence particularly attractive to the comparativist, there is no consensus regarding what national literary canon Kafka belongs to. Though he wrote exclusively in German, it is not clear if he belongs to German, Austrian, Czech, or Jewish literature. The query is relevant not only to Kafka's reader, but to Kafka himself, for while he never regarded himself as a specifically Jewish writer, his repeated assertions that he and his Jewish colleagues who wrote in German were really not at home in that language, were always predicated upon his being a member of the Jewish middle class in multi-cultural central Europe. The language problem and its implications has been dealt with in detail by G. Deleuze and F. Guattari.[2]

Often cited as the most characteristic modernist, i.e., twentieth-century writer, precisely because of his universality, Kafka's specific cultural background has been well documented by such writers as Ernst Pawel, Ronald Hayman, and Marthe Robert who, in turn, rely upon volumes of Kafka scholarship, particularly that of Klaus Wagenbach and Chris Bezzel. It is the world of the middle class Jewish community of Prague, prosperous but harried by rising exclusionary Czech and German nationalism, proud of its long history—the synagogues, the old cemetery, the legend of the Golem—but uneasy with it. For Kafka, as for most of his friends in Prague, being Jewish was an ineluctable fact of existence. You could live with it; you could try to escape it; you could try to repress it. But you could never ignore or forget it. For all his diary and letter writing, Kafka never mentioned the antisemitic riots which raged for three days in Prague in 1897, or the Polna Blood Libel leading to the Hilsner Trial of 1899–1900, events in his crucial, impressionable, adolescent years; but it is inconceivable that he was indifferent to them. For all his individuality, the cultural milieu from which Kafka sprung is familiar to anyone conversant with modern Jewish history. Prague, between 1880 and 1914, was undergoing rapid urbanization and industrialization and its Jewish residents were profoundly affected by these processes. Hermann Kafka, for instance, had moved to the city from a Bohemian town in 1882, only a year before his son Franz was born. Like many Jews of his generation, he had served in the Austrian army, made his living as a peddler in the Czech-speaking countryside, and moved to the city where business opportunities were more promising. Shortly after his arrival, he met Julie Löwy, the daughter of a wealthy brewer, well established by then in Prague. The Löwy family was much more advanced than Hermann Kafka on the road to acculturation: they had money; Julie's siblings were mostly professional men or administrators; they spoke German well.

Given the bourgeois mores of the times, it is not at all clear why the Löwys married off their daughter to Hermann Kafka, who had no more in 1882 than his ambition and energy. Nevertheless, the marriage was apparently successful and lasted until their death in the 1930s. Julie Kafka, always the dutiful wife, devoted her energies to supporting Hermann's ambitions: she worked in his increasingly prosperous haberdashery business (a trade usually identified with Jews in the cities of Central Europe), and bore him six children. Of these, Franz was the eldest; the two boys born immediately after him died in childhood; the following three daughters grew up, married, and reared families. They were murdered in Nazi concentration camps together with most of Prague Jewry including many of Kafka's acquaintances, one of his fiancées, Grete Bloch, and his lover, Milena Jasenska. Kafka, himself, was saved from this fate by his death of tuberculosis in 1924, a fact usually overlooked, but nonetheless crucial, for any consideration of his life and works: slaughter in Theresienstadt or Auschwitz was the *final solution* of the group whose destiny he shared.

Though he traveled frequently for business, or vacations, or recuperation to a variety of places mostly in Central Europe, he lived until the last few years of his life with his parents in one of the many apartments they occupied, not far from the family haberdashery shop on the Altstadtring (Old Town Square) at the center of the Old City of Prague with its medieval and baroque buildings, its churches, synagogues, town hall, and historical monuments. This was the Josefstadt, primarily a Jewish district, part of which—the old ghetto area—was razed and rebuilt in one of the Hapsburg urban renewal programs in the 1890s. Many of the resorts where he spent his vacations were patronized primarily by Jews. Both the elementary school and the gymnasium, where he spent his childhood and adolescence were populated mainly by Jews; culturally German, they catered mainly to the Jewish middle class. Naturally, the various friendships he formed there and later in the university, were with young men of the same class.

Though Kafka noted in his diary that he was named after his mother's grandfather, Amschel (Adam) Porias, a learned, pious Jew (whose wife committed suicide and whose son went mad), the man had died forty years before Franz' birth; Jewish learning and observance had long been a faint memory in both the Löwy and Kafka houses. Kafka's wide intellectual interests were acquired not at home, but in the gymnasium, the university, and, most important, the ever-changing circles of fascinating friends one could find in Prague, almost all young Jewish men of similar backgrounds. Their dazzling intellectual passions were acquired and cultivated in conversations with other Jews, the sons of businessmen subject to the same social, political, and ethnic pressures as Hermann Kafka was. Kafka's Jewishness, then, was not traditional, learned from childhood through ritual observance and study, but situational, an amalgam of the varied responses to historical forces.

Like most contemporary Jewish intellectuals in Prague, he did not join in the efforts of the organized Jewish community to cope with the pressing needs of the times such as the outbreaks of antisemitic activities or the massive influx of Galician Jews fleeing the ravages of war on the Eastern Front in 1915. Unlike most of his contemporaries, he did not settle upon one specific option such as Zionism or Socialism or Aestheticism or religious orthodoxy. Given his complex temperament and the subtlety of his mind—both so evident in everything he wrote—it is easy to understand why none of the many suggested solutions to the problematics of Jewish existence in the modern world were acceptable to him. After 1911, when his consciousness of the richness of the Jewish past was awakened by his reading of Graetz's *History of the Jews* and his attending the performances of Itzik Löwy's traveling Yiddish theatre, concerns of the Jewish world as expressed in the Prague Zionist weekly, *Selbstwehr*, written and edited by friends and acquaintances, were always an integral part of his life.

Read against this background, "In the Penal Colony" (1914) assumes a very specific meaning. While it would be exaggerated to claim that the story is a commentary upon the predicament of the modern, secular Jew who has abandoned the traditional religious norms, but is still unsatisfied with his existence in the modern world, the central themes: the Law, the authority of the old Commandant (Moses?), guilt, the uncanny (*unheimlich* in the Freudian sense) nature of writing, are all unmistakably Jewish, especially when found in juxtaposition. And yet, there is no clear reference to anything Jewish in the story, a feature of Kafka's writing which must elicit from the informed reader a peculiar response. If the referents are unmistakably Jewish but their named specifics have been erased or repressed, what is really going on in this story? And when one couples this enigmatic style to the constant shifts of consciousness in the story, not only between the characters but even within the same character, one begins to land as an explorer upon the prison colony of Kafka's consciousness, there to discover a new world of thought and feeling, frightening, though often funny, but always intriguing. To facilitate the exploration of this self-imposed penal colony, I shall investigate two seminal documents Kafka has left us: one, a letter to his closest friend, Max Brod; the other, the famous "Letter to His Father."

❊ ❊ ❊

Most young Jews who began to write German wanted to leave Jewishness behind them, and their fathers approved of this, but vaguely (this vagueness was what was outrageous to them). But with their posterior legs they were still glued to their father's Jewishness and with their waving anterior legs they found no new ground. The ensuing despair became their inspiration. (p. 289)[3]

These almost aphoristic statements from this most quotable author are usually taken out of context and rarely properly analyzed. They are, to begin with, from a letter Kafka wrote from the Matliary sanatorium to Max Brod in Prague sometime in June, 1921. Though already advanced in his consumption, Kafka was at the peak of his creative powers: *The Castle,* for instance, was written during the first nine months of 1922. The appellation "most young Jews who began to write German," refers not only to the letter writer and the addressee, a widely published novelist and music critic, but to a whole generation of intellectuals and, by extension, to the German speaking Central European Jewish society that produced them. The reference to the frustratingly vague approbation of the fathers reveals that Kafka envisages the writer's problems as integral to the society. The animal or insect imagery of the writer's grotesque posture evokes memories of Gregor Samsa in "The Metamorphosis," struggling between humanity and insecthood. Most striking, however, is the concluding insight: "The ensuing despair became their inspiration,"(289) which sums up Kafka's explanation of Jewish cultural creativity in Central Europe in his days, certainly one of the most intriguing phenomena in modern cultural history. The cultural history of Central Europe, after all, cannot be written without some attempt to comprehend the remarkable prominence of what we ordinarily call *assimilated Jews* in the cultural life of Berlin, Prague, Vienna, Budapest, and some lesser centers. That Kafka is referring to this specific phenomenon we can easily corroborate from the first sentence of the paragraph often omitted in quotations:

> Psychoanalysis lays stress on the father-complex and many find the complex intellectually fruitful. In this case I prefer another version, where the issue revolves not around innocent fathers, but the father's Jewishness. (pp. 288–289)

"Psychoanalysis" and "the father complex" obviously refer to Freud, another Central European Jew, whose ideas Kafka had fully assimilated as early as 1912. In his diary entry describing his ecstasy at having finished his first great story, "The Judgment," in one night, he records that during the writing he had "thoughts of Freud, of course." Here, his "other version" amounts to a rejection of Freud's universalizing for a particularized explanation: not the general father complex, i.e. the Oedipus complex, with an innocent father caught in an inescapable father/son relationship, but the Jewish father who rejects his own Jewish identity by *vaguely* approving the son's writing in German. The father sends confusing, contradictory signals since he himself is conflicted as to his identity; the son is caught between the father's desire that he abandon his Jewishness yet remain vaguely faithful to it.

Behind Kafka's remarks lies an awareness of the three generational pattern so common, with its variants, to Jews of his period: the still pious ancestors who lived in small market-towns, the oft-cited shtetlach of Central and Eastern Europe; the fathers who moved to the city, succeeded in business, and abandoned most of the religious practices of their fathers; the sons who found the bourgeois ethic of their fathers unfulfilling. In their desperation and frustration, the sons sought expression in politics, science, or the arts. Though Kafka could formulate in his diary entry of December 25, 1911[4], an interesting portrait of his maternal ancestors, going back to his pious grandfather, Amschel, after whom he was named, he usually concentrates on the generations of his father, who named him Franz, after the emperor Franz Joseph. Compounding the confusion in identity was the problem of national affiliation manifested most sharply in language. Kafka, like many of his friends, lived in a bilingual world: the Jewish middle-class usually spoke German and sent their sons to German schools, but the majority of the population spoke Czech. Hermann Kafka, his father, spoke Czech better than German while his mother, Julie Löwy, spoke German better. Both parents worked in the family business on the Old Town Square where most of the hired help and customers spoke Czech as did Franz's Jewish governess. By the beginning of this century over half the Jews registered their language as Czech. Consider the writer's name: Franz, German; Kafka, Czech (meaning either jackdaw or some diminutive of Yankev); his Jewish name, Amschel, standard Yiddish. In the highly politicized atmosphere of Kafka's Prague, language was both the most obvious and most profound token of identification hence the preoccupation with the writer's choice of language.

The remarks concerning the inter-generational conflict cited above, actually follow two paragraphs which discuss what Kafka remembered of Karl Kraus' provocative book, *Literatur* (Vienna, 1921), a polemic against Franz Werfel who had attacked Kraus in his *Spiegelmensch* (Munich, 1920). The polemic naturally interested both Kafka and Brod, not only because Werfel was a boyhood friend, but because Kraus, whom both had met in Prague, satirized with his bitter, perceptive wit, the speech and writing patterns of German-speaking Jews—what is called *mauscheln*, a derogatory term with antisemitic overtones derived, apparently, from Moshe (Moses), implying to speak like Moses, the Jewish peddler. Kafka asserts that Kraus, the antisemitic Jew, is, in the world of German-Jewish letters, the "dominant" figure—or that the principle represented by him is the dominant principle. Ironically, Kraus' acerbic wit consists of *mauscheln*: "...no one can mauscheln like Kraus, although in the German-Jewish world hardly anyone can do anything else." Sander Gilman in his study, *Jewish Self Hatred*, subtitled *The Secret Language of the Jews*,[5] demonstrates how the term *mauscheln* is so central to the vocabulary of modern anti-Semitism and, in that assimilated Jews accepted as true the accusations of antisemites, to the vocabulary of these marginal Jews. Kafka, too, accepts Kraus' stricture that all Jews *mauscheln*, that "'mauscheln'...consists in a bumptious, tacit, or self-pitying appropriation of someone else's property, something not earned but stolen by means of a relatively casual gesture. Yet it remains someone else's property, even though there is no evidence of a single solecism"(288).Though Kafka seems to accept the Krausian definition of "mauscheln," he actually uses Kraus as a foil by arguing for the positive value of *mauscheln*, i.e. the concrete contribution of Jews to German literature:

> This is not to say anything against mauscheln—in itself it is fine: it is an organic compound of bookish German and pantomime....What we have here is the product of a sensitive feeling for language which has recognized that in German only the dialects are really alive, and, except for them, only the most individual High German, while all the rest, the linguistic middle ground, is nothing but embers which can only be brought to a semblance of life when excessively lively Jewish hands rummage through them. (p. 288)

Struck with the startling impression this might make on Brod, Kafka hastens to conclude this paragraph with: "That is a fact, funny or terrible as you like" (p. 288). Kafka develops the argument by stating that Jews are irresistibly drawn to German because "...there is a relationship between all this and Jewishness, or more precisely between young Jews and their Jewishness, with all the frightful inner predicament of these generations"(288). In the light of this argument which connects the usage of German with the predicament of the assimilated Jew of central Europe, the passage from the letter which we first quoted assumes a new sense. Writing in German becomes an expression of the Jewish predicament with all its desperation which is the source of the writer's inspiration.

The last of the four paragraphs of this discourse on writing—in a sense, Kafka's *ars poetica*—develops the central notion of literature born of despair. While this inspiration is credited with being as honorable as any other, the literature produced could not be German literature—but something else. That the writers of this literature of *otherness* had to be what they were, Kafka proves by his oft-quoted theory of the impossibilities of German-Jewish writers:

> They existed among *three impossibilities*. It is simplest to call them that. But they may also be called something entirely different. These are: the impossibility of not writing, the impossibility of writing in German, the impossibility of writing differently. One might add a fourth impossibility, the impossibility of writing (since the despair could not be assuaged by writing, was hostile to both life and writing; writing is only an expedient, as for someone who is writing his will shortly before he hangs himself—an expedient that may well last a whole life). (p. 289)

In presenting these impossibilities, Kafka is indulging in one of his characteristic verbal constructs: by spinning a series of fine distinctions, he entraps himself or his hero in a tight web from which any escape is impossible. The weaving of the trap is as Kafkaesque as is the preoccupation with suicide. Suicide, furthermore, is not a one-time act as it is in "The Judgment" (1912), but rather "an expedient that may well last a whole life" as it is in "The Metamorphosis" (1912) or *The Trial* (1914), the two latter being suicides integral to the hero's character. The suicide theme or posture is subtly continued in the last gambit of this passage, a typically Kafkaesque statement of self effacement:

> Thus what resulted was a literature impossible in all respects, a gypsy literature which had stolen the German child out of its cradle and in haste put it through some kind of training, for someone has to dance on the tightrope. (p. 289)

The two standard motifs evoked here, the gypsy who steals a child from its cradle and the dancing on a tight-rope, are particularly revelatory since the first refers to spurious parentage, and the second, to the precariousness of artistic creativity, two of Kafka's life-long obsessions. The link between them is, of course, language, in this case, German as used by Jews.

In his biography of Kafka, tellingly titled *The Nightmare of Reason,*[6] Ernst Pawel deftly portrays what it meant to be a Jew in Kafka's Prague. He derides those who would hail Kafka the writer as a crypto-Christian or a pseudo-Marxist and faults literary scholars for lack of imagination:

> ...the absence of explicitly Jewish references in the surviving texts has made literary pedants feel justified in dismissing his religion as an incidental biographical detail...Yet who he was, and what he did cannot possibly be understood without a clear realization that his being Jewish—not faith, to begin with, not observance, but the mere fact of being Jewish in turn-of-the-century Prague—was at least as vital a component of his identity as his face or his voice. (p.45)

Pursuing Pawel's argument further, if we take Kafka's reflections on literature written by Jews in German as a meaningful myth for Franz Kafka the writer—and it is at least precisely that—what he and his colleagues were writing was not German, but Jewish literature, an elegant type of *mauscheln.* However he might repress references to Jewish matters in his fictions—and there are almost no readily identifiable references of this sort—his language, taken in the context of his times, was, as far as he was concerned, not quite German, perhaps not quite Jewish, but somewhere in the margins of both.

Kafka's sense of his marginality developed slowly throughout his youth and young adulthood, and seems to have found its focus under the pressures of the events of 1911–1912: his struggle with his father over his obligations to assist in the family asbestos factory; the intense preoccupation with things Jewish: the Yiddish theatre, the Beilis Affair, his reading of Graetz's *History of the Jews;* his meeting with Felice Bauer, later to become his fiancée. It is significant that he found the proper metaphor for embracing all the tensions wracking his consciousness in the father/son relationship so pronounced in the works of late 1912. In a similar vein, almost at the mid-point between these early stories and the letter to Brod discussed above, he wrote the moving "Letter to His Father" (1917), a reading of which enriches our argument.

✿ ✿ ✿

> Marrying, founding a family, accepting all the children that come, supporting them in this insecure world and perhaps guiding them a little, is, I am convinced, the utmost a human being can succeed in doing at all. (p. 99)[7]

> My writing was all about you. (p. 87)

Neither the first nor the greatest of Kafka's works, the "Letter to his Father" (*Brief an den Vater*), offers the reader an opening to the labyrinth of Kafka's writing—an opening but not necessarily a thread through it. Written in November, 1919, when Kafka was already tuberculoid and suffering from a worsening in his relations with his father—the result, perhaps, of his engagement to Julie Wohryczek—the letter purports to be an answer to Hermann Kafka's question why his son was afraid of him. What the son produced was much more than an answer to the father's question: the *letter* is a passionate accusation and confession, subtly articulated and carefully crafted, more an attempt at self-definition than a communication to an addressee. We know that Hermann Kafka never received this letter and we doubt that he would have understood the intricacy of the argument had he received it. And while we have no proof that the son's formulation of the father's role in the shaping of his character and entire world-view is as accurate as it is devastating, the rhetorical force of Kafka's sentiments and beliefs is unquestionable. The strategies of exposition are shrewdly designed to depict a complex, dynamic situation that will both justify his behavior and shed light upon his writing. The reader cannot escape the characteristic Kafkan mixture of painful self-awareness and confident, even triumphal verbal command. In this linguistic duel between the *Ich* and the *Du*, between the dazzlingly agile son and the caricatured father who is even assigned a final repartee by the son and in the son's voice, there is no question who wins. This document and the verdict of history have assigned all the points to Franz, not to Hermann Kafka, precisely as the son knew it would.

The letter posits as an axiomatic, given the adversarial relationship between the father and the son, a relationship structured linguistically by the repeated, variegated opposition of *Ich* and *Du* throughout the first ten pages of this forty-five page manuscript. (Though Buber's *Ich und Du* was published later, Kafka was familiar with Buber's emerging ideas and might very well be playing with them here.) And while the writer expressedly exonerates his father as being guiltless (*schuldlos*), the entire, lengthy disquisition on the father's methods of educating his son is an irrefutable accusation. It is no accident that much attention is devoted to education, to *Bildung*, since the frame of reference throughout this letter is that of the bourgeois family and the bourgeois novel, with their ideals of family, education, economic security, diligence, and respectability—in sum, the formation of character and capital. The bourgeoisie that the writer repeatedly invokes in this document is very specific, and epitomized in his mind by his father: it is the circumscribed society of Jewish businessmen in Prague, often relatively recent arrivals in the city who had earned an enviable, though precarious, position for themselves by dint of hard work and enterprise. Kafka admires his father's energy, his appetites, his economic achievement, his devotion to his wife; he deplores his vulgarity, his callousness, his desire for respectability, his tyrannical rule over his subordinates—especially his son.

The general social situation, though not detailed here, is fully acknowledged: the son realizes that the father has struggled to rise from the penury of the newcomer from the countryside to the provincial capital. It explains the father's indifference to the Jewish religious heritage, a central topic in the letter, and the dominance of social scruples over religious ones. Kafka typifies his father's complaints as those of middle-class fathers regarding their sons: they are ungrateful, rebellious, alienated. What the son cannot condone is the father's unwillingness to concede that his overbearing nature has not built, but actually destroyed his son's character.

Kafka's analysis of the effect of his father's domineering personality is closely argued and graphically detailed, a classic depiction of bourgeois guilt formation. Looking back upon his childhood from a distance of some thirty years, he describes his father as a tyrannical giant, brimming with confidence and energy, always judging, sitting regally at the head of his dinner table, uttering statements which were taken as divine commandments. In his presence, the young Franz was crushed by a pervasive sense of inadequacy that engendered inescapable guilt.

Accepting his father's estimation of him as vermin *(Ungeziefer)*, he could not act independently and was often reduced to stammering or silence. The father's threats and warnings of failure became inevitable realities; punishment was meted out before the deed was committed; and since there was no proportion between any deed and paternal anger, the world became incomprehensible. Though threats of punishment were rarely executed, they were paralyzing since release was granted only through the father's grace. The only weapons the child—and even the mature Franz—could resort to were sulking, furtive ridicule, and escape plots all doomed to fail.

Three avenues of escape from this unbearable emotional maze are mentioned: Judaism, marriage, and writing. The participation of father and son in a common ancestral heritage is suggested as a possible meeting ground, but rejected after lengthy discussion, since it was clear that Hermann Kafka was not interested in Jewish religious practice. When Franz was a boy, synagogue or home observance of Jewish customs or laws bored him; when he matured and began to develop an abiding passion for Jewish history and current Jewish affairs, his father resented this rekindled interest and called it nauseating (*Ekel*). The very fact that Kafka could imagine that Judaism might have been an area of reconciliation is, in itself, a reflection of his sharing in the renewal of Judaism in certain circles of Jewish intellectuals in Central Europe during that period. On the other hand, he utilizes the notion of orbits of shared interests to explain why writing was, indeed, a viable avenue of escape from his father: Hermann Kafka harbored a deep aversion towards writing and this encouraged Franz to consider it an area of independent activity. The writer of this letter is by no means naive or contrite.

Moving systematically from general considerations of the father-son relationship, to techniques of education, the other members of the family, Judaism, writing, and the choice of a career, Kafka reaches his designated climax when he comes to the issue of his inability to marry, apparently the proximate cause of the friction with his father in 1919. The inability to marry, even though he considered marriage and founding a family a consummate achievement, engendered profound anxiety and reams of explanations, particularly to his twice-betrothed Felice. This was the ultimate test of his energy and determination, and here he failed repeatedly, involving not only his self-esteem, but his fiancée and the two families. Here, too, the burden of blame is placed on his father who prepared him badly for marriage. It is evident that the need to offer some explanation for this disastrous failure inspired the letter; it is precisely at this point that he comments on the excruciating effort to explain something so intimate and intricate with little hope of it being understood:

> I am afraid that, because in this sphere everything I try is a failure, I shall also fail to make these attempts to marry comprehensible to you. And yet the success of this whole letter depends on it, for in these attempts there was, on the one hand, concentrated everything I had at my disposal in the way of positive forces, and, on the other hand, there also accumulated, and with downright fury, all the negative forces that I have described as being the result in part of your method of upbringing, that is to say, the weakness, the lack of self-confidence, the sense of guilt, and they positively drew a cordon between myself and marriage. The explanation will be hard for me also because I have spent so many days and nights thinking and burrowing through the whole thing over and over again that now even I myself am bewildered by the mere sight of it. The only thing that makes the explanation easier for me is your—in my opinion—complete misunderstanding of

the matter; slightly to correct so complete a misunderstanding does not seem excessively difficult. (p.97)

Characteristic of the entire letter, this passage is a model of rhetorical control. While confessing weakness and anticipating failure to make himself understood, Kafka writes from an intellectual and morally superior position. He has worked out the explanation in agonized nights of thinking through and burrowing (*Ich...durchdacht und durchgrabe habe*) and finds it crucial to correct his father's misunderstanding on the matter—at least partially. All the negative forces result from the father's method of upbringing (*Erziehung*), especially the three traits we find repeated throughout the letter: weakness (*die Schwäche*), the lack of self-confidence (*der Mangel an Selbstvertrauen*), and, of course, the sense of guilt (*das Schuldbewusstein*). By this time the reader certainly is aware that the sense of guilt derives from the lack of self-confidence, and both are the result of the father's overpowering presence in the dialogue of *Ich* and *Du*; here, the *Du*, the father, is trapped in the tight rhetorical web spun by the *Ich*, the son.

Kafka demonstrates the father's pernicious education of his son by telling, in a disarmingly peculiar way, an incident which took place when he was out for a walk with his parents when he was about sixteen years old. He began to discuss sex with them in what he describes as "a stupidly boastful, superior, proud, detached (that was spurious), cold (that was genuine), and stammering manner" reproaching them for having left him "uninstructed." He admits, at length, that he probably acted so despicably to avenge himself on the two of them. Nevertheless, he proceeds to berate his father for answering that he "could give [him] advice about how [he] could go in for these things without danger," an answer which, given the relationship between the two, the son found staggering since it induced the son to consider himself as filth in opposition to the father's, and the family's, purity.

The impassioned reasoning here strains the reader's credulity: while admitting he was arrogantly embarrassing his father and his mother, the writer asserts that the father's reply (so typical of the period) was so monstrous that it precluded the son's development of a healthy attitude towards sex. Repeatedly, he resorts to the argument that given the unequal relationship between the two, any response would have had a negative effect, just as the granting of freedom to choose a career was interpreted as no freedom at all since the crippling relationship had rendered any concept of freedom meaningless. His summary argument explaining his inability to marry, is a courtroom tour-de-force designed to shift the blame from the (self) accused, to the putative accuser.

> The most important obstacle to marriage, however, is the no longer eradicable conviction that what is essential to the support of the family and especially to its guidance, is what I have recognized in you; and indeed everything rolled into one, good and bad, as it is organically combined in you—strength, and scorn of others, health, and a certain immoderation, eloquence and inadequacy, self-confidence and dissatisfaction with everyone else, a worldly wisdom and tyranny, knowledge of human nature and mistrust of most people; then also good qualities without any drawback, such as industry, endurance, presence of mind, and fearlessness. By comparison I had almost nothing or very little of all this; and it was on this basis that I wanted to risk marrying, when I could see for myself that even you had to fight hard in marriage and, where the children were concerned, had even failed?(119)

The rhetorical virtuosity which characterizes the letter after the introduction of the marriage theme is climaxed by the writer's construction of a hypothetical rejoinder by the father, Hermann Kafka, to his son Franz in reply to the lengthy letter of accusations, "the reasons I offer for the fear I have of you"(121). The *Ich* and *Du* relationship which marked the first pages of the letter is deliberately inverted here. The ventriloquist's voice selected here is revelatory. The writer could have parodied the father's voice, but didn't; he has the father speak in the son's voice with its unmistakably psychological perceptivity and formidable persuasive powers. He has literally swallowed his father and eliminated him as an independent individual. His reshaping of the father in accordance with his image of him is complete. When he has Hermann Kafka accuse him of fighting not like the knight, but like the vermin (again *Ungeziefer*) which "sucks your blood in order to sustain their own life," he has employed an apt image. The opening passage of the father's hypothetical rejoinder speaks volumes.

> You maintain I make things easy for myself by explaining my relation to you simply as being your fault, but I believe that despite your outward effort, you do not make things more difficult for yourself, but much more profitable. At first you repudiate all guilt and responsibility; in this our methods are the same. But whereas I then attribute the sole guilt to you as frankly as I mean it, you want to be 'overly clever' and 'overly affectionate' at the same time and acquit me also of all guilt. Of course, in the latter you only seem to succeed (and more you do not even want), and what appears between the lines, in spite of all the 'turns of phrase' about character and nature and antagonism and helplessness, is that actually I have been the aggressor while everything you were up to was self-defense. (121-122)

The letter-writer here displays the same obsession with the disparity between avowed or assumed human motivation and true motivation, i.e. that perceived by a relentlessly omniscient narrator, which we find in the mature fiction of Franz Kafka.

The letter therefore not only sums up the problematic relationship between the son and the father that is structurally so central in both the life and writings of Franz Kafka; it introduces us to Kafka's nuclear topoi and rhetorical devices; and, no less important, it forces us to consider what the writer has deleted or distorted. Without denying the pained reality of the letter for Kafka, we should not abandon our critical judgment, as most readers have, and accept this rendition of the truth as the only possible version of the relationship. We have not heard from Hermann or Julie Kafka, the parents, and we have next to nothing from the sisters.

A sober contemplation of the letter should prepare us for a cautious reading of all of Kafka's works, those we ordinarily call fiction, on the one hand, and the letters and diaries (that we group together for convenience), on the other. We are dealing with an artist no less controlled and deliberate than Flaubert, Kleist, and Goethe, the three writers he admires most frequently. And yet, despite Kafka's suppression of specific realistic detail in his fictions, we have abundant information about the community in which he traveled—middle-class Prague Jewry at the turn of the twentieth century—and can enrich our reading by observing what he did with the specifics of the community that nourished him spiritually, even as it suffocated him.

The accepted notion that human relations in Kafka's fiction, on the one hand, and his diaries and letters, on the other, are usually adversarial appears, upon reflection, to be simplistic. The *Ich–Du* relationship is less adversarial than dialectic, strictly speaking: Franz's negation of Hermann's efforts to educate him—in the broader sense of *Bildung*—finds its synthesis in Franz Kafka's texts (though not in his life) and energizes them with their peculiar, intriguing interweaving of accusation and confession. Without the one, the other is ordinary, even stereotypical. Franz has so internalized Hermann that he acts the role of both Franz and Hermann at the same time, hence the constant presentation of multiple points of view, often overlapping, so evocative as they merge and dissolve. Franz was not entirely accurate in his assertion "my writing was all about you;"(87) by assimilating Hermann so totally and painfully, he is not writing "about" him—perhaps *through* him, but not *about* him. He is writing Franz's recreation of the world, including Hermann's central role in it, as Franz envisages it.

While one could argue that all writers ultimately do precisely this, in Kafka's case, the self-conscious obsession with the wavering problematic relationship between consciousness and being was so acute that the traditional authorial process is essentially doubled. The narrator's repeated ambivalencies, shifts in point-of-view, and rhetorical dexterity are so complex, yet controlled, that the reader senses the author is conscious of another author who engages him in a continuous dialogue about his writing and perhaps contributes to it. The reader is therefore forced to comprehend a multi-voiced, subtly nuanced conversation of personae, observing and speculating about perplexed or anxious human beings.

❍   ❍   ❍

However reactive, this world of fluid consciousness, of consciousness of consciousness, has its own solid existence which is ultimately the literary articulation of one complex writer to a complex existential situation. The literary *oeuvre* of this Prague Jewish writer, Franz Kafka, raises endless questions of interpretation, many inspired by the puzzling fact that the diaries and letters are replete with specific references to places and people in Prague, not the least to Jewish Prague, while the fiction is almost free of such references. Clearly a sustained process of repression is going on here.

Whatever the final, and larger, analysis of these complex matters, the example provided by Kafka's life and work should force us to re-examine the notions of assimilation and marginality that we have inherited from classical nineteenth century nationalism. More often than not, our notions are shaped by two parameters: religious observance and affiliation with some activist Jewish group. For Kafka, so bedeviled by the problematics of Jewish existence, neither of these parameters presented a meaningful option. Logic would dictate that the time has come to consider assimilation and marginality as central—not marginal—phenomena in modern Jewish history.

NOTES

1. *Franz Kafka. The Complete Stories,* (ed.) Nahum N. Glatzer (New York, 1971), 166–167.

2. G. Deleuze and F. Guattari, *Kafka: for a Minor Literature* (Minneapolis, 1986).

3. *Kafka: Letters to Friends, Family and Editors,* translated by Richard and Clara Winston (New York, 1977), 286-289. Since all subsequent quotes from this remarkable letter are from the same source, I do not cite them by page.

4. *The Diaries of Franz Kafka*, 1910-1913 (New York, 1946).

5. Sander Gilman, *Jewish Self Hatred* (Baltimore, 1986).

6. Ernst Pawel, *The Nightmare of Reason* (New York, 1985).

7. *Kafka: Letter to his Father,* translated by Ernst Kaiser and Eithine Wilkins (New York, 1953).

INTERPRETATION OF
TRADITIONAL TEXTS

⮑ Swallowing Jonah: The Eclipse of Parody

Nineveh and Tarshish, understood literally or figuratively, are obvious polar opposites in the Book of Jonah. From the author's unnamed vantage point, apparently Jerusalem, they are directions in the prophet's career. For the reader, they are two cardinal modes of human behavior: engagement and flight. Since these two modes involve the relationship between an individual and his God, the text of Jonah has attracted special attention in each of the three Scripture-based religions and has generated countless interpretations, some serious, some whimsical. Most modern scholars note that the reader is immediately confronted with a strange paradox: the book was canonized as part of the classical prophetic literature by the second century, B.C.E., but the portrayal of the prophet, Jonah, is strange, to say the least. It is precisely this paradox and this *strangeness* that intrigues us and establishes the point of our departure. In our attempt to understand the strangeness of the book, its intriguing hermeneutic history, i.e. its canonization despite its whimsicality, we shall have recourse to some theoretical studies generated by the recent renewed interest in parody. Foremost among these is Margaret A. Rose's *Parody//Metafiction* (1979), which deftly fuses many strands of critical thought on parody from traditional poetics to Russian Formalism, Structuralism, Post-Structuralism, and Reception Theory.[1] *Strangeness*, we should recall, is a basic feature of the poetics formulated by the Russian Formalists.

It is Elias Bickerman who most forcefully called attention to the book's strangeness. In introducing his English essay on Jonah as one of the *Four Strange Books of the Bible*,[2] Bickerman indulges in several paragraphs of scholarly play by simply cataloguing an artfully chosen disconnected series of facts. He begins:

> The Book of Jonah contains only forty-eight verses according to the reckoning of the ancient Hebrew scribes. But the name of no prophet is better known to the man in the street. Jonah is that man who was swallowed alive by a whale and was spewed up three days later, unhurt. The Hebrew Bible contains fifteen prophetic books, but Mahomet speaks only of Jonah, "him of the fish." As early as the second century B.C.E. Jonah in the belly of the sea monster and Daniel among the lions appeared as outstanding examples of deliverance, and in the eyes of the first Christians the emergence of Jonah alive from the depths of the sea prefigured the Resurrection. (p. 3)

Bickerman continues with a desultory history of the book's interpretation designed to convince the attentive reader that the book is a literary creation which has generated the most disparate interpretations, then shifts to an implicit attack upon modern readers:

> Despite the discomfort the story aroused in the faithful, its literal historicity was declared as late as 1956 in a Catholic Encyclopedia, and admitted, albeit halfheartedly, in a Protestant biblical dictionary in 1962. In a mosque bearing the name of Jonah near the oil derricks of Mosul the pious visitor can still admire the remains of Jonah's whale. (p. 4)

The essay that follows this whimsical introduction is sober, thorough, erudite, but the author could not refrain from introducing it with his comic, parodic introduction named, naturally, "Jonah and the Whale." Ironically, writing at precisely the same time in *Irony in the Old Testament*,[3] E. M. Good can declare with relief:

> Controversies over the Book of Jonah have apparently all but ceased. One's viewpoint on the historicity of the "great fish"…no longer determines his orthodoxy or heterodoxy….That theological battle has been finished. There is even a remarkable unanimity on the interpretation of the book among Old Testament scholars (a notably quarrelsome lot), which seems suspicious were it not so welcome. (p. 39)

And yet, Good, the professed lover of irenic, dispassionate scholarship can state near the end of his essay on Jonah:

> But the author of the Book of Jonah challenges this isolationism to consider the implications of such a reign and such a compassion. In that sense, we may see Jonah as a representative of Israel. Such an untenable understanding of God's ways with man as that held by Jonah was a persistent notion in Israel. Jesus was battling the same pattern of belief when he said to the chief

priests and elders, "The tax collectors and harlots go into the kingdom of God before you." (Matt. 21:31) (p. 54)

We shall forgive Good his religious zeal which has him attribute too much importance to this caricature of a prophet who dealt in fish and gourds, not tax collectors and harlots. What is particularly surprising is his espousal of a specific religious truth, here: Christianity, in a book which purports to be an exploration of irony in the text of the Hebrew Scriptures, those texts that he calls the Old Testament. Irony usually suggests the capacity or the need to entertain two contradictory positions simultaneously; there can, however, be no irony in a position which insists upon one exclusive claim to the truth. If the lengthy and varied history of interpretation teaches us anything it is respect for the amazing fecundity of the human interpretive imagination.

The Book of Jonah has inspired this interpretive activity not only because of its theme, flight from commitment to a divine injunction, but because it is itself a conscious interpretation of many literary texts. Most Biblical scholars agree on two facts: the Book of Jonah is certainly post-exilic and was probably first published in the late fifth century, B.C.E.; obvious and repeated references to other, previous literary works energize this text from beginning to end. The *competent* reader of the Hebrew scriptures, familiar with those texts dateable as antecedent to Jonah, cannot escape the impression that this evocation of previous texts is relentless, exceptional, and hence peculiarly meaningful.[4]

The intertexual density of the book suggests that the book was originally published as a parody, i.e. as a composition imitating and distorting another, usually serious, piece of work. By definition, any parodic text has one or more pre-texts to which it relates often satirically. These pre-texts must be fairly obvious to the reader; otherwise, the parody simply does not work. The role of the reader's ability to respond to parodic signals is central to my approach which builds upon that of such scholars as M. Burrows, J. Miles, B. Halpern, R. Friedman, J.C.Hulbert, and J. Ackerman all of whom argued for a reading of the Book of Jonah as satire or parody.[5] The argument in this article builds upon the work of these—and many other—scholars, but differs in two respects: it attempts to utilize more recent thinking about the genre of parody; it asks what happened to those parodic aspects of the Jonah text once the book was canonized as prophetic literature in the second century B.C.E.

Since it is clear that even those scholars who have suggested that the text of the Book of Jonah embodies certain parodic features often write without a clear idea of what parody actually is, how it differs from satire or irony, or what it entails, it will be helpful to outline at this point specifically what we mean by parody. There are a number of aspects of parody that have been accepted by those theoreticians who have followed the lead of Margaret A. Rose, and it is useful to reformulate them here in brief. One can hear in them echoes of Shklovsky, Tynjanov, Iser, Riffaterre, Bakhtin, and Foucault.

1. A parody is a composition that always assumes a pre-existing text which it imitates and distorts, often, but not always, for satiric purposes. While satire "censures wickedness and folly" in human society in general, parody is a literary genre which deals with the refunctioning, or criticism, of other preformed literary and linguistic material. Though parody is usually a literary genre, there are parodies in painting and music and, for the purpose of discussion, they too can be treated as texts.

2. The parodic text raises expectations in the reader that it is, in some way, e.g. in style or implication, similar to the parodied text, but it deliberately frustrates these expectations by being markedly different from the parodied text.

3. The parodic text thus consists of two text-worlds: that of the parodist and that of the parodied text. The co-existence of these two text worlds within one linguistic structure (in the case of literature) lends parody both its inherent interest and its difficulty.

4. The parodist utilizes a variety of devices ranging from puns and sound play to exaggerations, incongruities, and allusions which generate, in effect, two sets of signals: one evoking the parodied text; the other playing with or against it.

5. For the parody to be effective, the reader must respond to the two—often mixed—sets of signals embodied in the text. Not all readers are competent to respond to these signals.

6. While the attitude of the parodist to the parodied text might be contempt or sympathy, it might more often be one of ambivalence.

7. The target of the parodist might be the text parodied or the world it represents, but it might also be an unidentified contemporary text that aspires to achieve the norms of the parodied text, but fails to do so.

8. In that the parodist assumes implicitly that the reader can respond to his mixed signals, i.e. can discover and interpret the two text-worlds which constitute the parody, there exists a world of shared discourse, an episteme. Parody, therefore, raises a host of ques-

tions concerning varying norms and expectations, audiences, interpretation, and canonization.

By focusing on these parodic features in the Book of Jonah, we should be able to account for some of the book's strangeness and the crucial fact that it has been accepted as part of the prophetic canon since the 2nd century, B.C.E. though, as we shall demonstrate, it was originally a brilliant composite parody of the stories dealing with the prophets. This line of investigation, furthermore, can contribute to our understanding of the complex process of canonization, a topic of much recent research, notably the work of Brevard S. Childs.[6] If, finally, Jonah can be firmly established as a parodic text, it can be studied as such among other parodic texts, thus both enriching the repertoire of parodic texts and the attendant literary theory on parody.

❉   ❉   ❉

The book assumes familiarity with a variety of Biblical passages. The first is a fleeting reference to a certain Jonah, son of Amitai, a prophet mentioned in II Kings 14:25 in connection with promises of national expansion made by Yahweh and executed by Jeroboam II, one of the more disreputable kings of the northern kingdom of Israel. There might have been in ancient Israel other stories of a prophet Jonah, as there were of Daniel or Job or Noah (Ezekiel 14:14), but we know nothing of them. Since Jonah is a prophet and is being called to bring the divine message to Nineveh, the call-scenes of the literary prophets—Jeremiah, Isaiah, Amos—is evoked as is their careers. The narratives in I and II Kings about Elijah and Elisha spring to mind. It contains allusions to a variety of prophetic oracles, notably Jeremiah 36. The storm at sea and the threat of death by drowning recall the Deluge; the brief oracle Jonah recites in Nineveh uses the fateful term used to portray the devastation of Sodom and Gomorrah; Jonah's querulous conversations with God echo Abraham's pleading for Sodom. These three referents are from Genesis, as is what might be a burlesque of the Tree and Serpent story, Jonah's dejection over the eating of the gourd by a worm. The song of thanksgiving in Chapter Two is obviously a Psalm. Even a superficial reading, then, situates one familiar with the Hebrew scriptures in a literary world that is extremely familiar. It thus affords the grounds for constructing the "horizons" (in the Jaussian sense) of the Hebrew reader in the fifth (?) century B.C.E.

Of cardinal importance for understanding the motivation of this *prophet*, his flight from his call, is the majestic passage in Exodus 34 describing the second encounter on Sinai between Moses and Yahweh, significantly less dramatic than the first, but still powerfully numinous. Yahweh appears here as the God of forgiveness and covenant. Moses, both the lawgiver and prime prophet of Israel is instructed: "Carve two tablets of stone like the first, as I will inscribe upon the tablets the words that were on the first tablets, which you shattered" (v. 1). When Moses arrived on Sinai with the new, blank tablets, the Lord descended in a cloud, stood with him and "proclaimed the name Yahweh" (v. 5). At this point, Yahweh, in an act that parallels the enigmatic name-revelation in Exodus 3:14 when Yahweh calls himself "Eheyeh Asher Eheyeh" ("I Am Who I Am"), names himself with a formula of epithets stressing his compassion and forgiveness (vs. 6-7): "Yahweh, Yahweh, a God compassionate and gracious, slow to anger, rich in steadfast kindness..."[7] And in response to Moses' prostration and request (v. 9): "...stiff-necked though this people be, pardon our iniquity and our sin, and take us for Your own." Yahweh re-invokes the covenant between His people and Himself, a covenant associated here with the *exclusion* of any covenant between Israel and any other nation. The dialogue implies a possible contradiction between God's universal compassion and his exclusive covenant with the particular people which Moses was leading.

The compassionate, forgiving God, who declares an exclusive covenant with His people, is the same God who sends Jonah on his mission to Nineveh from which he seeks to flee to Tarshish, a flight later (Chapter 4) explained by Jonah in the light of the possible contradictions one might infer from Exodus 34 between God's compassion and His demand from his people of an exclusive covenant. It is notable that this revelation on Sinai is secondary to the original, a belated re-inscription of the stone tablets after the greatest of all prophets, Moses, had broken the first tablets in his anger at the rebelliousness of the chosen people. Whatever the author of the Book of Jonah meant in his deceptively simple narrative that reaches its climax in Chapter 4, he surely had to confront the tension inherent in Exodus 34 and, perhaps, the notion of the belated inscription of the second pair of stone tablets. The involved hermeneutic history of the book certainly manifests this awareness. Exodus 34 thus provided the author of the Book of Jonah much more than the theme of God's compassion: it allows or even necessitates the ambiguities of the book and offers a cardinal model of re-inscription. It should be noted, however, that the re-inscription of the second pair of tablets differs from parody that implies a distortion of the original, not a duplication as in the case of the second tablets.

The very notion that the Book of Jonah, for centuries canonized as one of the Twelve Minor Prophets, could originally have been a parody of prophetic literature or Biblical literature, in general, is bound to encounter strong opposition by most readers of the Bible, who, following the tradition of Biblical interpretation since the canonization of these texts, take them to imply commitment, obedience to the will of God, the same God who sent Jonah on his mission to Nineveh. The *Nineveh orientation*, i.e. following God's commandment is the undeniable direction of the Bible in its canonized form—whatever might have been the import of specific books or passages in their pre-redacted phases. The opposite *Tarshish orientation*, of flight from God's presence is not only impossible; it is a violation of His will. Parody, in that it plays with texts considered by someone to be sacred, is clearly *Tarshish oriented*. The objections the pious reader would have to a parodic reading is more complicated than the reasons for failure to recognize or accept parodic signals that Rose formulates (p. 27):

1. The reader does not recognize the presence of parody, because he does not recognize the text world of the parodied text as a quotation from another work but reads it as part of the text world of the [parodic text].
2. The reader recognizes the quotation, and the presence of two text worlds, but does not comprehend the intention of the author or the relationship (usually one of discrepancy) between the two texts.
3. The [reader who is a] friend to the parodied text recognizes the parodistic effect of the work and feels both himself and the parodied text and its author to be the target of satire. The resistance to parodic signals on the part of a reader with a *Nineveh orientation* is more stringent than Rose's third reader, one friendly to the parodied text. Not only is our hypothetical pious reader friendly to the parodied text, passages of the Hebrew Bible, but he sincerely believes it to be Sacred Scripture. For him, even the parody, the Book of Jonah, is sacred text. For the Jewish reader, it is a prooftext of sin and repentance; for the Christian, a prefiguration of the Resurrection.

Fully realizing the perils of these waters, we are exploring the seas to Tarshish. We are going to follow a course charted partly by Good, who calls the book "ironic," Burrows, who concludes it is a satire, and more specifically, John A. Miles , Jr.[8] I am particularly indebted to Miles's article, "Laughing at the Bible: Jonah as Parody" since, by suggesting that Jonah is a parody of "Hebrew letters," of the prophetic writings, in particular, he has significantly shifted the grounds of the argument from speculation about the history of Israelite religion or early Judaism, to the plane of intertextuality where we can first examine the text against its previous literary background and speculate about the nature and effect of this literary play, its freedom, flexibility, and provocation of both laughter and indignation. By playing with an antecedent tradition, one both declares one's attraction to it (otherwise, why bother with it?) and one's desire to escape from it. The escape is, in a sense, futile, since the need to play with, to engage, implies the inability to reject or ignore. Hence the ambivalence of the parodist—a characteristic which all modern theorists of parody from Tynjanov on refer to. One can never reach Tarshish, but one might try to do so. And yet, the Tarshish orientation, the desire to escape through play, however futile, is an aspect of literary creativity we should note and explore, thus challenging the pervasive *Nineveh orientation*, the drive towards relentless commitment, which marks the history of the hermeneutics of the Book of Jonah. Miles' article is a first step in a new, significant direction.

A sample of the *Nineveh orientation* of most of the exegetical tradition can be found in Adele Berlin's critique of Miles's article.[9] Obviously incensed by Miles's irreverence, Berlin proclaims:

> ...the author has not explained how a parody of prophetic writings, which were looked upon with utmost seriousness throughout the rest of the Bible, came to gain enough acceptance to be included in the Prophets. That is, unless Dr. Miles is implying that the canonizers of the Bible did not understand the message of the book. They were obviously not alone in their ignorance; Jewish tradition regards the Book of Jonah with such reverence that it is read at the afternoon service of the Day of Atonement, hardly the appropriate occasion for a parody of the Bible. (227)

Berlin's assertion bears scrutiny since she raises the fundamental questions most readers of the Book of Jonah are likely to ask at this point. Two historical facts prevent her from even entertaining the possibility that the book might be satiric or parodic: it was canonized among the prophetic books; it is read in the synagogue as part of the ritual of repentance. By implication, she denies that books have their history of interpretation. The book could have been interpreted as parody before it was canonized as a serious prophetic text; it certainly wasn't always canonical because, as far as we know, no book of the Bible was canonized upon first publication. Canonization, as Childs reminds us, is a long, complicated process which actually contributes to shaping the text. The citation of its liturgical usage as proof of its meaning at the time of composition is pointless. The Book of Jonah was not always part of the Day of Atonement service; the first mention of this custom is apparently found in Megillah 31a, centuries after the period of canonization.

What we should ask is: "What might have been the understanding or the intent of the book before it was given a canonically acceptable interpretation?" Assuming that the standard dating of original composition is correct, i.e. the fifth or early fourth century B.C.E., at least two centuries passed before the canonization of the prophetic books was completed: the first reference to the Twelve Prophets is found in Ben Sira 49:10, ca.180 B.C.E. The Book of Jonah was therefore redacted in one of the most dynamic and least documented periods in Jewish history, the last century of Persian rule, a period described by Elias Bickerman and Morton Smith who rely primarily on ingenious yet plausible inferences.[10] Since this was clearly one of the most formative periods in the history of Judaism, and after it the paths of Judaism and Christianity diverged, interpretations of Biblical books dated in this period always bear the distorting weight of theological preconceptions, be they Jewish or Christian.

It is precisely for this reason that a "literary" analysis might be most fruitful since it attempts to understand the compositional dynamics of the text with its literary conventions, strategies of presentation, and point of view; while we can never hope to know exactly how a fifth or fourth century B.C.E. reader responded to a text, we are not totally ignorant of literary devices which are international and often timeless. Form Criticism often employed similar techniques, but it was usually bound to the search for a discernible, definable form and its Sitz im Leben. In calling Jonah a parody, we are not defining a form, but rather suggesting a generic convention implying certain attitudes and devices.

Miles, we believe, is, on the whole, accurate in stating "that the proximate target of the humor of the Book of Jonah is not Jewish life but Hebrew letters" (p. 170). That centuries of Jewish readers including the canonizers of the Bible "did not understand the message of the book," as Berlin suggests that Miles' implies, is no argument. Meanings change with readers, or, to use E.D. Hirsch's terms, the original meaning may be constant and possibly recuperable by research, but the significance changes. The questions to be examined are: Does the text of the Book of Jonah contain discernible parodic techniques (or signals) or doesn't it? If we can find these clear signals in the text, we are both entitled and obligated to ask a series of questions about the book: What is the effect of the parody? Who might have written it? What might the proximate target have been? What does the possibility of parodic composition and reception tell us about the episteme of the period? How, indeed, could the book have been accepted for canonization by a sober, pious group of religious authorities?

For the sake of convenience, we shall divide parodic techniques into two areas and two operations. The two areas are topoi (or situations) and stylistics. As a topos I would cite the standard call to prophecy and the prophet's reluctance to accept the call; as stylistics, I would call attention to the obvious usage of language taken from another text, but not exclusively a prophetic one. The two operations are inversion and exaggeration: a topos or a stylistic unit could be inverted to render a meaning opposite (this includes also higher and lower) to that intended in the original text, or it can be exaggerated by excessive comic repetition. Even a cursory consideration, furthermore, of the great parodic classics, Aristophanes' plays (contemporary, roughly, with the Book of Jonah), or *Don Quixote*, or Joyce's *Ulysses* should alert us to the variety of method and purpose. We should never forget, finally, that there is in parodic writing a self-indulgent pleasure which aims not only to criticize, but to provoke laughter. Our task, then, is to demonstrate that there are distinctive parodic elements in this text, a task admittedly hard to perform since we are working in a period about which we know very little and the dating of Biblical texts is always problematical. To establish the audience's horizons of expectations is therefore a speculative venture, but eminently worth the risk.

✿   ✿   ✿

Miles, Halpern, Friedman, and Ackerman have discussed these techniques in the Book of Jonah, though they were not always aware that it was parody they were talking about. By placing many of their insights into the proper analytical framework, i.e. by treating their examples as parodic techniques, and by expanding their arguments, we can amass an impressive body of literary evidence. We do not intend to be exhaustive.

Miles's treatment of the parody in the Book of Jonah is essentially situational or topical. He isolates five situations and demonstrates that they are inversions of recognizable topoi found in the literary prophets. We shall review them in order and comment upon them.

a. *The Prophet's Calling.* Played against known call scenes, e.g. that of Moses, Gideon, Isaiah and Jeremiah, Jonah's call and his reaction to it is a masterpiece of comic inversion. We expect the prophet to protest verbally, profess his inadequacy, but finally yield. Jonah says nothing (in general, he is the most reticent prophet in the Bible: his actual oracle contains but five words), flees in the direction opposite to the designated locale of his mission, Nineveh, books passage on a ship to Tarshish. That Nineveh no longer existed at the time of composition suggests that the author's "ideal intentional reader" not only knows this, but probably realizes that Tarshish is used as a mythical, or at least fanciful, destination. Anachronism, of course, is a familiar parodic convention. The booking of passage and Jonah's Chaplinesque falling asleep in the hold of the ship during the storm are deft touches of quasi-realistic, comic inversion. Prophets do not do such things. Jonah's behavior is particularly ridiculous when read against the background of "narratives about the prophets in the Hebrew Bible" collected and analyzed deftly by Alexander Rofé in *The Prophetical Stories*.[11]

b. *The sailors' prayers.* Miles's rendering of the second situation, the frantic activity to save the ship, is the weakest of the five he chooses to study since he concentrates on only one aspect, the sailors' prayer, which he shrewdly calls "the mockery of the mockery of idolatry in Second Isaiah (cf. 44: 15-17)." Miles would have improved his argument by expanding the scope of the genre parodied to include the romance which was obviously wide-spread by that period as we can see from Herodotus, for instance, who traversed the Middle East about that time collecting, among other things, fanciful tales. The fanciful background of the parody, the bizarre previous behavior of our foolish prophet, the sudden conversion of the sailors to Yahwism which Jonah tried to escape, the rapid dialogue and turns of plot, are all signs of skillful comic writing based on a genre which was not meant to be taken seriously in contradistinction to prophetic oracles which were, after all, the message of Yahweh. It is surprising that Miles missed this mixture of generic sources since he does admit, in the next situation, the parody of a Psalm.

We have no easily definable *romances* in the Hebrew Scriptures that precede the Book of Jonah, though Northrop Frye does succeed in finding elements of the romance in these texts.[12] Following his suggestions regarding the romance in general, we can outline roughly a pattern that the author of the Book of Jonah inverts. Frye posits three basic stages in the romance: the hero's quest; his trial and conquest; the final exaltation of the hero or his God. In this case, the quest (the prophetic mission) is refused; the storm scene is ignored since our hero would sleep through it; and the exaltation of the God, Yahweh, is concretized by the sudden acceptance of Jonah's God by the sailors. Even more characteristic of the romance is the appearance of a dragon or Leviathan which the hero must conquer; Jonah, naturally, does not crush the great fish, but is first swallowed then vomited by him. Written against the background of a romance-tradition of miraculous deliverance from a Leviathan—a monstrous figure certainly not unknown to the Hebrew author or his audience—the great fish scene could be hilarious.

c. *The Psalm of Thanksgiving.* Since Miles does treat the oft-discussed Psalm of Thanksgiving as a parody, it accords well with the tenor of the entire book. He concentrates on the water and pit images here which, he claims, is the most concentrated of any passage in the Bible. This would thus be a fine example of comic exaggeration characteristic of parody. Miles adds a keen insight: "...the power of sea-imagery is only effective if it is in fact imagery and not direct description. If it is not to be merely bombastic, it cannot refer to real oceans and real water. In Jonah 2, it does." One might formulate this argument slightly differently: what the author of Jonah is doing is the realization of clichéd imagery, a comic technique practiced from Aristophanes to Thomas Pynchon.

d. *The Rejection of the Prophet by a King.* Biblical kings were not particularly fond of prophets: Pharaoh disdained Moses; Ahab rebuffed Micaiah; Zedekiah rejected Jeremiah. But Jonah not only encounters no difficulties with the temporal authorities; he apparently persuades the unnamed king of Nineveh to repent after uttering only one five-word sentence. It would seem, therefore, that Jonah was the only successful prophet there ever was. The scene is thus a comic inversion of the topos we know from the classical prophets.

e. *Jonah's Peevish Wish to Die*. Not only Job prays for death as an end to his agonies. Moses (Numbers 11:10-15), Jeremiah (Jeremiah 20:7-8), and Elijah (I Kings 19:4) all utter a preference for death over their agonies. Jonah complains "I wish I were dead" twice, but for rather silly reasons: first, that Nineveh was saved—as God had willed; second, that the blasting east wind dried up the protective gourd. The background of Elijah is particularly illuminating since the figure of Elijah became increasingly dominant in the post-exilic period and, according to rabbinic tradition, Jonah was a disciple of Elisha, Elijah's leading disciple. The contrast with Elijah makes Jonah all the more foolish and petty. (Again, see Rofé.) Jonah under his gourd tree outside of Nineveh is a clear parody of Elijah under his broom bush outside of Beer Sheba (I Kings 19). After this incident, Elijah traveled to Horeb and had the dramatic encounter with Yahweh who speaks to him from the "soft murmuring sound" (or "a still, small voice") (19:12), surely one of the most moving passages in Biblical narrative. Notice the inversion: Elijah at Horeb, the ancestral locale of revelation, speaking as a faithful emissary with Yahweh; Jonah petulantly bickering with God about his personal discomfort.

Miles's assignment of the Book of Jonah to the literary category, parody, rather than irony (which is not a literary category) or satire (which does not necessarily have as its target another text) is much more than a matter of taxonomy; it opens the way for fuller, unencumbered literary exploration. My major complaint with Miles's argument is that it does not go far enough: it restricts itself to topoi and slights stylistics; it attempts to limit itself to prophecy, while there are other literary categories being parodied at the same time: psalmody, romance and the hagiographic tale. In fact, the book is more a parody of the narratives about the prophets, a type of hagiography, than of prophetic oracles. There are, after all, only five words of prophetic oracle in the book. The very mélange of literary categories parodied strengthens the argument for the presence of parody considerably since it betrays a keen awareness of these categories on the part of the author and, more important, a desire to mix them up in willful play. One might suggest that the primary plane of activity here is literary, not theological: the virtuosity of the parodic techniques is evidence of a keen literary awareness.

Stylistic operations, scarcely mentioned in Miles's essay, are supplied in abundance in "Composition and Paronomasia in the Book of Jonah" by Baruch Halpern and Richard Friedman.[13] Ironically, though the authors demonstrate that "the book is a rich, almost baroque sampler of paronomastic techniques" (80), and conclude, at one point: "These instances should, if nothing else, serve to indicate that the undercurrent of verbal frolic is not fortuitous" (84), they never take the next logical step, which is to identify the book as parody. The authors study three paronomastic techniques: the repetition of key words, i.e. Leitwörter; phonetic word plays that "seem thematically inconsequential" (p. 83); and word play "on a semantic level" (p. 85). Let us review these categories more closely:

1. The repetition of key words such as *'alah, yarad, kam, hetil, gadol, minah, avad, ra'ah, karah* might have a theological implication in the narrative as argued by the authors in the beginning of the article, or constitute structural links binding the first episode with the second as demonstrated in the latter half of the article, but it also could have a comic effect. The same word repeated in radically different contexts focuses our attention on the incongruities or discontinuities in the text. Here, indeed, we run the risk of the hermeneutic circle: we determine the effect or meaning, of the term by its context and the context by the term but this is the same circle all exegetes run into in all periods, particularly when other supporting evidence is lacking. I can only suggest: read the text as a parody and see if these Leitwörter assume a comic effect. They often do. In this sense, none of these paronomastic techniques are semantically neutral or thematically inconsequential.

2. In the second category, the authors have collected an amazing array of puns which they claim—erroneously, I believe—are semantically inconsequential. Even the first example they present has the potentiality of provoking hilarious laughter in a parody-prone reader. In 3:7 the king gives orders "mita'am hamelekh" that no people or livestock should taste a thing—"al yit'amu me'umah." A pun, we should recall, is a figure of speech depending on a similarity of sound and a disparity of meaning. It has, for many centuries and in diverse cultures, been a source of intellectual play and delight. Why rule out the possibility of the playful enjoyment of the pun here? Is it that we assume that all Jews mourned for the destroyed temple every hour of their earthly existence? Among the possible puns which Halpern and Friedman adduce is the varied

use of the root *kdm*, or the chain: *naki* (innocent), *vayake* (he vomited), and *kikayon* (the gourd). While these latter three may seem far fetched, they are certainly within the acceptable limits of puns and could have been detected by a reader. In fact, one could argue that the connection of *vayake* (he [the fish] vomited) with *kikayon* (the gourd or the castor tree) is a true stroke of paronomastic genius which explains the choice of the *kikayon* (a vomit tree?) as the tree under which Jonah takes shelter. One ordinarily takes shelter under some sort of succah or tabernacle which can readily be associated with God's providential protection. Halpern and Friedman assert quite plausibly: "Paronomasia pervades the book so patently, in fact, that one is intrigued even by the tie of the name of the primary setting, Nineveh, to the name of the central character, Jonah (nynwh/ywnh)."

3. The third category isolated by Halpern and Friedman: word play on a semantic level could have been merged with the previous category since, in our opinion, no pun is devoid of semantic significance. The prime example they adduce is well chosen, nevertheless, since it is well-known and allows for amplification:

> The author of Jonah, however, in a mere 48 verses, exploits the ambiguity of words at least three times. He rigs the usage in such a way that the acute reader can perceive meanings that Jonah himself does not. Thus, Jonah believes he has proclaimed a message that has not been realized— he has grunted, "Forty more days and Nineveh will be overthrown (nhpkt)," and the city has weathered the crisis. But Jonah does not fathom the delphic nature of his oracle. Nineveh is nhpkt: apart from meaning 'physical overthrow,' the verb hpk denotes a change of character...Nineveh's transformation fulfills profoundly Jonah's prohecy (see Rashi on 3:4). (p. 87)

We don't know if Rashi chuckled at this pun with its latent ambiguity, but he certainly got the messsage. This type of pun not only manifests the difference between God's perception of reality and Jonah's, but it demonstrates a far-reaching sophistication in the use of the pun: the generation of comic or even tragic irony. The same is true in the second example adduced. When the sailors ask "What is your vocation?" (1:8) "mah mela'khtekha" (from mela'kha) Jonah never answers. But the "acute reader" (or the competent reader) should know that Jonah's vocation is prophecy. He is a mal'akh—a prophet, a messenger of YHWH, a term found in this meaning in several Biblical texts certainly known in literate circles in Judaea in the 5th century: Judges 6:8, Isaiah 63:9,

Haggai 1:13, and Malachi 2:7. The reader knows something Jonah does not, the common feature of tragic irony found also in comedies.

The study of paronomastic techniques or, more simply, punning, has a long and respectable history from the Greek rhetoricians to modern formalist critics with an interest in semantics and literary theory such as William Empson[14] and Sigurd Burckhardt.[15] Burckhardt, in fact, finds in the pun the very essence of literary creativity since the pun gives density, both phonetically and semantically, to language, a medium which is devoid of natural density. It is the epitome of literature's signal characteristic: its literariness. The brilliant manipulation of paranomastic techniques should not be taken lightly, but rather as a sign of advanced literary culture and sensitivity. More often than not, it is an integral device in parody, itself a technique which implies a world of texts, be they oral or written.

James Ackerman has also followed the suggestions of his mentor, F.M. Cross in two recent articles replete with interesting insights regarding both satire and imagery in the Book of Jonah.[16] Though his articles are indispensable for anyone interested in this Biblical book, and he often refers to the genre of parody, he never distinguishes clearly between satire and parody and misses many opportunities to enrich his fine perceptions. Some of Ackerman's analyses of incongruities are the finest one can find. He notes that the poem purports to be a lament (it is even in the lament prosodic form), but turns out to be a supplication. He shrewdly details the disjunction between what Jonah declares about his fate and what actually happened. He uncovers a rich texture of imagery, part in the text and part in the sub-text, and points to some startling links and dissonances. Within this framework he treats the gourd and worm episode as a satiric diminution of the tree and serpent story in Genesis 3. He demonstrates that the message of the book is carried by inverted situations: the prophet is portrayed as ridiculous as he accuses God for having too much pity (hus) for Nineveh, a reversal of Abraham's pleading for Sodom and Gomorrah in Genesis 18. This comic inversion is then connected with enclosure imagery by paronomasia: hus (pity) with hasah (shelter).

Ackerman does not refine his notion of parodistic composition since his interests lie elsewhere. His main thesis in his first, more original article is:

> ...that the song of Jonah plays a most important function in the story: it establishes major dissonances between the prophet's perception of reality and that of his narrative world. These dissonances, I suggest, are set in the

context of the bizarre and the unexpected. Thus, they move the entire work in the direction of satire and compel an ironic reading throughout. (219)

Given both this statement of purpose and Ackerman's fine literary sensitivity, one would expect a focused formulation of the role of parody in the Book of Jonah. But this never takes place. He is deflected from this by his other interests, i.e. Biblical exegesis and a Jungian (or Frommian) analysis of imagery. He pursues two arguments vigorously: the second chapter, a poem often considered a later addition, can be demonstrated to be integral to the book if it—and the book—are read as satires; the poem and other parts of the book are suffused with imagery of descent, death, and enclosures. These two arguments seem to deflect him from fully developing his thinking on satire to reach the logical discrimination between satire and parody.

While he has read widely in the standard works on satire (see notes on pages 227–229), he has not utilized the literature on parody. It is interesting to note that the two major theorists he cites are Northrop Frye and Wayne Booth. There is no mention or echo of those continental critics from the Formalists through the Post-Structuralists and the Reception theorists who inform much of the current theory on parody. A case in point is his discerning statement:

> The closest parallel to the Jonah story is Menippean satire, in which characters speak for themselves and are made to look ridiculous through their actions. In classical satire the events are wildly incongruous and distorted. The writer uses a mishmash of literary genres, often swinging from narrative prose to a song interlude and inverting those forms through parody. (228)

Ackerman, however, seems to be unaware that the Menippean satire of the Hellenistic period is repeatedly cited as a prooftext for much modern theory about intertextuality and narratology by scores of critics who adopted it from Bakhtin and Kristeva.[17] What interests them in this satire, really a composite of parodic texts, is its internally varied discourse, often free from historical generic restraints, its carnivalesque spirit capable of insinuating itself into other genres. Like the novel which, Bakhtin would argue, resembles it in many ways, the Menippean satire is constituted from many genres that it, in a sense, parodies.

✿   ✿   ✿

The evidence of parodic play is so abundant that one can ignore it today only by hermeneutic contrivance. We should not be troubled by

A. Berlin's argument—often advanced by traditional readers—that readers from the second century B.C.E. until the twentieth century C.E. did not read it as parody. Berlin finds it absurd to imagine "that the canonizers of the Bible did not understand the message of the book."[18] I would argue that it is entirely possible that a sage involved in the canonizing process could "misunderstand" a text; it may, in fact, be his sacred mission to "misunderstand" the text so that it could conform to his world view. The text, originally produced in the fifth century as a parody of prior texts, would have been understood as such by many, but not all contemporary readers. During the next two or three centuries, the audience changed and its capacity to grasp the parodistic elements in the text diminished, even disappeared. Certainly, the type of text produced in the early Second century, notably Ben Sira, reflects a world remote from parodistic impulses. Here the distinction between parody and satire is helpful, even crucial. Satire, even literary satire, does not necessarily incorporate materials from a text it is attacking; it may simply censure observed human behavior, human wickedness and folly. Parody must include a pre-text and is therefore more susceptible to "misunderstanding."

The author of the Book of Jonah, a master parodist, depicts the central character as a bit of a fool, peevish and tiring. Yet he is nominally a prophet. Since the author's attitude to the prophet, one of the leading character types in the Bible, is essentially negative, some scholars regard this book as an attack on prophecy, or the narrow nationalism of this prophetic stance, or the intensification of piety in the post exilic, or rather, post Ezra-Nehemiah era (cf. Miles and Good, for instance). Ackerman suggests that the object of attack was the Zadokite priesthood.

It seems to us, however, that the scholarship has missed the point by confusing life with literature. If we accept the scholarly consensus that prophecy, as a respectable religious phenomenon that could produce oracles worth saving, petered out after Haggai, Zechariah, and Malachai at the end of the sixth century or the first half of the fifth century B.C.E., and that the Book of Jonah was written about a century later, after the time of Ezra and Nehemiah, we are dealing with an author who was not concerned with real, practicing prophets, but rather with the *image* of the prophet as it appeared in the prophetic books, and, probably more likely, in the historical books such as Samuel, Kings, and Chronicles. This is the image formulated in Alexander Rofé's study mentioned above. The Pentateuch had been canonized by the end of the fifth century, but the canonization of the Prophetic Books was in process between 400 B.C.E.

(circa) and 200 B.C.E. (circa). Describing the last century of the Persian period, Bickerman, in *From Ezra to the Last of the Maccabees* states:

> The Chronicler's historical work, Attic pottery unearthed in Palestine, Jewish coins bearing a Divine image, universalism and exclusiveness, all these together create a picture of Jewish life after the Restoration rather different from what is conveyed by the conventional clichés. They indicate that life was more vivid, more diversified than the rules of conduct as formulated in Scripture might suggest. (p. 31)

Since canonization is a protracted process and requires canonizers, we can imagine that there were rival factions involved in the work, factions that—consciously or unconsciously—shaped the image of the prophet according to their views either in the very work of redaction or in the oral interpretation which accompanies every text through history. We don't know exactly who constituted these factions, but we can deduce from the evidence of both prior and later centuries, that the Judaism of those two centuries was far from monolithic. According to Morton Smith, for instance, there were at least two classes or ideological tendencies: one which tolerated the worship of Yahweh together with other Gods (the Assimilationists) and one which worshipped Yahweh alone (the Separatists).[19] The original author of Jonah—or at least of what is known today as Chapters 1, 3, and 4—would have been a member of the Assimilationist class or party and thus opposed to the Separatist sentiment mocked in the text. The prophet of this book did not want God's compassion extended to the non-Hebrews.

Smith brings his two-party division up to the time of Nehemiah and in this he is on relatively firm ground. His description of the post-Nehemiah period is more speculative as it has to be since the firmly datable documentation between Nehemiah and the Hasmoneans is meager. He divides the articulate population of the period into three parties: the Judean gentry, the Levites, and the priests. According to this scheme, the book of Jonah was written from the viewpoint of "pious members of the assimilationist party", i.e. the gentry according to his characterization (pp. 157–163).

> All this material—Proverbs, Job, Ecclesiastes, Ruth, Jonah, Judith, Tobit, Esther—is essentially belletristic and as such is sharply distinguished from the national legend and history, laws and prophecies, preserved by the earlier Yahweh-alone tradition. This belletristic material testifies to the continued existence from the sixth to the second century of a lay circle enjoying wealth, leisure, and considerable culture (and of lay scribes and teachers

who copied this material and perpetuated it as part of a humane literary education).(p. 159)

Though one could conceive of a parodist in that sort of *party*, we have no solid proof that such a party ever existed. Two facts, however, are incontestable: by the end of this period, the Book of Jonah was canonized, was naturalized as part of the Twelve Prophets; the religious attitudes of the population of Judaea changed radically between Nehemiah and Ben Sira. One would assume that the oral interpretation that accompanied the text and allowed it to be canonized was consonant with that of the other prophetic books. The parodic elements and their implication were probably lost in the process since canonization implies selection and exclusion. That a book's original meaning can be changed radically prior to canonization is attested to by the paradigmatic instance of The Song of Solomon. There is no such evidence of any discussion regarding a problematic canonization of the Book of Jonah. Given what we know of the Jewish community in the second century B.C.E., it is reasonable to assume that the audience and its horizons had changed markedly. They had become more pious and could not perceive the parodic signals which former generations could appreciate. But they could accept the world of the texts parodied in the Book of Jonah; they could venerate Jonah as a story about a real prophet who, after all, was also mentioned in the book of Kings. It is conceivable that the psalm that constitutes Chapter 2 was inserted during the process of canonization since, taken as a true, i.e. nonparodic, psalm, it changes the character of the prophet: we get a Jonah who might be compatible to Pharisaic Judaism.

In this sense, the canonizing community could swallow the Book of Jonah just as the big fish had swallowed Jonah himself. In both cases the swallowing turns the prophet towards Nineveh, towards his mission to call mankind to repentance. A complex, often indeterminate parodic creation was simplified—perhaps only psychologically—by the canonizers and domesticated for consumption by a more docile audience. The text did not have to be altered. The parody in the book was eclipsed by the pious parable which the redactors gave us in their interpretation of the book. Pious parables are a respectable, wide-spread literary category designed to lead the reader to commitment, but the message they usually bear restricts the play of thought and language which is the joy of the parodic temper. The evidence of the text would suggest that for a brief period in the history of ancient Israel, the parodic *jeu d'esprit* flourished, but was later inhibited by subsequent exegetes.

If we are correct in our argument that the Book of Jonah was originally a master-work of parody, we are confronted with a literary phenomenon which has few (I can think of none) parallels. The parody, we have argued, was eclipsed in the exegetical process which thus allowed for its canonization. Unlike the Song of Solomon which was converted through allegorization, the Book of Jonah was reconverted by interpretation—or misinterpretation—to the genre which it was designed to parody. A parody of a prophet's career became a prophetic book with a prophetic message. The intriguing ambiguities of the book would therefore be attributed to this rare hermeneutical reversal.

NOTES

1. Margaret A. Rose, *Parody//Metafiction* (London, 1979); Linda Hutcheon, *A Theory of Parody* (London, 1985); Joseph Dane, *Parody: Critical Concepts vs. Literary Practices, Aristophanes to Sterne* (Norman [Oklahoma], University of Oklahoma Press, 1988); Michelle Hanoosh, *Parody and Decadence: Laforgue's Moralites Legendaires* (Athens, Ohio,1989). All these books contain rich bibliographies.

2. Elias Bickerman, *Four Strange Books of the Bible* (New York, 1967). Originally in French as: "Les deux erreurs du prophète Jonas," *Revue D'Histoire et de Philosophie Religieuse*, Vol. XL, No. 2 (1965) 232–264.

3. Edwin M. Good, *Irony in the Old Testament* (Philadelphia, 1965).

4. For a detailed study of the texts quoted or referred to in the Book of Jonah see: Jonathan Magonet, *Form and Meaning: Studies in Literary Techniques in the Book of Jonah* (The Almond Press: Sheffield, 1983); Moshe Pelli, "The Literary Art of Jonah," *Hebrew Studies*, Vol. XX-XXI, 1979–1980, 18–28. For intertextuality in the Hebrew Bible see Michael Fishbane's masterly study, *Biblical Interpretations in Ancient Israel* (Oxford, 1985).

5. Millar Burrows, "The Literary Category of the Book of Jonah," *Translating and Understanding the Old Testament: Essays in Honor of Herbert Gordon May*, ed. Harry Thomas Frank and William L. Reed (New York, 1970) 80–107; John A. Miles, Jr., "Laughing at the Bible: Jonah as Parody," *The Jewish Quarterly Review* (New Series) Vol. LXV, No. 3, January 1975, 168–181; Baruch Halpern and Richard Friedman, "Composition and Paronomasia in the Book of Jonah," *Hebrew Annual Review*, Vol. IV, 1980, 79–91; John C. Hulbert, "'The Deliverance Belongs to Yahweh!': Satire in the Book of Jonah," JSOT, 21, October 1981, 59–81; James S. Ackerman, " Satire and Symbolism in the Song of Jonah, *Traditions in Transformation*, ed. Baruch Halpern and Jon D. Levenson (Winona Lake, Indiana, 1982) 213–246 and "Jonah," *Literary Guide to the Bible*, ed. R. Alter and F. Kermode (Cambridge, 1987) 234–243. One finds in the notes of Ackerman's "Satire and Symbolism..." a rich listing of works on Jonah and on satire. Miles, Halpern, Friedman and Ackerman are all students of Frank M. Cross. It is evident both from the shared approach and Frank Cross' lecture notes which he has so kindly shared with me that the four younger scholars have adopted and furthered much of their teacher's basic interpretation of the Book of Jonah.

6. Brevard S. Childs, *The Old Testament as Scripture* (SMC Press: London, 1979).

7. The connection between Exodus 34 and Jonah (and Joel) has most recently been treated by Thomas B. Dozeman, "Inner-Biblical Interpretation of Yahweh's Graciousness and Compassionate Character," JBL, 108/2, Summer 1989, 207–223. Dozeman compares the formulaic recitation of God's attributes in Exodus 34 with that in Jonah and Joel.

8. See note 5.

9. Adele Berlin, "A Rejoinder to John A. Miles Jr., With Some Observations on the Nature of Prophecy," *The Jewish Quarterly Review* (New Series) Vol. LXVI, No. 4, April 1976, 227–235.

10. Elias Bickerman, *From Ezra to the Last of the Maccabees* (New York, 1962); Morton Smith, *Palestinian Parties and Politics that Shaped the Old Testament* (Columbia University Press: New York, 1971).

11. Alexander Rofé, *The Prophetical Stories* (Hebrew) (Magnes Press: Jerusalem, 1986, 2nd. ed.)

12. Northrop Frye, *Anatomy of Criticism* (Princeton, 1957), 187–192.

13. See note 4.

14. William Empson, *Seven Types of Ambiguity* (London, 1931). See Chapter 3.

15. Sigurd Burckhardt, "The Poet as Fool and Priest: A Discourse on Method," *Shakespearean Meanings* (Princeton, 1968), 22–46.

16. See note 5. The texts quoted in this article are from Ackerman's "Satire and Symbolism" of 1982. The 1987 article, "Jonah," in the Alter and Kermode volume though more comprehensive, still fails to distinguish between satire and parody.

17. Julia Kristeva, "Word, Dialogue, and the Novel," *The Kristeva Reader*, ed. Toril Moi (Columbia University Press: New York, 1986), 52–54.

18. See note 9.

19. Smith, op. cit.

✐ The Politics of Scripture: The Hasidic Tale

The "politics of scripture" is no oxymoron, but rather a straightforward assertion that even texts deemed scriptural are the products of circumstances which can properly be termed political. This assertion collapses the traditional opposition between the political and the spiritual by calling attention to the obvious facts that one grants authority to the text, and authority implies power. I prefer the term "authority" rather than the more current term "privilege" since it embraces both semantically and etymologically the notion of author, whether assumed to be divine or human. In the same conventional spirit, I mean by the term "scripture" precisely what users of English have generally meant by it, that is, a text to which a certain audience attributes divine authorship or inspiration. Here, too, I am constrained to call attention to my traditional usage of a simple English term since we live in a period during which avant-garde critics of Romantic poetry habitually refer to their subjects as visionaries or prophets while even a more conservative critic like Northrop Frye can write a book called *The Secular Scripture*, an oxymoron in more traditional parlance. This oxymoron obviously betrays an acute sense of cultural, and hence semantic, displacement which must engender both psychological and linguistic anxiety.

If there is any anxiety that I want to deal with in this essay, it is not that of the secular reaching out for an elusive source of authority, nor is it the anxiety of influence often discussed by Harold Bloom; rather it is the anxiety generated within a religious, scripturally-based society by the creation of a new authoritative text, a new scripture. I shall take for my prooftexts the opening tales of the first and foremost collection of

109

Hasidic tales, *Shivhe HaBesht (In Praise of the Baal Shem Tov)*, first published in 1815, but probably circulated either orally or in manuscript around 1780, if not earlier, during the lifetime of the Baal Shem Tov himself (1700-1760). The specific problem I shall attempt to confront is how the early masters of the Hasidic tale made the accommodation between their notion of the sanctity of the tale (*kedushat hasipur*) and the prior, immutable sanctity of the scriptural text, the traditional Hebrew Bible.[1]

The need for such accommodation is, to be sure, one of the pervasive problems of a scripture-based religion, particularly one in which the Lord created the world by what we call today a *speech act*, and, in a counterpoised episode, shattered both the linguistic (and topographic) unity of mankind when it tried to transcend its nature by building a huge tower on the flat plains of Shinar. Most biblical scholars today would argue that the entire redactional process of the Hebrew Scripture was shaped in some way by reverence for the sanctity of text and language. When scripture officially became Scripture (for shorthand I refer to Nehemiah 8), the power of language, of the text, was both increased and diminished by institutionalization: increased through the permanence of bureaucracy and text; diminished by the mediation of the same social forces. The various accommodations with Scripture would constitute a veritable catalogue of the genres of Jewish, and for that matter, Christian, and Islamic literature through the ages, ranging from allegory, to midrash, to exegesis of all sorts. All this is well known and needs no elaboration here. What, however, we may ask, happens when a new genre of composition suddenly emerges within the scripture-based religion and almost instantaneously becomes an independent scripture without even pretending to be a commentary upon previous scripture? This is what happened in the case of the Hasidic tale, an argument forcefully advanced both by Joseph Dan (1975) and Gedalya Nigal (1981), the authors of the two most seminal works devoted to this genre, which has received little scholarly attention to date.

❂   ❂   ❂

Hasidism, the religious and social movement which has embraced and revitalized much of Jewish spiritual life from the eighteenth century until today, has not been a neglected area of research and debate. Though several generations of intense research into the origins of the Hasidic movement have produced a host of contradictory theories regarding the nature and purpose of the original sects which appeared in the southwestern Ukraine in the early decades of the eighteenth century, several uncontestable facts have emerged. During these decades, there appeared a variety of individual groups led by forceful, pious men, many of whom did not fit the mold of traditional rabbinical leadership, which prided itself on the interpretation of the sacred law. While some of these new leaders were prodigiously learned, others were not; some adhered strictly to the traditional rabbinical norms of authoritarianism, but others indulged in charismatic practices including faith healing; some stressed asceticism, while others preached service of the Lord through joy and ecstasy. Their followers also varied: some were learned and wealthy; others were ignorant and poor. Within these divergent currents, one religious phenomenon seems to be constant. Each group developed an extraordinary allegiance to its specific leader, whose authority derived more from personal charisma than formally ordained traditional practices.

This new allegiance slowly replaced the traditional structure of Jewish communal life which had rapidly disintegrated during the wars and social upheavals in Eastern Europe during the latter half of the seventeenth century. And though these new leaders did not preach reform or even outwardly challenge the status quo in either praxis or belief, they did convey, often in vastly popularized form, many of the basic notions of Lurianic mysticism which had developed in Palestine in the late sixteenth and early seventeenth centuries and had rapidly spread from the Ottoman Empire into the Kingdom of Poland, with which it was contiguous.

The Lurianic portrayal of the catastrophe of creation and the possible redemptive process was dazzling in its complexity but even in its popularized versions sufficed to give the masses of downtrodden Jews, often recent exiles, some sense of the meaning of the world, an understanding of their repeated exiles, and hopes for redemption through prayer and praxis. It certainly helped prepare tens of thousands of Jews to accept the messianic claims of Shabbetai Zevi, the false messiah who later converted to Islam in 1666 and, despite the normative rabbinic reaction to all signs of messianic claims usually identified with Sabbateanism in the late seventeenth and early eighteenth centuries, it could infuse the early, often isolated groups of early Hasidim with religious ardor. This new ardor, coupled with the comforting sense of belonging to a cohesive sect led by a self-assured, forceful religious leader, contributed significantly to the emergence of dozens of these groups in the southwestern Ukraine or Podolia.

By the third and fourth decades of the century, many of these groups coalesced under the charismatic leadership of Israel Baal Shem Tov, usually called The Besht, the zaddik or holy man considered by all later Hasidim and historians as the founder of the movement.

Gershom Scholem has summarized, in his characteristic authoritative manner, the history and meaning of the Besht's title.

> The technical term *ba'al shem* "Master of the Divine Names," literally: "Possessor of the Name," was the title given in popular usage and in Jewish Literature, especially in Kabbalistic and Hasidic works, from the Middle Ages onward, to one who possessed the secret knowledge of the Tetragrammaton and the other "Holy Names" and who knew how to work miracles by the power of these names...In the 17th and 18th centuries the number of *ba'ale shem* who were not at all talmudic scholars increased. Such a *ba'al shem* was often a combination of practical Kabbalist, who performed his cures by means of prayers, amulets and incantations, and a popular healer familiar with *segullot* ("*remedies*") concocted from animal, vegetable, and mineral matter ...There is a variety to the title *ba'al shem* known as *ba'al shem tov*. The Besht, the founder of Hasidism, is the most famous bearer of this title ....

A popular though far from ignorant charismatic healer who employed amulets and magic spells, the Besht attracted masses of adherents who came to be cured and join him in ecstatic prayer, one of the special characteristics of his religious praxis. Precisely because of the dynamic relationship between the zaddik and his follower, the term *Hasid*, which formerly meant simply "pious," developed the connotation of a pious adherent of a certain charismatic leader, of a certain Rebbe or zaddik. Both the Besht and his Hasidim clearly believed in his supernatural powers and visions, which were featured in a wealth of anecdotes narrated either by the master himself or by his Hasidim. The Hasidic tale, in fact, was one of the prominent literary genres spawned by the Hasidic movement, though it did not neglect more traditional genres such as exegesis and homily. By the time of his death in 1760, the Besht had left behind him a group of dedicated disciples and other, more tangential sects which were attracted to his charismatic posture but had not yet adopted all his practices or the unquestioning adulation of his saintly figure.

The Hasidic tale was certainly not the first hagiographic tale to emerge in the long history of Jewish literature, but it did succeed in changing the prevalent attitude toward the tale and the very act of telling tales. If, within the rabbinic tradition, tales, even hagiographic tales, were not accorded the dignity of other genres such as halakha, homiletics, or exegesis, the Hasidic tale was endowed with dignity and sanctity even in the lifetime of the Besht. Part of this new valorization is due to the simple sociological fact that the zaddikim themselves told these tales or were the heroes in them. Joseph Dan has presented a more profound, theological explanation for the sanctity attributed to the Hasidic tale. He argues that the telling of the tale was the narrative correlative of the performance of commandments to which the individual, according to Lurianic doctrine, was to commit himself in order to contribute to the coming of the Messiah. In Lurianic Kabbalah, the creation of the world is described as a catastrophic process, the violent clash of forces within God himself, a rending apart called *shevirat hakelim* (the breaking of the vessels). This rending can be mended by the process of *tikkun* (remedying or repairing), in which man can take part by intense prayer, categorical belief, or fervent praxis.

The sanctity of the tale is encapsulated in an oft-quoted statement attributed to the Baal Shem Tov himself: "When one tells stories in praise of the zaddikim, it is as though he were engaged in *Ma'aseh Merkavah.* The term *Ma'aseh Merkavah* (throne mysticism), implied by this time some type of participation in the mystical act intended to cleanse the upper divine sphere through prayer and contemplation; the attribution of such dynamic effects to an activity, the telling of tales, which had not been held in high regard in previous generations, attests to a radical revision in values. I have demonstrated elsewhere that these stories are evidence of an impressive expansion and refinement of literary sensibility in the Jewish world and must be included in any consideration of *the making of the modern Jewish mind.* What I would like to demonstrate now is that these tales, or rather their dissemination and parts of their structure, display a sophisticated social and political awareness, an awareness which is manifest in the attempts not only to reconcile two conflicting claims to personal authority, but also to accommodate the scripturality of the later text with that of the former, biblical text, whose primacy can never be denied or challenged. We are therefore talking of politics in two senses: the literal, referring to the power struggle between two groups, in this case both Hasidic; the metaphoric, referring to the intellectual tension, the anxiety which a new scripture must generate in a community inextricably bound to an old, venerable scripture.This is not the *anxiety of influence* but an *anxiety of non-influence* spawned by the realization, or even the unarticulated intuition, that something has been violated by endowing the new text with sanctity.

While we would argue that the metaphorical sense of politics is essentially meaningless, divorced from the literal, political situation, it is the politics of scripturality which interests us here.

     ✿ ✿ ✿

While one can agree that these tales do not embody the theoretical richness of Hasidic thought, it is difficult to accept the notion that they have no other didactic purpose than the hagiographic presentation of the zaddik. It is no accident that both *Shivhe HaBesht (In Praise of the Baal Shem Tov)*, and the Bratslav Tales, the second major collection of classic Hasidic tales, were published in the same Hebrew calendrical year, 1814–15. By that time the Hasidic movement was well established in the Ukraine, in southern Volhynia, in eastern Galicia, and even in Belorussia. It had already encountered fierce opposition in Lithuania from the established rabbinic authorities and suffered some feeble attacks from the early maskilim (westernized, enlightened Jews). By 1815 we are talking not of small, isolated and secretive prayer sects, but of many well-organized courts, some large, some small, controlling masses of people, their way of life and their markets. Ironically, precisely at this period, both the compiler of *Shivhe HaBesht,* Dov Ber ben Samuel of Linitz, and its printer, Rabbi Israel Yoffe, felt that the movement had reached a critical juncture which required the collection and publication of these tales that they had been reluctant to publish before. Though both express their hesitation about committing these holy tales to print, each gives a different reason.

Dov Ber ben Samuel, the compiler, states "I myself have noticed that in the time between my youth and my old age miracles have become fewer every day and marvels have begun to disappear. This happens because of our many sins." The concept of decline is fairly normative for a pietist working within the confines of a traditional religious culture. Had he been able to conceive of his period as of historical value equal to that of the biblical patriarchs, or all subsequent rabbinic tradition, we would be forced to interpret this new valorization as a challenge to the sacred tradition or even as some form of messianism. The underlying difference between the Hasidic notion of new scripturality and that of the apostle Paul will be discussed further on; at present we shall simply note that this difference obviously must shape the respective attitudes toward allusions to the previous scripture. Modern historians of Hasidism, however, tend to discount Dov Ber's pessimism and see in Hasidism a revitalization of

Judaism and a dynamic restructuring of social forms. Precisely during the most dynamic period of Hasidic expansion, the compiler of the most authoritative text of Hasidic tales perceives that there has been a religious decline, hence there is need for such a compilation to buttress the faithful. These varying perceptions of the state of affairs, that held by modern historians and that held by an authoritative contemporary, lead one to wonder how to weigh the valuations of each.

Rabbi Israel Yoffe, the printer, is troubled by another phenomenon, this one perhaps more political than religious, though it is couched in religious terms. The printer, in his preface, tells a tale worth quoting in full:

> I heard, moreover, from the people of the Holy Land, that the first time there was a plague in the Holy Land, God forbid, the holy Rabbi Menahem Mendel (of Vitebsk), blessed be the memory of this righteous and holy man, locked himself in his home with a minyan. During all the time they were secluded, their prayers were successful. However, on the holy Sabbaths, he did not say Torah at the third meal as was his custom: instead he used to sit at the dinner table with his companions who hearkened to his voice. There was an old man with him, one of the Besht's disciples, who told stories in praise of the Besht. One time the rabbi, the Maggid (of Mezeritch), blessed be the memory of this righteous and holy man, appeared in a dream of Menahem Mendel and said to him: "Are you not my disciple? Why do you not tell tales in my praise also?" So he agreed to tell tales in praise of our Great Rabbi during the third meal. When Menahem Mendel began to relate the wonders of the Great Maggid, the old man began to tell him about the Besht, as was his custom. Menahem Mendel did not let him continue, and immediately realized that he would be punished for it. Indeed it happened that after the meal he became sick with an intestinal disease. In a few days he passed away.

In concluding this tale, the printer asserts: "The profundity of these things is easily understood." Attempting to understand the profundity of these things, we should consider the following facts.

Menahem Mendel immigrated to the Land of Israel in 1777 and died in 1788. By that time, it was already a custom among Hasidim to substitute pious tales about the Besht for the customary Torah reading at the third Sabbath meal, late on Saturday afternoon; the tale, that is, had already assumed a quasi-ritual function and could be substituted for the Torah lesson. Menahem Mendel was thus practicing a custom known among Hasidim and given ritual status. When he attempted to substitute for a tale about the Besht, a tale about his own Rebbe, the Great Maggid of Mezeritsh, the second major leader of the Hasidic movement, he was severely punished and died. The contesting demands for honoring the memory of the two departed, saintly rabbis reflects a broader contest within the Hasidic movement in general. While we do not have a clear picture of the relationship between the Besht, who ruled until his death in 1760, and the Maggid, who led and spread the movement between 1760 and 1772, we do know that by the 1780s there were tensions between the biological descendents of the Besht and those who could claim authentic discipleship either from the Besht directly or through the Maggid, the first major theoretician of the movement. This conflict over legitimacy of succession is not unparalleled in religious movements and often erupts in the third generation.

This conflict, I would suggest, explains the peculiar organization of the first seven tales of *Shivhe HaBesht*, those prefaced to Dov Ber's manuscript by the printer, Israel Yoffe, at the behest of his Rebbe, Shneour Zalman of Lyady. That these prefatory tales were added to the manuscript on the instructions of Shneour Zalman (1745–1813) is of major import. He, as the leader of Belorussian Hasidism, was engaged in bitter struggles with the leading opponent of the movement, the famous Gaon of Vilna (Elijah ben Solomon Zalman, 1720–1797), and also rivaled Baruch ben Jehiel of Medzibezh (1757–1810), who, as grandson of the Besht, regarded himself as the legitimate leader of all Hasidim. The Gaon of Vilna had excommunicated Hasidim, burned their books, closed their prayer rooms, and in 1772 refused to meet for discussions with Menahem Mendel of Vitebsk and Shneour Zalman, whose beliefs and practices he considered heretical. Shneour Zalman, in fact, was imprisoned by Czarist authorities in both 1798 and 1801 on charges raised by followers of the Gaon. Within the Hasidic camp, Shneour Zalman was one of the paradigms of the charismatic leader whose authority derived from personal spiritual and intellectual virtues, not from family lineage. In struggles with both the Gaon and Baruch, Shneour Zalman was engaged in the historic contest over legitimacy and privilege; this contest, I suggest, underlies the composition of the added passages, certainly the first seven stories, which, unlike the material collected by Dov ben Samuel of Linitz, pays scrupulous attention to chronology and sequence of events.

The first three tales are devoted to the miraculous adventures of Rabbi Eliezer, the father of the Besht: his kidnapping, his sagacity, his chastity, his miraculous delivery by the Lord, and the promise of a remarkable son as a reward for his chastity in captivity. Chapter four relates the well-known story of the Besht's childhood and adolescence.

Chapter five and six introduce an entirely different figure, the miraculous Rabbi Adam, "from whom the Besht received the manuscripts. Rabbi Adam had found these manuscripts containing the hidden secrets of the Torah in a cave." In the seventh chapter we learn of the involved mystical process through which Rabbi Adam tested the Besht and transmitted these manuscripts to him rather than to his own son, whom he told: "I have manuscripts here which hold the secrets of the Torah. But you do not merit them."

The delicate balance of this cycle of seven tales is no accident: it stressed the fact that the Besht actually has two fathers: his biological father, the saintly Rabbi Eliezer, and his mystical mentor, the miraculous and shrewd Rabbi Adam. I would suggest that this narrative cycle is an adroit attempt on the part of Shneour Zalman to heal the wounds incurred in the ideological conflict between the two camps claiming legitimacy of succession. The cycle says, in effect, that both are legitimate heirs of the charisma of the Besht. Like his contemporary Nahman of Bratslav, Shneour Zalman obviously realized that there are times when the telling of tales is the most effective way to communicate the truth of the Lord and, no less important, to preserve the integrity of the community. Not only among maskilim, but also among Hasidim, literature had established itself as a moving force in the life of Eastern European Jewry. Some scholars, in fact, would argue that Hasidism was the most cohesive force in Jewish communal life between the dissolution in 1764 of the Council of Four Lands, the representative assembly of Jewish notables in the Kingdom of Poland, and the politicization of Eastern European Jewry at the end of the nineteenth century. If this is so, the function of the Hasidic tale in enhancing this cohesiveness is a cardinal sociological factor in modern Jewish history.

          ✧   ✧   ✧

What we call the "politics of scripture" can only be demonstrated by reference to a specific text, and so we turn to the first three tales of *Shivhe HaBesht*. Though these tales were told in Yiddish, they were transcribed in both Yiddish and Hebrew. The transcription and collection of the tales in Hebrew immediately lent them the status of a conventional pious text and it is in this form that they were widely circulated and read. In the Hebrew text there are no titles or paragraphing; the paragraphing used in the English translation both facilitates discussion of the text and demonstrates the structure of the story.

✿   ✿   ✿

RABBI ELIEZER

Rabbi Eliezer, our teacher, the father of the Besht, lived in the state of Walachia near the border. He and his wife were old. Once bandits came to the city and captured him, but his wife managed to escape to another town. She was so poor that she became a midwife and in this way earned her living. Rabbi Eliezer's captors took him to a remote country where there were no Jews and sold him. Rabbi Eliezer served his master faithfully. His master liked him and he appointed him overseer over his house. He asked his master to allow him to observe the Sabbath and to rest on that day, and his master granted his request. And it came to pass that he remained there a long time. He wanted to escape and save himself, but a dream came to him: "Do not be too hasty, since you must still remain in this country."

It came to pass that his master had dealings with the king's viceroy and as a gift he gave him the rabbi, our teacher, our rabbi, Eliezer. He lavished praise on him and extolled him. As soon as he came to the home of the king's viceroy, he found favor in his eyes and was given a special chamber in which to stay. He had no duties to perform at all, except that when the king's viceroy came home Rabbi Eliezer would welcome him with a bowl of water to wash his feet, since this was the custom accorded to great men of state. During all that time he studied the Torah and prayed in his special chamber.

Once the king became embroiled in a great war and he sent for his viceroy to counsel him on tactics of attack and defense. Because it was difficult for the viceroy to grasp the actual situation, he did not know what to say. The king stormed with rage because the viceroy could not help him in this time of trouble. The king's viceroy went home dejected. When he arrived, Rabbi Eliezer, the rabbi, our rabbi and teacher, welcomed him as usual with a bowl of water, but the king's viceroy rejected it and lay down on this couch in a troubled mood. Rabbi Eliezer said to him: "My master, why are you so troubled? Please tell me."

The king's viceroy scolded him, but Rabbi Eliezer was a faithful servant to his master and wanted him to be treated justly. He endangered his life and repeatedly urged him until the king's viceroy was forced to tell him what had happened. And he said to his master: "Do not interpretations belong to God? The Lord is a man of war. I will keep fasts and I will ask the Lord, blessed be He, for this secret since He is a revealer of secrets." And he asked a dream-question and it was answered. All the tactics of war were revealed and clearly explained to him.

The next day he came to his master and told him the advice that had been revealed to him from heaven. The king's viceroy was very pleased with the information and he joyfully hastened to the king. And he said, "Oh, my master, this is the advice I have to give." And he answered every question.

When the king heard all the viceroy's words, he said: "This is marvelous advice. It is not from a human mind, unless it comes from a holy man who had inspiration from gods whose dwelling is not with flesh or from one who had contact with the Evil Spirit. Since I know that you are by no means a godly man, you must be a sorcerer." The king's viceroy was forced to confess the truth and tell him what had happened.

The narrative devices employed to domesticate this new scripture, i.e., to make the crucial accommodation between it and the traditional Hebrew Scripture accepted by the audience, are varied and effective. Before the narrative in the Hebrew text we find this statement by the printer, Israel Yoffe:

> Since in the manuscripts from which I have copied these tales the sequence of events and the revelation of the Besht—may his merit protect us, amen—are not in the right order, and because I heard everything as it came from Admor [Shneour Zalman], whose soul rests in heaven, in the proper order and with the proper interpretation, I will print them first as I heard them from his holy lips, and after that point in the story I will include what has been written in the manuscripts.

This attribution of source, though much longer than those of the stories in the main portion of the manuscript, is typical of the tales in *Shivhe HaBesht*: almost all of them begin with the statement: "I heard this from so-and-so," thus establishing the authenticity of the tale by attributing it to a respected authority and deliberately disclaiming all originality.

Once the actual tale begins, "Rabbi Eliezer, our teacher, the father of the Besht ..." the audience is immediately introduced into a familiar world. The themes and even the diction is that of the patriarchal narratives in the book of Genesis or of *midrashim* elaborated from them. We learn that Eliezer and his wife were old (like Abraham and Sarah) and presumably childless, a fact explicitly mentioned only in the third tale. Eliezer's capture by the brigands, his sale to a master in a distant land, his master's affection for him, all evoke memories of the Joseph story and are even climaxed by a direct quote from Genesis 39:4 where Potiphar appoints Joseph overseer in his house. The motifs patently culled from the Joseph story serve several purposes at once: they assure the reader that this tale is indeed within the patriarchal tradition; they identify Eliezer with Joseph, perhaps even suggesting that Joseph is a traditional model for Eliezer; they prepare us for accepting Eliezer's wondrous capacity to interpret dreams, to have access to knowledge not given to ordinary men, even kings. Eliezer, furthermore, is portrayed as a saintly person in the rabbinic tradition that embellished the biblical characterization of Joseph: he requests permission to observe the Sabbath, and he studies Torah in the seclusion of his room. Even the instructions he received in his dream when he wished to escape: "Do not be too hasty, since you must still remain in this country," echo the narrative technique of the Joseph story, which is self-consciously structured with a control of episodes paralleling divine control of human affairs. In the Joseph story, this parallelism is concealed until Joseph declares to his astonished brothers, that the Lord has all along controlled their behavior, hence the flow of the plot. Here, the theme of divine intervention in the plot is more obvious and is repeated in the second tale.

What the audience cannot know, upon first exposure to this tale, is that precisely those features that appear to be so conventional as to enhance the acceptability of the tale embody elements of the Hasidic claims to the legitimacy of the movement and its specific tenets. The patriarchal ambience endows Eliezer with the authority of the biblical patriarchs that pervades all Jewish literature. The identification with Joseph, so seemingly innocuous, might very well allude to messianic pretensions since the belief in the imminent appearance of the Messiah, son of Joseph (as opposed to the Messiah, son of David) was by no means a dormant issue in the Jewish world in the seventeenth and eighteenth centuries: the Sabbatean upheaval of the 1660s and the Frankist turmoil of the 1750s and 1780s generated by the heretical instigations and apostasy of Jacob Frank, were still fresh in the collective memory and are alluded to in *Shivhe HaBesht*. Even more crucial is the evidence of the fourth tale of this collection where we find clear intimations that the Besht might have the power to bring the Messiah, a very Lurianic notion. Satan, we are told, wanted to kill the young child who was to become the Besht since he "was afraid that the time was approaching when he (Satan) would disappear from the earth," i.e., the prayers of the child might bring the Messiah, who would annihilate Satan.

Eliezer is endowed with the gift of interpretation, a gift associated with Joseph and Daniel (many echoes of the Daniel stories are evident in the tale and at least two direct quotes from Daniel are inserted in the text), the two prototypical interpreters of dreams. This visionary gift has a broad range of manifestations: sensing the depression of the viceroy, divining military tactics, receiving in dreams instructions that the time to escape his captivity has not yet come. Throughout this collection of tales, the Besht is known to possess a variety of superhuman characteristics, many associated with the power of interpretation rooted in the traditional capacity of the *baal shem* to master the Divine Names. One decisive, hence controversial aspect of mastery of the Divine Names is the ability to interpret the truths embedded or hidden in the Torah;

these truths, though possibly new or even subversive of older truths, are in consonance with the Torah since they are demonstrably integrated in it and extractable by a master of Divine Names.

That the time to escape has not yet come, is more than an echo of the narrative device of Genesis since the correct time to escape captivity, i.e., to be redeemed from exile, is a pervasive theme in traditional Jewish thought and was given special urgency by Lurianic speculation. In *Shivhe HaBesht,* the specific time for revelation is transferred to the personal, biographical plane: the Besht, we are told, did not reveal his true self until 1736 when he was already thirty-six years old. Before that date, he lived as a humble worker or teacher, often humiliated, struggling to keep his secret until instructed to reveal it, a theme obviously central to the Hasidic tradition and touched on in this collection in several forms, including tales fourteen and fifteen, the last two of the tales admittedly added by Israel Yoffe. The doctrine of the hidden zaddik was prevalent both before and after the appearance of the Besht.

The saintliness and piety of Eliezer is necessary to establish the credentials for his son, who is to be the founder and authoritative source of a new religious movement; the pious father is a recognizable feature in hagiographies. From the point of view of narrative structure, these qualities are both given special importance and, in turn, actually shape the seemingly strange ending of the story. We would expect Eliezer to be rewarded for his services to the state in the final paragraph of the first tale, but this does not happen until the first statement of the second tale. Instead we are treated to a conversation between the king and his viceroy (Eliezer's master) who had just brought the king the brilliant military plan which, we understand, is to win the battle. The king remarks shrewdly:

> This is marvelous advice. It is not from a human mind, unless it comes from a holy man who had inspiration from gods whose dwelling is not with flesh [Daniel 2:11] or from one who had contact with the Evil Spirit. Since I know that you are by no means a godly man, you must be a sorcerer.

This statement, mouthed by a gentile king, is a perceptive encapsulation of fairly standard Kabbalistic doctrine which would have been widely known after the dissemination of popular Kabbalistic texts in the seventeenth and eighteenth centuries. It distinguishes between normatively human knowledge and that derived from superhuman sources; among superhuman sources, it distinguishes between God and the Evil Spirit and, on the earth, the corresponding agents of superhuman power, the godly man and the sorcerer. The king's logic is impeccable: the viceroy is not a godly man and since he has received this marvelous advice, he must be a sorcerer. The viceroy, confronted with this analysis, must confess the source of his inspired information.

This denouement subtly informs the audience that what has begun as a seemingly conventional retelling of a pious tale leaning heavily on biblical allusions, concludes with a logical, theological statement which both describes and legitimizes the charisma of the zaddik figure in general, and the Besht in particular, since it refers to his father, Eliezer. This statement is dramatized in narrative form in the fourth tale where we find both oppositions, that between human and divine knowledge, and that between the saintly man and the sorcerer who is an incarnation of Satan.

✿   ✿   ✿

The second tale both artfully reinforces the themes of the first and advances the plot.

✿   ✿   ✿

RABBI ELIEZER AND THE VICEROY'S DAUGHTER

The king elevated him and made him his battle commander, for he perceived that the Lord was with him and that all that he did prospered. He won every battle that the king sent him to fight. During this time Rabbi Eliezer became concerned about what would happen to him, and he thought that it might be the time to flee to his native land. It was then revealed to him from heaven: "You must still remain in this country."

Then it happened that the viceroy died, and since Rabbi Eliezer had found favor in the king's eyes the king appointed him as his advisor. He also gave him the viceroy's daughter as his wife. Yet with God's help, the rabbi did not touch her. He devised various ways to avoid remaining at home, and even if by chance it so happened that he was at home, he refrained from touching her.

It so happened that no Jew was allowed to live in that country. When they found a Jew, there was only one verdict: that he be put to death. It had been so for several years. Once, his wife asked him, "Tell me, what fault do you find in me that you do not touch me and you do not make me your wife?"

He said to her, "Swear to me that you'll not reveal this to anyone, and I'll tell you the truth." She swore to him, and he told her: "I am a Jew."

She immediately sent him home with a rich treasure of silver and gold. But on the way thieves robbed him and he lost everything that he possessed.

The parallel to the biblical Joseph is conveyed by (1) the elevation of Eliezer to general, then to viceroy (marked by a direct quote from Genesis 39:3); (2) a novel version of the temptation of Joseph, an episode with a rich midrashic history, Joseph's saintliness manifested in his resisting temptation; and (3) the awareness that the hero, for all his prestige, is an alien in a foreign land, an exile. Again we find the explicit manipulation of the plot by an external, divine force. Complementary to this thematic reinforcement, we find an ingenious concatenation of conventional themes: unlike the young bachelor Joseph, who is importuned by his master's wife, Eliezer, an elderly married man, is given the viceroy's daughter as wife. Instead of the lust of Potiphar's wife, we have the natural expectations of the new wife that the marriage be consummated sexually, a deed which Eliezer, a traditionally pious Jew, refuses to do. This complication of plot is designed to motivate Eliezer's release from his land of exile, precisely the opposite of Joseph's incarceration when false charges are brought against him by the woman he spurned. The separation of Hebrews and Egyptians in the Joseph story is radicalized and given contemporary, concrete substance: there were, indeed, European lands where Jews were not allowed to reside. Eliezer's piety is rewarded by his disappointed wife—clearly an instrument of divine will—with release from bondage which echoes the Exodus from Egypt: he leaves laden with wealth. In a purposeful surprise ending, this wealth is robbed from him by thieves, and he arrives home destitute, clearly setting the scene for the climactic dispensation: the appearance of Elijah at the beginning of the third tale, which brings us to the birth of the charismatic leader of the new movement.

❉ ❉ ❉

THE BIRTH OF THE BESHT

While he was on his journey, Elijah the Prophet revealed himself to him and said: "Because of the merit of your behavior a son will be born to you who will bring light to Israel, and in him this saying will be fulfilled: Israel in whom I will be glorified."

He came home and with God's help he found his wife still alive. The Besht was born to them in their old age, when both of them were close to a hundred. (The Besht said that it had been impossible for his father to draw his soul from heaven until he had lost his sexual desire.)

The boy grew up and was weaned. The time came for his father to die, and he took his son in his arms and he said, "I see that you will light my candle, and I will not enjoy the pleasure of raising you. My beloved son, remem-

ber this all your days: God is with you. Do not fear anything." (In the name of Admor, I heard that it is natural for a son and a father to be closely bound, for as our sages, God bless their memory, have said: "The talk of the child in the market place is either that of his father or of his mother." How much closer then are ties between parents and children who are born to them in their old age. For example, Jacob loved Joseph because he was born to him in his old age, and the ties between them were very great, as it is said in the holy Zohar. And it was true here. Although the Besht was a small child, because of the intensity and sincerity of the tie, the words were fixed in his heart.)

The tale relating the actual birth of the Besht is carefully constructed to maintain a balance of the traditionally acceptable and subtly insinuated new ideology and problematics. The appearance of Elijah the Prophet to an individual, particularly alone on a road, is by no means an exceptional occurrence in Jewish folk literature nor is the annunciation of the birth of a child who will bring light to Israel (an obvious play on the Besht's personal name, which was Israel). And the audience would not be surprised by the old age of the parents—almost 100 years—since this is one of the traditional ways to suggest divine involvement in the birth process of an important personality in Jewish history. The early orphaning of the Besht might indeed have been based on fact and could evoke, either in real life or in the folk narrative, the death-bed blessing: "God is with you. Do not fear anything."

Since this tale must function as the narrative transfer of charisma from Eliezer to his son (subsequent tales in the collection do not deal with this issue), the very act of transfer should be the theme. And it is. As Eliezer recedes from the center of our interest, the Joseph story features disappear completely. The biblical Joseph, after all, was not the progenitor of the main line of the Israelites. We sense here a slight disruption in the line of succession. While Israel is clearly Eliezer's child, he is portrayed both here and in the following tale as an orphan whose father dies soon after the child has been weaned. The narrator finds it necessary to comment upon two aspects of transmission: one biological, the other spiritual. The miraculous birth of a child to elderly parents elicits an explanation, attributed to the Besht, that "it had been impossible for his father to draw his [the Besht's] soul from heaven until he [Eliezer] had lost his sexual desire." The problematic of spiritual transmission is handled in what looks like a traditional rabbinical explanatory note attributed here to Shneour Zalman himself. In attempting to explain how the son who had just been weaned could have comprehended and remembered his dying father's behest, Shneour Zalman asserts that it is natural for a son to be close to his father, particularly a son born to elderly parents. These common-sensical insights, however, are confirmed by three prooftexts: one from the Talmud; one from the patriarchal narratives in Genesis (Jacob and Joseph are cited as models, but not as an analogue to Eliezer and Israel); and one from the Zohar.

In telling the story of the birth of the charismatic leader of the new movement, the narrator both adorns his narrative with traditional, recognizable features, such as the annunciation by Elijah, and subtly insinuates the issue of both biological and spiritual legitimacy which interests him. After establishing Eliezer as a patriarchal figure, Shneour Zalman must insist upon the demonstrable legitimacy of his son, the Besht.

The recourse to prooftexts to prove the possibility of a narrative item is not limited to this tale alone and indicates the tentativeness of the narrative: it cannot stand alone, free of the supports of traditional texts and traditional methods of reading them. Similarly, the crucial figure of Eliezer cannot stand alone but must be integrated with features from the Joseph story even when they are inverted or subverted in the narrative. I have therefore deliberately avoided in my analysis the term *prefiguration*: Joseph here is not a *figura* (as described so lucidly by Auerbach) and the type of interpretation involved is not figurative, since Joseph is not posited as an independent trans-textual reality in history.

❂   ❂   ❂

In a seminal essay on Nahmanides' symbolical reading of history, Amos Funkenstein has demonstrated the relative paucity of typological interpretation in the Jewish exegetical tradition.[2] Even when this mode was employed by so sophisticated an exegete as Nahmanides, it was limited to the patriarchs, thus omitting Joseph who, in Christian typology, prefigures Jesus. Nahmanides, Funkenstein argues, was certainly aware of the implications such typological interpretations had for "the Church Fathers [who] employed these images... to define the continuity and progress from the Old Testament to the New Testament." For Paul, too, the Old Testament was a series of prefigurations of Christ.

While Nahmanides's awareness of Christian exegesis and his sensitivity to its implications can be established, Hasidism seems to have been more introverted and reacts primarily to previous Jewish assumptions and practices. To my knowledge, no Hasidic thinker considered the teachings of the Besht or the Maggid a new dispensation which replaced the older dispensation; rather, the teachings were taken as a legitimate continuation of the Jewish tradition, if anything an enrichment of that tradition by the intensification of piety through adherence to charismatic leaders, fervent prayer, and devotions.

When the narrator of the first tales of *Shivhe HaBesht* relies heavily upon features and language from the Joseph story in order to portray Eliezer, he is presenting Joseph not as a prefiguration of Eliezer in the Pauline sense, but rather as a legitimizing literary forbearer. The Joseph imagery in these tales does not prefigure or predict the coming of the Besht, the charismatic zaddik who leads this new movement, but rather legitimates his father, Eliezer, by attaching him both to the patriarchal tradition, broadly conceived, i.e., Abraham and Joseph, and the late prophetic or apocalyptic tradition, by reference to Daniel. While exegetes of the New Testament, following the Pauline tradition, claim that the new scripture is a fulfillment of the older scripture, Shneour Zalman's version of these crucial tales implies that this new sacred text, which I take the liberty to call scripture, should be regarded as a sacred text in the tradition of prior Jewish sacred texts.

In sum, Shneour Zalman's claims are reverential, apologetic, and cautious. If Nahmanides was cautious because he was aware of the Christian usage of typological interpretation, Shneour Zalman was probably cautious because he had been engaged in the bitter struggle with the Gaon and his followers and realized the dangers inherent in the pretensions of his younger colleague, Nahman of Bratslav, who rashly denigrated the authenticity of all other Hasidic zaddikim, while hailing the true zaddik (himself), whom he describes as *behinat Moshe*, of the essence of Moses. Nahman claimed that he was the fifth of great Jewish masters of the spirit: Moses, Simeon bar Yohai (second century C.E.), Isaac Luria, the Besht, and Nahman himself. Since these historical persons are chronologically remote from one another, the connection between them must be on another plane, probably the figural. This claim was clearly unacceptable to Nahman's contemporaries. Nahman, furthermore, had strayed in another direction: he, too, told tales which were considered holy scripture by his followers; they were printed in 1815, the same year that witnessed the publication of *Shivhe HaBesht*.

NOTES

1. There are few serious analytical studies in English of the Hasidic tale. The reader might consult the introduction to the English translation of *Shivhe HaBesht: In Praise of the Baal Shem Tov*, translated and edited by Dan Ben-Amos and Jerome Mintz (Bloomington: Indiana University Press, 1970); the introduction by Arnold J. Band to

Nahman of Bratslav: The Tales (New York: Paulist Press, 1978), and also Band, "The Function of the Enigmatic in Two Hasidic Tales," *Studies in Jewish Mysticism*, ed. Joseph Dan and Frank Talmage (Cambridge, Mass., 1982), 185–210. All quotes from *Shivhe HaBesht* are taken from the Ben-Amos/Mintz translation, which also has a fine bibliography on Hasidism and the Hasidic tale. The lengthy quote from Gershom Scholem defining the term *ba'al shem* was originally published in the *Encyclopedia Judaica* (Jerusalem, 1972), IV, 6–7; it can also he found in his *Kabbalah* (New York: Quadrangle, 1974), 310–311. The two most complete books to date on the Hasidic tale are the Hebrew works of Joseph Dan, *HaSippur hahasidi (Jerusalem,* 1975), and Gedalya Nigal's *hasiporet hahasidit* (Jerusalem, 1981). I have used the Hebrew texts, both the 1947 Horodetzky edition cited by most scholars and reprints of the first (Kapust) edition of 1815, for the first three tales. The variations are minor. The numbers and names of the stories are those of Ben-Amos/Mintz; they do not appear in the Hebrew texts. I do not deal with the variant reading of the second tale (2a) since it adds nothing to my argument. Though Ben-Amos casts some doubt on the authenticity of the attribution of tales 5-8 to Shneour Zalman, I do not.

2. Amos Funkenstein, *Perceptions of Jewish History* (Berkeley, 1993) 98–120. For recent research on Hasidism see: Rachel Elior, "Hasidism—Historical Continuity and Spiritual Change," in *Gershom Scholem's Major Trends in Jewish Mysticism 50 years After*, ed. P. Schäfer and J. Dan (Tübingen, 1993); Moshe Idel, *Hasidism—Between Ecstasy and Magic* (Albany, 1995); Shaul Magid, ed., *God's Voice from the Void—Old and New Studies in Braslav Hasidism* (Albany, 2002); Ada Rapoport-Albert, *Hasidism Reappraised* (London, 1997); Ora Wiskind-Elper, *Tradition and Fantasy in the Stories of Reb Nahman of Bratslav* (Albany, 1998).

⁓ Folklore, Literature, and Scripture: The Bratslav Tale

The generic title, "Folklore, Literature, and Scripture" is neither a promise of an all embracing formulation pretending to solve a series of nagging methodological problems, nor a threat of pages groaning with tiring technical terminology. It is, rather, the preface to a cumbersome subtitle, too long to publish in a program: "A Study of the Bratslav Theory of the Folktale and Its Implication for Our Understanding of Narrative Art and Genres of Literary Composition." The basis for my theoretical discussion is the main cycle of Bratslav tales that are considered sacred scripture by Bratslav Hasidim, even today. Aside from their intrinsic charm, the Bratslav tales hold for the literary scholar a specific fascination in that they strategically straddle three genres we normally separate one from the other. And since this conference is dedicated to Jewish folklore, much of which is verbal, often considered sacred text by traditional Jews, we should not disregard this opportunity to continue the discussion that must always accompany a serious consideration of Jewish folklore.

At the thematic climax of the enigmatic story "Iddo Ve'Enam," Agnon has Mr. Gamzu, a traditional Jew who traffics in manuscripts, declare: "Folklore! Folklore! They have taken our Holy Torah and made it a topic of research or folklore."[1] Agnon thus raises pointedly one of the central issues of that story and, for that matter, of the far-reaching social and religious implications of *Die Wissenschaft des Judentums* (Judaic scholarship) for several generations. The story was written during the siege of Jerusalem in 1948, only three years after Gershom Scholem's seminal essay "Hirhurim al hokhmat Yisrael" (Reflections on Die Wissenschaft des Judentums) which impugned the cultural and psychological

129

presuppositions of the Judaic scholarship of the previous 125 years. It is, perhaps, no mere coincidence that when Agnon composed "Iddo Ve'Enam," he was living in Gershom Scholem's apartment in Rehaviah, since his own home in Talpiot had to be evacuated.

Agnon characteristically qualifies his thematic statement by a situational paradox: after all, Gamzu, who laments the desecration of these sacred texts by the ethnographer, Dr. Ginat, was the very man who often sold such texts to Ginat and his colleagues; and when Gamzu's wife, Gemulah, the personification of the sacred aura of the manuscripts, climbs to a rooftop to commit suicide, it is Dr. Ginat, not Gamzu, who climbs up to save her, and dies in the attempt. The implied author knows that the issue is serious, but not simple, that though right and wrong are not easily assigned, the basic act involves the soul of a culture, its history and its destiny. With these concerns in mind, I approach the study of the Bratslav tales, which have intrigued many critics and seduced many writers: I cannot ignore the fact that these tales, which are for me essentially the object of my literary concerns—for I am not a Bratslav Hasid—are for the faithful sacred texts. The Bratslav hagiography, we should note, lists a tradition of five Tzadikim: Moses, Shimeon bar Yohai, the Ari, the Besht, and Rav Nahman of Bratslav. This is the stuff that our studies are made of.

Before entering a discussion of Bratslav poetics, I should define some of my terms: by *folklore* I refer to subject matter and not to method or scholarly discipline. Within *subject matter* I restrict myself to what some call *verbal art*, of which I know something, and omit song, dance, and the crafts, of which I know little. Within the verbal arts, I will deal not with riddles, incantations, or sermons. This latter distinction is crucial since it eliminates the *sihah*, the reputed statements of the Tzadik, which were intensely cultivated by Hasidic writers. The distinction between the plot-dominated tale and the *sihah* was important enough to precipitate the dissolution of the contracted collaboration between Buber and Agnon in the 1920s. They had agreed to do an anthology of Hasidic tales together, but while Buber wanted to elucidate theological points and would stress the *sihah*, Agnon wanted to retell good tales. While I believe the collaboration would have disintegrated on personal grounds, the published evidence, i.e. what each writer collected independently, does confirm the account that there were varying concepts of anthologizing.

Literary research of the past generation has blurred the rigid boundaries once drawn between *folk-literature*, on the one hand, and literature, on the other. Anyone who has studied the structuralists, from Propp and Levi-Strauss through Greimas and Todorov, knows that from the point of view of the intrinsic structure of the verbal artifact, the fine definition is often both groundless and counterproductive. The researches of Albert Lord in the Homeric epic or Max Lüthi in the fairy tale suggest that it is difficult and pointless to hold to such disparate categories as folk-literature and belles-lettres. Finally, the notion of *fiction* advanced by Frank Kermode or Walter Benjamin, on the one hand, or the contemporary semiologists, on the other, argues persuasively against a rigid dichotomy between the two areas. In addition, it seems to me that the classical predication of folk-literature upon a vague notion of orality is confusing, particularly among a people as literate as the Jews, and should be discarded without further mention, unless one is discussing canonized religious texts and traditions deliberately and officially transmitted orally. The perennial question raised in any introductory course on the folktale with regard to the activity of the Grimm brothers should suffice to disabuse us of any simplistic dichotomies.

The publication of *Kinder und Hausmärchen* by Jacob and Wilhelm Grimm in 1812 and 1815 should serve as a convenient, oblique point of view for our discussion of the folktale as practiced by the Hasidim, and by Nahman of Bratslav in particular. During the same years, but about 1,000 miles east of Kassel and Göttingen, where the Grimm brothers lived, the first two collections of Hasidic tales, *Shivhe HaBesht (In Praise of the Baal Shem Tov)* and *Sippure Hamaasiyot* (The Tales) of Nahman of Bratslav, were being collected and edited. Just as there is no historical connection between the editorial activities in the west and those in the east (the identity of dates is purely accidental), there is no similarity in the aims of the collectors. The Grimm brothers, as both scholars and romantic nationalists, were motivated by a desire to recover the authentic Germanic folk tradition. The two Hasidic editors, Dov Ber ben Samuel, the compiler of *Shivhe HaBesht*, and Nathan Steinmetz of Nemirow, Nahman of Bratslav's disciple and amanuensis, were both pious men anxious to present tales about or by their respective charismatic leaders, thus glorifying the name of the Lord and inspiring the Hasidim to emulate the ways of their masters. At issue, here, is the meaning of the term *modern:* if we use the term generically, referring to a period of time—the last two centuries, for instance—all the above-mentioned collections are of the *modern* period. If modernity, however, is measured by the secular, inquisitive, and historicistic spirit, the Grimm brothers are *modern* while neither Dov Ber ben Samuel nor Nathan of Nemirow is. On the other hand, while these collections of

Hasidic tales have not generally been included in histories of modern Hebrew literature, the arguments Dov Sadan and others have proposed for their inclusion, are quite convincing.

Both Yosef Dan[2] and Mendel Piekarz[3] contend that the Hasidim, certainly by 1780, had effected a radical change in the attitude towards the tale. Whereas the telling of tales had previously been frowned upon by Jewish authorities, it was regarded as a worthy pastime by Hasidic masters for a variety of reasons: since God was immanent in this world, He could be present even in a seemingly idle tale, which, upon examination, might contain a deep theological truth; the tale projected before the devout the image of the Hasidic hero, the Tsadik, more often than not the Besht himself; the tale was an effective means of communicating basic religious notions.

The Bratslav concept of the tale and its role was somewhat more complex and self-conscious. Apart from the Bratslav tales themselves, we have, from the early nineteenth century, three striking *theoretical* statements on the essence of the tale and its function in society: two sermons delivered by Rav Nahman himself at the end of 1806 and included in *Likkute Muharan*,[4] and the first introduction to Nahman's tales, *Sippure Maasiyot*[5], written by his disciple, Nathan of Nemirow, in 1814. Since Nathan's introduction builds upon the sermons, we shall analyze the introduction and later refer to the sermons. The composite theory of the tale is one of the most coherent and remarkable in the history of Hebrew literature.

Written about four years after Rav Nahman's death in 1810, the introduction strikes a subtly balanced tone, fusing evangelic and apologetic overtones, both couched in terms taken from Ecclesiastes, thereby suggesting a parallel between Rav Nahman and King Solomon, who, after all, "spoke in riddles and parables, and dressed the Torah in several garments." The note is evangelic since it heralds the first publication of this new sacred text, the formal publication of the great tales delivered "from his holy mouth," from the holy mouth of Rav Nahman, the "perfection of mankind, our honorable lord, teacher, and master, our glorious and mighty pride, the holy and awesome rabbi, the great light, the supernal light, the precious and holy light, blessed is his name, Rav Nahman (the memory of the Tzadik is a blessing), the great grandson of the holy, awesome, and god-like Rabbi, the Baal Shem Tov (the memory of the Tzadik is a blessing)." In these stories, authentic since actually heard from his holy mouth, the master "pondered, and sought out, and set in order many proverbs (Eccles. 12:9) and garbed and hid lofty and mighty

concepts in tales *(Sippure Maasiyot)* in marvelous and wondrous ways."
Though new, the book follows the legitimizing precedent of the ancients,
who "would speak in riddles and parables and garb the Torah in several
different garments when they wanted to talk of divine secrets." These
sacred texts are being published primarily for the benefit of the faithful
followers of Rav Nahman, who wanted to know the precise text of these
awesome tales since "our master has told us that every statement in these
stories contains a potent meaning and he who changes one statement of
these stories omits much of the meaning."

It is obvious from the first section of the introduction that Nathan
was fully conscious of the novelty and daring of this publication, since
these tales are sacred scripture, "worthy to be expounded in public and
told in the synagogues, and whosoever is expert in sacred texts, especially
in the Zohar and Lurianic writings, can understand some of the allusions
in this text." Nathan also realizes that much of the impact of the stories
was due to the charisma of the storyteller, Rav Nahman. "It should be
clear to any intelligent person that he who hears statements from the
very mouth of the sage is not like he who sees them in a book, especially
in such illusory matters as those which cannot be understood without the
movement of the limbs and the nodding of the head and the wink of the
eye and the inclination of the hand, etc." Ever conscious of his mission,
Nathan brings as support of his project the striking statement of his master, Rav Nahman himself. Before he told the first tale of this book ("The
Loss of the Princess"), he said: "In the tales which other people tell are
many secrets and lofty matters, but the tales have been ruined in that
they are lacking much. They are confused and not told in the proper
sequence: what belongs at the beginning they tell at the end, and vice
versa. Nevertheless, there are in these tales which other people tell lofty
and hidden matters."

"The tales which other people tell" are obviously universal folktales
culled from many sources, some even Gentile. Nathan is defensive about
this point since he asserts several times that most of Rav Nahman's stories are original and that when he did use stories of foreign provenance,
he added, modified, and improved them. Normally, his stories are really
original ideas *garbed* in story form. Time and again we encounter the
three terms: *hasagah* = concept or idea; *maaseh* = the tale; and some
form of the root form *lavash* = to garb. The Bratslav story is supposed
to be the garb in narrative terms of a theological concept. The mundane
or Gentile origin of the story should not disqualify it for sacred usage,
once the material has been transmuted by the inspired master storyteller.

Nathan's obvious defensiveness about "the tales which other people tell" bears some elucidation. In his doctoral dissertation[6] Martin Mandel poses the question: "Is it possible to discern the models which taught Rabbi Nahman the art of storytelling and supplied the materials for his first venture in the summer of 1806?" To this crucial question he answers: "The answer is clearly yes," though he hastens to argue that there is no case for direct influence from the Grimm brothers or Afanasyev, two logical sources. By tracing in Aarne-Thompson's *The Types of the Folktale* and the Yiddish *Maaseh Buch* a variety of tale types found in several of the Bratslav stories, Mantel constructs an impressive array of tale types which Rav Nahman might have utilized and molded for his stories. While the method is highly speculative, it does provoke thoughts about the choices the author made in narrating the details of his stories. Mantel suggests (Vol II, p. 52): "What is required now is a new approach based upon the operative principle that literary effectiveness must be granted at least full parity in questions of interpretation along with speculations of biographical and metaphysical interest." In doing so he opens a new avenue of research which can contribute to an enhanced understanding of these stories, their composition, and the Bratslav theory of literature.

The following passage in the introduction seems at first to be a digression to the source of historical legitimization to the Besht, but, as Yosef Dan has pointed out, it forms with the first passage an integral theory of literary composition:

> And the Besht (may his holy memory be a blessing), could "unite unities" by means of tales. When he saw that the upper conduits were ruined and he could not repair them through prayer, he would repair and join them by means of a tale.[7]

Basing his reasoning on the pervasive Lurianic terminology, Dan explains the Bratslaver theory (a composite of Nahman's and Nathan's ideas) based on Lurianic Kabbalah.

1. The "lofty and hidden concepts" found in tales other people tell, be they Jews or Gentiles, are parallel to the "holy sparks" that fell into the created world at the time of the cataclysmic act of creation.
2. The tales themselves underwent a process similar to the Lurianic "breaking of vessels" at the time of creation; they are, therefore, confused, ruined, disorderly, and their original meaning has been lost.

3. The inspired Tzadik, in this case the Besht, is endowed with the power to reveal the holiness hidden in the stories by restructuring them according to their original, proper order. In this sense the Tzadik *repairs* the story.

4. Once the story has been repaired, it assumes enormous religious, even theurgic power, and a Tzadik like the Besht can use the story to "unite the unities," i.e., to reunite the *sefirot (tiferet* and *malkhut)* which had split asunder in the act of creation.

Dan's explanation derives from Rav Nahman's own theory concerning the relationship between the telling of stories and the details of sefirotic structure, a theory fully, yet circuitously expounded in the famous sermon: "Patah Rabbi Shim'on" *(Likkute Muharan 1:60),* a classical Bratslav homily based on the introductory passage of the *Idra Rabba* of the Zohar to *Parashat Naso* of the Book of Numbers (128). The gist of this sermon is found in Nathan's introduction to the *Sippure Maasiyot* which we have been analyzing. Nathan tells us that his master turned to the telling of tales in a deliberate attempt to achieve by this new method what he had failed to achieve by more conventional methods: the repentance of his flock, their return to the Lord as he, Rav Nahman, understood it.

> When our master, blessed be his memory, began to engage in the telling of tales, he stated explicitly as follows: "I am about to begin to tell tales," by which he meant that since he could not help them return to the Lord by means of Torah lessons or holy discourses... he is beginning to engage in tales. In the same period he delivered the sermon, "Patah Rabbi Shim'on." ... At the end of that sermon it is explained that by means of tales "the true Tzadik" awakens from their sleep those human beings who have fallen asleep and sleep away their days.

The sleep mentioned here is a specific spiritual sleep, the period of spiritual obtuseness when the true essence of one's soul, which should properly be connected to the upper world of *sefirot,* is dormant, hence disconnected from the source of illumination. The tale is a particularly convenient vehicle for the awakening of the soul from its dormancy since it is, by its very nature, a garb *(levush)* and can transmit the supernal illumination subtly, gradually, thus avoiding the risk of blinding the human being with the brilliant light from above.

Nathan's introduction includes one more intriguing notion culled from the sermon "Patah Rabbi Shim'on": there are tales in the category of "in the midst of days," and there are tales in the category of "the years of antiquity." Nathan refers here to a threefold classification of tales found in the sermon: (a) standard tales with no specific sefirotic association; (b) tales classified as "in the midst of days," thus connected with the lower seven spheres; (c) tales classified as "of the years of antiquity," thus associated with the three upper spheres. Tales in the second group recount great acts of divine beneficence in the past, such as the stories of the patriarchs or the exodus from Egypt; tales in the third group predict the great act of redemption in the future. Tales of the second group are connected with the lower spheres since they present accounts of incomplete redemption, a fact attested to by our experience of this imperfect world. Tales of the third, redemptive group are logically associated with the upper three spheres, but since the final redemption has not yet taken place and the Messiah has not yet come, these stories are usually left unfinished, e.g., "The Loss of the Princess."

The Bratslav theory of literature, its concept of the utilization of folktales, would be incomplete without reference to the notion of the Tzadik, especially as it appears in the model sermon "Bo El Par'oh," also delivered toward the end of 1806. After two introductory paragraphs describing the Lurianic cosmogony: *tsimtsum*, *shevira*, and *tikkun*, and two types of heresy, Nahman approaches his main theme, the nature and function of the Tzadik. Nahman refers not to the Tzadik generically, but to "the Great Tzadik of the category of Moses." (According to Yosef Weiss, when Nahman speaks of "the Great Tzadik" or "the Tzadik of the Generation," he refers to himself. Weiss bases his argument both on the original texts and on the commentary of Nahman of Cheryn, one of the leading nineteenth century Bratslav exegetes.)[8] The Great Tzadik must investigate the words of the heretics who have fallen into the *empty space* opened up in the previously harmonious cosmos when the infinite God contracted himself in order to create the world we live in. Since the *empty space* implies total absence of all divine presence, it is the locus of all evil. As such, it is the domain of silence, particularly since its opposite, the created world, was brought into existence by divine speech. The letters of the Holy Tongue by which the world was created and in which divine law is revealed, comprise the border between the created world and the *empty space*. In that the Great Tzadik belongs to the category of Moses, he partakes of the paradoxical nature of Moses: he is both a great leader and "heavy of tongue," i.e.—as interpreted by Nahman—a man of silence, hence the only man capable of descending to the realm of silence, the *empty space*, to redeem the souls that have fallen there. The Tzadik does this by means of the *nigun* (melody) or the *zemer* (song), which is peculiar to him, a manifestation of his essence as a man of faith.

Though this sermon does not mention the telling of tales as such, the literary implications of this adaptation of the Lurianic myth are far-reaching. Our teller of tales, Rav Nahman, is the Great Tzadik who, by his very nature, is distanced from his audience, his Hasidim. The gap between him and his audience, however, can be bridged through the telling of tales which are a garb of his divine concepts. The tales have a specific therapeutic, cosmic function: they redeem souls from the *empty space*. In this sense, the tales are marvelous, and the telling of tales, a redemptive act. But, following the usual Bratslav sense of paradox, the tales are an impure mode of expression, and the telling of tales is a "descent of the Tzadik" into a lesser realm of existence, for, as Nahman and Nathan tell us, the master resorted to this medium of communication *after* he felt he had failed miserably in his other modes of communication: prayer, homilies, and Torah lessons.

The paradox inherent in the telling of tales is a reflex of the remarkable analogue Nahman repeatedly draws between God's relationship to the created world and the Tzadik's relationship to his Hasidim. In both cases, the sense of vitality emanating from the source is so overwhelming, so far beyond the capacity of ordinary human beings, that special means are required for transmission of the illumination: in both cases *garb* must be used. God uses the letters of the Torah or the Shekhinah, the lowest sphere of the sefirotic system; the Tzadik uses his tales to talk to his Hasidim. The Torah of the Tzadik, like the Torah of the Creator of the universe, is garbed in tales since it would be impossible to transmit it as it is. For God, as for the Tzaddik, the telling of tales, the contact with the created world, is a deliberate, willed act of descent motivated by compassion. It is no coincidence that one of the *Leitwörter* in the sermon "Bo el Par'oh" is *rahamanut* (compassion).

Nathan's claim that these stories are original even when they utilize "tales other people tell" is correct to the extent that the master's intention and his audience's understanding were the presentation of a theological message in a carefully contrived garb. In this sense, the Bratslav tales differ radically from the Beshtean tales which, for instance, do not pretend to be a garb (though Nathan does introduce this notion) of a preconceived theological message. The Bratslav tales conform to the known pattern of allegory in that they embody an obvious and continuing reference to a system of ideas (or events). Behind the stories stands the elaborate system of the *sefirot* with all their dynamic, cosmic implications. Unlike Philo and many medieval interpreters of scriptures, the reader of the Bratslav tales which are, in a sense, scriptural, does not engage in allegorical interpretation, because the plot and figurative language of the text are embarrassingly frank and concrete, too much like the life of ordinary human beings as we know it. The reader of the Bratslav tale is presented an allegorically structured text. Within the conventional categories of modes of allegorical interpretation best summarized by Dante in the Tenth Epistle to Cangrande, the meaning called for in the Bratslav tale is anagogic in that it illuminates the entire scheme of creation, the governance of the universe and—most important—of redemption.

Given the amazing self-awareness of Nahman and Nathan concerning the nature of garbing—really the allegorical technique—it is surprising that they did not succumb to a mechanical equation of narrative and ideational systems. One can, perhaps, ascribe this deliverance from potentially tedious contrivance to several features unique to Rav Nahman, the teller of tales, who, as Yosef Weiss would argue, identified with the redemptive heroes of his own tales, be it the "Mishneh lamelekh" or the "tzadik emet," and thus suffused his tales with an anxious immediacy. Furthermore, Nahman, as we have stated, conceived of the telling of tales as an act analogous to the redemption of the cosmos by God at the end of days. This concept of narrative, coupled with his identification with his heroes, prevented the dissociation of sense from sensibility, of idea from image, which critics from Coleridge on have assailed so relentlessly. The narrative concretization of his ingenious concept of the narrative art is to be found in what we—parodying Frank Kermode—would like to call "the sense of a non-ending," when one tells a tale involving the third, redemptive group, those of "the years of antiquity," one does not finish the tale, since the very act of fiction and the dynamics of the cosmos are concomitant. While we, today, often tend to glorify fiction as the consummate and characteristic human activity, Rav Nahman considered the proper telling of his tales of such cosmic import that only "the Tzadik of the generation" or his authorized disciples should perform this act.[9]

Whether or not the thirteen canonical Bratslav tales actually conform to the theory expressed in these three early and authentic Bratslav documents—and there is good reason to state that many of them do not—the very self-consciousness of the theoretical statements betrays an awareness of an implicit crossing of genre borders. Nathan knows that there is a difference between the telling of tales and traditional Torah literature, homilies, commentaries, etc.; he also knows that there is a difference between traditional Torah literature, however sacred it might be, and these stories which were uttered "by the holy mouth" of the Tzadik of the generation. While these three genres are not at all similar to the three genres we have referred to at the beginning of our paper, we should at least share Nathan of Nemirow's consciousness that there are genres with their implicit assumptions even when the borderlines are blurred. Not all genre borders, finally, are equally distinct. The crossing of the border from folk-literature to *literature* might raise serious problems of definition, but not grave concerns of intentionality. The crossing from folk-literature or literature to scripture does raise the problem of intentionality; the scholar dismisses, with peril to his perspective, the notion that these utterances were regarded as scripture by their audience.

NOTES

1. S. Y. Agnon, *Kol sipurav shel Sh. Y. Agnon* (Jerusalem, 1953), vol. VII *(Ad hena)*: 382.

2. Yoseph Dan, *Hasipur hahasidi* (Jerusalem, 1975): *3 ff.*

3. Mendel Piekarz, *Hasidut Bratslav* (Jerusalem, 1972): 83–131.

4. Chap. LX: Patah Rabbi Shim'on. Chap. LXIV: "Bo El Par'oh."

5. The First Introduction is found in all the standard editions of the *Sippure Maasiyot.*

6. Martin Mantel (Princeton, 1977). The second volume of the dissertation is devoted to annotation and commentary.

7. Dan, op. cit.: 50.

8. Yoseph Weiss, *Mehkarim bahasidut Bratslav* (Jerusalem, 1974):150–171. In his thoroughly researched biography of Rav Nahman, *Tormented Master: A Life of Rabbi Nahman of Bratslav* (Alabama, 1979) Arthur Green supports Weiss's analysis.

9. In his doctoral dissertation (UCLA, 1974), Yoav Elstein studies the first tale, "Avedat bat hamelekh" as archetypical of the Bratslav technique. For recent scholarship on these tales, see: Shaul Magid, ed., *God's Voice from the Void–Old and New Studies in Bratslav Hasidism* (Albany, 2002); Marianna Schleicher, *A Theology of Redemption: An Analysis of the Thirteen Tales in Rabbi Nahman of Bratslav's 'Sippurey Ma'asiyot.'* Ph.D. diss. (University of Aarhus, 2002); Ora Wiskind-Elper, *Tradition and Fantasy in the Tales of Reb Nahman of Bratslav* (Albany, 1998).

ISRAEL AND ZIONISM

From Diaspora to Homeland: the Transfer of the Hebrew Literary Center to Eretz Yisrael

The crystallization of a Hebrew cultural center in Eretz Yisrael between the two World Wars is a remarkable example of Diaspora–Homeland relationship, but it has never been satisfactorily described. There are two reasons for this: first, until recently we have not had adequate studies of what happened in the Yishuv during those years; second, the portrayal of the growth of the Tel Aviv center is usually detached from the decline of the Diaspora centers. Thanks to the basic research done by Zohar Shavit and her colleagues assembled in the recently published massive volume: *Beniyata shel tarbut ivrit be'Eretz Yisrael* (The Construction of Hebrew Culture in Eretz-Yisrael), we can draw a coherent picture of what happened in the Yishuv.[1] Though I am profoundly indebted to this collective study, I differ from Shavit on two major, interrelated issues. First, the volume pays scant attention to the precipitous decline of Hebrew culture in Europe after World War I and the complex political situation that caused it. Second, Shavit and her colleagues assume that precisely because the Tel Aviv center became dominant, it was destined to do so. This is based on a reductionist and teleological view of Zionist history, and resembles the theories advanced by Yaakov Klatzkin (1882–1948) in Berlin in the 1910s and 1920s. While I do not accept the implied assumption that the decline of the Diaspora or the crystallization of the Eretz Yisrael center was inevitable, I do agree that the facts of the production and distribution of Hebrew literature, first in the Diaspora then in Eretz Yisrael, must convince any objective scholar that the dramatis personae of this powerful drama were passionately devoted individuals whose ideals and perseverance created a vibrant center in Eretz Yisrael. In the most desperate circumstances, they believed that they were bringing light, beauty, and even salvation to the Jewish people.

This transfer of a cultural center is one of many in the long history of the Jewish people, but unlike many of its antecedents, it can be studied in some detail since here we have abundant sources. While it is widely known that the center of Hebrew culture is in Israel today, it is not common knowledge that Israel, or Eretz Yisrael, achieved Hebrew cultural hegemony long before the official establishment of the State in 1948, or before the decimation of European Jewry in the Shoah, between 1939 and 1945. Note I refer to "cultural hegemony," a specific political-cultural concept by which I mean that one center is more or less universally recognized as the center of creativity and, hence, of leadership and authority. The transfer of cultural centers from country to country was one of the basic historical concepts formulated by Simon Dubnow (1860–1941), one of the great historians of the Jewish people. Zohar Shavit and others assign this rise in hegemony to the period between the two World Wars.[2] I would be more specific and narrow this dramatic shift to the years between 1924 and 1928. And since I contend that one cannot describe the establishment of hegemony in Eretz Israel without consideration of the decline of Hebrew creativity in the European Diasporan communities, Russia, Poland, and Germany, I will concentrate here on the shift in hegemonic centers rather than on the construction of the Tel Aviv center itself. The shift of the hegemonic center from the Diaspora to the ancestral homeland is, in itself, a fascinating phenomenon, highly significant for comparative Diasporan studies. To situate this event, we shall begin with a focal point in the history of the Russian Jewish community, where most European Jews resided before World War I.

In the spring of 1917, after several years of the virtual cessation of Hebrew publishing in Russia, there appeared in Odessa a new periodical, *Keneset*, edited by Hayim Nahman Bialik, by then the iconic figure of modern Hebrew literature. In the editor's preface to this famous volume, Bialik explains to his readers, in prose ringing with Biblical phrases of lamentation and historical import, the reasons for the delay of the volume:

> At this moment, while the press is busy issuing the last sheets of the collection "Keneset" and I am writing these lines—relief has come. The iron yoke has been broken from our neck, and heaven and earth delight in the

downfall of the wicked. A year and one half ago, when this selection was first conceived, the rod of perversity still tyrannized us ferociously. A burning storm arose to uproot the cities of Israel and scatter their inhabitants like mountain-chaff in all directions. Then there gathered in Odessa, the only place where Hebrew publishing still flickered a bit—a small group, a refugee-remnant, of Hebrew authors who, because of the decree, a Hadrianic decree against the Hebrew language, lost all literary shelter.

The decree referred to was the Russian governmental ban of July 5, 1915 on the publication of all Hebrew and Yiddish in the country at war. Bialik explains that in this situation, a private subsidy was provided to publish a volume, but after he had edited it in full compliance with all possible censorship regulations, the censor would still not approve it. Suddenly, "the revolution came and 'turned the saucer upside down.'" The efforts to obviate the censor were unnecessary since "the hour of the collection's birth was greater than its conception." He ends the preface with the exclamation: "Hayta harevaha! Besiman tov uvemazal tov!" (Relief has come! Good omen! Good Luck!)

There were grounds for greeting this new birth of a literary miscellany into the Jewish community. The Tsarist government had been overthrown in the February Revolution. After decades of oppression and censorship, the evil rule was over. Bialik himself proceeded to establish the new publishing house, Dvir, with its ambitious plans to publish the classics of all periods. The philanthropist, Avraham Stybel would soon engage Tchernichowski, still in St. Petersburg, but soon to return to Odessa, to translate the Iliad and the Odyssey into Hebrew. In the spring of 1917, the future looked rosy.

By January 1918, however, the Bolshevik regime had created the Yevsektsia to dismantle the institutions of the Jewish community and with them, the use of Hebrew. The process was confused and painful, often resisted, but finally depressingly victorious. There would be no place for Hebrew in the Soviet Union. Within four years, on June 21, 1921, Bialik and many of his colleagues were on a ship leaving Odessa for Istanbul, escaping Communist Russia never to return. After two months in Istanbul, Bialik traveled to the Zionist Congress in Carlsbad, and onward to Berlin where he lived until 1924 when he finally settled in Tel Aviv.

Bialik's editorial preface evokes two historical phenomena that will constitute the axes of this paper: first, the nature of Hebrew literary productivity in the modern period until the consolidation of the institutions of culture in Eretz Yisrael during the British mandate; second, the impact of specific, definable historic events on the fortunes of Hebrew literature and the final transfer of the center of Hebrew culture from Europe to Tel Aviv in the late 1920s. Hebrew publishing, always at the mercy of the censor, the volatile economic situation, and severe political oppression, was a complicated history of contingencies, of bold enterprises and desperate failures, of occasional exuberance, but frequently, despondency. When one recognizes the utter fragility of the entire enterprise from Moses Mendelssohn through Bialik, one comes to admire the amazing crystallization of a hegemonic center in Eretz Yisrael by the late 1920s. An exploration of the relationship between these two axes raises a host of interesting questions that tend to subvert some of the myths we have all been brought up with.

I place the term "Hebrew literary centers" in quotation marks since I contest that it is, at best, a dubious term, as one can see from study of Glenda Abramson's *The Great Transition*. The history of Hebrew literature from the *Meassfim* in Berlin of the 1780s until Tel Aviv of the 1920s and 1930s is essentially the collective biography of a series of determined individuals who believed that Hebrew, the ancestral language of the Jews, could be used as a vehicle of enlightenment in the modern world, or as the instrument for the revolutionary modernization of Jewish life, including the establishment of a Jewish homeland in Eretz Yisrael. Their devotion to the Hebrew language and Hebrew literature was passionate, approaching or substituting for religious fervor; it is impossible to imagine the great cultural achievements in Hebrew without their vision. While we often talk of centers of Hebrew literature or creativity, these centers are really contingent assemblages of scattered individual writers, editors, and publishers in convenient major cities, mostly in Europe. Historians, furthermore, sometimes confuse major centers of Jewish residence with centers of Jewish creative activity. (Certainly, such industrial centers as Lodz and Bialystok were not major centers of Jewish learning.) Not every major city where Jews resided in the past 150 years, for instance, was also a center of Hebrew culture, though historians of Hebrew literature invariably confuse the two by implying that every Jew in Odessa, Warsaw, or Berlin knew the names of the Hebrew writers who dwelled among them. Returning to Bialik's moving preface to *Keneset*, we might ask: How many of Odessa's 150,000 Jews shared Bialik's excitement about the new-born freedom he felt in the spring of 1917?

Hebrew literature before World War I is marked by a strange paradox, for while works of great literary quality were indeed produced (one can list such formidable figures as Mendele, Ahad HaAm, Bialik,

Tchernichowski, Berdyczewski, Gnessin, all still studied today), there never emerged a stable, supportive community of readers. In the first generation of Haskalah literature, in Prussia of the late eighteenth and early nineteenth centuries, once the Hebrew readers learned enough of the local language to read newspapers, journals, or books, they abandoned the Hebrew periodicals that had been their path to modern, general culture, to enlightenment. While the situation in each subsequent *center* was different, the abandonment of Hebrew for national European literatures was repeated. The history of this recurring process is well described by Dan Miron in his *Bodedim bemo'adam* (When loners come together).[3] Miron's account deals with the period before World War I, but it is applicable for the 1920s, the period of our immediate concern. Bialik's preface is thus a strategic point of departure for a consideration— or reconsideration—of the transfer of centers I wish to discuss: it reflects a major juncture in the history of the political events which shaped the Eretz Yisrael center that emerges as hegemonic by the end the 1920s. That Tel Aviv would emerge as the hegemonic center is often treated as a foregone conclusion, as an inevitable phase of history, and so it is regarded in Zohar Shavit's book. A study of the broader contexts of this cultural transfer will show that the situation was much more contingent than it is usually presented. Much depended on the determination of the writers, editors, and publishers, but much was the result of adverse political circumstances beyond the control of the Jews.

To understand these circumstances, we have to breach the intellectual barrier that has been raised after World War II. The enormity of the two events of the 1940s: the Shoah, on the one hand, and the establishment of the sovereign State of Israel, on the other, has dwarfed the catastrophic events of World War I and its immediate aftermath that left much of East European Jewry decimated or displaced. While it is possible that we can never put the years 1914–1922 in proper perspective, we should not attempt to evaluate them without first acknowledging this barrier to such an assessment.

Shai Agnon, among others, alludes, on several occasions, that in August 1914 the world changed radically for the worse. The guns of August opened a new cataclysmic period that introduced massive slaughter, the dissolution of Empires, the reshuffling of borders, and the unleashing of both rabid nationalism and violent communism. And yet, even before that eruption, we see that Jews were on the move, less to Eretz Yisrael as Zionists, than to America, both North and South, and to South Africa, as individuals seeking better lives for themselves and their families. They came from both Tsarist Russia and the Austro-Hungarian Empire fleeing poverty, discrimination, and pogroms. The grim, absurd world they fled was brilliantly portrayed in the novels of Mendele, both in Yiddish and, after 1885, in Hebrew. Between 1890 and 1914, thirty percent of East and East Central European Jewry left Europe, but by 1914 there were only 85,000 Jews in Eretz Yisrael, half of them immigrants of the Second Aliya (1904–14). The trend would have likely continued were it not for the Johnson Act of 1921 which first restricted immigration to the United States from Eastern Europe and virtually cut it off by 1925.

The trajectory of Hebrew literature during this period seems to defy all logic, for between 1885 and 1914, precisely when masses of Jews were leaving Europe, Hebrew literature enjoyed one of its most glorious, creative periods. And yet, this creativity is selective, for while great works were written and published, the audience for these writers diminished, so much so that in 1904 both *HaShiloah* and *HaDor*, the leading periodicals of Odessa and Warsaw respectively, collapsed. The situation in Eretz Yisrael was no better in 1904, and were it not for the infusion of new forces after the failure of the 1905 Russian Revolution, the prospects for the future of the Yishuv would have been dimmer. Despite the outstanding talents of these writers who made a versatile modern literature out of feeble and unpromising precedents, there was never a stable market for modern Hebrew writing and, as early as the 1870s, it was obvious to a writer like Mendele that the market for Yiddish, a language spoken by masses of potential readers, was substantial and growing. By the first decade of the twentieth century, when the Yiddish press was finally allowed to publish dailies in Russia and a mass community of readers assembled in New York, most Jewish readers of journals did so in Yiddish.

While the market for Hebrew books and periodicals was usually weak, significant educational institutions were established in the Yishuv in its early years. By the end of the nineteenth century, there were twenty schools where modern Hebrew was taught, using the Ivrit be'Ivrit method. By 1903, Ussishkin organized a coherent teachers' union (Agudat hamorim ha'ivrim). More advanced institutions emerged: the Lemel Teachers College in Jerusalem in 1904; the Gymnasia Ivrit in Jerusalem in 1905; the Herzeliyah Gymnasium in Tel Aviv in 1906. These teachers (truly, the unsung heroes of the Yishuv) and the parents of their students were powerful enough in 1913 to defeat the attempts of the *Hilfsverein der deutschen Jüden* to introduce German as the language of instruction in the new Technion in Haifa. They embodied and were animated by a new concept in the Jewish world: the teaching of Hebrew as the living language of an organic society. The crucial importance of these triumphs would become clear only in the mid-1920s, in the period of the crystallization of a hegemonic center. They served as an inspiration to the Hebraists of the Diaspora who were still struggling to create a literature for an ever dwindling audience.

The fragility of the Diasporan Hebrew centers was exacerbated during the disastrous days of World War I to which Bialik refers: after July 1915, publication was outlawed in Tsarist Russia which still included Poland; in the Yishuv, even the weekly *HaPoel Hatzair* ceased publication since much of the population of Tel Aviv and Jaffa was evacuated by the Turkish army; the weekly *HaToren* continued to come out in New York, but even its impressive circulation figures, some 13,000 subscribers, pales in comparison with the huge readership of the Yiddish daily press which had reached over 250,000. To put matters in perspective, in 1917, the year of the Russian Revolutions and the Balfour Declaration, the number of Jews in the world was about 14,000,000, while the number of persons who both could and would read a modern Hebrew book or journal could not have exceeded 100,000 and the number of real speakers of Hebrew might not have been several thousand, mostly teachers and their students. Large numbers of pious Jews knew Hebrew, but most of them would not be interested in modern Hebrew texts and they rarely bought modern journals and books.

In the three years after the publication of Bialik's preface, several events, crucial for the later growth of the Hebrew cultural center in Eretz Yisrael, took place. First, the British conquered Palestine from the Turks and issued the Balfour Declaration; both acts opened possibilities for a new type of Jewish settlement in Eretz Yisrael, more official, under a western government that recognized Hebrew in 1922 as an official language. Second, the immigration of Jews to Palestine that had ceased because of the war in 1914 recommenced in late 1918, bringing some 35,000 new Jews by 1923. It must be said, however, that this number was little more than a replacement for those who had fled during the war, and for every Jew who migrated to Palestine in the Third Aliyah, about forty migrated to the United States in the same years. In Russia, the effects of the October Revolution began to be felt and thousands were slaughtered either in the Civil War or in the pogroms in the Ukraine. Third, in the Paris (Versailles) Peace Conference where Jewish lobbying was intense, new nations, including Poland, were established from the territories ceded by the great pre–World War I Empires: Russia, Austria, and Germany. The legal protection of minority rights, including the right to maintain schools in minority languages, including Hebrew and Yiddish, was grudgingly granted and enabled the creation of Tarbut Hebrew schools—and other Jewish schools—throughout central Europe and the Baltic nations. What few people realized at the time was the pernicious nature of resurgent nationalism; the same impulses that created minority rights for Jews quickly deprived them of much more than fundamental minority rights.

Even from the sketch of historical events I have offered to make my argument, it should be clear that the first two decades of the twentieth century were grim, punctuated by revolutions, pogroms, evacuations, migrations, and frantic political efforts to solve some of the problems of political deprivation and poverty. It is against this background that one must read the tortured novels and articles of Yosef Hayyim Brenner or the apocalyptic poetry of Uri Zvi Greenberg. Brenner's historical persona looms so large even today because his biography and writings reflected the disruptive upheavals of the period and his dynamic initiatives were what kept so many cultural enterprises alive, despite the absurdity of the circumstances in which he lived.

By 1922, the results of the war, the October Revolution, the pogroms, and the post-war political decisions were becoming all too clear. In the Soviet Union, the Jewish community institutions had been closed down, and Hebrew had been labeled as a bourgeois language. This meant not only the cessation of Hebrew creativity in Russia, but the closing of a significant potential market for Hebrew journals and books published elsewhere, especially since the borders were closed. This affected publishers in Poland and Germany. At first, Warsaw and Berlin became replacements for Odessa and St. Petersburg and, to a lesser extent, so did New York and Tel Aviv, which had begun to reveal signs of cultural life after 1905. Since the New York Hebrew center never developed self-sufficiency, and we will turn at some length to Tel Aviv towards the end of this paper, a brief examination of the peculiar fates of Berlin and Warsaw are in order.

In the early days of the Weimar Republic, Berlin enjoyed a sudden and rare efflorescence in both Hebrew and Yiddish publications. Bialik arrived from Odessa (via Istanbul) and re-established the Dvir publishing house in Berlin with an ambitious program for publication. Other significant publishing ventures were initiated in Berlin and Bad-Homburg. In a gala celebration of Bialik's fiftieth birthday held in the hall of the Berlin Philharmonic in 1923, we find: Bialik, Tchernichowsky, Sokolow, Jabotinsky, Schneour, Frischman, Greenberg, Kleinman, Klatzkin, Fichman, Dinaburg, Yehezkel Kaufmann, Rawidowicz, etc. And yet, within a year, many if not most of these Hebrew luminaries had already left Germany, as did Agnon and Goitein, for Eretz Yisrael, mostly to Tel Aviv, which had become the cultural center of the Yishuv.

This sudden departure of such a significant group was not precipitated by any political threat. The proximate cause was really economic. During the period of the great inflation in Germany, many writers and scholars were supported by Avraham Stybel who had business interests in countries with hard currency. For ten dollars a month he could support a writer and his family. When the mark was revalued at the end of 1923 by the Finance Minister, Hjalmar Schacht, this subsidy could not be continued and there was little support for either the writers or their publishing projects. Shimon Rawidowicz summed up the situation in a quip: "Dr. Schacht hegla et Bialik le'eretz yisrael." (Dr. Schacht exiled Bialik to Eretz Yisrael.) While this sudden loss of support might have impelled many to leave for Eretz Yisrael, there were obviously broader reasons. It was becoming clear that Berlin was really a temporary refugee center, a fleeting *Nachtasyl*, as it were, with no real Hebrew hinterland. All these writers and publishers were Russian or Polish Jews. Even the writers who preceded them in Berlin, Shai Hurwitz and Berdyczewski, were not German born or trained. They were fully aware that with Russia now a communist country, a massive Jewish audience was lost. As for Poland, the severe discriminatory Grabski economic measures of 1923 accelerated the pauperization of Polish Jewry. The relocation of this group of Hebrew writers and scholars from Berlin and Frankfurt to Eretz Yisrael in 1924 marks, I would argue, the beginning of the final phase of Hebrew culture in Europe where it had existed, often thrived, since the tenth century.

While the brevity of the dynamic period of the Weimar Hebrew group is easy to understand, the rapid disintegration of the Hebrew community in Poland requires more analysis.[4] Poland, after all, was the center of vibrant, though turbulent, Jewish life between the wars. With three million Jews—350,000 in Warsaw alone—and the success of the Tarbut schools, one of the most noble experiments in Hebrew education going from kindergarten through gymnasium, one might expect a burgeoning Hebrew public. But Polish Jewry, including Vilna, then part of Poland, could not maintain a Hebrew daily throughout this period and by the 1930s few modern Hebrew books were published annually. By 1928 there was only one bookstore in all of Warsaw dedicated to modern Hebrew books and periodicals, most published in Eretz Yisrael. By the mid-1930s few Hebrew writers or editors were left in the country. One usually attributes this decline to the harsh economic boycotts and political discrimination, and these were certainly a factor, but they could not be the only explanation since the interwar period, for all its dark moments, was a period of astounding social and cultural activity of Polish Jewry as a whole, particularly in the Yiddish press. There are two other, less famous reasons that explain this decline. First, despite the increasing hostility of the Polish Christian population and government to the Jews, Polonization of Jews proceeded at a dizzying rate. Shmeruk (citing Paul Glickson) states that 100,000 Polish language newspapers published by Jews for Jews were sold daily in Warsaw in the 1930s.[5] He concludes, as does Ezra Mendelssohn, that given the rapid Polonization of the Jews of Poland, the future of the community was in doubt even had there been no Shoah. Second, the Hebrew language Tarbut schools were not designed to perpetuate the Jewish community of Poland; their curricula and teachers, consciously or unconsciously, were preparing their students for life in a Hebrew speaking society which implied aliyah to Eretz Yisrael. Certainly, more than a few of the 67,000 olim in the Fourth (Grabski) Aliyah and of the 94,000 Polish Jews among the Fifth Aliyah had been educated in the Tarbut schools or the various Zionist youth movements. The very success of this education spelled its ultimate doom. Usually societies create education institutions to preserve their values and structures, but the implicit goal of the Hebrew/Zionist oriented schools and youth movements was to remove the Jews from Poland. By doing so, they precluded the possibility of a Hebrew reading audience in that country.

The basic outlines of the actual institutionalization of the Tel Aviv center in the 1920s have been formulated and documented over the past twenty years, and I intend, in the last phase of this essay, to summarize some of the main points and to interpret them in light of the broader portrait I have painted above. A simple comparison of publication figures will set the parameters of the change. In the years 1920–1923, the total numbers of Hebrew books published annually in Eretz Yisrael are: 48, 56, 63, 75. In the years 1925–1928 they are: 152, 254, 316, 321.[6] The number of books sold rises from 4,000 in 1918 and 6,900 in 1919 to 150,000 in 1928. While the Jewish population in the Eretz Yisrael almost tripled in that period from about 60,000 to about 175,000, the amount of books sold multiplies by a factor of twenty. By 1925 when the Histadrut begins to publish *Davar* under the editorship of Berl Katznelson, there were three Hebrew dailies in Tel Aviv, and the schools in Eretz Yisrael were beginning to turn out successive classes of Hebrew-speaking youngsters. In that same year, the Hebrew University was formally opened in Jerusalem, and while the early classes were very small, the symbolism of the Hebrew University in Jerusalem was overwhelming.

In Poland, the trend of publications of Hebrew books moves in the opposite direction and by 1930 reaches the disastrous number of eighteen per annum. This does not mean that the Yishuv was an independent cultural center by the late 1920s. The economy was fragile and underwent two depressing recessions in that decade, in 1922 and 1928–30. Editors and publishers were constantly seeking financial subsidies from both America and Europe. But it was clear to most involved parties by 1929 when the Agudat HaSofrim was formally organized in Tel Aviv, that the center of the Hebrew world was there, not in Berlin or Warsaw or New York.

One can enumerate a variety of reasons contributing to this success. The Yishuv showed remarkable talents for self-organization, for establishing institutional structures especially through the labor movement, particularly after 1904, but even before then. While public life was often chaotic and contentious, the Jews of Eretz Yisrael could work together especially when led by charismatic figures like Brenner and Katznelson. Foremost among the institutions contributing to the crystallization of a coherent cultural center was the Histadrut, founded in 1920. The labor-oriented society the Histadrut was intent upon creating was to be Hebrew speaking; the three *kibushim* (conquests) were of labor, of the soil, and of the language, and these slogans were taken seriously. Second, the conquest of Palestine by the British Army in 1917 rid the Yishuv of Ottoman control that was repressive and certainly not conducive to the realization of Jewish aspirations.[7] While the Mandatory powers were an extension of British colonialist goals and Albion could indeed be perfidious, the Balfour Declaration, the recognition of Hebrew as an official language, the lack of interference in the internal affairs of the Jewish settlers, and the introduction of many western norms of public behavior, all contributed to the strengthening of the Yishuv. Third, the disastrous political events in Europe and the restriction of immigration to the United States, both diverted immigration waves towards Eretz Yisrael and induced many to draw certain conclusions about the destiny of the Jews in the modern world with its intensified nationalisms. Last, but by no means least, the ideology that animated much, but not all of Hebrew literature from the 1880s on, first as Hibbat Tzion, then as Zionism, offered a coherent interpretation of history and the political events of the times. While the leadership of the Zionist movement was not always interested in the development of a Hebrew culture, and Bialik himself was not an eager settler, and a Berdyczewski or a Frischmann never made aliyah, the basic Ahad Ha'Amic formulation of cultural Zionism made much sense to many people. The Yishuv could, indeed, be a cultural center for the Jews of the Diaspora. It was also a refuge that still accepted Jews after the Johnson Act.

The passing of hegemony to Eretz Yisrael was not regarded with a sense of triumph by the more sensitive writers. When one reads the correspondence generated by the independent literary journal *Hedim* in its early years, 1922–1923, one cannot escape the note of desperation among writers like Yaakov Rabinovitz, Barash, Shlonsky, Lamdan who realized that they now had the responsibility to keep Hebrew literature alive and vital. The apocalyptic mood of the period was most forcefully captured in Yitzhak Lamdan's epic poem *Masada* (1927), an expressionistic evocation of the inescapable terrors and false options facing Jews after World War I, all leading to the desperate, absurdist conclusion that the only solution lies in Masada, his mythical name for Eretz Yisrael.

As the political situation worsened in Europe in the 1930s, the stream of Jews seeking refuge in Eretz Yisrael widened and, as is well known, some 250,000 olim arrived between 1930 and 1939. This Aliyah, often erroneously called the "German Aliyah," actually included 94,000 Polish Jews, in addition to significant numbers from the Baltic nations and Romania, many of whom had excellent Hebrew training in a variety of schools thus adding measurably to the potential reading audience for both Hebrew books and journals. The hegemony of Tel Aviv, already well established by 1929, was corroborated. It is significant to note, however, that of the 137 Hebrew writers listed by Agudat Hasoferim as residing in Eretz Yisrael between the wars, only twenty-eight arrived in the 1930s precisely when the population doubled. The happy result of this massive Hebrew Aliyah was not only the strengthening of the new creative center in Eretz Yisrael, but the saving of this group from the slaughter of the Nazi period. For while hundreds of Yiddish writers were killed in the Shoah, significantly fewer Hebrew writers suffered this fate.[8] The impact of the differing fates of these two groups of writers, the Hebraists and the Yiddishists, have had the obvious consequence. After World War II, Yiddish literature could have no real future: most of its writers and many of its readers were killed in the Shoah.

These two groups read the same political signs differently because of their different ideologies, and one might cite this as a crucial example of the destined triumph of the Zionist concept of history. And yet, the picture is far from simple since many Jews did not appreciate the true dangers of Nazism and in the 1930s no one imagined the death camps. An historian as intelligent as Salo Baron, no anti-Zionist, could write in the late 1930s that the Nazi threat was a passing phenomenon. More important are two military events. First, Montgomery did succeed in stopping Rommel at El Alemein in 1942, but this was not a foregone conclusion. The Yishuv was justifiably panicked by the threat of a Nazi invasion from Africa, and there were Vichy forces in the Lebanon. Second, despite the questionable analysis made in the 1980s and 1990s by Benny Morris and others of the contesting forces in the War of Independence, those battles were bitterly fought and took 6000 Jewish lives. The stated Arab purpose was the liquidation of the Yishuv, and that had to be taken seriously. Nazi or Arab victories in Palestine would have annihilated the Yishuv and the new hegemonic center in it.

Given the combination of historical forces described above, the development of Eretz Yisrael as the hegemonic center of Hebrew culture is understandable, but not essentially inevitable. The equation is complicated, charged with many variables, most contingent on human desires and behavior, certainly not components one can easily predict. The one constant in the equation has been the devotion of those individuals who accepted the Ahad HaAmist vision of a vibrant Hebrew cultural center in Eretz Yisrael, a vision which, fused with a Brennerian sense of desperation and absurdity, inspired many to act and write. Until the State of Israel was established, much depended on the voluntary acts of many highly motivated, even heroic individuals. Even those who channeled their energies and talents through existing institutions like the Histadrut or the Palmah, could have done otherwise. But these ideals, as we have suggested, are not free from the contingencies of history. A homeland was constituted for modern Hebrew literature as it was for the Jews who settled in Mandatory Palestine or later, in the State of Israel. After many centuries of achievement in Hebrew literary creativity, the European Diaspora was silent—and no other Jewish Diaspora has showed any vital signs of life. As early as 1914, Yaakov Klatzkin projected in his collection of essays, *Tehumim* (Borders) that there would be no future for a viable Galut culture if a Hebrew speaking center were firmly established in Erestz Yisrael. If we interpret his statement to mean a Hebrew oriented culture, we would have to concede that he was right.

NOTES

1. *Toldot hayishuv hayehudi be'Eretz Yisrael me'az ha'aliyah harishonah.* ed. Moshe Lissak. Part I,(Mosad Bialik: Tel Aviv, 1999).

2. See articles by G. Shaked, Y. Shavit, and Z. Shavit in *The Great Transition*, eds. Glenda Abramson and Tudor Parfitt (Rowland and Alanheld: New Jersey, 1985).

3. (Am Oved: Tel Aviv, 1987), 9–429.

4. My information on Poland has been culled from a variety of sources. Ezra Mendelson, *The Jews of East Central Europe Between the World Wars,* (Indiana Press: Bloomington, 1983); *The Jews of Poland Between Two World Wars*, ed. Yisrael Gutman, et.al. (University Press of New England: Hanover and London, 1989); *The Jews in Poland*, ed. Chmen Abramsky et. al. (Blackwell: Oxford, 1986); *Polin: Studies in Polish Jewry,* Vols 1–15.

5. "Hebrew-Yiddish-Polish: A Trilingual Jewish Culture," in *The Jews of Poland Between Two World Wars*, ed. Yisrael Gutman et al. (University Press of New England: Hanover and London, 1989).

6. These numbers and those for Warsaw are taken from The Harvard On Line Public Access Catalogue (HOLIS).

7. For life under the British Mandate, see Tom Segev, *One Palestine, Complete: Jews and Arabs under the British Mandate* (Little Brown: London, 2000).

8. In a study published anonymously in 1973, Yisrael Cohen lists sixty-five Hebrew writers killed in the Shoah. *Yediot Genazim*, no. 81, vol 5, yr 10, Nissan.

❧ The New Diasporism and the Old Diaspora

Now that diasporan studies are spreading over the land like chaff scattered by the wind, it might be helpful to revisit the Diaspora from which all notions of diaspora have been disseminated: the Diaspora of the Jews. Diasporan discourse today, deriving from post-structural and post-colonial circles, differs so radically in concept and language from traditional discourse about the historic Diaspora of the Jews that one wonders about the propriety of the usage of the term. Precisely because of contemporary confusion about the term and its historic origins, it is imperative to attempt a brief presentation of what the Diaspora originally was. I revisit this historical phenomenon with all due hesitation since the literature on the Diaspora is so voluminous, and the term itself is so differently nuanced in each instance over a period of at least twenty-five hundred years, that any statement one makes must be qualified repeatedly, often beyond practical definition. On the other hand, the opportunity to discuss the Diaspora in response to the "new Diasporism" (my nomenclature) is challenging, since this new angle affords both fresh thoughts and perhaps better focus. For example: to ask the question, "How does a diaspora continue to exist over centuries without sustained territorial cohesiveness and despite the frequent hostility of foreign host populations?" forces us to raise several other questions: Do we assume that a diaspora must have a center, a homeland? What is the relationship of the diaspora to that center? Does the diaspora community create within it certain institutions and narratives that enable it to exist as a diaspora community? How do the newly created institutions and narratives relate to actual or mythic public spaces in the *home* community? When we

157

begin to examine the variety of diasporas discussed, for instance, in the periodical, *Diaspora*,[1] we begin to realize that this is one of the most slippery terms in critical usage today—slippery and emotionally charged.

The new Diasporism is succinctly and authoritatively summarized in the short article "The Nation-State and its Others: in Lieu of a Preface" by Khachig Tololyan, the editor of *Diaspora* as the manifesto of the new periodical when it first appeared in the Spring of 1991. The articles published in subsequent issues of the periodical hew to the ideological line set forth in this manifesto which therefore deserves our close attention.

The title of the article situates us in its world of discourse for the "new Diasporism" is a modern—or, perhaps more properly: post-modern—phenomenon focusing on the *others* found in the nation-state. Otherness is predicated here on the nation-state, not on pre-modern political entities such as the medieval European estates. Consequently, the two literary prooftexts adduced in this piece are Shakespeare's *Henry V* and Joyce's *Ulysses*, conceived as the two brackets delineating a period moving from the Renaissance to High Modernism, the period of the rise of the nation-state, capitalism, and imperialism. Actually, though reference is made to this period, the point-of-view of the author is defined by the cultural currents of the post-World War II world that has witnessed a major reshuffling of boundaries and peoples, and a new awareness of the lives of migrant populations all over the entire earth. This is the world of the jet, the multi-national corporation, and electronic communication.

It is also the world of discourse of Michel Foucault, Frederick Jameson, and Benedict Anderson. Note the language of the statement of purpose:

> Diaspora is concerned with the ways in which nations, real yet imagined communities (Anderson), are fabulated, brought into being made and unmade, in culture and politics, both on land people call their own and in exile. Above all, this journal will focus on such processes as they shape and are shaped by the infranational and transnational Other of the nation-state.[2]

The key term here is "transnational," since it is the defining phenomenon of the new Diasporism. People originating in one region or nation are scattered among a variety of nation-states and form a coherent transnational community. More often than not, these migrant populations leave their native lands to seek better working conditions elsewhere, though some populations have been forcibly expelled from their homelands.

Diaspora is concerned as well with all of the other forces and phenomena that constitute the transnational moment. These include massive and instantaneous movements of capital; the introduction of previously *alien* cultures through the practice of *media imperialism*; and "issues of the double allegiance of populations and the plural affiliations of transnational corporations. All these developments point to the need to interrogate the national context in which certain assumptions about collective identity once prevailed; they also raise questions about the global context."[3]

The author/editor is keenly aware that he is formulating a definition of diasporism which is very specific to his times, though he finds adumbrations of it throughout the last five centuries. Furthermore, he senses that the term should be used "provisionally to indicate our belief that the term that once described Jewish, Greek, and Armenian dispersion, now shares meanings with a larger semantic domain that includes words like immigrant, expatriate, refugee, guest-worker, exile-community, overseas community, ethnic community."[4] Indeed, this reader finds the semantic domain so capacious as to be unwieldy and misleading. The desire to universalize, to find structural similarity and simplicity flattens the variety of human experience, and is, in itself, an intellectual imperialism. The yearning to universalize leads him into the problematic grouping of the Jews, the Greeks, and the Armenians as undifferentiated models of the pre-transnational diasporism. Even a casual acquaintance with the historic experiences of these three peoples should alert one to the vast differences between their diasporan experiences. Precisely because of this tendency to homogenize all so-called diasporan experiences, it is crucial to revisit the original Diaspora, that of the Jews. In doing so, we should, however, be mindful of the differences between this experience and that of the Greeks and Armenians, on the one hand, and that of the migratory millions of the past two or three decades.

And so, risking the possibility of belaboring the obvious, I will open with some basic facts about the historical Jewish Diaspora. The term, of course, is Greek, deriving from "diasporein", the scattering of seeds, and it is usually assumed that the Jewish Diaspora was a product of the Hellenistic period during which more Jews established permanent residence outside of the Holy Land than in the Holy Land itself with its Holy City, Jerusalem, often referred to as Zion. Prior to this dispersion there were two significant recorded and vividly remembered events that shaped for the Jews, all subsequent notions of dispersion or exile: the conquest of the Northern Kingdom of Israel in 722 B.C.E. with the attendant deportation of a significant portion of the population to Assyria; the conquest of the Southern Kingdom centered around Jerusalem in 586 B.C.E., causing exiles or dispersions to Babylonia and Egypt.

We have coupled the term *dispersion* (diaspora) with the term *exile* to broach a key question to be raised: How did the Jews regard their residence in communities outside the Holy Land? Ordinarily, the meta-narrative of the Jews as formulated no later than the Deuteronomic historians (seventh to fifth centuries, B.C.E.) considered this dispersion an exile from God's Holy Land, and punishment for disobeying his commandments. This pervasive concept engendered a relentless tension, for though residence outside the land was considered a state of punishment, and one yearned for a redemption that entailed a return to the pre-exilic state, one often lived in large communities outside the land. This very tension, I would suggest, defines the specific nature of the Jewish Diaspora in all subsequent periods (until the modern) and all other diasporas may conveniently be measured by their obsession with or freedom from such a tension. To what extent, we should ask, does diaspora residence entail a sense of guilt, of betrayal of a cherished ideal—or commandment—requiring residence in the homeland. The case of the Jews is instructive. Though there were, in the sixth and fifth centuries B.C.E., several waves of return to Judaea from the lands of exile (never, incidentally, involving large numbers of people) and though an independent or semi-independent Jewish polity was established in Judaea between 175 B.C.E. and 70 C.E., it appears that by the period under discussion, from about 300 B.C.E. to 200 C.E., most Jews lived outside their ancestral Holy Land, thus creating a well defined diaspora, regarded as such in contemporary documents (e.g. certain books of Rabbinic literature, Josephus, and the New Testament).

The numbers given for this diaspora and its motherland, are impressive: about 6,000,000 souls, one tenth of the inhabitants of the Roman Empire at the time, scattered throughout the empire, but mostly concentrated in the cities and market-towns of the eastern Mediterranean. This diaspora fits, on the whole, the definition of "the dispersion of an originally homogeneous people;" or "the dispersion of an originally homogeneous entity, such as a language or culture." Homogeneity is a key concept, but requires some qualification. On the one hand, there seems to have been a significant movement of conversion to Judaism during the period, not very well documented, but still sufficiently attested. On the other hand, though there were obviously a variety of religious positions among the Jews of the Holy Land, they manifested a distinct homogeneity since they agreed on a significant number of cultural items, not the least was their personal involvement in the meta-narrative of the Chosen People of Israel as described in the Hebrew Scriptures. In one way or another, they were devoted to the Torah, its revelatory authenticity, and its authority as a guide for behavior. They were, furthermore, repeatedly enjoined to remember this meta-narrative and their part in it. Consequently, we can describe this diaspora in terms of both the geographic matrix to which it relates (i.e. the ancestral home land, the Holy Land, centered on Jerusalem), and the ideological matrix to which it related (the Torah, as it began to take shape in the fifth century B.C.E.). Both are types of public space, the first real, geographical, the second, ideological, metaphysical. It required, however, a third type of public space to provide cohesion to the tensions mentioned above.

For while the Diaspora is, indeed, a Hellenistic phenomenon, what gave it its specific shape and force was an event—an account of an event in the middle fifth century, B.C.E.—that we find in Chapter 8 of the Book of Nehemiah. (One can go back even further to the early sixth century to pertinent chapters in Jeremiah and Ezekiel.) There we read that Ezra the scribe brought to the congregation assembled in the square before the Water Gate—men and women and all who could listen with understanding—the scroll of the Teaching of Moses with which the Lord had charged Israel. "They read from the scroll of the Teaching of God, translating it and giving the sense; so they understood the reading." The text loses much in translation since in the original it conveys the entire process of the public reading of a historically significant and consequential text, its explanation and communication to an attentive, receptive audience. ("Vayikre'u basefer betorat ha'elohim meforash vesom sekhel vayavinu bamikra.") I stress this text because of what it dramatizes: the public communication of the master-narrative and the divinely ordered legal system embedded in it are more central to the binding of all Jewish communities, including those in the Diaspora, than any sense of kinship or folkways or vague memories of shared historical experience. The Jews of both the homeland and the diaspora shared a public space, a synagogue in Greek or a *bet keneset* in Hebrew, where the congregation performed a designated process of public communication that invariably included study of the Torah, its exegesis, both homiletical and halakhic (legal). This, in turn, required a degree of literacy for all male participants, ordained no later than the second century C.E. This public space is one of discourse with specific parameters: it deals with scripture, its exegesis, and its control of human behavior. (To complete the picture, one should speak of the necessary private space, the home, and, more specifically, the kitchen where women were probably determinative.) And since the language of the Jewish scripture is Hebrew, the Hebraism of the discourse is a significant parameter.

The question of language is crucial. One should not merely accept the modern nationalist Hebraist view that it was the Hebrew language that bound the various diasporas of Jews throughout all centuries. The picture is far more complex than one would surmise, once confronted with the simple fact that few Jews spoke Hebrew in the diaspora, or even in the Holy Land, after the second century C.E. and that even in the earlier centuries of the Hellenistic period, the third, second, and first centuries B.C.E., the picture—however fragmentary—was clearly mixed. While Hebrew was certainly used for prayer and Bible readings, the international language of commerce was Aramaic and, after the penetration of Greeks and Romans to the area, obviously part Greek and part Latin, more the former than the latter. To say that most Jewish males were at least bi-lingual (i.e. Hebrew plus another language) for the past 2,500 years, is to cite a commonplace. It is obvious that Hebrew was used in prayer, in Bible reading (mostly for those portions read in the synagogues) and a variety of other religious occasions, while daily discourse was usually carried on in the other language. Naturally, the learned elite, the rabbis, would know more Hebrew than the average Jew. It is fair to say that by the second century C.E., Hebrew was still better known in Palestine than in most cities of the Diaspora with the possible exception of several centers in Mesopotamia.

Their bi-lingualism tells us little. Of greater importance is the fact that in the public space—the world of the synagogue with its house of study—the *language orientation* was toward Hebrew, even if Hebrew was not spoken there. By *language orientation* I mean that since the language of the determinative texts was Hebrew (the prayers, the Bible, the Mishnah, the Midrashim, etc.). Hebrew was the language of holiness and dignity, and even if the discussion about the text was in Aramaic, say, or later, in Arabic, or Yiddish to take three examples,the language of the public space was "oriented" toward Hebrew: it absorbed Hebrew locutions of all sorts and, even more important, was considered a vehicle to make the word of God clear to the Jew who lived in the public space.

The daily language of the Jew, furthermore, was never linguistically identical with the language of the host population, but was rather a

Jewish sub-dialect of that language. The situation varied from place to place of course, but the evidence is abundant. The study of the languages of the Jews is now well developed: Jews, for instance, often wrote the host language in Hebrew letters and the Jewish peculiarities of the languages spoken by Jews is well known. When we speak of the bi-lingualism of the Diaspora communities, therefore, we clearly refer to a phenomenon of great flexibility and variety. Either of the two languages, Hebrew and the host language of the diaspora communities, was thus not merely a member of a bi-lingual pair, but was rather a constituent of a diglossic continuum in which, as in any diglossic situation, complementary social functions were distributed between two varieties of a language. Here I would prefer to treat language in the broadest sense, as the vehicle of cultural communication. I am thus treating the language range of the diasporan community as one language, divisible into a variety of glosses, at least two, as in a digloss, or more.

What endowed these two orientations legitimacy and cogency was, of course, the belief in the meta-narrative of the Jews, that there is a providential God who created the universe, revealed his Torah to his chosen people at Sinai, and will, in time, bring about their redemption including a restoration to the national homeland. This structure of beliefs and behavioral entailments, was both binding enough to create group cohesion despite widely differing geographical locations in the Diaspora, yet flexible enough to allow each community to adapt to new situations in the Diaspora. The political structures of the countries of the diaspora were not yet organized on the basis of the modern nation state that generated a new set of relations with its resident populations; in pre-modern states, Jews lived in partially autonomic communities and their status was both negotiable and often viable. Obviously, life was not always pleasant for the diasporan communities, but not all migrations were determined by persecution by the host population; clearly, at times, better trading and occupational opportunities beckoned from other lands. Our records are often fragmentary since diasporan communities rarely develop the archival bases of settled communities, but we have enough information to form a picture of repeated ventures into new territories. For example, the five volume study, *A Mediterranean Society*, by S.D. Goitein, describes the trading and living patterns of Jews in the Mediterranean basin between the eleventh and fourteenth centuries. Here we see a network of communities, some large, some small, some traders, some craftsmen, carrying out their daily lives, in contact with other Jewish diasporan communities at great distances.

Two major events in the last few centuries have forced a reconceptualisation of the diasporism which was more or less normative from the Hellenistic period on: the creation of the modern nation-state in Europe with its concepts of citizenship; the creation of the State of Israel, a modern nation state in the ancestral homeland of the Jews. Once France, for instance, raised the question of citizenship for Jews, demanding, in return, allegiance to the state, the diaspora status of Jews, predicated on their allegiance—however hypothetical—to Zion, or to their own public spaces that were Zion and Hebrew oriented, was called into question, and they had to chose between French citizenship and diaspora existence. Naturally, most chose the former and the motto, "Paris is our Jerusalem" or "Berlin is our Jerusalem" became the new calculus of public space. The attrition of religious life in many urban centers in the west has further loosened the diasporan bonds described above.

The establishment of Israel, on the other hand, together with the dazzling improvement of communications in the modern period, has induced many far-reaching changes in the concept of Diaspora existence. To begin with, one can easily end a diaspora existence by settling in Zion. One can visit Zion freely and easily. Zion thus becomes a presence in the Diaspora even for non-religious Jews. But residence in a modern national state with its demands and affiliation with the ancestral homeland with its demands might generate certain ambiguities not known before 1948. As we approach the end of the fifth decade of Israel's existence, we note that the concept of the Jewish Diaspora has undergone radical revision.

Though the revival of the Hebrew language as a modern, sophisticated tool of expression is closely associated with the rise of modern Zionism, its development is unparalleled among new-nation languages. For while many new nations have been established since World War II, no ancestral language has experienced such expansion and adoption. While a variety of reasons have been suggested for this phenomenon (see B. Harshav, *Language in the Time of Revolution*) most linguists would agree that the above-described language status of Hebrew among diasporan Jews was a key factor. Hebrew had an active and honored role in the public space of Diaspora Jews.[5]

We end with two intriguing linguistic ironies. As the Jews have moved out of the ghetto, the term *ghetto* was appropriated for describing depressed, inner city spaces mostly populated by African Americans. As the Jews focussed much of their attention on the new Jewish national state in Zion, and thus had to undergo an agonizing and far from resolved redefinition of their diaspora status, the term "diaspora" is used to describe Armenians, Chinese, Indians, Latinos, Palestinians etc.

The contemporary diasporan discourse, as we suggested at the open-ing of this paper, reflects the currents of thought prevalent today: post-modern, post-structuralist. The dominant theoretical paradigm is Frederick Jameson's late global capitalism which attempts to explain the spread of multi-national corporations and the migration of jobs and masses of peoples. The leading names among these theorists are Said, Spivak, and Bhabha. The spokespersons of this diasporism are often from the Indian subcontinent, the Middle East, and Latin America. They have moved to the west where they have received their education and often occupy academic positions in prestigious universities. In their articles, they bemoan the plight of the poorer masses of their countrymen who are the poorly paid employees of the multi-national corporation (seen as a neo-colonial phenomenon) in their homeland, or in the cities of the industrialized west.

While much of what they describe is the plight of immigrants throughout history, the specificity of the situation today is shaped by global capitalism. There is, in their discourse, however, little discussion of the emotional or ideological sway the homeland holds over the mem-bers of the diasporan communities. Yearning, alienation, concern for the identity of the next generation are pervasive, but one finds little of the ideological obligations and the guilt generated by the Jewish Diaspora.

Finally, certain of the preoccupations of the new diasporan theory, may indeed help us to distinguish between some concomitant phenom-ena. We notice, for instance, the significant settlement of Israeli born and educated Jews in a variety of nation-states, mostly in western indus-trial countries, most specifically in the United States. How do we cate-gorize these communities? Are they similar to the Jewish communities in the same countries in which they settle or do we define them differ-ently? Do they define themselves differently? Are they part of the tra-ditional Diaspora, or are they a totally new phenomenon, coming as they do from a sovereign Jewish nation-state where they often visit, hold pass-ports, and even return for military service. If they comprise a new type of trans-national diasporan community, does their very existence call for a redefinition of the nation-state from which they come?

NOTES

1. *Diaspora: A Journal of Transnational Studies*, edited by Khachig Tololyan, has been published by Oxford University Press since 1991.

2. Khachig Tololyan, "The Nation-State and its Others: in Lieu of a Preface," *Diaspora* 1(1) (1991):3.

3. Ibid., 5.

4. Ibid., 4.

5. See B. Harshav, *Language in a Time of Revolution* (Berkeley, CA 1993).

Adumbrations of the Israeli "Identity Crisis" In Hebrew Literature of the 1960s

> But is there a more terrible tyranny in the world than the tyranny of the saints? The wicked may condemn you to suffering, torment, terror. But the righteous don't let you live!

Towards the end of his 1965 novel, *The Living on the Dead* (208), Aharon Meged has the plaintiff's lawyer, Evrat, read before the author-defendant, Mr. Jonas, a transcript of a brief statement the latter had made at a party. Jonas is being charged with breach of contract: he did not write a contracted book about the prototypical Zionist hero of the previous generation, one Abrasha Davidov. Jonas's own lawyer finally claims that he couldn't write it because of "a mental crisis" in his life. To disprove this claim, Evrat reads Jonas's statement that Davidov, in his heroic righteousness, was a tyrant and "If we want to live, it is our sacred duty to wipe out his memory for ever and ever!" The breach of contract was therefore deliberate. I cite this passage because it captures so vividly the matrix of the turbulent attitudes animating so much of Israeli fiction of the 1960s, fiction which so eerily adumbrates the so-called identity crisis of Israeli society discussed by social scientists in the 1980s and 1990s.

I refer to this *identity crisis* with hesitation because I think it is time to retire this tired cliché. Recent sociological studies including one by James Clifford[1] have taught us that identity is not stable and reifiable, but rather a flexible concept contingent upon changes in a person, his circumstances, and those he interacts with. Rather than speak of identity crises, we would be better advised to talk of transformations over a period of time, at times very rapidly. In literary criticism the reification of identity crises is normal and frequent; what we often view as an identity crisis in fiction, for instance, is really the product of the conflict necessary to heighten the interest in plot. What we see is transformation structured and condensed to yield tense drama.

The transformation that interests me in this paper is one that has been developing for some time in Israeli society, namely the gradual moving away from the so-called Zionist narrative that reigned supreme in the Jewish society of pre-Israel Palestine, then in Israel from about 1920 through the 1950s. This was the narrative that educated generations of students and mobilized the Jewish society of the Yishuv to create the state and its many institutions. Viewing the past with the hopefully dispassionate eyes of the historian, we can indeed trace the crystallization of this narrative and its transformations. A fine example of this type of study is Yael Zerubavel's *Recovered Roots*.[2] Frequently, contemporary sociologists or political scientists, in studying the state of Israeli society in the 1990s, a society in which ideals of the founders are notably attenuated, perhaps noticeably absent, tend to attribute this dissipation to specific political events. Reaching backward from the present, they offer as candidates such events as the Lebanese War of 1982, or the decline of the Labor Party after the Yom Kippur War, or, at most, the problems engendered by the battle-field successes of the Six Day War of 1967. The last is a favorite candidate for speculation, especially since it fits in with the pressing political issues of the 1990s, the Intifada and the Peace Negotiations.

Anyone familiar with the developments in Israeli literature in the past two generations is fully aware that these political markers are inadequate for the task of tracing these transformations for two reasons: first, many aspects of the Zionist narrative began to change shortly after the establishment of the State in 1948, and, second, there are many facets of Israeli life—or of any human existence—that are not necessarily the products of political conflict.[3] Yizhar's early stories, "The Prisoner" (1948) and "Hirbet Hiza'ah" (1949), are obvious literary articulations of the rejection of the optimism and triumphalism of the period, as are several novels portraying the disenchantment with kibbutz life.[4] The 1950 fictions of M. Shamir, A. Meged, N. Shaham, etc. reflect a brooding meditation over the failures of the state to fulfill the dreams of its founders.[5] This disappointment is not unique to Israel: it is characteristic of most writers who are sensitive to the inevitable gap between the dreams they had inherited and the realities they must live with. It is most acute in the early years after a revolution or the establishment of a new political entity. If we do not find this expression of disappointment, we can usually expect to discover that the regimes in which the writers live do not tolerate such expressions of disappointment.

Israeli literary critics have noticed this critique embedded in Israeli fiction long ago. In the 1960s, it was obvious, as one can see from Shaked's essays, collected in 1971[6] that a new generation, with new perspectives, had appeared; this has subsequently been more fully documented by Nurit Gertz (1983),[7] among others. It is now abundantly clear that in the imagination of the writers of Israeli fiction, the transformations often attributed to the 1967 War were well developed in the decade before the 1967 War.

This is the subject of a much later article by Hannan Hever in *Prooftexts* 1990, which I deliberately cite because it is replete with brilliant readings; but it is—in my opinion—fundamentally flawed, since in its *cultural critical*, post-colonialist mode, it reduces everything to the tensions between the majority and minority cultures, leaning heavily on the theories of Deleuze and Guattari as evident even in its title, "Minority Discourse of a National Majority: Israeli Fiction of the Early 1960s."[8] The majority/minority pair refers in Hever's writing to the Jewish/Arab tension which, he suggests, defines much of what one might call the Israeli identity. In doing so he joins forces with the *New Historians* and the *Critical Sociologists*, whose work is found, among other places, in the periodical *Te'oria uvikoret*.[9] These scholars, however, in their sweeping effort to reinvestigate and rewrite Israeli history, couple with the repression of the Arab voice, other repressions, including those of Mizrahim (Middle Eastern and North African Jews), and women. Hever is far more reductive. Obviously deeply influenced by the publication of Anton Shammas's *Arabeskot* (1986), the first impressive book in Hebrew by an Israeli Arab, Hever reduces his focus to this one aspect of Israeli life and seeks to find manifestations of the Arab theme twenty years earlier in the literature of the sixties.[10]

Here, as elsewhere, I reject the attribution of any complex human event to any one cause or set of causes, such as the definition of self by the suppression of the other. Identities in both real life and in sophisticated literature are much too complex for this reductionism. While I agree that there are radical and new perspectives that inform the literature of the 1960s, I will offer an alternative—and, in my mind, less reductionist—rubric. Instead of limiting my focus to the Arab-Israeli tension which, I believe, is still a minor theme in the literature of the period, I will expand it to include the entire range of intergenerational conflict, between that of the founding fathers of the nation, and that of the first generation of Israeli writers. To do so I will deliberately use a different set of examples. I will use one of Hever's three examples, but will change the other two. Hever dealt with Yehoshua's "Facing the Forests" (1963), Amos Oz's "Beduins and Viper"(1964), and Amaliah Kahana-Carmon's, "Heart of Summer, Heart of Light"(1965).[11] I will examine the Yehoshua story, too, but will replace the Oz story for his longer novel, *My Michael* (1968) and begin my study with Aharon Meged's *The Living on the Dead* (1965).[12] Like Hever, I select my examples to support my thesis, but I would argue that my thesis and examples are more representative of the literature of the 1960s as experienced by the readers of that period. I believe that my selection of specimens and the attendant analytic strategy will yield a more varied and authentic picture.

We begin with Meged's *The Living On the Dead* (1965) not because it is the best novel of the period—it is far from that—but because it captures the generational transition more clearly (in fact, too clearly) than any other book of the period. Though now relegated to a deserved secondary position among the books of the sixties, it was, upon its publication, hugely successful and influential. It purports to be the story, told by a young writer, of his inability to write a contracted book about a hero of the previous generation, the typical hero of Labor Zionist fiction from the 1920s to the 1950s. In the process of telling how his life has disintegrated after he signed the contract, he actually records the story of this hero as background to his present problems. His narration is set in three different situations: his interviews with friends and relatives of the deceased hero; the court scenes; his dissolute carousing with artist friends mostly in a Tel Aviv night club. The stories he records in his notebook are typical hagiographic tales of devoted hard labor and prodigious heroism characteristic of the literature of the Third Aliyah and the school textbooks, so characteristic, in fact, that they border on parody.

We learn, of course, as the story progresses, that Davidov was far from an ideal family man: he was rarely home, often sought out other women, was excessively demanding of his son, and frequently beat his daughter. But precisely because Jonas was contracted to tell a hagiographic tale of the Zionist hero, he couldn't write it. The Oedipal relationship is obvious: the saintly reputation of the dead Davidov repressed Jonas. Jonas, on his part, portrays his own life as the antithesis of

Davidov's; a writer who could not write, he is often drunk, and after divorcing his caring wife, he pursues several different women. So while he claims he must wipe out Davidov's memory, he cannot do it, and has nothing to replace it. We must deduce that part of the failure of the founders' generation lies in their failure to rear worthy sons and daughters. The bleakness of the picture that Meged paints here has nothing to do with the Holocaust, or with the Arab problem, or with the exploitation of Oriental Jews by Ashkenazic Jews. The heroes here are not defined by these three crucial moments in Israeli history, but rather by the internal dynamic of Zionist efforts of state building and social engineering. While other motifs adhere to this matrix and complicate it, I would submit that without a clear understanding of this matrix, no reliable reading of Israeli literature is possible.

Meged's novel is particularly poignant since it was written not by a member of the generation that appeared on the scene in the 1960s, but by a veteran writer, a long-time member of a kibbutz, who earned his reputation in the early, more *heroic* years of the state. When he wrote *The Living on the Dead*, Oz and Yehoshua were already rising stars in the literary pantheon. The problematics of Meged's novel provides an interesting and illuminating backdrop for Amos Oz's first novel, *My Michael*, which appeared three years later in 1968, and may help us fill what I consider a gaping lacuna in the many interpretations of the novel I have read.

At the end of his novel, Oz is careful, incidentally, to indicate the date of completion of his novel as May, 1967, that is, before the outbreak of the Six Day War. Clearly, he does not want the reader to confuse the issues he is dealing with anything having to do with that war. The story, in fact, takes place in the 1950s and purports to be a memoir written by an unhappy woman, Hanah Gonen, in 1961 after ten years of her marriage to Dr. Michael Gonen, a geologist. Though she claims she is writing this memoir "because people I loved have died" and she wants to recapture and revitalize her power to love, one senses that revenge might also be a motive for her writing.

She traces the story of their marriage from their first encounter as students, their meetings with future in-laws, their wedding, his grinding away at his doctorate, her pregnancy—briefly, all the normal stages of a young couple in a bourgeois society, an ambiance which she, in her vague aspirations for an ideally romantic union, detests. She seeks to escape bourgeois mediocrity by fantasizing about scenes of domination and violence, and, in anger at her responsible husband, goes on wild shopping sprees. Her refusal to accept reality is often so acute and provokes such outbreaks of violence that it easily borders on psychosis. For while one can sympathize with her disdain of bourgeois acquisitiveness and careerism—which she, incidentally, also shares—one cannot condone her wild fantasies about violence and rape. In the final passage of the novel, Hannah, in her rage against her husband who seems to be having an affair with a student (an outrage she cannot tolerate since she has always considered him so dull and unimaginative) invokes in her fantasy the twin Arab brothers she had befriended in childhood, to slip across the Jerusalem border as terrorists to blow up a symbolic water tower. The description of their deed in her fantasy is conveyed in an orgy of verbal realization, and its consummation seems to bring her temporary psychic calm.

What is missing in the standard interpretation of the novel is any interrogation of the possible cause of Hannah Gonen's sense of desolation, her *shemamah*, her acute malaise fueling her wild fantasies. If this were merely a novelistic portrait of a psychotic young lady, all the detailed social scenes and references to politics—the Sinai War, for instance—would be unnecessary. If Hannah were merely an Israeli version of Emma Bovary, seeking erotic excitement as an escape from humdrum bourgeois life, we would have her involvement in routine adulterous affairs rather than her violent fantasies. The heroine's family background is not sufficiently delineated to allow us to determine a specific source of her psychosis. We know that upon her father's death in 1943 when Hannah was thirteen, the family broke up and Hannah was sent to a religious boarding school. We have little information about the crucial years between 1943 and 1950 when she turns up as a student at the Hebrew University in Jerusalem where she meets her Michael. There is no hint of anything in her childhood or adolescence that might motivate her adult behavior.

I suggest that this powerful, relentless, malaise, this sense of alienation from society and even from nature, is an expression of the collapse of the ideological certitudes of the Zionist narrative in the 1950s and 1960s. For once the state had been established and people had to turn the normal routines of making a living, buying household goods, raising families, the dreams were obsolete, even absurd. The days of the halutzim were over, but their rhetoric lingered on; the gap between language and reality was palpable, a rich subject for satire. Michael Gonen does adapt to this new, unromantic reality, because he was never a romantic figure, had never, for instance, been in the Palmah. But

Hannah Gonen was a student of literature at the Hebrew University in Jerusalem and her aspirations for fulfillment are boundless, hence unrealistic. She could never adapt to the realities of the *day after the Revolution*. As her communication with reality collapses, she turns to violence in a futile attempt to recapture a sense of existence and identity.

We turn, finally, to the Yehoshua story, "Facing the Forests" (1963), precisely because it contains the most obvious pairing of Jew and Arab and is the model for Hannan Hever's argument that the story centers on the adoption by the majority figure, the Israeli, of the discourse of the minority, the Arab. Briefly, in this story a peculiar, alienated Israeli graduate student takes a job as a forest-watcher for the Jewish National Fund, and at the end of his six month tour of duty, the forest seems to be burned down by a mute Arab, also employed by the same Jewish reforestation agency. As the forest burns down, one can detect the ruins of the Arab village that the forest, planted by the Jews, had covered. The plot, in its bare outlines, obviously criticizes the violence done to the indigenous Arab population of the country by the Zionist enterprise, which prided itself in the reforestation of the desolate land. This aspect of the story is undeniable, as is the adoption by the unnamed forest-watcher of some of the characteristics of the aged Arab; one can, therefore, understand why Hever found the schema of Deleuze and Guattari helpful.

Yet there is much more to the story than this; the Jewish Arab relationship is, at best, only one of many interlocking themes and a secondary one at that. The story centers on the nameless hero, one of the typical passive, pathetic men who populate Yehoshua's fiction in the 1960s and even later. This type of rootless hero is the inverse image of the purposive, active hero of Zionist fiction of the previous period, which had become a tiresome cliché by the early 1950s. The entire story, as Yael Zerubavel has demonstrated, is the inverse of a story, "Anshe Bereshit" (The Founders) published by Eliezer Smolly in 1933.[13] In that story, an archetypical halutz, named Hermoni, heroically tends a forest that is burned down by a malevolent Arab. Pushing Zerubavel's statement one step further, I would argue that the intertextual comparisons are so striking that one must read the Yehoshua story as a parody of the Smolly story, and, most important, the listless Yehoshua hero as a parody of the dynamic Smolly hero. Following the pattern discerned by Shaked and Gertz, among others, we note that here, too, the hero seeks to revive his sense of being and belonging by an act of violence, such as the burning of a cherished forest which he, incidentally, does not actually perform, but rather seems to tacitly inspire the Arab to do so. The act of violence, however, does not succeed in redeeming the hero from his ennui; he returns to the city as forlorn and depressed as he was before. Though the story does impart a greater sense of realism than Yehoshua's previous stories, we are, I would argue, still in the genre of magic realism; the consciousness of the narrator is often so close to that of his hero, that we often wonder if the story is actually taking place in any identifiable reality or in the mind of this very peculiar hero. Certainly, there are many scenes—the stillness of the forest, the relationship to the aged Arab and his pre-adolescent daughter, even the fire, itself,—that make more sense and are, indeed, more compelling if seen as figments of the hero's fervid imagination.

The Hebrew reader can easily recognize the place of such a character in the evolution of the Hebrew literary hero, which has been fully described by Simon Halkin in several seminal works.[14] Writers of the nineteenth century imagined an enlightened, westernized hero, a *maskil*, who would bring redemption to his benighted brethren of Eastern Europe. The *maskil* type was mostly discredited after the pogroms of 1881–1882; he was replaced in the late nineteenth and early twentieth centuries by romanticized traditional pious Jewish hero types or by the *talush*, the deracinated, alienated hero found in the works of Yosef Hayyim Brenner, Uri Nisan Gnessin, and S.Y. Agnon, later fused, perhaps, with echoes of Camus and Sartre. The *talush*, in turn, was replaced at least in the pre-state literature of Palestine, by the halutz of the Zionist narrative. Following this evolutionary pattern, we can say that with the disintegration of the Zionist narrative, we are back again to the *talush*, albeit in an Israeli guise, but still a *talush*. Yehoshua's *talush* is thus defined not so much by the other, the *minority* figure that he tries to emulate, as Hever would see it, as by the lack of any authoritative model, now that the halutz model is passé.

In rejecting Hever's majority-minority model for the broader collapse of the halutz model, understood broadly as the literary manifestation of the dissipation of the ideals of the Zionist narrative, we are not substituting one reductionism for another, but are rather offering a complex multi-faceted explanation for a wide array of transformations in what we might call the evolving Israeli identity. Certainly, the abundant evidence, marshalled by Shaked and Gertz, support our contention that we are dealing here with a gradual transformation of many aspects of Israeli life, not merely of the attitude of Israeli writers to the Arab minority. We should place these heroes in the broader context of Hebrew literature, as it has undergone significant transformations over the past century.

These transformations are manifold and involve the constant shifting of centers and peripheries, the emergence of new, hitherto repressed voices, such as that of women, Oriental Jews, and Arabs. Societies are not static, but change at times with greater velocity than at other times. The velocity of change in the first years of any state or revolution are so understandably intense that radical, wrenching displacements should be accepted as the norm, not the exception. The literary historian should comprehend these changes, however bewildering and chaotic, as the normal process of history.

NOTES

1. James Clifford, *The Predicament of Culture: Twentieth Century Ethnography, Literature, and Art* (Cambridge: Harvard University Press, 1988).

2. Yael Zerubavel, *Recovered Roots: Collective Memory and the Making of the Israeli National Tradition* (Chicago: Chicago University Press, 1995).

3. This transformation is traced in Gerson Shaked, *HaSipporet ha'ivrit: 1880–1980* (Tel Aviv: Keter,1993) Volume IV.

4. See Shaked, *HaSipporet ha'ivrit* and Nurit Gertz, *Hirbet Hiza'ah vehaboker lemohorat* (Tel Aviv: Porter Institute, 1983)

5. See Shaked, *HaSipporet ha'ivrit.*

6. Gershon Shaked, *Gal hadash basipporet ha'ivrit* (Merhavyah: Sifriat Poalim,1971).

7. See both Nurit Gertz, *Hirbet Hiza'ah* and more recently *Shevuyah bahaloma* (Tel Aviv: Am Oved, 1995).

8. Hannan Hever, "Minority Discourse of a National Majority: Israeli Fiction in the Early Sixties." *Prooftexts,* 10/1(January, 1990), 129–148.

9. The emergence of the "New Historians" and the "Critical Sociologists" in Israel over the past decade has generated a broad literature in both books and perodicals. For a tentative summary and bibliographies see: *History and Memory* 7, 1 (Spring-Summer 1995) and, more recently, *Te'oria uvikoret* (Summer 1996). For literary criticism in the light of the "New Historians," see Yitzhak Laor's *Anu kotevim otkha moledet* (Tel Aviv: HaKibbutz hame'uhad, 1995). This collection of essays has been critiqued by Gerson Shaked, "Aher-al *Anu kotevim otkha moledtet* (1995) me'et Yithak Laor" in *Alpayim* 1(1996), 1–72.

10. Hever's reliance on the theories of Gilles Deleuze and Felix Guattari as presented in their *Kafka: Towards a Minor Literature,* trans. Dana Polan (Minneapolis: University of Minnesota Press, 1986) are standard for *cultural critics,* particularly those who follow the post-colonialist theories of Edward Said. The applicability of these theories is convincing in Hever's article on Shammas's *Arabesques,* in "Hebrew in an Israeli Arab Hand: Six Miniatures on Anton Shammas's *Arabesques,*" *Cultural Critique* 7 (1987), 47–76, reprinted in *The Nature and Context of Minority Discourse,* ed. Abdul R. JanMohamed and David Lloyd (New York: Oxford University Press, 1990), 264–293. They become less convincing as he attempts to apply his ideas to the entire corpus of Israeli literature. In a subsequent article, "Lehakot be'akevo shel Achilles" in *Alpayim* 1 (June 1989), 186–193, (English version in *Tikkun* 4/5 (Sept./Oct. 1989), 30–33, Hever

considers the new openness of Israeli literature to Palestinian writers, usually translated from Arabic, as a major cultural breakthrough, an attack on the *Achilles heel* of the Zionist narrative that has dominated Israeli Hebrew literature. The theories of Deleuze and Guattari, especially "deterritorialization," work only if inverted, only if the features of the minority culture are appropriated—consciously or unconsciously—by the majority literature.

11. The first appearances of these stories are noteworthy: A.B. Yehoshua's "Mul haya'rot," *Keshet* 5 (Spring, 1963), 18–45; Amos Oz's "Navadim vatsefa," *HaArets,* Feb. 7, 1964; Amaliah Kahana-Carmon's "Lev hakayits, lev ha'or," *Molad* 23 (dated Dec. 1965; actually appeared in Sept.1966), 576–613.

12. Aharon Meged, *Ha-hay al hamet* (Tel Aviv: Am Oved, 1965); Amos Oz, *Mikhael sheli* (Tel Aviv: Am Oved, 1968).

13. Yael Zerubavael, " The Forest as National Idiom," *Israel Studies,* 1/1 (Spring, 1996), 60–99.

14. Simon Halkin, *Mavo lasipporet ha'ivrit* (reshimot lefi hartsa'ot) (Jerusalem, 1955); *Derakhim vetside derakhim besifrutenu* 1–3 (Jerusalem, 1969).

⁓ The Impact of Statehood on the Israeli Literary Imagination

The intimate relationship between modern Hebrew literature and the development of the Jewish community in Eretz Yisrael, first in the Yishuv and then in the sovereign State of Israel, is one of the fundamental, intriguing phenomena of modern Jewish history. During the pre-state period, the Hebrew literary establishment was one of the salient components of *ha-medinah baderekh*, the crystallization of interlocking institutions which grew from the First Aliya onwards and were in place and operative when the state was declared. In fact, most of the Hebrew literary establishment: writers, publishers, booksellers, had settled in mandatory Palestine by the late 1920s. To use the current discourse, we can say that the Hebrew literary establishment was a major agent in the formation of *the Zionist narrative*, i.e. the system of narratives, symbols, and attitudes which the Zionist movement generated, wittingly or unwittingly, in its attempt to mobilize the Jewish population in both the Yishuv and the Diaspora, for actions leading to the creation of a Jewish sovereign state in the ancestral homeland. In turn, the establishment of a sovereign state has generated a host of new circumstances that have contributed to the burgeoning of Hebrew literature in Israel over the past two generations.

While this story has often been told, the parallel between the growth of the state and the development of Israeli literature has distorted the historiographic perspective on the period. The model has been fundamentally biological: both the state and Israeli literature are described as twins growing up together. Recognition is accorded to the pre-state writing of such figures as S. Yizhar, Aharon Meged, and Moshe Shamir, for

instance, but little attention is devoted to the impact of the establishment of a sovereign Jewish state upon more established writers such as
S.Y. Agnon and Haim Hazaz, in prose, or Avraham Shlonsky, Natan
Alterman, and Amir Gilboa, in poetry. While it is normal to focus upon
what seems to be the new voices that gave expression to the emerging
reality of statehood, the resulting picture is incomplete.

Even when writing a literary history at a distance of a generation or
two, most critics choose to cluster the writers of a literary generation
together and then treat writers and works separately, tracing their development from period to period in their lives. This is probably the most
coherent way to present the variety and flux of artistic productivity.
Ultimately, diachronicity dominates over synchronicity, since that is how
we comprehend history. But if we want to understand the synchronic status of a literature in a specific decade, how writers and audiences of different ages interact in *real time* how political and social conditions might
have affected them as a group, we rarely find a synchronic martialing
of material.

These preliminary observations on the tension between the diachronic
and synchronic axes in the historiography of Israel literature provide a
necessary framework for the main project of this paper: a consideration
of how the prose writer, Haim Hazaz, contributed significantly to the
shaping of the Zionist narrative. While much has been written on Hazaz
and the Zionist narrative, I have not found an adequate assessment of his
central role in this crucial project. Mention is often made of his story/essay
"ha-Derashah" (The sermon) (1943), but the persistent presence of Hazaz
in the center of the literary stage as the normative, admired writer of the
Labor Party, the central political, hence cultural, force of the Yishuv and
the state in its first 25 years, has not been appreciated.[1] This failure is the
logical outcome of the normative historiographic bias that stresses the cutting edge in each generation or decade to the neglect of the total picture
of literary production in any period. Writers are situated in the period
when they first made a significant impact.

Take the most obvious example relevant to our topic: Israeli literature in its first decade. If we ask who were the leading prose writers of
the 1950s, we would probably agree upon three names: Agnon, Hazaz,
and Yizhar. When we want to study what Gershon Shaked, the leading
literary historian of the period, has to say about these writers in his
HaSipporet ha'ivrit (Hebrew fiction) (1880-1980), we will find Agnon in
Volume II, Hazaz in Volume III, and Yizhar in Volume IV.[2] This diffu-
sion is inevitable, given the need to select and organize, to lend coherent

shape to the chaos of history. The loss, nevertheless, is regrettable. Our consciousness of the loss of historical specificity becomes more acute when we peruse a study, however inchoate, like that of Reuven Kritz, who, in attempting to survey the prose productivity of the "Struggle for Independence Era," during roughly the decade before Israeli independence, in his *HaSipporet ha'ivrit shel dor hama'avak le'atsma'ut* (Hebrew fiction of the generation of the struggle for independence) (1978) we discover scores of names and hundreds of stories that are never mentioned by Shaked, certainly because the latter did not consider them of equal importance to those whom he did present.[3]

To further focus the historiographic problem that affects not only the literary historian, we shall ask a very specific question: How did the creation of a sovereign Jewish state in 1948—certainly a major event in modern Jewish history—affect the literary imaginations of such established writers as Agnon and Hazaz, Alterman and Shlonsky, writers in their prime years of creativity in 1948? By doing so, I hope to call attention to the problem described above and help rectify a distorted picture. In the process, I shall ask other fascinating questions such as: How did writers whose imaginative and metaphorical coordinates were shaped by non-state or exilic or diasporan existence adapt to the new social, psychological, and philosophical realities of political sovereignty and all that they imply? Can one detect in their work an imaginative confrontation with this new phenomenon in Jewish history? Did they assimilate these changes successfully? More generally, what happens to firmly held perspectives and ideologies when they are rendered obsolete by historical events? What happens to the Zionist narrative? It should be obvious that these literary preoccupations are by no means indifferent to the historical debate precipitated by the Israeli New Historians and Critical Sociologists over the past decade.[4] While I would agree that the decisions made by the founding fathers of the state were motivated primarily by the exigencies of the period, they were abundantly aware that they were involved in a momentous event in Jewish history and were often shaped by the same cultural experiences as the writers who interest me in this project. All Hebrew writers of the period were deeply involved in and committed to the basic principles of classical Zionism and their reaction to the realization of the Zionist dream is of cardinal importance.

I have chosen for our initial study the figure of Haim Hazaz (1898–1973), not that he is the best writer of the period, but because his literary career offers the richest opportunities for an examination of the questions that interest me. More than any respected writer of the first decade of Israeli sovereignty, Hazaz resembles most closely the profile of the leadership of the new state, mostly Russian or Polish Jews born about the turn of the century, those clustered under the rubric of the Third Aliyah which, in many ways, absorbed the more prominent leaders of the Second Aliyah like Ben Gurion and Berl Katznelson. Born in the Ukraine in 1898, reared in a pious home, Hazaz was old enough to comprehend the violent upheavals of the Great War and the October Revolution. Never distant from the sweep of armies and marauding bands during the civil war in the Ukraine, he witnessed the uprooting and brutality which have become part of the fabric of human experience. As a Jew, furthermore, he experienced at first hand the ever-accelerating disintegration of the once clearly defined forms of Eastern European Jewish society. The years between the Bolshevik Revolution and his escape in 1921 to Istanbul were the formative experiences of his creative life to which he devoted all his fiction through 1931 when he moved from Paris, where he had lived for eight years, to Palestine. He returned obsessively to themes of the Revolution even in the 1940s and the early 1950s, the first years of Israeli statehood. While brutality and force are never distant from the scene of action, Hazaz is more interested in the phenomenon of historic upheavals and their implications for both individuals and Jewry as an historic entity.

Like other writers who had experienced the Russian Revolution, Hazaz was obsessed with the dialectics of history. For him, however, the dialectics of history do not involve Hegelian or Marxist notions regarding the swings of universal history; rather, they are limited to the history of the Jews. Within this framework, he often vacillates between two radical attitudes. On the on hand, Jewish history is the history par excellence because its major theme is the striving for redemption, the transcendence of history in a messianic period free of the agonies and contingencies of history; on the other hand, Jewish history does not exist, for history implies action, extension in space, while Jews, after their loss of political sovereignty, have been passive and bereft of space. The first view derives mostly from traditional Jewish, perhaps kabbalistic sources; the second, from modern themes of nationalism. Given the pressure of political and social events in Russia from 1914 on, Hazaz had to confront these two complementary, but radically different vectors. His personal experience led him to conceive of history not as evolving processes, but as a series of radical ruptures. This tension lends intensity to his stories, to his Hebrew style in which rhythms are jagged and the individual words are frequently thrust forward in unexpected verbal, nominal, or adjectival modes, vibrating with an excitement on the verge of the apocalyptic. The kinship to the various offshoots of expressionism is clear. And while Zionism is an option of action in these "stories of the Revolution," it is by no means the dominant, driving option. Hazaz himself, apparently did not feel compelled in the 1920s to seek the Zionist solution of aliyah, of settlement in the ancestral homeland, but rather spent some eight years, from 1923–31 in Paris—writing about the postrevolutionary experiences of Russian Jews.

Highly regarded even before his settling in Jerusalem, he quickly became part of the literary establishment once he did settle there. He was embraced by leading figures in the dominant labor party, MAPAI; he published most of his stories in their newspaper, *Davar*, and his books in their publishing house, Am Oved. He garnered many honors throughout his career: the Bialik Prize twice (1942, 1971); the first Israel Prize for Literature in 1954; membership in the Hebrew Language Academy (1953); the Presidency of Agudat Hasoferim (the writer's association) (1970); several honorary doctorates, including one delivered posthumously from the Hebrew University. He was repeatedly invited to deliver what were considered significant cultural policy statements.[5] For some fifteen years, between the late 1950s and the early 1970s, he was Labor's senior cultural spokesman, constantly lecturing, eulogizing, commenting on cultural issues, responding to audiences that assembled to honor him, especially upon the publication of the second edition of his collected works in 1968. He was called upon to comment on the significance of the victory of the Six Day War and joined the Eretz Yisrael Hashelemah (the whole Land of Israel) movement together with Natan Alterman and Moshe Shamir. In many senses he was the quintessential establishment prose-writer over forty years.

And yet, so radical have tastes changed in the past two decades, that even in Shaked's history, Hazaz is accorded only 24 pages (Vol III, 1993) to 80 for Agnon (Vol.II, 1983) and he is known today by younger readers only for several anthologized stories in textbooks and mostly "HaDerashah." (Ironically, though a natural object of attack by the literary critics associated with the New Historians, he has almost been ignored by them.) Hazaz, I would argue, has lost his potential readers since the mid-1970s for the same reason that he captivated his contemporary readers during his lifetime: his fiction is always shaped by meditations on Jewish history and, after his aliyah in 1931, by meditations on Zionism. Inevitably, he intuitively envisages each situation as a point in a broad historical framework. Even when he is not writing what we might call *historical fiction* he focuses upon moments or aspects of the dynamic process of Jewish history, primarily in this century. And even when he is focusing on the past, for example when he deals with Shabbetai Zevi in his play *Bekets hayamim* (In the end of days), or in his many chapters on the life of Jesus, he tries to embody in his fiction the essence or meaning of Jewish suffering, of yearning for redemption, for the Messiah.[6] This characteristic is at once both his strongest and weakest point. When the historical resonance increases the body and depth of the realistic situation, the story vibrates with a certain excitement and scope which transcend that of ordinary realistic writing. This is fairly characteristic of Hazaz of the 1920s. But when the historical import outweighs the situation itself, realistic contours are so flattened that the result in embarrassingly (to today's reader) sermonic and tendentious. This is how Hazaz developed after his aliyah in 1931. Actually, this is precisely what his audience wanted then: a literature not only engaged with contemporary issues, but offering ideological discussion and suggesting direction.

His four "Zionist" stories: "Harat olam" (1937), "Havit akhura" (1937), "Drabkin" (1938), and "haDerashah" (1942) are a case in point. In these stories he creates characters, Moroshke in the first two, Drabkin in the third, and Yudka in the fourth, who are more expositors of various Zionist positions under discussion in those turbulent years than fictive characters. In fact, these stories are major constituents of the "Zionist narrative" and are still quoted as such. Even his "Yemenite novel," *HaYoshevet baganim* (She who sits in the garden) (1944), finds its positive solution when Rumiyeh, the lovely granddaughter of the pious hero, Mori Sa'id, settles in a kibbutz to work the soil in a paradigmatic Zionist gesture. These stories and the novel have supported the elevation of Hazaz, the writer, to an iconic status in the *Zionist narrative*, a status reinforced by the loss of his son in the battles for the defense of Jerusalem in 1948. A comparison with Agnon's literary output of the same period is illuminating for in those years Agnon published: "Sippur pashut" (A simple story) (1935), *Ore'ah nata lalun* (A guest for the night) (1938–39), many of the stories of "Sefer hama'asim" (The Book of Deeds) (1941), "Shevuat emunim" (Betrothed) (1943), and *Temol shilshom* (Only yesterday) (1945). Even the last two of these fictions can hardly be considered supportive elements of the *Zionist narrative* even though they are set in Palestine of the Second Aliyah.

It was only logical, therefore, that with the rapid loss in the 1970s of the hegemony of the Labor Party which was, for all practical purposes, the major political and cultural establishment of Israel, its icons would also topple, and among them Hayim Hazaz. Though Hazaz was honored with his second Bialik Prize in 1971 and the Presidency of the Writers Association in 1970, it is clear that by then the shift in interest had raised such writers as Amos Oz and A.B. Yehoshua to critical acclaim. They, in turn, had replaced the first generation of Israeli writers, i.e. Yizhar, A. Meged, and N. Shaham. In 1965, Aharon Meged published his *HaHay al hamet* (The living on the dead), the most open and forceful novelistic attack on the halutzic leadership of the Third Aliyah, Hazaz's contemporaries and admirers. I have suggested since the very outset of this paper that a more synchronic view of literary history presents a picture closer to the real time existence of the literature, its production and reception. By adding a few dates to those we have just given, the complexity of the picture begins to emerge.

1963: A.B. Yehoshua, "Mul haya'arot" (Facing the forests)
1965: Aharon Meged, *HaHay 'al hamet*
1966: S.Y. Agnon, Nobel Prize for Literature
1968: Amos Oz, *Mikhael sheli* (My Michael)
1968: Hayim Hazaz, *Kol Kitvei* (Second, revised edition of collected works)

This list, spanning only five years, notes significant events in the careers of three generations of Israeli writers. The interaction of these generations is illuminating: for instance, the attitude of the younger generations to their seniors may be one of emulation, of rejection, of parody.

Hazaz is thus the logical candidate for the question we have posed: How did the establishment of the state influence already established writers? When we list his works of the first decade of the state, we discover that the scholarly problems are truly formidable.

1948: "Hupah vetaba'at"
1950: *Bekets hayamim*
1952: *Ya'ish* III, IV
1955: "Nahar shotef"
1956: *Daltot nehoshet*
1958: "Ofek natuy" in *Hagorat mazalot*, 7–135

Of these six items, only the first and the last were first created in the period under discussion.

Bekets hayamim, the only play Hazaz ever wrote, was first published in serial form in late 1933–34, but was not produced on stage until 1950 when it was also published for the first time as a complete work. A historic drama set in the period of the Sabbatean messianic upheavals of the seventeenth century, it affords abundant opportunities for monologues on the agony of exile and the glory of redemption, two of the author's favorite themes. While the play certainly fits the euphoric, almost apocalyptic mood of 1950, the year of its production, it was conceived and written in the months after the accession of Hitler to power in Germany. Since the differences between the early and later versions are relatively insignificant, they certainly do not warrant our characterizing this powerful play as a work written under the influence of the establishment of the state. We have, furthermore, no way to compare the reception of the play in 1934 (only as a read document), with its reception as a stage production in 1950.

One of Hazaz's two "Yemenite novels," *Ya'ish*, has an intricate publication history. The first of its four volumes was published serially in 1940–41 under the Yemenite sounding pseudonym "Zekhariah Uzali." The novel was then published in four parts, the first in 1947 as Volume IV of Hazaz's *Ketavim* (Writings), the second in 1948 as Volume V of *Ketavim*, the third in 1952 as Volume VI of *Ketavim*, and the fourth in 1952 as Volume VIII of *Ketavim*. Clearly, this novel was long in the works, and at least half of it was published before the establishment of the State. It is a rambling Bildungsroman, tracing the spiritual and sensual development of a young Yemenite boy, Ya'ish, beginning in his home in Yemen and ending in the latter volumes, in the Land of Israel. The book parallels Hazaz's other Yemenite novel, *HaYoshevet baganim* (1944), in that it was partially composed at the same time, and follows the same broad developmental stages: the pre-modern world of religious piety suffused with fantasies of messianism; the dissipation of that world of faith and the concomitant dissolution of the hero's moral stature; a type of redemption through settlement in the Land of Israel. Since settlement in Israel is already posited as a novelistic solution in *HaYoshevet baganim* published five years before the establishment of the state, it is impossible to attribute any of the Zionist motifs of the latter two parts of Ya'ish to the impact of the new reality: Jewish political sovereignty.

During the first five years of Israeli sovereignty, Hazaz invested much of his energies in rewriting two of his stories dealing with the period after the October Revolution. "Nahar shotef" (1955) is a radical recast of his first published story, "Mizeh umizeh" (1923) while *Daltot nehoshet* (1956) is a massive expansion of "Pirkei mahapekha" (1923). Though any connection between these stories and the impact of the new political reality must be speculative because both stories are detailed efforts to recreate the realities of the immediate post-revolutionary period in the Soviet Union, two suggestions can be made. First, it is productive to develop a suggestion made by Bargad regarding why Hazaz chose, at this point in his career, to rework his early stories on the Revolution.

> It may well be that certain socio-political issues of the early fifties had influenced Hazaz in this regard. Israel itself was going through the early stages of a political revisionism; it was beginning to turn away from the Soviet Union (particularly in response the U.S.S.R.'s embracing of the Arab cause) and gradually moving towards western spheres of influence. (117)[7]

While Israel was, indeed, shifting towards a more western orientation in the early 1950s, Hazaz, it should be remembered, had fled from the Soviet Union in 1921, had lived in Paris for eight years, had never written in support of Communism, and regarded the Revolution as a catastrophe for Russian Jewry. While closely associated with the hegemonic MAPAI party of the Labor block throughout his days in Palestine, then Israel, he was more interested in Zionism than in Socialism as the redemptive solution to the Jewish problem. In the early fifties, the Labor block was embroiled in a vicious internecine battle over this issue. The catalyst was Stalin's anti-Semitism, as manifested in the "Doctors' Trial" and the murder of the last Yiddish writers in the Soviet Union. When one reads both "Nahar shotef" and *Daltot nehoshet* against this background, one sees how the political controversy of the years 1951–53 energizes many aspects of these texts. Unfortunately, Hazaz is so interested in recreating the realistic milieu of the revolutionary period that plot, character, and even ideology are obscured by the detail.

Second, Hazaz's concept of history, of narrative, was shaped by the ruptures of World War I, the October Revolution, and the turmoil following the Revolution: civil wars and pogroms. It is highly likely that in trying to comprehend the momentous changes in Jewish history wrought by the creation of a sovereign Jewish state, he found his objective correlative in the post-revolutionary milieu that he knew well and was distant enough for fictional manipulation. The daily events of the new Israel might have been too difficult for him to handle artistically.

Of the two works first created after the establishment of the state, "Hupah vetaba'at" (1948) was well received, probably because it was published only several months after the declaration of the State and the death of the author's son in battle, both in May, 1948. Because it seemed to give expression to the emotions evoked by the momentous events of those months—the struggle for the defense of the state and the arrival of many refugees from Europe bringing tangible evidence of the ravages of the Holocaust—it answered the needs of the reading audience. The story focuses upon the thoughts and actions of one desolate widow, a Mrs. Porat, who ruminates relentlessly about the death of her children in the Holocaust. The slow flow of the plot from one mournful situation to another, is barely—and somewhat ironically—relieved when we hear, outside her bedroom, the jubilant noise of the crowd celebrating the declaration of the state. Hazaz thus fuses the two epochal events together, devoting most of the attention to mourning rather than jubilation. The reader is forced to connect the two events and to dwell upon the agony and death that preceded and accompanied the public joy of the realization of the Zionist dream. The story gains a certain poignancy when seen as a personal statement of the author's continued mourning for the loss of his only son who fell in the battle for Jerusalem only twelve days before the official declaration of Israeli Statehood.

The short novel, "Ofek natuy" (Extended horizon) (1958) deserves more detailed attention, not that it is an artistic triumph—it is far from that—but in that it is the author's most transparent attempt to deal with the overwhelming historical events of the decade in novelistic form. Read today with our heightened sensitivity to the elitist prejudices of the Labor party and Haim Hazaz as an occasional spokesman for its ideology, its biases are glaring and illustrative. The shift to the first person narrative from his more customary third person distancing makes the ideological positions even more transparent than usual. Always verging on a travelogue, "Ofek natuy" is the account of the author's trip to the Lachish sector of the Israeli coastal plain to visit the new settlements comprised mostly of Oriental immigrants. The given situation is most felicitous: the sophisticated urbanite European plunges himself into the midst of a society supposedly free from Western contamination. That these Orientals are also Galut Jews, invariably so backward that they require instruction and constant surveillance by their modern, Western brethren, does not deflect Hazaz from his quest. And a quest it is. Superficially, the author is inspecting the material progress of the new settlements; actually, he is searching for a new hero-type with the virtues of the imaginary pristine Hebrew. As the story progresses, however, these virtues prove to be insufficient.

The author is engulfed by Oriental Jews from the very moment he boards the bus for Lachish. Gentle but raucous in their endless bickering, their childish naiveté literally charms the narrator. The vignettes depicting the new immigrants at work and at play are posed picturesque snapshots taken by a paternalistic tourist who is always conscious of the gulf between him and the quaint primitives. They constantly remind him of Assyrian bas-reliefs, of Sphinxes, or of primitive cave paintings. Their daily activity is the background for the experiences and reflections of the narrator and endows the novel with whatever unity it has. All the primary characters are calculated to represent various sentiments or traits that serve to form the image of the new hero. The author's first hosts are Shimon and Miriam Zayit (Olive), the administrative heads of the area. Though of both middle age and the middle class, they had abandoned the settled life of public officials in Jerusalem to guide and educate the new immigrants. Imbued with a sense of mission and haunted by the past, Shimon consistently quotes biblical verses. (The author, too, always carries his pocket Bible with him.) In their conversations, the degenerating complexity of city life is always contrasted with the salutary simplicity of life on the land; the whipping boy of their jests is the public official or orator. In educating the Orientals, they and their staff of teachers who join the conversation feel a sense of personal fulfillment; they are doing a constructive act in a disintegrating world. Premonitions of the very real danger of Levantinism, which threaten Israel, are voiced by Uri, a teacher:

> In several years the children of the Oriental groups will comprise a majority in the country. And immigration continues to come from the East. Ultimately we will turn into an Oriental nation…All the traits which have rooted themselves in us during the 2000 years of exile in Europe and by which we have become a European entity [will disappear]. The question is: Is it possible to deposit in the hands of an Oriental the destiny of the Hebrew nation, Hebrew history, and, more than this, the destiny of the country?…The East is indifferent, sunk in the routine of generations upon generations…anarchic, individualistic, fanatic, lazy….One can't rely upon education. Primal traits and tendencies always return, and return precisely at crucial, decisive moments. (p. 29)[8]

Since the harsh realism of these views is not in consonance with Hazaz's romantic vision of the Orientals, he refutes Uri's case by depicting its pleader as a student of sociology, a neurotic intellectual. One may wonder, in passing, why this exilic stereotype had not been redeemed by his contact with the soil—or, for that mater, what Hazaz's personal position really is.

The antithesis of Uri is present in Yuval, the regional supervisor who is rarely seen without his jeep. Youthful and vigorous, efficient and businesslike, his reserve bespeaks stability and, technically, allows the author to indulge in interim mystical reveries on the broad fields they are passing: reflections upon the freshness and force of raw nature, the distant Israelite past, the bond between the ancient Israelite and the modern Israeli farmer. In several remarkable passages the author describes his exhaustion after hours in the open fields at the mercy of the crushing desert sun. The terrain, itself, assumes symbolic value: the "outstretched horizon" (ofek natuy) reaches back to the past and forward to the future. The naked force of nature is identified with the natural past when the Hebrew was a farmer and closer to nature. This is a specifically Zionist category of naturalism, for coupled with the adoration of naked natural forces and a flight from civilized sophistication, we find a yearning for an imaginary preexilic Hebrew past and a possible future.

At a second encounter several months later, the taciturn Yuval is discovered to be effusive, even sentimental, concerning the education of the immigrants and the dignity of farm labor. Similar sentiments are expressed even more emphatically by the rabbi of Mesharim (rightness or directness), one of the villages of the sector: "We have at our disposal three cures which are effective for every disease and plague—and they are: Torah, loyal citizenship, and tilling the soil" (p. 88). The reader will perhaps find it a bit disingenuous that the rabbi holds a law degree from the Sorbonne and is an expert marksman with a pistol. His talk of missionary work and universal religion coupled with his earthly bearing preclude any possibility of identifying him with a rabbi of the Galut.

The narrator becomes personally involved in his narrative upon meeting Rehela, the fiery Moroccan maiden whose desert beauty enchants him. Embarrassed at his infatuation with an adolescent, yet unable to resist her charms, he lingers in the sun-baked fields to catch a glimpse of his beloved. In his mind she obviously symbolizes the legendary Hebrew beauty who seems to be at home in a primitive setting. Her name, in fact, is a derivative of Rachel—a name which her literary cousins often bear. And though she spurns him, he cannot forget her.

In his wandering through the fields, the narrator meets Binyamin Oppenheim. Binyamin's characterization is a realization of the very views he represents. Tall and handsome, Binyamin is a young American rabbi who has come to tour Israel. But he cannot simply be an American: actually, Binyamin, the last of a long line of distinguished European Jews, had survived the concentration camps and spent four years in Israel before migrating to America. He looks and acts like an Israeli. Though a product of the Galut, he has already been partly redeemed. In their conversation, Binyamin verbalizes many of the leitmotivs of Hazaz's literary creations, with the significant exception that here the Galut is evaluated more objectively.

Though it is posited that the Galut is drawing to a close because of its inability to sustain itself, Binyamin regards its passing ruefully since "it was a mighty deed, one of the greatest things that happened in the world" (p. 124). The Jewish people accepted Galut voluntarily, even proudly: the ancestral land was not of prime significance; God was the center of the universe and his adoration, the sublime purpose of all life. The Galut, therefore, was the peculiar ennobling characteristic of Jewish experience. In its transcendence of temporal interests and its devotion to God, it pointed the way to the salvation of mankind; "in it was hidden the secret of the redemption of humanity" (p. 126). But now that the Galut is drawing to a close, all that is left is a national state.

> The land of Israel is a decline, a submission, bankruptcy and despair. It is not for this that we have struggled among the nations for two thousand years from one end of the world to the other and have borne all kind of harsh and evil afflictions, and have been killed in all kinds of harsh deaths, and have suffered for the sins of all of them—so that finally we will return to the Land of Israel. Folly! Absurdity! A thing which makes no sense. This is as if…Jesus, let us say, after they lowered him from the cross and he rose from the dead, returns to Nazareth and works at his carpentry. (p. 125)

As the discussion ends, Binyamin parts with the narrator, each continuing on his own way through the fields. Had the story ended here, one might imagine that Hazaz regretted the alleged end of the Galut and feared for the future of the State of Israel. The ending of the story, though abrupt and artificial, would seem to indicate, however, that Hazaz had not changed his position. Visiting a kibbutz in the Negev a year later, the narrator meets a pregnant woman who turns out to be Rehela. She rushes into the barn to summon her husband who, of course, could be none other than Binyamin. We are lead to understand that he, too, has undergone the transition from Galut to complete redemption, particularly through his love for Rehela, the primitive Hebrew beauty. Their child will naturally be the new ideal hero.

The search for a new hero type is not a new phenomenon in modern Hebrew Literature. By the 1880s the stereotype of the enlightened Jew battling the forces of darkness was rejected and authors sought heroism in the romanticized portrayals of pious, often Hasidic types. Towards the end of the century, this type gave way to the *talush*, the uprooted, almost, *superfluous man*, common in late nineteenth century European literature.

In Hebrew literature created in Palestine of the Second Aliyah, the *talush* was often replaced by the halutz, the pioneer rebuilding the ancestral homeland. (The many deracinated heroes of Yosef Hayyim Brenner are perfect examples of *telushim* even when they seek to root themselves in the ancestral soil.)[9] The highly idealized swamp-drainer and desert-reclaimer always volunteered—as some did in real life—to undergo severe hardship and danger to realize the dream of Zionist redemption; he felt fulfillment through self-sacrifice and an unflagging devotion to this vision of personal and national salvation. But by the 1950s the halutz, too, had outlived his capacity to focus and personify the moral issues of the day. The creation of the State of Israel predicated the realization and hence, the dissipation of an inspiring dream; the formation of an organized political entity based on prescribed duties and rights robbed pioneering and volunteerism of its appeal.

Since the creation of the State, therefore, the Israeli novelist has been presented with a new cultural and artistic problem. Ordinarily, the individuality of a created character, his decisions and actions must bear some relationship to an accepted set of values and an identifiable social group, but the coordinates of Israeli society have become more and more tenuous. The identifiable outlines of the Palestinian community on the eve of statehood were blurred by the successive waves of immigrants of diverse ethnic backgrounds. The much discussed return to normalcy precipitated a moral crisis among writers not habituated to *normalcy*. To what society or set of values could a hero be related, either as a reflector or a rebel?

Although this quandary was shared by writers of fiction in many Western countries throughout the postwar world, historical circumstances particularized the experience of the Hebrew writer. The disintegration of the mold of Western society during the past two centuries was exacerbated in the instance of the Jewish community by extraordinary circumstances: violent geographical displacements, partial extermination, and the shift from a unique situation and concept of exile to landed statehood. However, the situation was temporarily assuaged by the application of interim ideologies, most of which proved fruitless. The astounding material success of political Zionism, however, both de-energized it as a moving ideology and, now that the uniqueness of the exilic situation had been eliminated, confronted the Hebrew writer in Israel more squarely with the problems that had been besetting his colleagues in other countries. He now had to face the enraging fact that the *normalcy* that he had been taught to equate with social health—even with salvation—often implies precisely the opposite in this century. Problems of the spirit are not necessarily solved by the valiant reclamation of barren wastes or even the creation of a welfare state. The Israeli writer, indeed, had to return to the universally human questions which obsessed those of his predecessors who did not succumb to the temptation to reduce all human situations to an obvious personification of the plight of Jewry in the Galut. His quest to redefine the human condition, furthermore, must necessarily be conditioned by the wealth of the historic associations that his language constantly evokes. He had to decide, for instance, whether the redemption he often writes of is that of normative Judaism or of Herzen and Bakunin.

Hazaz's shift from the third to the first person, we have noted, both uncovered and unleashed the obsession with ideology that was always present in his previous works. But this alone does not explain the grotesquerie of "Ofek natuy." The ideology of his earlier stories was less verbalized than felt, emerging, as it did, from actual situations in a definable society. But in "Ofek natuy" everything is invented, even pre-fabricated. The new hero, as yet unborn, is a product of will and not of the imagination—an artificial harlequinade of disparate elements. Born of Binyamin and Rehela, educated and trained by the likes of the Zayits, Yuval, and the rabbi, the future hero will stand entrenched in the ancestral soil of Lachish and scan "the outstretched horizon" beckoning towards the future. Bereft of truly imaginative creations, the story disintegrates into a secular morality play from which God is absent, Satan is the decadent Galut, and Everyman is the unwritten result of an ideological equation.

In December 1955, probably shortly before he began work on "Ofek natuy," Hazaz wrote one of his first major articles on the mission of Hebrew literature in the newly created sovereign state of Israel.[10] He lamented the failure of Hebrew writers to capture and express in their fictions the majesty of the momentous events of the period viewed from a broad historical perspective. After centuries of Exile, the Jewish people had returned to their ancestral homeland and created there a viable sovereign state. The description of these events are always couched in messianic rhetoric, however secularized Hazaz might have been. One of the aspects of the Jewish messianic dream has always been the ingathering of exiles, the return of Jews from all the corners of their exile to their homeland.

In "Ofek natuy," Hazaz is clearly attempting, however feebly, to realize this authorial aspiration. He yearned to write the great Israeli novel.

To fully appreciate the ambitions and failures of the novel, however, one must view it not only as a late novel in the author's career, but as an integral part of the literary effort of the decade, a proposal we have made at the beginning of this essay. At about the same time, S. Yizhar, a generation younger than Hazaz, was deep into his expansive novel on the Israeli War of Independence, *Yeme Tsiklag*, (Days of Tsiklag) (1957), certainly the most impressive novel of Israel's first decade, and A.B. Yehoshua, a generation younger than Yizhar, published his first short story, "Mot hazaken,"(The Death of the Old Man) (1957), an ironic elegy on the death of a Zionist hero. While Hazaz's "Ofek natuy" is a paean to the Zionist achievement, Yizar's novel and Yehoshua's short story both raise questions about this grand human project and suggest areas of failure or disappointment. While I do not claim that any of these writers, however talented, has succeeded in meeting the high demands that Hazaz established in his essay on the mission of Israeli literature—Yizhar and Yehoshua would question whether Israeli literature should have any such mission—I suggest that a synchronic comparison of these three more or less contemporary works would open new, extensive horizons in our understanding of the dynamics of literary change in the first decade of Israel's existence. We would also learn that many of the ideas that find articulation in the "New Historians" and "Critical Sociologists" of the 1980s and 1990s, are already evident in the fiction of the younger writers of the 1950s. The disenchantment with the myths and ideals of Zionism and declared Israeli norms was already present in the late 1950s and early 1960s in the work of such influential writers as Yehoshua and Oz in prose, and Yehuda Amichai and Natan Zach in poetry. The student of Hebrew literature often wonders why this realization has come to political scientists and sociologists so belatedly.

NOTES

1. Haym Hazaz, "The Sermon," in *Israeli Stories* (New York, 1965), pp. 65–86.
2. Gershon Shaked, *HaSipporet ha'ivrit: 1880–1980* (Tel Aviv: HaKibbutz hame'uhad-Keter) vol II–1983, vol III–1988, vol IV–1993.
3. Reuven Kritz, *HaSipporet shel dor hama'avak le'atsma'ut* (Kiryat Motzkin: Purah, 1978).
4. The emergence of the "New Historians" and the "Critical Sociologists" in Israel over the past decade has generated a broad literature in both books and periodicals. For a tentative summary and bibliographies see: *History and Memory* 7,1 (Spring-Summer 1995) and, *Te'oria uvikoret* (Summer 1996). For literary criticism in the light of the "New Historians," see Yitzhak Laor's *Anu kotevim otkha moledet* (Tel Aviv: HaKibbutz hame'uhad, 1995). This collection of essays has been critiqued by Gerson Shaked,

"Aher–al *Anu kotevim otkha moledet* me'et Yithak Laor" in *Alpayim* 12, 1996, 51–72. See also Hannah Hever, *Paytanim uviryonim* (Jerusalem: Mosad Bialik, 1994).

5. For a listing of Hazaz's articles and speeches, see Rafael Weiser, *Annotated Bibliography of the Writing of Haym Hazaz* (Jerusalem: Hebrew University Press, 1992), items 250 ff. (in Hebrew). All these items were collected by his widow, Aviva Hazaz in *Mishpat hage'ula* (Tel Aviv: Am Oved, 1977). In general, Weiser's bibliography is an indispensable source for the study of Hazaz's writings, since it organizes in coherent form one of the most chaotic publication careers imaginable. Many of Hazaz's publications were revised and republished, or were parts of novels, many unfinished and published serially. During the 1940s, Hazaz was writing some six novels simultaneously and published at least two items per month in *Davar*. For a less complete, yet eminently serviceable English bibliography, see Warren Bargad, *Ideas in Fiction: The Works of Hayim Hazaz* (Providence: Scholars Press, 1982), 133–136. For the sake of clarity in this paper, I have simplified the bibliographic complexity.

6. As indicated in Weiser, "Bekets hayamim" was first published serially in 1933 ff, but actually finished in early 1932. The full play, adapted for theatre production, was redone in 1950 and published as a separate volume that year. Many chapters of Hazaz's novel on the life of Jesus were published in the late 1940s, but were never collected.

7. Warren Bargad, *Ideas in Fiction: The Works of Hayim Hazaz* (Providence: Scholars Press, 1982). The obvious, often contradictory, ideological statements that we and Bargad find so troubling are justified by Nurit Gertz in an article dealing with Hazaz's fiction of the 1930s ("Ideology versus Literature in the Stories of Hazaz," *Prooftexts*, vol 8, no. 2, May 1988). Gertz claims that this ideological confusion is deliberate, actually the result of a "poetics of contradictions," which is the author's response to the "heavy pressure exerted upon writers to express a political ideology and be mobilized in the Zionist national struggle" (194).

8. All translations of "Ofek natuy" are mine. The Hebrew text of "Ofek natuy" used is the original edition of 1958 published in *Hagorat mazalot* (Tel Aviv: Am Oved, 1958). All future citations from this work are noted in parentheses in the body of the text.

9. See Joseph Hayyim Brenner, *Breakdown and Bereavement*, trans. Hillel Halkin (Philadelphia, 1971) and *Out of the Depths*, trans. David Patterson (Boulder, 1992).

10. "HaSifrut ha'ivrit bazeman hazeh," *HaBoker*, 12.16.55. Republished in *Davar*, 12.23.55; and in *Lamerhav*, 12.23.55; and in *Daf*, vol 11, pp. 3–5.

MODERN HEBREW
LITERATURE

✍ A Jewish Existentialist Hero: Agnon's "A Whole Loaf"

Though virtually unknown outside the Hebrew reading public before he was awarded the Nobel Prize for Literature in 1966, S. J. Agnon (1888–1970) had enjoyed almost unanimous critical acclaim in the Hebrew press since the 1920s. His many published volumes of novels, short stories, and folktales have attracted attention not only for their literary virtuosity, but also they deal with the vexatious problems of the spirit which have beset twentieth century man.[1]

Interestingly enough, only in the 1920s did critics succeed in penetrating through the ostensibly classical composure of his prose style and glimpse the murky spiritual anguish below, a veritable "dark night of the soul" that had persisted unnoticed for a quarter of a century. Beginning in the 1930s, Agnon developed a highly compressed and suggestive narrative technique, not unlike Kafka's, which was obviously designed to convey the doubt and confusion of the pious, traditional Jew who is also intellectually a citizen of Western Europe with its broad humanistic tradition. Once apprised so shockingly of the power of blackness in the nonrealistic short stories of the thirties and forties, critics returned to the earlier works and found there what they had overlooked before. It is in this sense, therefore, that these later stories, collectively entitled "Sefer hama'asim" ("The book of tales"), provide the proper introduction to the entire corpus.[2]

Fortunately, one of the major stories in this collection, "A Whole Loaf" ("Pat shelema"), has been published in English, affording the English reader an opportunity to enter the world of Agnon with the proper perspective.[3] The translator's selection of this particular story could not have been fortuitous inasmuch as it had been singled out by B. Kurzweil, one of the foremost Israeli critics, as the most characteristic in "Sefer hama'asim."[4] In our discussion of the symbolic structure of "Pat shelema" we shall refer frequently to Kurzweil's pioneering analysis both because it has set the precedent for subsequent treatments of Agnon, and we feel that it is essentially wrong.

Though Kurzweil's analysis is highly suggestive, it is far from exhaustive and therefore dangerously subjective: instead of tracing the symbolic structure rigorously he hovers impressionistically over the prime symbols and disregards the objective details, the essential questions of technique, and, not of least importance, the significance of the title. Quite often, when a critic concentrates only upon prime symbols to the neglect of their position among the many ramifications and allusions that hold the symbols in a coherent structure, he can easily force the meaning and import of these symbols quite unwittingly. Kurzweil begins and ends with a formula which seems to derive from Faust: the hero fails to recapture his lost spiritual unity because of his unbridled yearning for material things (symbolized by "the whole loaf") and his egotism. Whatever deflects him from the true path is "demonic"; to Kurzweil, in fact, one of the characters in the story is Mephistopheles.

As we shall demonstrate in our analysis, Kurzweil overlooked both the fact that the loaf was "whole" (*pat shelema* is a technical term in Hebrew),[5] and the obvious allusion offered at the beginning of the story to a Talmudic saying that equates the preparation for the Sabbath to preparation for the world to come. The problem is far more complicated than the opposition of the material to the spiritual, and the outcome is not a partial return, as Kurzweil would have us believe, but frustration. Finally, but of utmost concern, Kurzweil fails to distinguish between the author Agnon who created the story, and the story's hero, the narrating introspective "I."

Even a cursory reading of the story cannot fail to alert the reader to two features, two lines of force around which all the other particles of the story are poised: The point of view of the narrative "I"; and the specific religious atmosphere through which the action moves. Though the first is a rather common phenomenon in this century, we should never lose sight of the fact, so formative in this story, that all objects, characters, and moments are seen through the psyche of the narrator and exist only in their relation to it. The narrator is less egotistical than solipsistic, and his alienation less a willed, selfish aloofness from society (according to Kurzweil) than an ineluctable, haunting perspective on reality.

Furthermore, aside from its subjective peculiarities, the psyche operative in the story is clearly that of a pious Jew; its concern and reactions
are those of one whose frame of reference is "the religion of Moses and
Israel."

Since the reader must adopt the point of view of the pious, traditional
Jew while reading this story, the specific religious aspects of the given
situation should be elucidated. The story takes place on and after the
Sabbath. According to Jewish law and lore, the holy Sabbath is taken to
be the sign of the covenant between Israel and the Lord, a reminder of
the fundamental belief that the world was created by Him.[6] The
Sabbath, then, should be observed with joyous sanctity; a man, for
instance, should both prepare for the Sabbath and eat abundantly on it
in honor of the day.

More specifically, the following quotes from *Hayyei Adam* concerning the bread eaten on the Sabbath will be found germane to "A Whole
Loaf."

> It is the custom among all Jewry to bake breads in honor of the Sabbath.
> There are two reasons for this: in order that a woman might take a *halla*
> because on Sabbath Eve the first man, who was the *halla* of the world was
> created; in order that he (the husband) may eat the bread of a Jew.[7]

This passage assumes that the reader knows that *halla* is not merely
a white bread eaten on Sabbath and holidays, but a memory of sacred
ritual, and even in contemporary practice, the woman baking the *halla*,
sets aside and burns a piece of it. To explain the standard practice of baking bread in honor of the Sabbath, the author here suggests two reasons:
first, a commemoration of the creation of man; second, the importance
of eating bread baked by a Jew. The seemingly simple act is endowed
with broad meaning. Later in the text, we read :"A man must slice two
whole loaves at each Sabbath meal."[8]

The term *pat shelema* appears shortly afterwards and thus triggers
off a chain of interlocking association: the Sabbath meals; the sanctity of
the Sabbath; wholeness; wholeness of family; wholeness of spirit; the life
of the spirit; the life according to the law; life within the society of the
Law; personal identity. The "whole loaf," therefore, symbolizes a coherent cluster of spiritual, not material values; the narrator's unfulfilled
desire for a "whole loaf" represents modern man's yearning for spiritual
wholeness. Many of the incorrect readings of this story derive from the
failure to discern the connotation of the central symbol. Bread, to be
sure, is ordinarily a symbol of materiality; but Agnon is not speaking of

bread in general, but of *pat shelema*, a technical term with religious overtones.

Furthermore, since, as we shall see, the narrator seems to totter on the brinks of Heaven and Hell, it is pertinent to mention that in Jewish lore the righteous in Heaven are often regaled with sumptuous meals. Only when the precise usage of the term is grasped, together with its logical associations, does the story begin to unlock its meanings. The following detailed analysis will demonstrate, among other things, how scrupulously precise Agnon is in the meaning of his key symbol.

❖   ❖   ❖

> I had not tasted anything all day long. I had made no preparations on Sabbath eve, so I had nothing to eat on the Sabbath. At that time I was on my own. My wife and my children were abroad, and I had remained all by myself at home, so that the bother of attending to my food fell upon myself.[9]

It is no mere coincidence that the situation set by the first three sentences of the story is the exact opposite of the traditional Sabbath situation symbolized by the term *pat shelema*: the Sabbath is not dignified by feasting but desecrated by the involuntary fast of the narrator who simply did not prepare for the Sabbath; instead of enjoying the company of his family on the Sabbath the narrator is "on his own [alone]"; and, what is worse, his family was "abroad [outside the Holy Land]" while he obviously was in Jerusalem. The underlying tone, then, is one of alienation— alienation from the sanctity of the Sabbath, from family. The narrator is dependent for his food on outside, impersonal sources: hotels, restaurants, cafés.

The implications of the situation are magnified sevenfold when one recalls that it is actually a veiled allusion to a popular Talmudic statement: "He who has made preparations on Friday shall eat on the Sabbath,"[10] often interpreted to mean that he who makes preparations in this world can expect reward in the hereafter. This is not the story of one man's hunger and confusion in Jerusalem on a particular Sabbath, but rather the anguished meditations of a highly sophisticated, pious Jew on the state and destiny of his soul. Throughout the story, Agnon consistently externalizes and concretizes, in realistic situations, the internal throbbing of his soul.

The following paragraphs in this chapter prove the relevance of the Talmudic statement. The first, describing the oppressive heat in a vivid accumulation of nouns, verbs, and adjectives all signifying fire and intense heat, is a realistic reworking of verbal pictures of Gehenna, of Hell, often painted in Jewish ethical literature. Significantly, it is cooler at home. As the sun sets and the air cools, the narrator goes out to the street in anticipation of a fine meal. The thronged streets of Jerusalem on a late Saturday afternoon comprise a realistic picture of an idyllic situation: "They came out to glean a little of the atmosphere of Sabbath twilight which Jerusalem borrows from The Garden of Eden [Paradise]." These intentional references to Hell and Heaven serve to expand the metaphysical aspects of the situation stated in the first paragraph.

Once the stage is set, the narrator tells us: "I was borne along with them [the passers-by] till I came to my own path [to a solitary path]." Whatever the narrator must undergo, he must undergo alone, precisely because these events are really externalizations of highly personal internal conditions.

✿   ✿   ✿

The old man knocking at the window and appearing, by no means coincidentally, while the narrator is alone in the street, is also an externalization, representing his conscience as a pious Jew, a conscience which takes for its points of reference traditional Jewish Law, the Law of Moses. Baruch Kurzweil has judiciously identified the old man, Dr. Yekutiel Ne'eman with the historical figure of Moses, the lawgiver. The very name is significant: Yekutiel is a name for Moses in legends; Ne'eman means "faithful," alluding to Moses, the faithful shepherd of the people. He "is a very considerable sage and his words are pleasant." But the narrator is not worthy of hearing the "magnificent thoughts we are accustomed to hear from him." Echoing the opening sentences of alienation from the beginning of the first chapter, Dr. Ne'eman rebukes the narrator for having left his family "outside the land" (of Israel), and thereby implies that the narrator himself, and not external conditions, is responsible for his own alienation: conscience stricken, the narrator attempts vainly to save himself from the rebuke, and changes the subject to an objective discussion of Dr. Ne'eman's famous book.

Dr. Ne'eman's book is, of course, the Torah, the Five Books of Moses and all they represent. While the narrator praises the book to placate Dr. Ne'eman, we are presented with two possible attitudes toward the Pentateuch: the scholar's scientific questioning of its authorship; the moralist's approbation of its salutary effect upon human behavior. The scholars are divided in their opinion: some attribute its authorship to a Lord (. . . .) (the four dots correctly interpreted by Kurzweil to represent the ineffable tetragrammaton); others claim Ne'eman wrote it by himself but ascribed it to "a certain Lord whom no man ever saw." The moralist, however, regarding the book not as a matter of scholarship, but a way of life, rejoices that "since it first became known the world has grown slightly better." The relevance of the two attitudes grows clearer as the story progresses, but given the pervasive religious aspect of the story, the moralistic and not the scholarly attitude should be the correct one for the repentant sinner.

The narrator apparently angers Dr. Ne'eman by his empty, ingratiating praise of his book for the latter turns away without answering. The venerable doctor, however, "returned with a pocket of letters to be taken to the post office and sent by registered mail." (The term "registered mail" is conveyed by the Hebrew word *ahrayut* which also means "responsibility.") Putting the letters in his breast pocket, the narrator promises to perform his mission faithfully.

The letters and the narrator's obligation to dispatch them appear obsessively in each of the remaining chapters of the story and are always contrasted with the narrator's desire to eat, later particularized as the yearning for "the whole loaf." Though we agree that Kurzweil has correctly identified the letters as the commandments, both oral and written, by which a pious Jew must live, we dissent from his view of their function in the story and the meaning of the story as a whole. The antithesis, in our opinion, is not between spirituality and materiality, but, more precisely, between the life lived by the commandments, well-defined and binding, and the vague yearning for wholeness and sanctity, a yearning with a definable object but no definite means of realization. The point of the story is that all means, except the traditional means, are doomed to failure. But the narrative "I" is plagued by a psychological ambivalence which, in effect, is the unresolved tension between the yearning for the end without traditional means and the deeply inculcated sentiment that the means, the commandments, are an obligation which must be discharged faithfully and unquestioningly.

⚬　　⚬　　⚬

In the first three chapters we are presented with the situation that is both the backdrop and cause of the action about to take place in the seven subsequent chapters. This division between situation, setting and action corresponds to the realistic division in time. The first three chapters take place while it is still technically Sabbath; the ensuing quest for "the whole loaf" takes place after sunset when the sanctity and laws of the Sabbath have expired and man must face the workaday world.

The workaday world is ushered in by a brief episode that characterizes post-Sabbath time and adumbrates the narrator's hesitation to dispatch the letters of Dr. Ne'eman. On account of the tradition that Moses died on the expiration of the Sabbath, the congregation in the House of Study refrained from the study of the *humash* (The Five Books of Moses). It is obvious that the Sabbath and the *humash* both represent sanctity and wholeness, perhaps in different ways. Since the narrator had not prepared for the Sabbath, he could not eat on the Sabbath and had to defer his quest for food until after the Sabbath. The mournful darkness in the House of Study is an omen of things to come. The same failure of unquestioning religious purpose that prevented him from preparing for the Sabbath also motivates his constant vacillation between his obligation to Dr. Ne'eman and his yearning for food, for unmediated spiritual satisfaction. Several times in chapters four, five, and six, the narrator changes his mind, tormented by his own decision. His feverish imagination conjures up visions of the consequences of his pending decision; his taxed reason invents one rationalization after another for his mixed sentiments. Even the final decision to go to the post office is sullied by reservations and regrets: The road is rough; the postal officials will be slow; the food in the restaurants will get cold. The decision lacks the sincerity and devotion, the *kavvana*, which the performance of commandments must have.

Though he stands before the post office, the narrator cannot enter for lack of *kavvana*. The actual obstacle to or distraction from the dispatching of the letters appears in the form of Mr. Gressler, supposedly a friend of the narrator. Like Dr. Ne'eman, Mr. Gressler is an externalization of a part of the narrator's psyche. As his name (probably of Yiddish or Germanic origin) would suggest, Gressler is a figure of worldly importance as opposed to Dr. Ne'eman, whose significance transcends time and space. Kurzweil's identification of Gressler with Mephistopheles injects a foreign element into a story in which all attitudes, problems, and symbols are those of normative Judaism. Only when we consider both Dr. Ne'eman and Gressler as opposing parts of the narrator's psyche, do the details of their descriptions and their actions, both past and present, assume meaning and form a coherent pattern.

Both Gressler's entrance and exit break the realistic illusion of the story: he appears driving a two-horse carriage scattering the pedestrians before him with a malicious glee at a time when there were no longer horses in the city; his disappearance after the chariot overturns (chapter eight) is not even mentioned by the narrator. And yet, in spite of, or perhaps because of, the air of unreality which envelops him, Mr. Gressler is the most clearly defined figure in the story. Recalling the past, the narrator tells us "he was an intelligent and polite person, and although he was a fleshy fellow, his fleshiness was not noticed by reason of his intelligence [wide learning]." A man of affairs, Gressler "is gifted with exceptional wisdom, of the kind which undermines all the wisdom you may have learned elsewhere"; furthermore, he has taken the trouble to show the narrator "all kinds of pleasures." He "had something about him which attracted all who saw him," even those who were fleeing his horses' hooves; the narrator, moreover, is firmly convinced that Gressler prefers him to all other people. Worldly, fleshy, brilliant, attractive, known to the author "from the day [he] reached a maturity of knowledge," Gressler represents all the qualities that, in this story, are opposed to those ideals represented by Dr. Ne'eman.

We learn, for instance, that the first falling out between the narrator and Gressler is the result of the latter's part in the burning of the former's books, probably books of traditional law and lore. While playing cards on the floor beneath the narrator's apartment, in the home of a converted Jew (i.e. one who has abandoned the life of the Law), Gressler inspired him to set fire to his worthless ersatz merchandise in order to collect the insurance. After the fire (which corresponds to the fire of Gehinnom in the first chapter) the convert collected his insurance but the narrator not only lost everything, but was embroiled in frustrating and costly law suits in a claim against the municipality. But there is a second reason for the estrangement: since, in preparation for his journey to the Land of Israel, the narrator "was devoting [himself] to Dr. Ne'eman's book," and "was neglecting these worldly affairs...Mr. Gressler let [him] be."

Inasmuch as Gressler is actually a part of the narrator, the latter cannot escape him. Gressler turns up on the boat to Palestine, travelling first class, and even assists the narrator to clear customs. Gressler can take care of himself. In Jerusalem the friendship was rekindled "particularly in those days when my wife was away from the country." Again, the very state of alienation, which is the setting for the story as a whole, is also the state favorable for the friendship between them. And though Gressler's company was pleasant and his knowledge prestigious, almost prophetic, the narrator's conscience bothered him. The real significance of Gressler having been copiously documented, the reader need not assume demonology with Kurzweil, or homosexuality, as intimated by Y. Levinger.[11]

Returning to the time of the action of the story (chapter eight) we find the narrator entering Gressler's carriage in front of the post office. It is not insignificant that it is the narrator who signals and calls Gressler and not the opposite. In Gressler's presence *both* the hunger and the sense of obligation to post the letters recede from the narrator's consciousness. If the desire for food, later particularized as "a whole loaf," represents man's lust for material satisfaction, as Kurzweil would have us believe, this passage would be pointless. Why should Gressler, Kurzweil's Mephistopheles, distract the narrator from his quest for gratification of the sense and the ego, the very vices that this Mephistopheles is supposed to signify? The passage does assume meaning, however, when we realize that food, or "the whole loaf," symbolizes unmediated spiritual satisfaction.

The tension between the narrator and Gressler or, to verbalize it more explicitly, between the narrator's *entire* psyche and that part which is eminently at home in the world of affairs, is strained to the breaking point by the appearance of Mr. Hofni; the narrator would prefer to avoid him, but Gressler invites him to enter the carriage. Hofni (probably an allusion to one of the rapacious sons of Eli, the priest [I Samuel 3 and 4]), is a "bothersome fellow" whose pride in life is his invention of a new mouse-trap. But Hofni is more than a garrulous gadgeteer who, "when [he] goes gnawing at your brains, it's quite likely that you would prefer the mice to the conversation of the trapmaker." The translator has unfortunately mistranslated the statement "and the mouse-trap is very useful." Agnon says here that the mousetrap is a great *tikkun*, a metaphysical term suggesting the *repair* or *correction* of the imperfections of this world. Looking forward to Chapter 11, we notice the presence there of mice or rats, representing remorse or spiritual disgust. It is obvious, then, that Hofni and his mouse-traps symbolize the artificial and mechanical—futile though apparently facile—approach to correct the imperfections of this world.

In his rage, the narrator seizes the reins from Gressler and clumsily overturns the carriage in his frantic attempt to escape Hofni. As they roll in the dust the narrator screams in pain and indignation but Gressler "kept on laughing, as though he found pleasure in dusting himself with the dust of the horses legs and fluttering between life and death." As the narrator, who yearns for the whole life, realizes that Gressler delights in the presence of death, the latter disappears from the scene and the entire story. Though Gressler's exit seems to be as enigmatic as his entrance, we should recall that he enters to distract the narrator from the post office and exits when the latter is utterly disgusted with him. Both acts are quite plausible when we realize what Gressler actually represents.

Gathering his bones from the dust and cleaning himself off, the narrator remembers his hunger and enters "the first hotel that came [his] way"—clearly a rash mistake. Though at first impressed by the fact that this hotel has "fine arrangements and polite and quick service and good food and excellent wine and worthy guests," the light of the dining hall blinds him, the scent of the good food confuses him. In this palace of alien splendor it is quite unlikely that he will find satisfaction. Though he wants to snatch something to eat, the sight of the room and its grave guests inhibit him; sitting at the table and perusing the menu, he feels uneasy. The imposing air of social convention seems to doom his quest. "How many good things there are which a happy man can eat his full of, and how long it seems to take until they are brought to him!" The narrator's exclamation adumbrates the frustration of the final chapters and in a broader sense, that of the entire story.

✿　　✿　　✿

The frustration of the last three chapters, during which the narrator is never served his food, echoes his inner distraction and indecisiveness. Since he seeks spiritual satisfaction by unspecified means, or by obviating the means, he has no sure guide to his actions and desires. He fumbles and hesitates. A modern Tantalus, the food escapes his grasp precisely when it seems nearest. The unbreakable concatenation of frustrations begins most accidentally when the narrator attempts to impress the waiter by ordering a *pat shelema*, "a whole loaf." Time after time the waiter brings trays laden with food to other guests but not to the narrator who invents many excuses to explain the delay. He "began rebuking [himself] for asking for a whole loaf, when [he] would have been satisfied even with a small slice."

The feeling of remorse evokes a revealing side incident. The narrator sees a child holding a halla "of the kind that my mother, may she rest in peace, used to bake us for Purim, and which I can still taste now." Remorse kindles nostalgia for the carefree innocence of childhood, the security of family life, and the familiar, still meaningful pattern of religions observance, i. e. the cluster of associations that one might ordinarily connect with the term *pat shelema*. He "would have given the world for just a mouthful from that loaf." One mouthful or a small slice would have sufficed, he realizes all too late. In his frantic desire for the totality of experiences associated with *pat shelema*, he unwittingly forfeits his opportunity to enjoy the slightest experience.

Though he wanted to tell the waiter he would do without the whole loaf, he could not open his mouth. As the striking of the clock reminds him of the passage of time, he recalls his obligation to post Dr. Ne'eman's letters. In his panic, he jumps up, overturning a tray in the waiter's hands. From the hotelkeeper he learns that it was his own long-awaited meal that he overturned. His own anxiety and guilt regarding the letter prevent his achieving unmediated spiritual satisfaction. By the end of chapter ten his frustration is complete: not only has he overturned the tray with his meal but he realizes that "the post office doors were already closed, and even if [he] were to go there it would be no use." The closing of the doors, of gates, is a common Rabbinic metaphor suggesting the end of a period of divine grace or compassion. As in the scenes of frustration in Greek mythology, his spirit flits back and forth from the kitchen to the post office, free of the body but caged by its insatiable yearning.

If the story, up to this point, has always been on the verge of fantasy, chapter eleven introduces us into the realm of nightmare. "They did not fetch me any other meal," sighs the narrator, and as the guests rise to leave, he is left alone in the litter of "bones and leavings and empty bottles and a dirty tablecloth" still obsessively waiting for his meal. The room is darkened, except for one light burning faintly. Even the letters "had become dirty with the muck and the mire and the wine." The creaking of a key in the lock "like the sound of a nail being hammered into the flesh" informs him that he is locked in. The rustling of mice nibbling at the food (an externalization of his own remorse) terrifies him: "he'll gnaw at me." Even the cat, hailed by the narrator as "my salvation" does not frighten the mice but rather joins in the nibbling. When the last light goes out, the cat's eyes glow in the dark. At this climax of the phantasmagoria, he both falls again and hears Gressler's carriage outside. Here, for the first time, Gressler does not heed his call: the practical, worldly side of his personality cannot help him now. The narrator is now completely alone in this dark infernal setting.

Dozing off, he sleeps through the night amidst the refuse of the restaurant. In the morning he is wakened by the cleaners who are astonished to find him among the litter, perhaps a part of the litter. As they laugh, a waiter (probably the one who was to serve him the previous night) identifies him by his absurd request: "This is the one who was asking for the whole loaf," His absurdity has become his identity.

For the second time in this story the narrator picks himself up, dirty, aching, and still hungry. Leaving the hotel, he goes home to wash, his mind constantly bedeviled by his obligation to post the letters, an obligation which could not be discharged since it was already Sunday when post offices were closed "for things that the clerk did not consider important." Significantly, the story's end resonates with terms from its beginning. The narrator remarks as he sets out again on a quest for food: "I was all alone at that time. My wife and children were out of the country, and all the bother of my food fell on me alone." We, the readers, are left with an indeterminate ending: will the narrator begin again the agonized process in search of "the whole loaf" or will he simply go out to buy food while looking back upon his narrated experience.

✿   ✿   ✿

The indeterminate ending and the enigmatic characters constitute a daunting interpretive challenge. While other interpretations have been and will be presented, we would argue that the text of *A Whole Loaf* provides abundant material for the above interpretation.[12] For though the actual story-telling must be the beginning and the end of all our considerations, taken literally, the narrator's quest for a whole loaf cannot, by itself, organize the various incidents and allusions into a coherent, meaningful artistic whole. It cannot give structure to the story. The structure is rather built up painstakingly by the consistency of the referents of the surface incidents. The totality of referents lend the story its coherence and its meaning.

In this sense, then, we can speak of the symbolic structure of the story. Each incident, each character, each allusion, functions not only on the level of realistic storytelling, but refers to general concepts and transcendent values. The recurrence of key signs such as the "whole loaf" and the letters of Dr. Ne'eman, and the logic with which other elements of the story adhere to them, justifies their being called symbols. And though the use or implication of some symbols may be peculiar to Agnon, this is not a *private* symbolism. Both the key symbol and the atmosphere in which the symbols breathe are easily identified with a known culture pattern: traditional, normative Judaism. The entire story can be regarded as an extensive, complex modern *midrash* upon the implied Talmudic statement: "He who has made preparations on Friday shall eat on the Sabbath." Agnon is thereby saved from the hermeticism of many symbolist writers, and his stories of the type of "A Whole Loaf," can command and effect wider audiences.

The common comparison of Agnon to Kafka, therefore, requires careful modification. One might, for instance, see parallels between this story and Kafka's "Hunger Artist." But there are significant differences. The referents in a Kafka story belong to no specific tradition, a phenomenon which explains the proliferation of interpretations; in Kafka criticism, the line between exegesis and eisegesis is indeed tenuous. The comparison with Rabbi Nahman of Bratslav, whose tales Agnon imbibed in his youth, is more rewarding for in Agnon, as in Nahman, symbolism is not merely a private method of grasping reality; their symbols are palpably religious symbols transferred into literature.[13] In both writers, doubt propels their fictions as well as the desire for redemption, for the "whole loaf."

Looking through the symbols toward the broader implication of the story, we notice that here, too, the comparison with Kafka is misleading. Though, like Josef K., the nameless narrator of "A Whole Loaf" *is* quite alone, his loneliness is neither eternal nor complete: his family can be brought home to Jerusalem; he can post the letters for Dr. Ne'eman which, we are given to understand, would end his indecision and even allow him to eat something; and, above all, his God is not dead. Though God does not appear in the story, His presence is implied in the religious setting: the Sabbath, the "whole loaf," Dr. Ne'eman and his book, the letters. God exists but the narrator, representative man, is not properly attuned to His presence. It is precisely in this crucial aspect of the story that the dichotomy between the author, Agnon, and the narrator, is of utmost significance. The author has created a world in which God's presence is implicit and has put into this world a narrator who cannot feel this presence at all, or at least with sufficient force to motivate action, even though he obviously knows of God and His specific manifestation in Jewish tradition. And yet, we, the readers, are not sure what the narrator has learned from his experience. Herein lies the haunting power of the story.

If "A Whole Loaf" and, therefore, more than twenty other stories of Agnon are to be classed as existentialistic literature, the specificity of their existentialism must be defined. To be sure, the narrator is neither a Sisyphus doomed to eternal frustration, nor a hero for whom any *engagement* whatsoever is a commendable feat of moral courage, nor one for whom a vague form of human *tendresse* is satisfying, nor even the "man of faith" who has made his leap of commitment. The usual existential hero comes into the story without a background, personal or traditional, which could be a moving force in his life. The narrator of "A Whole Loaf," however, comes to the story with an *essence*: he is obviously a tradition-oriented Jew. The story is an account of a temporary suspension of this *essence, a* "dark night of the soul" in the life of the narrator. The sense of temporary suspension of belief is, incidentally, also typical of Bratslav theology. The phrase "I was all alone at that time," which resounds at the beginning and end of the story, indicates that the event narrated is now a matter of the past, a past, the memory of which, lives on in the subjective *presence of* the narrator. During this past period of temporary suspension, the narrator could be considered an existential hero who must make a crucial decision, an act of will that shall define him. Our narrator's act of will, however, is more a quest to regain a lost identity, an attempt at redefinition. The right way is both open and clearly delineated: by posting Dr. Ne'eman's letters, i.e. by observing the Mosaic commandments, he can regain the state of spiritual contentment symbolized by the "whole loaf."

NOTES

1. S. J. Agnon, *Kol Sipurav Shel Sh.Y. Agnon*, 7 vols. (Jerusalem 1952). To this set, Agnon added an eighth volume in 1962. After he died in 1970, his daughter, Emunah Yaron, published eight more volumes of his writings.

2. In the 1952 edition, "Sefer hama'asim" is found on 103–249 of Vol. VI entitled *Samukh Venir'eh.*

3. "A Whole Loaf" trans. I. M. Lask. *A Whole Loaf*, ed. Sholom J. Kahn, (Tel-Aviv. 1957): 316–331. The Hebrew original first appeared in *Moznayim* Vols. 28–29, 1933.

4. "Nituah hasipur 'Pat shelema,'" *Masekhet haroman* (Jerusalem, 1953), 84–89.

5. In his notes on "A Whole Loaf" appended to the anthology by the same name on 340–341, S. J. Kahn asserts: "But I feel in it, also, a somewhat pathetic desire for completeness and 'wholeness' in a drastically imperfect world." Unfortunately, his espousal of Kurzweil's reading blocks his further penetration into the story. Y. Levinger, in his article on this story (in the Festschrift *LeAgnon Shai,* 179–183) seems to be on the verge of an adequate insight into the nature of this 'wholeness' when he asserts that whatever value we attribute to 'the whole loaf' must stem from religious categories. However, Levinger fails to explain the crucial antithesis of the story between 'the whole loaf' and the letters. Furthermore, since the emphasis here is upon the narrator as an isolated individual, there seems to be no point to Levinger's remarks about society or his innuendos concerning illicit relations.

6. I take as my source of law and lore Abraham Danzig's *Hayyei Adam* of 1810 both because of its great popularity and its date which approximates the period which, to

Agnon, represents the Golden Age against which he measures the spiritual ills of modern man. The references are to the section dealing with the Laws of Sabbath, Article I, paragraphs 1 and 2.

7. Danzig, op. cit. Laws of Sabbath, Article I, paragraph 4.

8. Danzig, op. cit. Laws of Sabbath, Article VII, paragraph 2.

9. Inasmuch as we are writing a running commentary on the story, the citation of pages is unnecessary. Brackets are used to indicate a substitution of a more precise translation or the substitution of the third person for the first person of the text.

10. Babylonian Talmud, *Avoda Zara* 3a.

11. Levinger, op. cit., 182–183.

12. For a well-argued alternative interpretation see Avraham Holtz, "Mishelemut la'avoda zara: Iyyunim be 'Pat shelema' leShai Agnon," *HaSifrut* Vol. III, no. 2, (Tel-Aviv 1971), 295–311.

13. *Nahman of Bratslav: The Tales,* translation, introduction, and commentary. Arnold J. Band (New York 1978).

The Evolving Masks of S. J. Agnon

The growing interest of both the general reader and the professional literary critic in the writings of S. J. Agnon is doubtless one of the most fascinating phenomena in Hebrew literature in the twentieth century. Having first attracted considerable attention in 1908 with his story *Agunot*, Agnon has risen decade after decade in critical esteem. This phenomenon, extraordinary in literature as a whole, is all the more remarkable in Hebrew literature of this century with its violent upheavals and rapid shifts in taste. In Israel, one often finds the eight-volume set of Agnon's stories and novels in an amazingly wide range of homes, among the old and the young, the religious and the non-religious. For some readers, Agnon is the epitome of traditional Jewish folk-literature; for others, he is the most daring of modernists. For the older reader, Agnon conjures up memories of Jewish life in Eastern Europe; for the younger reader, he wrestles with the central universal problems of our agonized century. And though he appeals to such a wide range of devoted readers, Agnon is the most individualistic of writers whose indelible imprint remains upon the pages of those who try to imitate him.

Since Agnon is so protean, displaying several masks at the same time while concealing several others, it is only natural that literary critics have often fallen into the trap of homily and personal confession; each critic finds in Agnon what he was looking for. When one plows through the hundreds upon hundreds of articles written on Agnon's works, the question arises: which is the real Agnon—that of Brenner or of E. M. Lifshitz, of Sadan or Kurzweil, of Kariv or Tochner? The answer probably is: all of them, not separately but together, complementing and correcting each other. Objective control over all the conflicting views can be gained only by the application of historically oriented scholarship, tracing the growth of artistic talent, the evolution of motifs, the permutations of obsessions. Agnon at twenty-five offered an entirely different portrait of an artist than Agnon at fifty, or today at seventy-six. The ultimate portrait must be a gallery of individual portraits observed in time sequence rather than the last member of the series. It is the last member of the series of portraits that we ordinarily see: the standard collected works of Agnon used by most readers is the eight-volume 1953–1962 edition that was edited and arranged by the author himself. What we have, therefore, is an edition that is aesthetically satisfying but confusing for the critic; the stories presented were written over a period of over fifty years and were edited several times each by Agnon as his taste changed.

Any sensible treatment of Agnon's works should, therefore, be historical. And inasmuch as his writing is often so autobiographical, the dichotomy conventionally drawn between the man and the writer has to be rejected. We should remember the oft-proven guide rule that the relationship between the life and the works is never direct, and one must always lean heavily on common sense to avoid over-psychologizing. But the danger of excessive reliance upon biography is slight in comparison with the opposite danger: the complete divorcing of the works from the man who wrote them.

✿   ✿   ✿

If Buczacz, the town of Agnon's birth and childhood, has gained a widespread reputation in the last half century, it is primarily because Agnon has made it the focal point of much of his writing, at times using the exact name of the town and at times calling the town of his story Shibbush, which is but a lightly veiled disguise for Buczacz. Buczacz was hardly different from several dozen other middle-sized towns with sizable Jewish populations in Eastern Europe, and it was actually overshadowed by other towns of Eastern Galicia such as Lemberg, Brody, and Tarnopol. Treating the town of his childhood and its history with love, and with nostalgia tempered with irony (after all, he did betray his town by leaving it to go to Palestine in 1908), Agnon has succeeded in shaping a literary world with which many readers can identify since Buczacz was so similar to other towns.

Shmuel Yosef Czaczkes, later to be known as Agnon, was born and raised in a middle-class family in Buczacz during the last decades of the

Austro-Hungarian Empire, a period in which the sharp dividing lines between Hasid, Mitnaged, and Maskil had been somewhat dulled, and political movements such as Zionism, anarchism, socialism, etc., had begun to capture the imagination of the young. The Czaczkes family itself was an interesting mixture: the father, Shalom Mordechai, an ordained rabbi and learned in medieval philosophy, prayed and studied with the Tchortkov Hasidim; his maternal grandfather, Yehuda Farb, a dominant figure in Agnon's life, was an influential merchant in town and a keen Talmudist; his mother, Esther, was well-versed in German literature. Shmuel Yosef, the eldest of the five Czaczkes children, unquestionably owes the shaping of his intellectual profile to the joint influence of these three figures and their individual interests. Aside from six years in various private *hadarim* in his childhood and a short period in the Baron Hirsch school in his early teens, the young Czaczkes had no formal education to speak of but profited enormously from the tutelage of his father, his studies in the Beth Midrash of Buczacz, which had a well-stocked library, and from his private reading.

Agnon's early years varied little from those of scores of other writers and public figures whose biographies have been recorded. In his adolescence he was active among the young Zionists in town: these were the days of the early Zionist Congresses, of the Kishinev pogrom, of Herzl's death. Much of his time was taken up by early attempts at writing both in Hebrew and in Yiddish. And though there is nothing in these stories, poems, and incidental articles which adumbrates the great literary talent of later years, or which distinguishes them from other stories and poems that appeared in the same periodicals, the years of intensive practice in Buczacz provided the basis for the growth of the later years. Galicia was on the verge of a new renaissance of Hebrew literature during the first decade of the twentieth century, after over a generation of aridity, and Agnon served his early apprenticeship under several of the more energetic figures of the period: Elazar Rokeah, Gershon Bader, and Yitzhak Fernhoff. Nonetheless, had he not left Galicia for Jaffa in the heady days of the Second Aliya, it is highly doubtful whether we would have heard of him afterwards. Agnon did not produce great literary works in Buczacz, but the experiences of the period provided him with an inexhaustible source of material for his creative imagination, and the very fact that his experiences were far from atypical of his generation explains how this highly individualistic writer could appeal to so wide an audience.

✿   ✿   ✿

The emotional and literary atmosphere of Jaffa of the Second Aliya was far more challenging than Buczacz: a new society was being formed; great personalities such as Brenner, Rav Kook, Ruppin. Aharonovitz, S. Ben-Zion, A. D. Gordon either lived in Jaffa or visited it frequently. Serving as the secretary of several of the more important committees in Jaffa, Agnon was in the center of affairs. The contact with the resurgent yishuv and the trips throughout the country, to Jerusalem in particular, were invigorating, and the young writer's writing reflected the new burst of creative energy: though some of the themes first struck in Buczacz are repeated in Jaffa, the quality of writing here is so superior to that in Buczacz that it is difficult to identify Czaczkes of Buczacz with the Agnon of Jaffa (Agnon adopted his pen-name, which was later to become his legal name, from the title of "Agunot" his first story published in Jaffa). To this day, both "Agunot" and "Vehaya he'akov lemishor" of the Jaffa period stand out as two of Agnon's better stories, and the latter is certainly one of the finest literary works in Hebrew of this century.

In each of these stories we can already detect a considerable mastery of two types of narrative that recur frequently in later years: the folktale bordering on fantasy in "Agunot"; the realistic description of society charged with deft usage of symbolic detail in "Vehaya he'akov lemishor." "Agunot" is the story of chained souls, of young lovers whose love cannot be realized, of a world turned into nightmare and desolation. "Vehaya he'akov lemishor" begins with the economic failure of its hero, the childless Menashe Hayyim who descends to beggary, degradation, loss of identity; finally he suffers the loss of his wife who marries another man on the assumption that her beloved Menashe Hayyim is dead. In both cases, the traditionally Jewish milieu is the situation of a plot whose implications suggest that something is horribly out of joint in this mileu, though its various aspects are described lovingly and nostalgically. The reader who is charmed by the warm ambience of the traditional Jewish way of life, and the peculiar style that Agnon employs to convey it, might not feel the shudders of nightmare. Certainly, most of Agnon's early readers either did not feel or could not describe this shudder. But the reader who follows the plot-line to its logical conclusion cannot escape it.

The ambivalence of sentiment that we feel even in these stories, published over fifty years ago, continues throughout most of Agnon's works and is one of the identifying marks of his narrative style. There is, furthermore, one salient aspect of Agnon's narrative technique that also begins to appear as early as the Jaffa period, albeit in rudimentary form. Among the other stories written in those years, we find several highly romantic fantasies in which the young artist-lover describes his yearning for an imaginary girl Salsebila. The haunting tone of these stories, with their shifting planes of consciousness, are so unlike "Agunot" or "Vehaya he'akov lemishor" in style and tone that it is difficult to imagine that they were written by Agnon. Indeed, in later years, Agnon himself either remodelled them completely (a practice he had adopted throughout his career) or simply eliminated them from his collected works. These personal fantasies, unknown to the general reader and usually neglected by critics, are essential for forming a comprehensive image of the writer before he left Jaffa for Berlin at the end of 1912. There is hardly a motif or a narrative technique in Agnon's later works that cannot be found at least in embryonic form in the Jaffa period.

❉   ❉   ❉

When Agnon arrived in Berlin at the age of 24, he was already an experienced short-story writer with an enviable reputation: some of the major literary critics of the day hailed him as a young man of literary genius. He had not only acquired much experience in writing but had also read widely both in Hebrew literature of all periods and in German and Scandinavian literatures (in German translations). Agnon's early familiarity with Schiller, Jean Paul, and Chamisso, on the one hand, and Hamsun, Ibsen, and Bjornson, on the other hand, deserves special attention, inasmuch as many critics tend to attribute this familiarity to his twelve-year sojourn in Germany. In Germany, Agnon expanded his previous knowledge of European literature, including the major Russian and French novelists that he read in German translation. To attribute Agnon's literary technique to Jewish folk-literature alone, as many tend to do, is sheer nonsense: Agnon was well-acquainted with the best in modern European literature at a relatively early age; the writers of Jewish folk-tales rarely achieved the formal perfection which Agnon did by the end of the 1920s.

And yet, when we survey his output during the years in Germany and the five following years (1924–29) in Jerusalem, leading up to the first edition of his collected works published in Berlin in 1931, we are struck by the paradoxical fact that most of the stories of the period are folk-tales that reflect Jewish life in Galicia. Precisely when he was confronted by the sophisticated culture of Berlin and Frankfort, Agnon wrote some of his most charming tales of the lives of the pious Jews of past generations and different regions, such as "Agadat Ha-Sofer," "Maase Rabi Gadiel

Ha-Tinok," and "Maase Ha-Ez." One group of tales was collected under the rubric *Polin*, and a second group was incorporated into his major effort of this period, the two-volume novel, *Hakhnasat Kalla.*

To this day *Hakhnasat Kalla* remains the favorite novel of many of Agnon's readers of more traditional backgrounds. The delightful tales of the adventures of the lovable hero, Reb Yudel, traveling the roads of Eastern Galicia in order to collect dowry money to marry off his daughters, is unquestionably one of the major artistic achievements of modern Hebrew prose. Dozens of well-wrought episodes portraying the inner life of the pious Jews of the area, bathing them in an aura of affection, are strung together around the main character whose charming innocence is so beguiling that we accept the world he moves in as plausible even though it is now quite remote from us.

It was logical, then, that critics writing of Agnon upon the publication of the four-volume 1931 edition, stressed the fact that his greatness lay in his ability to bring the Jewish folk-tale to artistic perfection in his short stories and to epic scope in *Hakhnasat Kalla.* That these stories often contained inner tensions that undermined or negated the placid surface texture, at times leading to death or nothingness, was completely overlooked. Agnon struck a responsive chord in the hearts of many who, like him, had abandoned the small towns of Eastern Europe and their families for the cities of Europe and America or the new *yishuv* in Eretz Yisrael, but who could somehow never recapture the wholeness and coherence of the society from which they had uprooted themselves. In their alienation, however unconscious and undefined, they found solace in the innocent reaction of Reb Yudel to a way of life which they wished they could have embraced.

❖   ❖   ❖

In retrospect, the appearance of the bewildering stories of "Sefer Ha-Maasim" in the early 1930s was a natural development of Agnon's creative personality, but the reaction it then evoked was utter consternation. Here were stories apparently unlike anything Agnon or, for that matter, any other Hebrew writer had published before. Densely written, bristling with symbolic reference, they conveyed an air of anxiety of the spirit, a confession of the profound difficulties involved in the maintenance of traditional faith and the practices prescribed by Jewish law. Many of the symbols had not yet been interpreted, many of the stories were not fully understood, but the spiritual perplexity was unmistakable.

Some readers found these stories an incongruously modernistic departure for so traditional a writer, or an aping of the techniques of Kafka. As the years passed and these stories were elucidated, the Hebrew reader began to find this strain in Agnon no less natural than the folk-tales that he continued to publish at the same time. Though there is a world of difference between the atmosphere of Kafka and that of Agnon, we are struck by similarities in narrative technique: we should recall that both grew up in the last decades of the Austro-Hungarian Empire; both read extensively the German and Scandinavian writers popular at the time; both were fascinated by the tales of Rabbi Nahman of Bratslav. The relevant question is not one of influences, but rather of the artistic necessity to employ the bizarre narrative technique.

We can only speculate on the writer's motivation that prompted the injection of this new element: perhaps it was the evacuation of his home in Talpiot during the Arab riots of 1929; perhaps it was the confrontation with Buczacz the following winter during a brief tour of Galicia, a confrontation that was patently painful since the Buczacz of his dreams, of Reb Yudel, could not possibly withstand the brutal comparison with the Buczacz of reality, a community clearly in ruins. Of greater significance, however, is the fact that the very existence of the stories of "Sefer Ha-Maasim" forces us to reconsider Agnon's previous works, which seemed so tranquil, and we then discover that the nostalgia of the *Polin* cycle or of *Hakhnasat Kalla* is the counterpart of the nightmare of "Sefer Ha-Maasim" and the stories of that type. Inasmuch as Agnon has continued to write in both modes for the last thirty years, it is inconceivable that there is no internal relationship between them. Many of Agnon's most avid readers delight in only one of these two basic modes: Agnon himself delights in both.

In addition to the nostalgia of the folk-stories and the nightmare of "Sefer Ha-Maasim," a third significant mode emerges with great frequency in the 1930s—as early as "Vehaya he'akov lemishor," in 1912, Agnon displayed an amazing ability to handle realistic situations, rendering both the sensual surface and the psychological undertones with telling accuracy. This ability develops slowly in the early 20s in such stories as "Bidmi Yameha", the second version of "Givat Ha-Hol", or the satire "Bine'arenu Uvizkenenu." Agnon, we should remember, read Hamsun and Bjornson at an early age, and could also draw upon his predecessors in Hebrew and Yiddish, the two languages he knew most intimately: Mendele, Peretz, Sholom Aleichem, and Berdichevsky. Agnon suffered no lack of models of excellent realistic writing. It is little wonder, then, that in the middle thirties, along with the folk-tales and "Sefer Ha-Maasim," we find *Sippur Pashut,* his most sustained attempt at that time at purely realistic composition.

Obviously, in the great tradition of the European novel of the nineteenth and early twentieth centuries, *Sippur Pashut is* the portrayal of a segment of middle-class Jewish society in a small Eastern European town, here Shibbush again. The situation is the essence of simplicity: Hershel, the son of middle-class shopkeepers, loves Bluma, a girl of lower social status than he, but is forced by his domineering mother to marry Mina whom he does not love; unable to bear the strain, Hershel goes mad, but is finally cured and returns to Mina whom he learns to love. Around this conventional situation Agnon drew a picture of Shibbush, not of the pious and the saintly but of the practical shopkeepers, salesmen, and their mundane affairs. In that world there is little room for sanctity or romantic love. The tone of the novel is all the more remarkable when we compare it with "Agunot," *Polin,* or *Hakhnasat Kalla.*

❖   ❖   ❖

The young writer who had just come to Berlin from Jaffa and was about to reach his twenty-fifth birthday in 1913 had already attracted considerable critical attention, particularly with his two stories "Agunot" and "Vehaya he'akov lemishor." Twenty-five years later in 1938, the Hebrew literary world celebrated his fiftieth birthday with great fanfare, in the realization that here was one of the major figures of modern Hebrew literature. And yet, the years proved that much of his greatest writing was still ahead of him. The very same year Agnon published both his *Yamim Noraim,* an anthology of source material relating to the High Holydays, and the newspaper installments of his novel, *Oreah Nata Lalun* (A Guest for the Night), which appeared daily throughout the winter of 1938–39. Indeed, when one peruses the chronological bibliography of Agnon's publications, one is struck by the fact that considerably more than half of his works were written after the age of fifty. And at the same time Agnon was constantly revising and reworking previously published stories.

In many aspects, *Oreah Nata Lalun* is the central literary creation in Agnon's career: it contains all the major themes and techniques of his other stories; it is the link between his previous and subsequent works. The hero of the novel is a narrative "I" who returns to his home town,

Shibbush, after an absence of many years and finds it in physical and moral ruin. The confrontation is crushing, since the real decay of the town, so pervasive and unavoidable, is accentuated by contrast with the childhood image the grown man had held of the town in his imagination. The hero makes an attempt to revive the spiritual life of his town, but it is all in vain; one man cannot stem the relentless flow of history. Technically, the novel is a series of confrontations with the various characters still left in town; through these confrontations we begin to see a complex, horrifying canvas conveying the tragic fate of a generation. The hero can maintain his identity and integrity in these surroundings only because he realizes that at the end of his sojourn he will join his wife and children in their return to Eretz Yisrael where there is a future. In Shibbush there is only a past and a grotesque present. Some of the glory of the past can be recalled in folk-tales told by the aged in wistful nostalgia; but the present is to be treated either in grim realism or in nightmarish sequences reminiscent of "Sefer Ha-Maasim." As we follow the hero in his walks through the desolate streets of his childhood, we share in his sorrow, which generates the peculiar but mercilessly authentic blend of nostalgia and nightmare. These are probably the two dominant emotions of Jewish experience in the twentieth century, and Agnon has captured them poignantly in his novel.

There is very little in the thousands of pages Agnon has written since *Oreah Nata Lalun* that cannot be directly related to this novel of his fiftieth year, either thematically or stylistically. Though the narrative "I" cannot be directly related to Agnon himself, it is undeniable that he draws upon his personal experience for the material of his writing; the personal experience is viewed from a distance and molded by aesthetic needs. The hero sees himself as representative, yet somewhat beyond the characters he portrays; they, in turn, are the feeble descendants of a stronger and nobler generation when Torah and sanctity were revered, and society had a coherent form. The world today is peopled by cripples and empty shells who can sense no divine order in the cosmos. Beyond the area of desolation there still gleams the ideal of renewed life in Eretz Yisrael, an ideal which combines both the aspirations of modern Zionism and an almost mystic vision of Jerusalem which somehow reflects, however palely, the Jerusalem of pious yearning. The hero experiencing all this is fundamentally a man alone, alienated from meaningful social relations, even from his family. He is not challenged by momentous moral decisions but rather seems to float along, bewildered in a stream which he does not control.

The notion of man's inability to control his own destiny is also felt throughout the novel *Temol Shilshom* (Only yesterday) in which the hero, Yitzhak Kummer, unlike the narrative "I" of *Oreah Nata Lalun*, is incapable of comprehending the world around him. Significantly, the novel takes place in Jaffa and Jerusalem of the Second Aliya, since these cities in that period are second only to Buczacz as focal points of Agnon's creative imagination. (It is interesting that Germany, where Agnon spent almost twelve years, appears several times as the locale of a story, but it never looms in his imagination as a coherent unit which he might portray epically.) As a literary subject, Buczacz presented two possible approaches: the sphere of love, on the one hand, which Agnon described tenderly in his folk-tales and clearly employed as a base or criterion of moral values against which he could measure the decline of society; his own personal experience, on the other hand, which, with the exception of childhood family memories, were not identified in his psyche with his intuitive notions of meaningful living. Agnon's attitude toward Buczacz, therefore, has always been singularly ambivalent. His attitude toward Jaffa and Jerusalem of the Second Aliya, however, is infinitely more complicated. While it was the period of youth, of young love, of warm, care-free nights by the sea at Jaffa, it was also the period of ideological challenge that is ultimately charged by sentiments concerning the town of his childhood and his family there, both of which he abandoned when he left for Palestine.

The story of the clumsy experiences and the tragic end of Yitzhak Kummer is fabricated out of the personal experiences of thirty-five years earlier, and though it is idle to consider the novel as autobiography, it is, nonetheless, impossible to comprehend the total meaning of the book or its artistic coherence, in spite of the variety of styles, unless we realize that the writer is taking stock of his past and, through it, of the world whose streets he walked. So obsessive were the memory of this period and its evaluation that Agnon wrote an entire novella, *Shevuat Emunim*, and several other stories describing various facets of the period. The novel *Temol Shilshom*, then, is not so much a realistic epic of the Second Aliya as a highly personal projection of conscience through memory. The hero, Yitzhak Kummer, is presented as a fairly typical *halutz* of the Second Aliya, and his experiences are treated as normative for the group he represents. We should, however, be mindful of the fact that this novel is utterly unlike any other novel dealing with the period. Yitzhak does not fulfill his ideal to settle on the soil, but becomes a house-painter in Jaffa and Jerusalem. In neither of these two cities (the former embodying the values of the new *yishuv;* the latter, of the old) does Yitzhak seem comfortable. And when he does make a final decision in favor of Jerusalem and all it implies, while marrying Shifrah, the daughter of the fanatically religious Reb Payish, he is bitten by a rabid dog and dies a dog's death.

Both *Oreah Nata Lalun* and *Temol Shilshom* were molded from fragments of memories; both are testaments of disintegrated values and broken dreams. In the former, the tone is uniform, and if the society described is a living graveyard, there is at least hope for revival elsewhere, in Eretz Yisrael; in the latter, however, the style varies from satire of the legendary heroes of the Second Aliya, to realistic narrative, to expressionistic description of the flight of the dog Balak, and all add up to a nihilistic rejection of the values of the new *yishuv* and the fanaticism of the old. *Oreah Nata Lalun* captured the pessimism and sense of impending doom which were the inescapable, radical sentiment of Jewish communal life on the eve of the Second World War; *Temol Shilshom* was a more daring, individualistic expression of deep-seated doubts about some of the sanctified ideals of Jewish life and, with it, a savage condemnation of a generation "whose face was the face of a dog." Though set in the early part of the century, *Temol Shilshom* was composed during World War II, a fact not without meaning in the case of a Hebrew writer whose sense of history is so keen. Both chronologically and thematically these novels are correlatives of the nightmarish stories of "Sefer Ha-Maasim."

❊   ❊   ❊

Unlike most writers who seem to lose their public after they reach fifty, Agnon's popularity has increased enormously since then. This is partly due to the improvement in the considerable body of literary criticism written on Agnon's works, particularly noticeable in the articles of Kurzweil, Sadan, and Tochner. Of greater importance, however, is the often overlooked fact that the reader of the 1950s had at his disposal a much more impressive corpus of writings than the reader of the 1930s. The Agnon we envisage in the light of the 1953 edition is a much greater writer than the one we envisage in the light of the 1931 edition. Between them loom such memorable works as we have discussed above, and many of his best short stories. And inasmuch as Agnon's writings include such a wide variety of milieus and narrative techniques, any conscientious reader of good literature can find among the seven volumes many pieces to his taste. The 1950s, furthermore, were marked by a de-emphasis in criticism of the ideological aspects of Hebrew literature and a concomitant interest in the problems of aesthetic form and the existential facts facing the individual as individual. It was Agnon in particular, of all Hebrew prose writers, who seemed able to fulfill these two needs: the aesthetic and the psychological.

No Hebrew prose writer of the modern period has been as scrupulously dedicated to the perfection of expressive form as Agnon. More than anyone else he has worked assiduously at his craft, developing style, narrative technique, and final mastery over his material. Though a born story-teller, Agnon has always spent much effort to find the right word, the proper phrase, the telling cadence. No manuscript is submitted for publication without much reworking and even those stories that have been published are revised for subsequent editions. As a result, there is always a finished, well-polished feeling about all Agnon's stories, a quality that some critics feel is somewhat overdone: at times, stories seem over-structured. The example of conscientious craftsmanship, however, is one that can only have a salubrious effect on younger writers.

Tutored by the articles of Baruch Kurzweil, the Hebrew reader has learned to realize that Agnon, in many of his works, probes the problems of the spirit that seem to be shared by many people in the twentieth century. And though Agnon's milieu is almost always specifically Jewish, the problems he deals with can be related to the preoccupations of serious writers in Europe and America. We find the disintegration of conventional social patterns and with it the loss of orientation in a world of bestiality. Under the seemingly placid surface of Agnon's prose style, there clearly boil whirlpools of spiritual torment. The tension between the surface calm and the stormy deep energizes many ostensibly simple stories and illuminates even homely detail with symbolic significance. Like much of Bialik's poetry, Agnon's stories are a radical expression of the loss of innocence of the modern Jew, however orthodox and observant he may be. Reb Yudel of *Hakhnasat Kalla* is a figure to be admired, but he exists no more, and his descendants are the bewildered, often nameless heroes of a certain strain in Agnon's later prose. The spiritual confusion seems to have found its natural expression in the enigmatic atmosphere of such stories as "Ido Ve'Einam" or "Ad Olam," two of the most discussed stories of the fifties and sixties. It is no wonder that we find unmistakable traces of Agnon's style in the later stories of Aharon Meged, in Amichai's prose, and, more recently, in Yoram Kaniuk and Avraham B. Yehoshua; for the mode of consciousness which they try to capture, the logical precedent in Hebrew is Agnon.

Agnon, then, has enjoyed what few writers ever enjoy in their lifetime—continued admiration by intelligent readers over a span of two generations. Many of his works have already been adopted as school texts, as classics of modern Hebrew literature. And yet, Agnon's writings are still in the stage of a work in progress. The *Complete Stories*, recently expanded to eight volumes, does not include many of the hundreds of pages published since the 1953 edition found in thousands of homes. The longer of the uncollected works have not been published in their entirety. We anxiously await the publication of the last half or two-thirds of *Shira*, the intriguing novel of the foibles and follies of academic life in Jerusalem. Of a two or three volume work on the history of Buczacz told anecdotally, only fragments have been published in the weekly literary supplements. The two anthologies, *Atem Re'item* dealing with Shavuot, and *Sefer, Sofer, veSippur* containing stories about books and their writers, are each less than one-quarter published. Add to these, dozens of items which do not fit into any of these larger rubrics, and it becomes quite clear that at the age of seventy-six, the major Hebrew prose writer of our times still has many surprises and delights in store for us.

POSTSCRIPT: FORTY YEARS LATER

This article was written during the preparation of my lengthy study of Agnon's fiction, *Nostalgia and Nightmare* (Berkeley and Los Angeles, 1968). Both the article and the book presented for the first time a historical analysis of Agnon's fiction. This study, though never translated into Hebrew, is still widely used in both Israel and elsewhere. It has not yet been supplanted. Dan Laor's *Hayye Agnon* (Tel Aviv, 1998), a biography but not a literary study, builds on the first chapter of my book, but adds much rich archival material.

➤ The Author, His Code, and His Reader: The Kafka-Agnon Polarities

"I tell you, 'Rabbi Binyomin,' that Mendele's style is not the last word in Hebrew fiction."

In a retrospective article written in 1933, the addressee of this statement, "Rabbi Binyomin"[1] recalls his meetings with Agnon in Jaffa in 1908–11, when both were young, aspiring writers. In one memorable scene, the two were walking along the Mediterranean shore when Agnon protested that Mendele's style, for all its monumental stature, did not lend itself to the description of nuanced psychological states and, as such, was not "the last word in Hebrew fiction."[2] The implication, of course, was that he (Agnon) would do better. The author, recording this event after Agnon had published the four volumes of the first edition of his collected works in 1931, implies that Agnon had indeed succeeded in forging a new prose idiom in Hebrew, something that transcended Mendele, even though in 1908 when Agnon expressed these aspirations, "Rabbi Binyomin" thought his claims presumptuous.

While the sequence of events in this reminiscence might not be entirely accurate, the statements and descriptions of personalities and sentiments have a ring of authenticity and coherence. Mendele, after all, was the giant of modern Hebrew prose fiction in those days and every young writer had to confront this looming figure. Some aped him, but others like Brenner, Agnon, Gnessin, and Shofman found their own individual style and voice. "Rabbi Binyomin's" analysis of the situation is, in general, precise; Agnon's prodigious energies, his dandyish playfulness, his friendship with Brenner, the favorable reception of two of his Jaffa stories, "Agunot"(1908) and "Vehaya he'akov lemishor" (1911) are all attested to in many other sources of the period. What "Rabbi Binyomin" seems to fail to comprehend, however, is the complex seriousness of the young writer's aspirations.

When Agnon protested against Mendele, he was not merely seeking a more adequate linguistic medium to express psychological realism. Mendele's Hebrew style was the quintessence of the Europeanization of Hebrew prose. Despite Mendele's richly textured Jewish ambiance and his dazzling mastery of Hebrew sources, his syntax and modes of narration are those one would recognize in the great nineteenth century European authors. As a dedicated proponent of *Haskalah*, his use of this Europeanized style was, in itself, an ideological statement. In rebelling against Mendele, Agnon was not only exploring new modes of expression; he was making a statement about Jewish history.

We should not forget where and when he said what he said and wrote what he wrote. This was Jaffa of the Second Aliyah, the concrete embodiment of secular Zionist aspirations, young pioneers returning to the ancestral homeland to rebuild it from its desolation. Agnon was an anomaly in Jaffa. He was not a pioneer; he never worked on the soil; he came from the Galician province of the Austo-Hungarian Empire, not from Russia, the homeland of most pioneers in Jaffa. To fix Agnon's ideological position among his contemporaries of the Second Aliyah, it is interesting to compare him to the two other figures prominent in "Rabbi Binyomin's" essay: "Rabbi Binyomin" himself and the writer, Yosef Hayyim Brenner. "Rabbi Binyomin," also a Galician, had no doubts about the viability of the Zionist enterprise and was busily engaged in a variety of colonizing activities. Brenner, on the other hand, was the paragon doubter, but nonetheless chose to immerse himself in a host of political and literary activities, in addition to writing his own fiction. Agnon's stance was marginal, fraught with ambiguities, and led to no easily definable commitment. His choice of both style and theme in this period was crucial for the development of his career and reveals much about his attitude towards Jewish history. What interests me, therefore, in this paper, is the ideological implications of the choice of style.

The question of style emerges not only when we study a text, but even when we address any of the large questions seriously. When asked to identify what is Agnon's forte as a writer of fiction, we are usually hard pressed. No careful reader would claim that Agnon's plots are particularly inventive, or that his characters are well-drawn and memorable.

And while his psychological remarks are often insightful and his land-scapes evocative, these narrative features would never suffice to justify the unflagging critical attention he has enjoyed. Agnon's oblique but demonstrably pervasive preoccupation with some of the more profound issues of modern Jewish life or his deft weaving of a texture of polyse-mous motifs generate a textual density that sustains repeated close read-ing. The latter, in turn, alerts the reader to what is specifically, unmistakably Agnonic: the playful dialogue the author conducts with his implicit reader through a carefully modulated narrative voice that speaks in an ingenious style, which sounds like speech, but is unlike any other discourse in modern Hebrew fiction.

Agnon's style has, to be sure, inspired numerous studies, mostly trac-ing his sources in Biblical or post-Biblical literature. Frequently, this style is characterized as *midrashic*, a term so vague and varied in common parlance as to be useless. One can, of course, identify the unmistakable Agnonic style as being derived from late-rabbinic models, that is, texts of the past three centuries deriving from rabbinic or Hasidic mileu in Eastern Europe, where the authors spoke Yiddish that left its imprint on their Hebrew diction and syntax. Rather than trace sources, I would ask: Why did Agnon choose to adopt and cultivate this peculiar style which must convey to the sensitive Hebrew reader the connotations of the world of pious East European Jews? This question is, unfortunately, rarely raised today, for not only is Agnon's style routinely recognized as that of pious writers, but many readers learn the stylistic norms of East European Jewry primarily through Agnon's writing. This style, however, was not the only one available to Agnon when he first adopted it in 1911, after several years of experimentation with other styles, but actually rep-resents a radical departure from the developing norms of Hebrew style at that time. When we remember that such powerful models as Mendele, Brenner, Bialik, or Berdyczewski were still alive and publish-ing, and that the use of Hebrew, or even a particular type of Hebrew, was an ideological statement, Agnon's choice begins to assume its proper historical dimensions.

Both individual Agnonic texts and the totality of his fictional works (and, all the more so, his anthologies of traditional materials having to do with such matters as The Days of Awe, or the Revelation at Sinai, or Hasidic Tales) are evidence of his *negotiations* with Jewish history. *Negotiation* and *appropriation* are two of the more colorful terms that have insinuated themselves into our critical vocabulary in the past decade and merit usage only upon examination and qualification. Usually they are employed when one wants to describe an author's use of material taken from earlier authors. By talking of *negotiation* or *appropriation* we both restore the author and treat him as an active agent rather than a passive receptor of *influences*. Despite their often mindless fadishness, these terms represent a conceptual gain. This gain, however, might be offset by the potential metaphorical obfuscation: because they derive from the world of property acquisition or capital exchange, they evoke overtones of their origins. I prefer *negotiation* to *appropriation* since the latter implies an act of domination, even violence in which the object appropriated, here the text, is inert and cannot possibly resist or shape the act of appropriation. *Negotiation*, on the other hand, assumes that there is an active, on-going process in which the other side is active. It forces us to remember what we often forget—that all texts have to be activated by a reader. The process of negotiation, then, is dynamic and complex. The author—Agnon, for instance—*negotiates* with a text that he has already activated by his reading. What makes the Agnonic text so intriguing is that a careful reading brings you to the conclusion that the author is supremely conscious of his negotiations with the text and, inasmuch as these are historical Jewish texts, the concrete manifestations of what we ordinarily call Jewish history; he is negotiating with Jewish history.

For the reader, then, reading an Agnonic text is also a "negotiation with Jewish history," and should be perceived as such. And since Agnon is so patently conscious of the historical contexts of his linguistic sources and fictive situations, we should also strive to acquire some expertise in these historical contexts. An awareness of this interpretive requirement should free us of some of the subjectivism that is an inevitable component of the interpretive act. In dealing with the text of an author so linguistically manipulative as Agnon, such awareness and added historical controls are not only advisable—they are imperative. Aside from the author's well-known habit of revising his texts for successive publications, we are forced to read his fictions through the voice of one of the most conflicted yet controlled narrative voices any modern writer has created. We should realize that almost every story has more than one published version, that the narrator's perspective—and personality—might change from work to work, from version to version of the same work, and even from phrase to phrase in the same sentence.

In suggesting that Agnon "negotiates with Jewish history," we do not imply that Agnon tries to render faithful representations of specific moments in Jewish history. The contrary is true; he was too shrewd a writer to succumb to that temptation. His writing career, we should remember, embraced one of the most turbulent centuries in Jewish history. To have lived through that period in some of the most important centers of Jewish historical experience: Galicia, Jerusalem, Germany, and to survive it as a writer in control of his materials is, in itself, a tour de force of the human imagination. I would argue that Agnon succeeded in doing so precisely because he fashioned a mode of narrative discourse that was not based on the norms of Hebrew discourse that we usually associate with the regeneration of modern Hebrew literature. These norms, to be sure, could not be fashioned after Hebrew speech norms at the beginning of this century, because few people spoke Hebrew then, even in *Eretz Yisrael* of the Second Aliyah. Since, however, Hebrew was in an advanced stage of *revival* and had already established a viable modern literary tradition by 1905, there were what one might call evolving *quasi-speech* norms, and the major Hebrew prose-writers strived to shape and/or approach those norms. In general, Hebrew writers from the last decade of the nineteenth century on linked Hebrew with the national revival movement and, specifically, the creation of a Hebrew community in Palestine. Agnon, on the contrary, persisted in refining his highly literary style which enabled him to keep his distance from the worlds of experience that he wished to describe, to recast in his own distinctive language. Until we realize that this manneristic style is both a resistance to the hegemony of a ruling culture and a device for containing the centrifugal, contradictory sentiments of the modernist sensibility, we will not fashion an adequate interpretive control.

In order to assess the import of Agnon's negotiation with Jewish history, I shall examine one of the stereotypes of Agnon research, the comparison drawn between his writings and those of Kafka. Since I have dealt with aspects of this comparison elsewhere and for different purposes, I shall refer to my previous research on this topic to illustrate my argument.[3]

Agnon's name was first connected with Kafka in the early 1930s. In 1931, Agnon published the first four volumes of the *Berlin Edition* of his collected works and thereby solidified his reputation as a modern version of the traditional teller of Jewish pious tales. In late 1932, he startled his readers by publishing a new cluster of five stories, titled enigmatically *Sefer ha-ma'asim* (The book of deeds). Most readers found them impenetrable since they suspended the realistic canons of time, space, and causality in ways that went far beyond even his most fantastic quasi-Hasidic tales. Several critics who knew both German literature well and the extent of Agnon's library suggested that he had been reading

Kafka. Though my recent studies have convinced me that the picture was much more complex, that the text behind *Sefer ha-ma'asim* is probably Freud's *Traumdeutung* (Interpretation of Dreams) rather than Kafka's stories, the Kafka suggestion was plausible.[4]

Kafka was, of course, not a well-known writer in the early 1930s, certainly not the oft-cited prooftext he is today, but the attribution was logical, given the literary situation in Jerusalem and Tel Aviv. By the late 1920s and early 1930s there had formed in those two cities a colony of sophisticated German-reading emigrés, many from Berlin and Prague, some of them Kafka's close associates. Hugo Bergmann, for instance, came in 1920 and was prominent in cultural circles; Leo Hermann, the editor of *Selbstwehr*, the Zionist newspaper published in Prague and which Kafka read faithfully, migrated in 1926. Among the refugees who came after the *Anschluss* and *Kristallnacht*, were Max Brod, Kafka's friend and literary executor (1939), and the two Weltsches, Felix and Robert (1940). Together with such luminaries as Gershon Scholem who came in 1923 and Martin Buber, who came in 1933—and, to be sure, many other less known intellectuals—they formed one of the first centers of Kafkaists. Their personal libraries contained at least the three novels, published in the late 1920s, some of the short stories, and, if they left after the *Anschluss* or *Kristallnacht*, the first edition of *Gesammelte Werke*, 1936–37. To be sure, those libraries contained many other treasures, such as the *Gesammelte Werke* of Sigmund Freud.

Agnon, though an *Ostjude*, was part of these circles since he had spent 11 years from 1913 to 1924 in Germany, was an Austrian citizen because he came from Galicia, and had shrewdly capitalized on the romanticization of the *Ostjude* which began to surface in Germany in the first decade of this century. While Agnon protested that he had never read Kafka except for "Der Verwandlung" (Metamorphosis), and that his wife read these works, he probably knew more than a little of Kafka and Freud since his wife would read to him from these two writers in the 1930s.

When one observes both Agnon and Kafka from the perspective of general history, the comparison is far from gratuitous: both were born in the 1880s (Kafka in 1883; Agnon in 1888) and reared in the homes of relatively successful businessmen, both in marketing, in the last decades of the Habsburg Empire. While Kafka's Prague was far more westernized than Agnon's Buczacz, connections of the latter with Lemberg and Vienna were well established; the latest newspapers were available and political life was intense. If one were to compare the news of the Jewish world published in *Selbstwehr*, the Zionist weekly whose centrality in Kafka's life has been well established by Hartmut Binder, with the Hebrew and Yiddish newspapers which Agnon was reading (and in which he published) one finds a remarkable commonality of content and concern: reports of Zionist activities, the settlement of Palestine, anti-Semitism as in reports of pogroms in Russia, blood libels throughout all of Eastern Europe, and, between 1911–13, the Beilis Trial which reopened the festering wounds of the Dreyfus Affair. The improved communications available with the building of the railroads and the telegraph contributed mightily to the formation of an international sense of Jewish solidarity: the Kishinev pogrom (1903) or the death of Herzl (1904), for instance, were widely covered and the news was immediately available in Jewish homes everywhere.

During Agnon's stay in Germany between 1913 and 1924, mostly in Berlin, but also in Leipzig, Munich, Frankfort, and Bad-Homburg, the intellectual circles of our two writers actually intersected in some places. Agnon probably read "Der Verwandlung" (Metamorphosis) during this period and it is inconceivable that Kafka did not come across the name of Agnon since the latter was very popular in the circles of German Jews who were Zionists and disposed to harbor a strange nostalgia for anything that smacked of *Ostjudentum*, as manifested in Buber's *Der Jude*, which certainly reached Kafka, who published in it "Ein Bericht für eine Akademie" (A Report for an Academy) in 1917. Agnon published six stories in *Der Jude* between 1917 and 1924, several translated from the Hebrew manuscript by Gershon Scholem and one, "Agadat ha-sofer" ("Die Erzählung vom Toraschreiber" in its German translation)[5] appeared in the same volume, though not in the same issue, as Kafka's "Ein Bericht für eine Akademie." Agnon also published stories in three anthologies which were very popular in the same circles: *Chad Gadja: Das Pesachbuch*, ed. Hugo Hermann (Berlin, 1914); *Treue: Eine Jüdisches Sammelschrift*, ed. Leo Hermann (Berlin, 1915); *Das Buch von den Polnischen Juden*, ed. S.J. Agnon and A. Eliasberg (Berlin, 1916).

The grounds for comparison between Kafka and Agnon are historically attested. We should not, however, rush into the facile comparisons that usually assert that Kafka *influenced* Agnon because some of his most significant works were published in German in 1912-14 and Agnon spent the years between 1913 and 1924, in a German-speaking environment. Agnon had, in fact, written a story in Yiddish in 1907 with the intriguing name "Toyten-Tants" which manifested many of the calculated indeterminacies of Kafka's mature style—and this before Kafka had published anything. Both writers had read widely in neo-Romantic German and Scandinavian authors; both had read and admired Dostoyevski and Flaubert. While grounds for comparison exist, historical research suggests that we should avoid misleading and simplistic notions of *influence*. There are, to be sure, major differences between these two writers, as there are between any two writers. The major difference in their backgrounds was their mastery of the texts and texture of Eastern European Jewish life. In this crucial area, Agnon was the prodigiously erudite insider while Kafka was the sympathetic, perceptive, outsider. The difference, we shall demonstrate, manifests itself most sharply in their attitude towards language.

This essential difference did not seem to trouble many critics, even the prestigious Hebrew critic, Baruch Kurzweil—also a Prague Jew. In many articles and books published in Israel, Kurzweil argued that under the deceptively pious surface of Agnon's prose lurk serious religious doubts. He compared Agnon repeatedly to other modern writers such as Kafka, Musil, and Joyce; more than any other student of Agnon's prose, he disabused the Hebrew reader of the naive view of Agnon which prevailed through the 1940s. Kurzweil correctly noted the obvious fact that while Kafka was only marginal to the Jewish tradition, Agnon was fully in the tradition—despite all his doubts. And yet, by slighting the differences in attitude towards language—and their implications— Kurzweil essentially constricted and subverted the grounds for comparison. Furthermore, his critical perspective was usually theologically oriented and deliberately avoided literary history.

Following Kurzweil, many critics have offered lavish comparisons between Kafka and Agnon. We should, however, establish some guidelines for research in this area by defining what is possible and productive. What, we should ask, are the perimeters of our investigation? Do we compare—or contrast—all of Agnon with all of Kafka? Obviously this is impossible because much of Agnon bears no resemblance whatsoever to Kafka's normative mode of expression. Even if we were to go beyond the twenty-odd stories of *Sefer ha-ma'asim* (ordinarily recognized as *Kafkaesque*, though my recent research indicates that it is more Freud than Kafka) to include such formidable pieces as "Shevu'at emunim" (The betrothed), "Ido ve-'Einam" (Ido and Enam), "Ad 'olam" (Forevermore), "Hadom ve-khiseh" (The stool and the throne), and the "Kelev meshuga" (Mad dog) portions of the novel *Temol Shilshom* (Only yesterday) altogether some 700 pages of dense fiction, we would still be left with several thousand pages of stories, novels, quasi-historical compilations of tales, collections of rewritten customs interlarded with anecdotes, eulogies, commemorative pieces, and so on. When we speak of Agnon's "resemblance" to Kafka, we are actually referring to about ten percent of the former's work.

To focus on the problem of style-choice and its implication we turn to two stories, one by each writer, both first published in 1912—not that these stories are thematically related, but that each, in its own way, was crucial in the artistic development of the author: Agnon's "Vehaya he-'akov le-mishor," (And the crooked shall become straight), and Kafka's "Das Urteil" (The judgment). In each case, the story represents a *breakthrough*—to use Politzer's term concerning Kafka—a breakthrough from fragments and experimentation to a sudden mastery involving decisions regarding stylistic and thematic features which subsequently mark the author's work for the rest of his career.

Kafka's "Das Urteil," written during the night of September 22–23, 1912, deals with the clash between a son, Georg Bendemann, and his seemingly ailing, aged father, who, by the end of the story, condemns his son to death by drowning. Bound by this injunction or command (*Urteil*), Georg jumps off the bridge near their apartment. In this story we already find the seemingly lucid sentence which, upon examination, is often indeterminate; the obsession with guilt and trials; the subject-object inversion; the varied and often contradictory identifications; and the unique fusion of disparate experiences—all characteristic features of Kafka's art.

Here as in some of Kafka's other well integrated stories, a central, generalized concept is presented as the title, for example "The Judgment" or "Metamorphosis" and the narrative is a taut examination of the term, situation by situation. The term may have several mutually contradictory meanings and the story is then a narrative concretization of the frustrating yet exhilarating complexities of language. Elsewhere,[6] I have traced the term *Urteil* to both the Jewish High Holiday Prayer Book and the famous Beilis Trial (1911–13). Echoes of the Rosh HaShanah or Yom Kippur service illuminate the process of judgment, the figure of the father or of all systems of authority which, by their very nature, must fail, despite their oppressiveness. Where the term *Urteil* appears in the service, it is attributed to the divinity envisaged as a domineering king and judge of the world, the source of all authority and thus of guilt, too. Muffled echoes of the Beilis Trial can be found in the text: the friend in Russia, the scene of an overturned shop, the priest raising his hand, the obsession with unmotivated guilt. Given Kafka's family background and his recently rekindled Jewish consciousness, an event so central to the consciousness of Prague Jewry as the Beilis Trial in Kiev could not have left him unaffected. Identification with Mendel Beilis, or even a remote though prolonged observation of his plight, could have provided Kafka with the validation of his own feelings of insecurity and loneliness, an objectification of his Oedipal torment, corroboration of his doubts about the validity and viability of language, and a moral justification for the bewildering dialectic between self-corrosive guilt and subtle imposture that marks so many of his protagonists.

In this story, as in most of his stories and novels, Kafka scrupulously suppresses any reference to specific persons, places, or events. When a specific place is named, Russia, for instance, it is not as a realistic item, but as a symbolic detail away from the presence of the protagonist. The German also avoids reference to recognizable literary texts; it evokes no historical echoes. This *clean* style is the product of deliberate artistic choices: the tight, Flaubertian technique which leaves nothing to choice; the plot strategies that take the reader from an apparently bourgeois setting into the abyss lurking beneath it; in all, a departure from the limitations of realistic prose narrative.

Agnon, in writing "Vehaya he'akov lemishor" also made several decisions concerning his craft that determined the direction of his writing for the rest of his long career. Though six years younger than Kafka during the writing of this crucial story, he had already published about seventy pieces in Hebrew and in Yiddish, both in Buczacz and Jaffa. Most of these were, to be sure, embarrassingly clumsy and were published only because the editor of a provincial newspaper often has to fill space. Those published in Jaffa attest to experiments in more serious writing, usually macabre, neo-romantic tales of frustrated love, bizarre deaths, strange women—all conveyed in an agitated, often lush Hebrew prose style. Agnon, himself, obviously realized that this was not the medium he was seeking since, after the success of "Vehaya he'akov lemishor," he scrapped most of what he had previously written and either rewrote or totally discarded every line he had published. Few of these seventy items were ever republished in the many collections of his works.

Instead of paring down contemporary prose style to the threshold of meaning as Kafka would do, Agnon adopted the late rabbinic style his grandfather might have used, but kept it under scrupulously tight control. The lexical, morphological, and phrase syntax are clearly late rabbinic. The sentence, however, is an ingenious fusion of the modern and the traditional: while carefully measured and modern in its stratagems, it nevertheless echoes the syntax of more folkish genres, the Hasidic tale for instance. The Hebrew reader cannot escape the fusion of these two registers, the traditional and the modern. In that Agnon deliberately shaped this style after experimenting with other styles prevalent in his youth and after the massive efforts by Mendele Mokher Seforim to Europeanize Hebrew prose, his choice of a style, which was historically regressive in certain aspects, implies a deliberate literary and ideological position. In that no Hebrew writer can escape consciousness of the various historical strata of the Hebrew language that are present and meaningful in modern Hebrew prose, linguistic choice involves some sort of attitude towards specific periods in Jewish history and what they mean in the modern period. For instance: the choice of a biblicizing style by *Haskalah* writers implied a revolt against rabbinical norms while the choice of a composite classical rabbinic fused with biblical style by Mendele implied a distancing from *Haskalah* norms. Agnon, whose knowledge of Hebrew of all periods was prodigious, was obviously conscious of the historical provenance and implication of any phrase or syntactical structure he might use. The *negotiation* with Jewish history is obvious in every line. Agnon could thus generate the tension he sought between historical linguistic resonance (so important in an ancient, text-oriented culture), and a controlled reticence that often conceals more than it tells. The sensitive reader is thus forced to share the implied author's ambivalence about the world he has chosen to describe.

The technique worked wonders even in the first story in which it was used: "Vehaya he 'akov lemishor." The author faced a crucial choice in writing this story: in the society described, mid-nineteenth century Galicia, the norms of traditional piety and the bourgeois ethic are at odds. The hero, Menashe Hayyim, a pious shopkeeper of some means, is forced into bankruptcy by a new competitor. To recoup his capital, he reluctantly takes to the road as an itinerant beggar armed with a letter of recommendation certifying his identity, his former position in society, and his rectitude. This seemingly bizarre technique for recovering lost capital was not unheard of in earlier centuries, but had become the butt of satire by the nineteenth century. Begging for funds even for acceptable charities like family support and dowries for indigent brides were stock subjects of satire in the works of such seminal authors as Mendele. Agnon wrote his story against the background of Mendele's works, which had been published in a three volume edition the previous year. Agnon's story is thus a deliberate deviation from Mendele's narrative technique: it is more attentive to psychological realism or to bourgeois attitudes, and strives to achieve effects which are less formally rabbinic, less balanced in their syntax. By refusing to avoid both late-rabbinic or Hasidic locutions and Yiddish speech patterns, he shaped an ambiguous, flexible style which does not let the reader know exactly what the author thinks about Menashe Hayyim's beggary, which is kept in the background while the hero's reactions to situations are foregrounded. With this style Agnon could fuse the pious with the bourgeois and neutralize the satirical Mendelean bite.

Since Menashe Hayyim is conceived as a person and not a type, he can lose both status and identity, themes Agnon learned from his reading in European literature. The hero succumbs to temptation once he has recouped some of his money and sells his letter to another beggar. As one might anticipate, he then loses his money and all his possessions and must return to the road to beg, sans letter of recommendation. The beggar who bought the letter naturally dies and is buried as Menashe Hayyim: the latter's wife, now a widow, remarries and bears children which she could not do before when married to Menashe Hayyim. When the hero finally returns home, he finds his wife both married and a mother.

Here, too, Agnon dwells upon the conflict inherent in the situation: according to Jewish law, Menashe Hayyim should reveal that he is alive, thus embarrassing his wife and condemning her child to bastardry; but since he loves his wife, a bourgeois-romantic sentiment, he leaves town beset by the guilt of his concealment. He spends the last days of his life living in a cemetery where, by chance, he finds the cemetery guard inscribing his name on a handsome gravestone that his wife, thinking that the beggar carrying the letter was indeed her husband, had ordered to memorialize him. Several days later, happy in the thought that his wife still loved him and that he had resisted the temptation to reveal the truth, thereby ruining her life, Menashe Hayyim dies and the guard, who knew the story, places over his grave the stone ordered by his wife for the beggar's grave that she thought was his.

Even in bald plot outline, this novella does not sound like the pious tale it was taken to be by most critics for over thirty years: the quasi-rabbinic style, the pious milieu succeeded in deflecting the reader from such topoi obvious today as the loss of identity and the descent into hell, let alone the ambiguous ending in the graveyard or the hero's impotence. Kurzweil noticed in the early 1950s that there are, indeed, many discordant elements in the story, but following his theological bias, he read the story and much of modern Hebrew literature as a literary manifestation of secularism. The story, for him, implies an accusation against the cruelty of God who lets the hero descend into a world of chaos for no glaring sin, if any at all. The hero is forced to leave his home and wife, to depart on a journey from which there is no return, since his return can be effected only by a miracle. But there are no miracles today.

Some fifteen years later I argued that Kurzweil did not address himself to the totality of the story, to the title which—taken from Isaiah 40—implies that "the crooked is made straight" and to the ending, which seems to vindicate the hero and restores the reader's confidence in the possibility of justice in this world. Menashe Hayyim does die happy in the knowledge that he has withstood temptation (to reveal his true identity: that he was still alive) and has been rewarded with the two gifts most important to him, after he had despaired of ever recouping his fortune and his status: assurance of his wife's continuing love for him, and confidence that he would have his posterity even if it were merely his name on a tombstone.

More important, Kurzweil, like most critics, has not come to grips with the implications of Agnon's choice of this peculiar style, with what I call his *negotiation* with Jewish history. If we consider the mode of production crucial for an interpretation of the work of art, we must account for this choice which changed the direction of his artistic enterprise. After four years of experimentation in a neoromantic style with themes taken from the world of Jaffa where he lived, he abandoned both this stylistic and thematic course. He obviously realized that the neoromantic direction did not afford him the opportunities to confront the cultural and psychological problems that possessed him or to exploit his prodigious knowledge of Hebrew. Ultimately, these Jaffa stories were embarrassingly self-indulgent, even frivolous, and remained so unless recast in his new style. (Many, as I have said, were simply discarded.)

Here, the contrast with Kafka is instructive. Kafka selected situations that were to him either intolerable, or absurd, or comically grotesque, and struggled to fashion an unmediated linguistic medium, contemporary yet timeless, concrete yet constantly plumbing the depths of human consciousness. Agnon's style, beginning with "Vehaya he 'akov lemishor," immediately directs the reader to a world of texts and textuality, a specific textuality at that, one that embodies in all its features a traditional, recognizable milieu. No competent reader of Hebrew could conceivably miss the multifarious implications of this style.

Realizing he could never fashion a neutral text, free of referentiality to previous texts—for such is the nature of the Hebrew language in the beginning of the century and, to a lesser degree, even today—Agnon fashioned an artful pastiche of an older style so convincing that it took most readers some thirty years to realize that under the *pious* text of the novella lay a subtext which qualified, ironized, or even subverted the text. The seemingly *pious* text can thus be used for a variety of purposes: as a mask hiding or modifying the author's bold or revelatory sentiments on religion or sensuality; or as a mediating barrier that allows the author to distance himself from too direct and immediate responses to the dynamic, demanding events of contemporary Jewish history. Without it, Agnon's *negotiation* with Jewish history would have been impossible since he, as a writer of fiction, would have been overwhelmed by the flood of events.

Though criticized for this style by such formidable figures as Berdyczewski and S. Tzemah, Agnon succeeded admirably in creating a voice that allows for a wide range of authorial attitudes towards the text and the situations created, a subtle modulation between authorial and narrative voice, hence the possibility of a variety of *unreliable narrators*. Applied to those stories that most closely resemble those of Kafka, the manneristic style adds another level of indeterminacy. If, furthermore, one, were to speak of Kafka and Agnon in terms of self-referentiality and the concomitant *play* of signification, one could say that Kafka creates the space for play by precluding clear signification of the represented world, while Agnon creates space for play by precluding clear signification of the textual world. Again, it is the artist's deliberate choice of style that makes all the difference. Two narrative situations may be thematically identical, but if they are conveyed in radically different styles, their impact on the reader has to be radically different.

NOTES

1. The Hebrew author Yehoshua Radler-Feldman.

2. Yehosua Radler-Feldman, *Mishpehot soferim: partzufim* (Tel Aviv, 1960).

3. Some of the material in the following pages can be found in a different context in my article "The Kafka-Agnon Polarities," in *The Dove and the Mole (Interplay 5)*, ed. M. Lazar and R. Gottesman (Malibu, 1987), 151–160.

4. My remarks on Agnon's reading of Freud's *Interpretation of Dreams* can be found in my article "Agnon Encounters Freud" in this volume. Delivered in two conferences in Israel in 1988, these were the first specific connections between Agnon's writing and a text of Freud's.

5. "The Story of a Torah Scribe."

6. See my essay "The Beilis Trial in Literature: Notes on History and Fiction" in this volume.

Agnon Encounters Freud

In the engaging discussions of texts and their interpreters held over the past twenty years, the author has been treated as a nuisance or a pariah. Increasingly, the reader or critic emerges as the producer of meaning. We, the critics, either brazenly usurp the title of author or patronizingly relegate the author to a fiction of our imagination or implication. My argument here should therefore be understood as a reaction to this arrogant posture, to what I would call "the critical fallacy." In simple terms, I am going to ask: What do we readers do with an author who won't go away? What do we do with an author who asserts his presence in every line, who virtually challenges his reader to a duel—a friendly duel, to be sure, since no one is killed and no blood is spilled—but a duel from which the reader comes away humbled.

That Agnon asserts his presence in every line should be obvious to anyone who has read one page of his Hebrew, written in a style that is flagrantly non-normative, though correct, dazzlingly dense, relentlessly demanding the reader's full participation. The reader's encounter with that peculiar style is the background against which all other considerations must take place. Though I shall make few references to style in the following remarks, I assume that you realize that style and what it implies, informs, and underlies everything I say.

Readers familiar either with Agnon's writings after the 1931 Berlin Edition or with the criticism that attended it, are fully aware of the critical dictum that many of these works echo Kafka because, we are told, Agnon was influenced by Kafka—whatever the word *influence* means. Since I have dealt with that problem elsewhere I won't address it now. What I would like to present here is the exciting and far reaching notion that Agnon in mid-career, i.e. sometime after 1931, became keenly aware of the broader implications of the Freudian concepts of language in general, and dream language, in particular; he understood both their challenges and opportunities, and struggled to master this language. I will suggest, then, that much of what we have thought was *Kafka* is really *Freud*. The implications of the shift in perspective should be immediately obvious. At the very least, it opens new avenues of interpretation and might aid us in understanding what was hidden from us before.

Two distinctions should be drawn at the very outset of our argument. Critics have referred vaguely to something Freudian in Agnon since the 1930s, but they have, to my knowledge, neither proved the point, nor specified what they mean by Freudian, nor suggested implications for our reading. Second, we are not primarily conducting an exercise in psychoanalytic interpretation, but rather an historical investigation.

First, a grounding in history. What evidence do we have that Agnon ever heard of Freud? For those who need strictly positivistic proof, there are, to my knowledge, at least two significant references in Agnon's writing to Freud, his "system" (*shita*) or his "circle" (*siya*). The first is found in a letter to his wife, Esther, dated February 16, 1925, and demonstrates knowledge of Freud's theory of the latent meaning of slips of the tongue. The second is so revelatory that it deserves fuller citation. In the first version (*Davar*: December, 1932) of the well-known story, "Panim aherot" (A different face) the hero, Michael Hartmann, tells his ex-wife, Toni, a frightening dream he had. The narrator then comments:

> Hartmann was grateful that she did not interpret his dream as would Freud and his circle. His dream was fine just as it was [without interpretation], like snow before it melts.

In the first sentence, Freud is connected with the interpretation of dreams; the Hebrew roots (psr) or (prs) and (hlm) appear together. The interpretation of dreams, I submit, is the central aspect of the Freudian enterprise that intrigued Agnon; my studies, in fact, convince me that the specific Freudian work that intrigued Agnon was *Die Traumdeutung* (The Interpretation of Dreams) (1899) and I would suggest that in that book he focused upon Chapters V and VI (though Chapter II is possible). In the second sentence about Michael Hartmann, where we are told that Hartmann preferred his dreams uninterpreted since they are then "like snow before it melts," we find an acute awareness of the problematic, disturbing feature of Freudian dream-interpretation. It reveals many dirty facts of our psychic life that we would rather hide or repress under a surface of white snow.

In addition to these two references—and there are probably more—let me adduce two other biographical facts:

1. There was, in the personal library of Mrs. Esther Agnon, a set of *Die Gesammelte Werk* (The Collected Works) of Sigmund Freud.
2. According to Mrs. Emunah Yaron, Agnon's daughter, the tireless editor of his posthumous works, Mrs. Agnon would read sections of Freud out loud to Agnon in the late 1930s, perhaps into the 1940s, together with Kafka and Margaret Mitchell's *Gone with the Wind*.

To expand the picture, I would like to refer to what I call "The Eitingon connection," which I offer as one of a variety of personal connections Agnon had with individuals for whom Freud was not merely the name of a controversial Viennese doctor who created a scandal in Vienna as early as the first decade of this century, but one of the revolutionary intellectual giants of the twentieth century. Max Eitingon, a psychiatrist with strong Jewish and even Zionist sympathies (he first visited Jerusalem in 1910), was one of Freud's staunchest disciples, a trusted member of the inner circle. Independently wealthy until the Crash of 1929, he often supported Freud financially in a variety of enterprises. Though outwardly unpretentious, he was clearly an aggressive organizer with a sense of mission. He was the chief Freudian in Berlin from 1909 until 1933 when he migrated to Jerusalem, where he and his wife struck up a friendship with the Agnons. Eitingon founded the Berlin Psychiatric Society in 1920, the International Psychiatric Association in 1930, and the Palestine Psychoanalytic Society in 1933. From 1934 through 1938 he made annual trips to Vienna and London to visit Freud. The memorial volume published in his honor in 1950 contains contributions by such an array of authors as Anna Freud, Marie Bonaparte, Arnold Zweig, and Shai Agnon. The psychoanalytic institute in Jerusalem is named after him.

The "Eitingon connection" is one definite personal linkage of Agnon with the world of the Freudians, but there may be others. Agnon could not escape a familiarity with Freudian concepts after 1934 and probably knew something about Freud much earlier from his sojourn in Germany, Berlin in particular, from 1913-1924. I find it hard to conceive of Agnon's ignorance of Freud in Germany of that period, particularly since Otto Weininger's *Geschlecht und Charakter* (Sex and character) (1903) continued to generate all sorts of debates about sexuality and Judaism. It is also possible that Agnon as an adolescent in Buczacz, a provincial town of the Hapsburg empire, knew something of the furor created by Dr. Freud in the Hapsburg capital, Vienna. At some time, finally, Agnon must have discovered that Freud's father's family stemmed from his own town, Buczacz, and Agnon never forgot who came from Buczacz and who didn't.

Now that I have established plausible historical grounds for Agnon's encounter with Freud, I can ask what exactly do we mean when we use the cultural term Freud. There are three areas of Freudian interest that we should explore:

1. The most accessible and popularly known area is that of dream symbols, or rather, the specific items of symbolism found in *Die Traumdeutung*, Chapters 2, 5, and 6. Any literate adult in the past two generations knows all about the erotic equivalences of umbrellas, and keys, and walking sticks, and staircases, and ladders, and boxes, and mounds, and keyholes, and so forth. There is no aspect of Freud's writing that lends itself so readily to vulgar interpretation and parody as these symbols. I suggest that Agnon realized the potential of these symbols, both for his craft as a writer of fiction and, perhaps, for parody. It is very possible that certain passages in his stories should be read in this light, as parody. The story "Panim aherot" (A different face) is full of these symbols and they could serve both purposes.

2. The boundaries of psychological realism were substantially expanded by Freud's investigations and a writer with Agnon's interests both in the psychodynamics of guilt and doubt, on the one hand, and the relations between the sexes, on the other, would be eager to expand his narrative capabilities in these areas. The publication of "Panim aherot" and "Pat shelema" (A whole loaf) within one month of each other in December 1932 and January 1933, respectively, is no accident. They represent the two facets of Agnon's narrative interests that were most enriched by his encounter with Freud. In 1942, when he published the volume entitled *Elu va'elu*, (These and those) he contrasted his pious tales category with another category that includes two subcategories: the surrealistic stories of *Sefer hama'asim* (The book of deeds) and the two love stories, "Panim aherot" and "Harofe ugerushato" (The doctor and his divorcee). This fact has escaped most critics, as has the possibility that the doctor in "The Doctor and his Divorcee" might be a parody of Max Eitingon himself.

3. Freud, more cogently than anyone before him, systematically presented dreams and free-associated thoughts as a language that can be read and for which he has discovered the key. In the famous opening paragraphs to Chapter VI of the *Interpretation of Dreams* we read:

> The dream-thoughts and the dream-content are presented to us like two versions of the same subject-matter in two different languages. Or, more properly, the dream-content seems like a transcript of the dream-thoughts into another mode of expression, whose characters and syntactic laws it is our business to discover by comparing the original and the translation.

If it is our business to read the grammar of these languages, it is within the power of a talented writer to reproduce these languages in his fictions. I would suggest that Agnon's obsession with arcane language, both verbal and non-verbal, which we find in such stories as "Shevuat emunim'" (The Betrothal) "Ido ve'Einam" (Ido and Einam), "Ad olam" (Forevermore) and the novel, *Shirah* all stem from these powerful Freudian notions.

There are, to be sure, many other aspects of the Freudian universe which would have interested Agnon, more specific items like the contrast between Eros and Thanatos, the Oedipus Complex, the role of the fantasy life, the categorization of various types of mental illness, or simply Freud's prodigious talents as a writer, as a spinner of tales called "case-studies"—but I shall focus for the present on the first three areas: dream symbolism, the new concept of psychological realism, and the readability of all aspects of human behavior. And since these do not appear separately, but are usually interwoven, we shall refer to them in passing while looking at several specimen stories. In our brief analysis, we shall present examples of possible investigation.

The novel *Sippur pashut* (A simple story) of 1935 immediately comes to mind since it deals with the madness of its main character, Hirshel Horowitz, and his cure in the sanatorium of Dr. Langsam in Lemberg. The story, set in the fictional Galician town of Shibush (the literary correlative of Agnon's home town, Buczacz) about 1907, brilliantly captures many aspects of life of those times and places. Its real strength lies in the portrayal of the relations between the various characters, primarily between Hirshel and his domineering mother Tsirel, Hirshel's frustrated love for Bluma Nacht, and his initially unhappy marriage with Mina Tsiemlich. We can see Agnon's assimilation of Freud in his detailed portrayal of Hirshel's derangement, in the subtle construction of plausible causes of this derangement in the behavior of the mother, and in the therapy offered by Dr. Langsam. The attention accorded to the therapeutic method evidences awareness of psychotherapy. While one critic has called this method Jungian (without really explaining why) I have argued elsewhere that the method is at least consciously non-Freudian and takes some of its main features from Nahman of Bratslav. Most important is the use of language, of narration, in the cure: Dr. Langsam cures Hirshel, not by guiding him along an analysis of his fantasies and screen-memories, but by relating to Hirshel pleasant, nostalgic stories of Dr. Langsam's own childhood in a shtetl which resembles Shibush. That the narrative art has the power to cure the insane, to repair the broken vessels of this world, is of course, a romantic concept, but employed here in this situation and with all the implications of the Agnonic narrative voice, argues forcefully for a keen awareness of Freudian concepts.

Let me move now to a comparison of two seemingly unrelated stories; "Ma'ase ha'ez" (A fable about a goat) (1925) and "El harofe" (To the doctor) (1932). The first story is a well known Agnonic pious tale while the second is one of his surrealistic stories of *Sefer hama'asim*. I have never seen these two compared, but when we look closely at them, we notice strikingly similar situations.

In both, the father is sick, the doctors really cannot help, and it is the obligation of the son to secure help for the father. In both cases, the son fails. In "Ma'ase ha'ez" the narrator speaks like a traditional pious story teller, opening his story with an Aggadic phrase, referring to Biblical verses, uttering pious asides, and creating a fantastic tale. The boy follows a magical goat through a cave that leads him to somewhere in Eretz Yisrael near Safed. While the story certainly lends itself to a Freudian psychoanalytic interpretation—which I will not enter into now—the technique of the story does not, in my opinion, evidence an accommodation to or exploitation of Freudian concepts.

"El harofe" (To the Doctor) leads us into an entirely different world. Here the tortured, hesitant protagonist tell us, in his own voice, that his father was sick and he, the son, had to get to the doctor to secure help. That the doctor might be a source of aid for the dying father is doubtful, since he is described as a wanton fellow who likes to drink and play cards. What we read is actually the narrator's description of his mental anguish. Our attention is directed to the agonized workings of his mind in which time and space can be condensed into simultaneous layered images, as it is in dreams: Bordeaux is in England; two alter egos, Mr. Andermann and a pious old cantor, struggle to lead the narrator, each in his own way; the narrator's resolve is distracted by peas or lentils on the steps or a hole in his pants; and reality begins to quake. The story ends, in fact, with the protagonist on the bridge over the heaving waters of a river, certainly a more disturbed scene than the pastoral, hopeful ending of "Ma'ase ha'ez" which suggests that the boy is still alive in Eretz Yisrael, that the way to Eretz Yisrael may no longer be gained by miracle and faith, but it is still possible to find it. When one compares the mode of production of one story with that of the other, the difference in narrative concept emerges in fascinating detail.

In comparing "Ma'ase ha'ez" with "El harofe", I have tried to demonstrate the advantages of analyzing two stories with similar kernels but different narrative treatments. Another fruitful technique is the comparison of an earlier version of a love story with a later version of the same story. In this case I shall refer to "Panim aherot" (A different face), which I have already mentioned: the first version was published in 1932, the second in 1941.

1. The first version contains, as I have mentioned, a specific reference to Freud. This reference was omitted in the second version.
2. In general, the revisions made in the text for the second version exhibit a greater awareness of psychological realism, of concretization of psychic states, than the first version.
3. The story contains two dream sequences, one composed of fragments of the hero's recent experiences, the other of childhood screen-memories. These are precisely the two main dream categories that Freud mentioned in *Die Traumdeutung*
4. The story is densely larded with standard Freudian dream symbols: the parasol, the flowers, the cigarette, the ladder, the mound, the fireflies, rooms, walls, etc. At times, the erotic symbolism is so dense that this reader begins to sense that Agnon is playing with us, that there might be, in this moving story of discovery of love after divorce, a note of parody. If this possible parody is dissonant to some readers, I would argue that the varied, ever-changing Agnonic narrative voice is one of the great inventions in modern Hebrew prose.

Comparing version with version, then, one can watch, with fascination, the development of this prodigious literary talent, its struggle with what I think are notions culled from Freud. Various types of evidence have allowed us to establish that Agnon was not only aware of sections of Freud's writings, but realized that here was a literary and cultural presence he had to confront. I would like, in closing, to push the argument one step further by returning to my point of departure, to the author. If we can demonstrate, or even imagine that Agnon could consciously manipulate and generate Freudian texts for narrative purposes just as he so obviously generates rabbinic texts, we might ask: In what way should this possibility condition our reading of certain stories of Agnon?

This question intrigued me as I recently reread two fine efforts at psychoanalytic criticism, that by Gerson Shaked of the death-wish etc., in "Shevuat emunim" (The betrothal) and that by Yael Feldman of the key motif in Agnon's novel of 1938–39, *Oreah nata lalun* (A guest for the night). Shaked argues cogently that the matrix of the story is to be found in the passive hero's ambiguous relationship to his mother. As a result of these relations, he cannot form a meaningful erotic attachment to any of the young women of Jaffa of the period (The Second Aliyah). This matrix situation is forcefully conveyed and given psychic depth by a variety of techniques and motifs that are unmistakenly Freudian: the condensation of the figures of the two mothers and a sister (here: Shoshana Ehrlich); the transferred Oedipal complex of Rechnitz; the "death wish," the attraction to care-free death both in situations and in motifs such as sleeping sickness, the sea, mummies, stuffed animals; the pervasive dread of incest; intimations of homosexuality, both female and male; the reference to Otto Weininger's *Geschlect und Charakter*, classical antiquity, Latin, Homer, the Mediterranean Sea, seaweeds.

Shaked's analysis of these clusters of topoi and motifs carries us to unprecedented depths in the understanding of this story. His argument is utterly persuasive—yet it leaves me with the uneasy feeling that the author of this story, "The Betrothal," is patently familiar with the entire world of Freudian concepts, symbols, and focal situations. I have argued at length that the hero of the story, Dr. Yaakov Rechnitz, is constructed from pieces of Sigmund Freud's life history. The young Freud began his career with a study of eels at the marine biology station at Trieste. Rechnitz, also from Vienna, studies primitive sea life in Jaffa. Both Freud and Rechnitz are fascinated with the world of Greek antiquity. If Agnon is that aware of that world, he may be manipulating it just as he manipulates the world of references to rabbinic literature by creating pseudo-midrashim or pseudo-proverbs. He is also a wizard at conjuring up mock-passages of Zionist pamphlets, standard bourgeois thought-patterns, political dribble, and academic nonsense. I realize, to be sure, that many psychoanalytically oriented critics might argue that it makes no difference whether or not Agnon deliberately inserts an erotic symbol here or an Oedipal projection there, or a death wish here and there, but given my sense of Agnon's dialogic play with his reader conveyed through that truly uncanny style (in the Freudian sense: *unheimlich*) I begin to get a bit wary—even suspicious. I ask myself: Is he doing it again? Is he "playing" with us? If we can now accept the fact that Agnon is parodying the style of the pious tale in *Hakhnasat kalla* (The bridal canopy) (1931), the style of Zionist or bourgeois thought-patterns in *Temol shilshom* (Only yesterday) (1945), the style of the academic world in *Shirah*—and many other styles in many other places—why, I ask, shouldn't we suspect that he is parodying the style of the psychoanalytic report, particularly that found in *Die Traumdeutung* where the self-dramatizing narrator/analyst is Sigmund Freud? This may seem preposterous to some, but then if you would claim in the late 1930s that *Hakhnasat kalla* is a comic/ironic/parodic novel, most readers would recommend you to Dr. Max. Eitingon's psychiatric clinic.

In conclusion, let me phrase my main point in another way. In a pair of perceptive articles, Yael Feldman has treated the key-motif in *Oreah nata lalun* to a searching, semiotic and psychoanalytic analysis. Among the many passages she treats, there are two, found towards the end of the novel, for which I would like to offer alternate readings.

As the narrator is about to leave the town of Shibush for Eretz Yisrael, he visits the Beth Midrash to take leave of it, for that was the focal point of the action of the entire novel. Since he no longer has a key, he peeps through the keyhole and remarks that "the Beth Midrash shrank within the ball of this man's eye." Feldman interprets this as an act of voyeurism, of looking in. I would read it more concretely to mean that from that point on the Beth Midrash exists only within the eye-ball or the consciousness of the narrator. There is nothing left to Shibush except the narrator's ability to portray it in his fictions. We, the readers, can know Shibush only through him, since outside of his consciousness, Shibush no longer exists; it cannot be visited. The author, then, controls all.

Following this idea, we come to the final chapter in which the narrator/author returns to Jerusalem and mysteriously finds the old, huge key to the Beth Midrash in his suitcase. He takes it, locks it up in a box, and ties the small key to the box on a string that he hangs from his neck. Feldman reads this locking up of the original key as the awareness that the authentic key can never really find a proper new home in Eretz Yisrael. I would suggest, however, that in locking up the key and keeping the new key to the keybox for himself, the author is telling us that the key to full understanding of his fictive world—and that, again, is all we have left—is something which he alone has.

We may possess or fashion all sorts of interpretive keys—old keys, new keys—but we will never possess the key to total understanding; we shall never totally possess the world of Agnon's fiction, Agnon's personal Beth Midrash. This, I find, is a sobering thought in an age when interpreters arrogate to themselves primacy over the author.

OTHER HEBREW
WRITERS

The Beginnings of Modern Hebrew Literature: Perspectives on "Modernity"

The traditional opening statements in the debate concerning the beginnings of modern Hebrew literature usually assume the form of claims or accusations of paternity. Claims, if the child is legitimate; accusations, if it is not. I wish to avoid the paternity issue because, as I shall argue, it is essentially groundless and precludes consideration of other perspectives. My strategy shall therefore be an oblique attack from an unexpected quarter using traditional camouflage, I begin with a prooftext.

> The Second Temple, completed seventy years after the destruction of the First by Nebuchadnezzar, differed in four ways especially from the Temple of Solomon. Though about the same in area, it was not so high. It was also less of a unit, being divided now into an outer and inner court. In equipment and decoration it was barer. Above all, the Holy of Holies was now an empty shrine, as it was also to remain in the magnificent third Temple built by Herod. The Ark of the covenant was gone, and no one felt at liberty to try to replace it with a substitute.

A careful reading should alert the reader to the fact that the author is probably not thinking in normative Jewish terms, in which there are ordinarily two temples, not three, even though the Temple destroyed in 70 C.E. was by no means the Temple built by Zerubavel in 516 B.C.E., but what the Mishnah and Josephus (Ant. 15:380 if.) knew as "Herod's Building." Dispensing with solicitation of conjectures, I shall simply reveal the source not really from a history of the Jews, but from W. Jackson Bate's *The Burden of the Past and the English Poet*, by now a classic essay

253

dealing with the difficulties the modern poet felt since the eighteenth century about achieving something new and significant.[1] Aware of the creative achievements of his predecessors and obsessed with his self-consciousness of the rich legacy of the past, Bate argues, the poet felt the past was a crushing burden that he had to bear and manipulate.

The sustained metaphor of the Second Temple, a revealing metaphor in itself, was not, of course, Bate's invention but rather a term current in the literature of the neoclassical period beginning with the Restoration. The employment of biblical tropes is by no means surprising in an age reared on Bible reading and sermons and for whom the most popular poet was unquestionably Milton. Bate extends the figure in his book by calling the romantic period, for him the creative solution of the problems induced by the burden of the past, "The Third Temple."

Since England has housed few Hebrew writers of any importance after the readmission of the Jews in the time of Cromwell (Ephraim Luzzatto and Shmuel Romanelli come to mind), one does not ordinarily think of its literary history as a ground for comparison with modern Hebrew literature.[2] The known direct eighteenth-century English influences upon Hebrew literature, for instance, are not considerable: Addison and the English periodical, Young's "Night Thoughts," Lowth's biblical studies, and the notion of Longinian sublimity, are important examples. Why England? one might ask. Why begin a discussion of early modern Hebrew literature with a reference to a country that never was a center for Hebrew creativity? The opening gambit is obviously deliberate: it aims to reject traditional tracing of *influences* in order to pose new questions.

The early eighteenth century in England should be of particular interest to students of Hebrew literature since it borrowed and further developed the Ancients vs. Moderns controversy from the French seventeenth-century critics and also witnessed many of the early phenomena we usually associate with modernism: secularization, enlightenment, industrialization, urbanization, the increase of literacy, democratization. The English experience was replicated on the continent, particularly in Germany. As Lawrence Marsden Price has demonstrated so convincingly in his *English Literature in Germany*, most of which deals with the eighteenth and early nineteenth century, one cannot form a coherent picture of German literature in Germany during that period without factoring in the English influence.[3] Price, for instance has fully documented chapters on the moral weeklies, Pope, Thomson, Milton, Young, MacPherson's "Ossian," Percy's "Reliques," Richardson, Fielding, Sterne,

Goldsmith, Locke, and Shaftesbury, and an entire section on Shakespeare. As one reads through studies of early modern Hebrew literature, particularly of the Berlin maskilim, one is struck by the gross neglect of the English connection. England, furthermore, presents a useful paradigm for modernization because of its priority in many areas, its relatively unbroken line of development, and the widespread commercial and cultural influence of England until World War I.

Much of the recent literary criticism written in France, England, and America has been obsessed with the problematics of modernity, often attributed to the subversion of the scriptural underpinnings of language since the eighteenth century, which has led to such notions as the indeterminacy of language, the crisis of consciousness, the abyss gaping between consciousness and reality, and the reinterpretation of Nietzsche and Freud, in short, the entire deconstructive enterprise. Since so much of the criticism of culture traces its roots back to the eighteenth century, it behooves us to examine the Hebrew writers of the period in this light even if we discover that the crisis of consciousness cannot be found there.

In the past twenty-five years, there has been little theoretical debate concerning either the beginnings of modern Hebrew literature, its secularity, or its consequent problematics. The energies of research in modern Hebrew literature have been invested elsewhere, in formalist, semiological, or narratological studies. The eighteenth century, in fact, has attracted relatively little attention. With the exception of pioneering work being conducted in the aesthetic analysis of the Hasidic tale (composed at the end of the eighteenth century, but published at the beginning of the nineteenth), the few articles devoted to eighteenth-century writers have essentially illuminated some dark corners in the work of the Berlin maskilim. The avoidance of theorizing about the beginnings and nature of modern Hebrew literature is concomitant with a recrudescence of interest in the problematics of modernism and literary history in Western Europe, England, and America, for this is the period of Foucault and Derrida in France, of Jauss in Germany, Bloom and Hartman in America, let alone Marxists of all stripes throughout the Western world. While I do not argue that all or any of these theoreticians should be applicable to our own field of study, I do find it curious that precisely when modernity becomes a burning issue in the more advanced Western literary societies, it is not an issue that exercises contemporary Hebrew literary criticism.

Bate, to be sure, is no deconstructionist, but even in his more traditional mode of criticism he points to an aspect of the anxiety of the eighteenth-century English poet. Contrasting him with Harold Bloom, one of the more influential American critics of crisis, is particularly illuminating, since Bloom tries to understand, and perhaps bridge, this abyss with ideas taken from Buber and Scholem. Bate's argument, put simply, is that the modern poet in general, and the eighteenth-century poet in particular, had to struggle with the poetic tradition of his forebears in order to create his own modes of expression. This struggle was beset with a psychological anxiety first alluded to by David Hume, but expanded upon in recent years by Bloom.[4] This anxiety engendered a pervasive self-consciousness which, Bate asserts, is one of the hallmarks of the literature to which we attribute the nebulous term "modern." Note that Bate's passage subtly suggests the themes that inform the self-consciousness of the poets and critics of the period: "not so high"; "less of a unit"; "barer"; "an empty shrine." Bate, furthermore, never forgets that the history of literature is the account of the struggles of a succession of creative writers to express themselves in their own idiom despite the burden of past writers, which is part of the linguistic and literary tradition that enables them to express themselves.[5] He nevertheless regards the transition from period to period as evolutionary, that through such new notions as sublimity and the imagination, romantic poets learned to bear the burden of the past and the problematics of modernity generated by it.

Bloom's position is a *revision* of the traditional one advanced by Bate in that where Bate sees evolution, Bloom sees cataclytic, but creative, disjunction. Bloom's version of this anxiety is, as is well known, formulated in Freudian terms: the struggle of the poet against his immediate ancestors is Oedipal and violent. Whatever we might think of Bloom's exotic ratios, or his often rash excursions into gnosticism and Kabbalah to seek metaphors for his theories, one must grant that he has revitalized the study of literary influence in the past decade. Since the periods discussed by both Bate and Bloom are what has commonly been recognized as the threshold of modernity, the eighteenth century, a testing of the applicability of their theories to Hebrew literature of that century to which we commonly attribute the beginnings of modern Hebrew literature, should be a fruitful heuristic exercise. It should, furthermore, provoke a sorely needed rethinking of the basic critical assumptions we utilize in approaching the materials of the period and make us conscious of the "tropics of our discourse," to use the term of Hayden White.

It is illuminating, for instance, to cite at least one sharp contrast between the problematics occupying Bate and Bloom and that facing the scholar of eighteenth-century Hebrew literature. When one speaks of the burden of the past suffered by the eighteenth-century English poets, one refers to the immediate past, to Milton and, a bit more removed, to Shakespeare. To escape parental authority, they espoused ancestral authority in the form of classical antiquity with canons of aesthetics often borrowed from the French, who had experienced somewhat similar problems. Bate (p.22) argues that "this is the first large scale example, in the modern history of the arts, of the leapfrog use of the past for authority or psychological comfort: the leap over the parental—the principal immediate predecessors—to what Northrop Frye calls 'the modal grandfather.'"

It should be immediately clear that none of the Hebrew writers we shall discuss, Moses Hayyim Luzzatto, N.H. Wessely, and the early Hasidic storytellers, suffered from this "burden of the past," since they were not preceded by towering literary talents which they had to overcome. To the extent that there was a burden to overcome, it was the burden of the present, more specifically, the repressive force of traditional rabbinical authorities. If we were to utilize the parental/ancestral terms proffered by Frye and Bate, we would have to designate the parental as the normative Judaism of the period of the author and the ancestral as an idealized biblical ethos, different in each case, upon which the author could draw to legitimize his activities in the face of the recognized, established authorities. While Luzzatto's and Wessely's long poems openly employ biblical diction and character-types, the Hasidic tales almost always have as prooftext or subtext some biblical image or reference. In each of the three cases we shall study, the composition of an aesthetically pleasing drama, or poem, or story—whatever the overt religious or social message may be—is an imminent goal. The formal qualities of the text are those of accomplished literary artifacts.

We must remember, furthermore, that the notion of *beauty* in all its manifestations is problematic in itself. While the admiration for *the beautiful* in life and literature was one of the basic Haskalah tenets, it is difficult to know when the preoccupation with aesthetics is inextricably bound up with the whole complex of Haskalah notions and impulses and when it is an independent value.[6] When a poet or a critic expresses his admiration for a certain work, e.g., Wessely's *Shirei Tiferet,* and extols its "beautiful poetry, the likes of which we have not seen since the Bible," what, we must ask, does he really mean? Aesthetic notions rarely exist in isolation from other ideological considerations.

❂   ❂   ❂

No consideration of any aspect of Hebrew belles-lettres of the eighteenth century can dispense with an orienting discussion of the various theories of beginnings and definitions.[7] Though the recognition of a new period in Hebrew poetry was recorded as early as Franz Delitzsch's *Zur Geschichte der Jüdischen Poesie* in 1836,[8] which reflected the awareness of such figures with whom he collaborated, such as S. D. Luzzatto and Meir Halevi Letteris, the now classical positions were fully formulated, as is well known, almost a century later by Y. F. Lachower (1928)[9] and J. Klausner (1930).[10] In each of these two cases we find a conceptual need to attribute the beginning of the modern period to an individual, either M. H. Luzzatto (by Lachower) or N. H. Wessely (Klausner). In neither instance does a specific word for *modern* appear; the term throughout all theoretical discussions in Hebrew of modern Hebrew literature is *hadashah*, simply *new* as opposed to *old* (cf. Lachower's book of essays: *Al gevul hayashan vehehadash*), suggesting that on the theoretical level, at least, there was little awareness of the problematics of modernity much discussed in other literatures and forcefully injected into the discourse on the topic by Baruch Kurzweil as late as the 1950s.[11]

When it comes to reasons and definitions, Lachower is irritatingly elusive. He refers to a "new spirit," a "new style" and "content," "immense literary talent"; but while he finds in Luzzatto's *Migdal Oz* clear echoes of the secular environment, he also finds in it unavoidable references to kabbalistic sources, particularly in the image of the tower, and yet seems to feel no need to reconcile the two strains. His claims of subsequent historical influences are sparse and undocumented.

Klausner's argument is more cohesive: he chooses Wessely as the key proponent of the new period, since his pamphlet *Divre shalom ve'emet* (1782) was a forthright statement espousing secular education and enlightenment, the ideals of the group known as the Me'asfim that generated such controversy at the end of the century.[12] He rejects Lachower's arguments for Luzzatto's primacy on three grounds: Luzzatto was essentially a religious author, a kabbalist even in his dramas; his plays were not known until a century after their composition; Luzzatto had never intended to begin a new age. The last reason is naïve at best, since it assumes that the individual writer to whom one can attribute a new departure has deliberately and consciously set upon a new path, a position which few historians would accept. Wessely, furthermore, did advocate educational reform, but had no dreams of being the father of a new epoch in Hebrew literature. On the matter of historical filiation, Klausner is on somewhat firmer ground: only some fifty copies of

Luzzatto's *Layesharim Tehilla* were published in 1743, while *Migdal Oz* was not published until 1837, and *Maase Shimshon* was not published until 1927. By the time *Migdal Oz* was finally published, the reputation of Wessely as the prime literary influence on such figures as Shalom HaCohen, Meir Letteris, and Adam HaCohen was firmly established. What Klausner neglects to mention (and I shall treat at length) is the great popularity of *Layesharim Tehilla* between 1780 and 1836.

Klausner's categorical identification of the new, i.e., modern litera-ture as secular was by no means new, but was decisive because of his rep-utation. Once secularism, however, ill-defined, was posited as the dominant characteristic of this new literature, the unanswered—perhaps unasked—question remaining was: What was this secularism? The more important question: What value does one assign to it? had been taken as a given, even though what would seem to be the prior question, the def-inition, had not yet been adequately clarified. Clearly both Lachower and Klausner considered this modernity a positive achievement. For Klausner, a militant Zionist, it was associated with worldly activism, which led through the Haskalah to the Jewish Renaissance and political Zionism, which he advocated. Lachower, no less a nationalist than Klausner, was more attuned to the vitality manifested in the expanded scope of the imagination, in linguistic expressiveness. His essays should be read in conjunction with Bialik's two essays: "HaBahur miPadova" ("The Youth from Padua" [on Luzzatto]) and "Giluy vekhisuy balashon" ("The Revealed and the Hidden in Language").[13] Bialik's editorial work on *Sefer HaAggadah* or the medieval Hebrew poets was later paralleled by Lachower's work with Y. Tishby on the Zohar.[14] In all these cases one finds a relentless preoccupation with language: How does one create in language? How does one write in Hebrew? What is figural language? How does one edit a legend to make it more attractive in literary terms? The Zohar, finally, self-consciously creates worlds of thought and emo-tion through language.

The clarification of the term "secular" (*hiloni*) is one of the tasks of H. N. Shapira's lengthy introduction to his *Toldot hasifrut ha'ivrit hahadashah* (1940).[15] Since he finds a mixture of *kodesh* (holiness) and *hol* (secular-ism) throughout Jewish history, he prefers a different set of concepts: "ter-restrialism" (the concrete reality of the terrestrial world) vs. "empyrealism" (Hebrew: *superliut*) (the etherealized reality of the spiritual world). These two terms are paralleled to "introcentrism" vs. "transcentrism." In the course of history, Jewish life has affirmed the preponderance of "terreal-ism" over "empyrealism"; modern Hebrew literature, in striving as an expression of the collective Jewish will to restore the preponderance of "terrealism," is thus an organic link in the unbroken chain of Jewish culture, a move in the dialectic between these antithetical forces. This latest dialectical swing, the beginning of modernism, began—for Shapira—after the expulsion of the Jews from Spain in 1492, when Jewish life had reached the extreme of landless spirituality and began to shift back to concerns for territorial, or terreal, realities. Following the suggestions of Gershom Scholem, Shapira regarded the Sabbatean movement as an abortive step in this direction which ultimately led to the Haskalah, in turn, a necessary move towards Zionist nationalism. Literature, of course, is a manifestation of this cosmic dialectic, not an isolated phenomenon to be regarded on aesthetic grounds alone.

Shapira's elaborate exposition and coinage of bizarre terms evidence his struggle with the definitional problem of modernity, not with its valorization, which he takes for granted. He also is not exercised by the psychological or spiritual implications of modernity, so defined. He is essentially in accord with Klausner's assignment of eighteenth-century secularism of modernism to the 1780s in Berlin, and not with Lachower's choice of Luzzatto, though many of his reasons are those that led Lachower to select Luzzatto as the beginning of the modern era: a greater power of expressivity, an expansion of the human imagination, etc.

The expansion of human capacities and horizons is also the criterion identified by Simon Halkin as the mark of modernity in modern Hebrew literature.[16] Though much less specific than Shapira, Halkin does assert that modern Hebrew literature is essentially the product of the past two centuries and also finds in the Sabbatean movement, as Scholem portrayed it, the desire for a "fuller life in the heart of the simple Jewish folk." While differing from Shapira regarding the terminus *a quo*, Halkin agrees with his basic criteria. Halkin thus includes Luzzatto in his concept of modern Hebrew literature and also the Hasidic folktale. Both Shapira and Halkin are obviously eager to demonstrate that modern Hebrew literature was a natural growth of literary or cultural phenomena that preceded it. They try to demonstrate the fallacy of the prevailing view that this modern literature represented a sudden, unanticipated jump from the medieval to the modern without the mediating period of gradual development in the Renaissance. During the centuries of the Renaissance in Italy, France, and England, most of world Jewry was not affected by the new humanism. Both Halkin and Shapira endeavor to fill this gap by reference to Kabbalism, hence their espousal of Scholem's ideas, which Shapira cites as early as 1939, as does Lachower.

Avoidance of the potentially critical issues posed by modernity and secularism seems to be the goal of Dov Sadan's holism,[17] which is actually an expansion of Zinberg's concept of "Jewish literature."[18] (Since Zinberg was a Marxist, it is possible that notions of totalizing informed his writing on Jewish literature.) Rather than focusing upon the narrow confines of the Hebrew Haskalah as delimited by either Klausner or Lachower, Sadan presents a concept of modern Hebrew literature that embraces the totality of literary creativity in Hebrew over the past three centuries, including traditional rabbinic and Hasidic literature. This holism, in fact, impells him to include in the field of his study, everything of Jewish content or concern written by Jews, not only in Hebrew, but also in Yiddish, Ladino, and any other language, even if not specifically Jewish, such as German or French or English. While Sadan grants that secularism is the distinguishing feature of Haskalah literature, he regards it as a minor, surface phenomenon under which the subconscious currents of Jewish creativity continue to course. Sadan's thesis has had far-reaching ideological and curricular effects since its formulation in 1950, but it contributes little to a clarification of the question of modernity.

It should be clear that all the above-mentioned positions are Ahad HaAmic rather than Berdyczewskian in their view of the structure of Jewish history. In all cases, Jewish history, for all its variety, was to be considered as a unitarian flow through time, always preserving its essential identity and source of energy, the will to survive of the Jewish people as a distinct cultural entity. Where Ahad HaAm saw essentially superficial changes, Berdyczewski detected radical disjunction and the concomitant relentless struggle by the forces of privilege and power to repress all dissent or change. The well-known provenance of their respective positions bears mentioning at this point in our argument. Ahad HaAm derived his evolutionary perspective from Spencer and other British social philosophers of the nineteenth century; Berdyczewski, admittedly Nietzschean, also read deeply in Schopenhauer and Faust. The comparison with Bate's evolutionary development and Bloom's cataclytic struggles is illuminating.

From Lachower's history (1928) through Halkin's and Sadan's books (1950) the secularity of modern Hebrew literature, however defined, was not seen as a disjunctive force or problematic from a cultural point of view. The problematics of this secularism, this modernity, was forcefully thrust into the public debate on the nature of modern Hebrew literature, affecting both the interpretive and evaluative processes, in the

1950s by Baruch Kurzweil, in a dazzling flurry of splenetic articles including attacks on Halkin, Shapira, Ahad HaAm, Scholem, and most native Israeli writing. Kurzweil derived his ideas from Max Wiener's *Jüdische Religion in Zeitalter der Emanzipation*[19] and Isaac Breuer's *Judenproblem.*[20] From the former, he learned the psychological or spiritual problematics of secularism; from the latter, the critique of secular Zionism seen from a traditional religious point of view. In a variety of different formulations, Kurzweil argued that modern Jewish secularism, the ethos that informed most of modern Hebrew literature, was a radical break from traditional Judaism and therefore an ethos that had been emptied of the fundamental certainty in the sacred that embraces all the phenomena of life and measures their value. Unlike all his predecessors mentioned above, Kurzweil considers this modernity a disaster, a radical discontinuity with the Jewish past, a specious attempt to claim its legitimacy as the rightful heir of historical Judaism, while it is actually its repudiation.

His answer to the loaded question posed by the title of his most influential book, *Sifrutenu hahadasha: hemshekh o mahpekha?* (Our Modern Literature: Continuity or Revolt?) is obvious; and the literature, in his opinion, is an accurate reflection of the calamitous results of this revolt: not the renewal of the Jewish spirit, but its fragmentation and desolation. This fragmentation of the Jewish consciousness was far more catastrophic than the similar fragmentation that appeared in European literature in the eighteenth century, since the European nations had a whole range of social institutions and traditions grounded in landed states of one sort or another, from which a viable literature could be sustained, even when traditional faith in an all-embracing divinity was undermined. The Jew had nothing but his faith, his halachically structured way of life, and when the sacral underpinnings of that were sapped, there was left a void that could not be filled even with the reestablishment of Jewish political sovereignty in the State of Israel.

Steeped in the phenomenological philosophy of his student years, Kurzweil holds that language flows from being and therefore insists that Hebrew, whose essence is sacral, used by secular authors, can only produce a disjointed, shallow literature, the literature of the Haskalah, for instance. Only when authors begin to sense the inadequacy of their secularism as a replacement for traditional belief, only when the problematic is intuited—as in the case of Feierberg, or Bialik, or Brenner, or Agnon—does Hebrew literature achieve an aesthetic, though tragic, quality. Kurzweil therefore devoted his literary studies to an examination of the "tragic paradox" which informs the works of some of the foremost modern Hebrew writers. The paradox is the product of their belated realization that their secularism was inadequate to sustain a spiritual way of life. Ruthlessly consistent, he could find little of value in Israeli literature (with the exception of some of Amichai and Ravikovich), and of all modern Hebrew writers, only Uri Zvi Greenberg, with his mystic view of Jewish destiny, elicited his unstinting approval.

Kurzweil has thus presented a theory of Hebrew modernism that is totalist and revisionist. It is totalist in that it comprehends all of modern Jewish life, hence modern Hebrew literature as the most accurate reflection of modern Jewish life, and allows for no phenomena that might not fit into his theory. As a hermeneutic philosophy, it determines the interpretation of every literary text, and though Kurzweil claims he reads with the authority of Dilthey, Heidegger, or Gadamer, it should be clear to any sensitive reader that he is not engaging in an open dialogue with the text, but searching in it for those passages which might corroborate his views of the catastrophic nature of modernism. It is revisionist in that it completely rejects the normative Zionist overview of Hebrew literature, which posits a dynamic that moves ever upward from traditionally informed texts, to maskilic works, to revival *(tehiyah)* creativity, culminating in the literature of the State of Israel. Kurzweil's periodization is significantly different from the normative: simplistic Haskalah; militant-reformist Haskalah; the tragic period (which corresponds to the Zionist *tehiyah*); and the period of the apocalyptic vision of redemption, which actually includes only one writer, Uri Zvi Greenberg.

As for eighteenth-century Hebrew literature, Kurzweil has little to offer that is new or even evidences close familiarity with the material. He follows others in regarding the Berlin Haskalah as the point of departure and relies upon Natan Rotenstreich's formulation of the period as a radical change in Jewish consciousness.[21] Though Rotenstreich was primarily concerned with the philosophers of the period, Mendelssohn in particular, and not literary texts, Kurzweil has no difficulty with this discrepancy. In general, one realizes that for all his assertions about the validity of his inherent reading of the text, Kurzweil is no less an ideologue than Klausner; neither exhibits much concern with the very nature of the literary text, its literariness, its basic figurality.

Since relatively little attention has been devoted for some time to these problems of beginnings—which are ultimately problems of self-definition—new departures are called for. The following paragraphs, therefore, comprise the beginning of an exploration of the three most influential works of the period in an attempt, not to solve problems, but to put them in such a way as to reopen the discussion, which has been neglected, perhaps deflected, for too long.

✿   ✿   ✿

We have seen that in refuting Lachower's attribution of the beginning of modern Hebrew literature to Luzzatto, Klausner cited both the belated publication, hence influence, of *Migdal Oz*, and Luzzatto's kabbalistic, hence anti-secular (i.e., anti-modern) bent. Klausner's citation of the belated publication of *Migdal Oz* offers a convenient point of departure for a theoretical excursion into several important aspects of literary history that are usually neglected. (Among these I find most useful the notion of *Rezeptionsgeschichte* introduced by Hans Robert Jauss.) While Klausner correctly established the fact that *Migdal Oz* was available only in manuscript, hence unknown in the formative decades of the Haskalah period, 1780–1830, he strangely neglected to record that Luzzatto's third play, *Layesharim Tehila*, though published in only fifty copies in 1743, was republished in Berlin in 1780 and 1799, precisely at the peak of the Berlin Haskalah. Note, furthermore, all the subsequent publications: in Lemberg, the publishing center of the subsequent Galician Haskalah, in 1799, 1813, 1823, 1825; in Lissa in 1824; in Yosefow in 1826; and in Bamberg in 1827.[22] By the time *Migdal Oz* was rediscovered (Almanzi bought it from the heirs of R. Elhanan HaCohen, a disciple of R. Israel Benjamin Bassan for whose wedding Luzzatto wrote the drama), *Layesharim Tehilla* was well known in both Berlin and Galicia, as was Luzzatto's famous ethical tract, *Mesillat Yesharim*, which had been published in ten different editions between 1740 (Amsterdam) and 1835 (Yosefow).

From the 1780s through the middle of the nineteenth century, the two belletristic books that every maskilic writer had were Wessely's *Shirei Tiferet* (1789–1811) and Luzzatto's *Mesillat Yesharim*. Simply from the point of view of factual *Rezeptionsgeschichte*, the Lachower-Klausner argument has been a futile exercise, since both writers, Luzzatto and Wessely, exerted a powerful influence simultaneously on Hebrew writers and readers during the formative decades: 1790-1830. The historical record was unfortunately blurred by Franz Delitzsch's influential statements, which both reflected the prevalent opinion of the 1830s and gave it authority for following generations: "Moshe Hayim Luzzatto is the founder of the modern school in Italy" (p. 89) The separation into geographic schools made little sense, since Hebrew readers were essentially trans-national. Of greater importance, however, is that Delitzsch and his colleagues, the members of the first generation with a realization that they were experiencing a new phrase in the history of Hebrew literature, determined what was modern.

It is at this point that Hans Robert Jauss has much to contribute to our argument.[23] *Rezeptionsgeschichte* is, for him, more than a history of the reception of a work of art by certain audiences; it is an ambitious attempt to rejuvenate literary history, which has been anesthetized by the formalists, on the one hand, and the Marxists, on the other. In the process, Jauss also rejects the standard philological approach. He quotes Walther Bulst's statement that "no text was ever written to be read and interpreted philologically by philologists," and adds "nor...historically by historians. Neither approach recognizes the true role of the reader to whom the literary work is primarily addressed, a role as unalterable for aesthetic as for historical appreciation" (pp. 7-8).

The history of literature, claims Jauss, "is a process of aesthetic reception and production which takes place in realization of literary texts on the part of the receptive reader, the reflective critic, and the author in his continued creativity" (p. 10). To dispel the doubts often voiced that an analysis of the aesthetic impact can approach the meaning of a work of art or serve as the basis for an objective history, Jauss introduces the notion of the horizon of expectations, by which he means the set of expectations with which the reader approaches the text, expectations that are historically contextualized since they are based on the reader's reading experience, his notion of genre, his sense of the implicit relationships to familiar works of the literary historical context, and by the contrast between the poetical and practical functions of language that the reflective reader can always realize while he is reading. (Note the similarities with Bate and Bloom.)

As to our ability to gauge the newness of a specific work for a specific audience, Jauss says:

> If the horizon of expectations of a work is reconstructed in this way, it is possible to determine its artistic nature by the nature and degree of its effect on a given audience. If the "aesthetic distance" is considered as the distance between the given horizon of expectations and the appearance of a new work, whose reception results in a "horizon change" because it negates familiar experience or articulates an experience for the first time, this aesthetic distance can be measured historically in the spectrum of the reaction of the audience and the judgment of criticism (spontaneous success, rejection or shock, scattered approval, gradual or later understanding). (p. 14)

Turning to Luzzatto and Wessely, it should be clear, in the light of Jauss's theory, that the combined reception of *Layesharim Tehilla* and *Shirei Tiferet* between the late 1780s and the middle of the nineteenth century is a central phenomenon in the history of modern Hebrew literature. These two books inspired a host of plays, translations, epic poems, even Avraham Mapu's *Ahavat Tzion* (1853), the first Hebrew novel. We can detect traces of these books in works by Franco-Mendes, Shalom HaCohen, Meir HaLevy Letteris, Adam HaCohen, Micah Yosef Levinson, and Y. L. Gordon, let alone dozens of less accomplished writers. No less important is the testimony about these books by many of these writers who were also critics and scholars. Nowhere does one find approval of these two books because they are *secular* (Klausner's argument), when they are admired for their praise of wisdom and derision of folly, these are not cited as their cardinal virtues.[24] The readers, after all, could and did read *enlightened* books in German or French. The recurring note of admiration, even adulation, however awkwardly articulated, is reserved for the sheer beauty of the poetry, its expressiveness, its openness to experience, which is always compared with the poetry of the Hebrew Scriptures. Time and again one encounters the phrase: "Poetry like this has not been written since the time of the Scriptures." The comparison with Scriptures has two effects: it legitimizes the new work and aestheticizes Scriptures.

The fact that Wessely and Luzzatto were pious Jews, that the former was attacked for his *new* though really moderate ideas on education, or that the latter was hounded out of Italy for his messianic intimations, seems to have meant little to the readers of their poetic works. For these readers and aspiring poets, schooled primarily on rabbinic texts and those portions of the Bible used in one form or another of religious worship, books like *Layesharim Tehilla* or *Shirei Tiferet* represented a major "change of horizon," for while they were written in a Biblicizing idiom, hence accessible and familiar, they offered a narrative sweep (Wessely), an enchanting portrayal of nature, of passion, and sensuous figural language (Luzzatto). Each, in fact, offered a different mode of poetic expression: *Shirei Tiferet* became the paradigm in modern Hebrew literature for the lengthy narrative poem, the *poema*; *Layesharim Tehilla* (and, after 1836, *Migdal Oz*), which was poor in plot but rich in figural language and lyrical passages, demonstrated for several generations of poets and novelists the potentialities of complex lyrical expression in a language that none of them spoke.

The most eloquent testimony to the impact of Luzzatto's achievement in expanding the linguistic horizons of Hebrew poetry is found a century later in Bialik's famous essay "HaBahur miPadova,"[25] written upon the publication of Luzzatto's book of plays by Simon Ginzburg in 1927.[26] Bialik, to be sure, was no historian or trained philologist. His enthusiastic, lavish praise is historically distorted: he attributes the entire upsurge of modern Jewish creativity to Luzzatto, the inspiration, he implies, for the three fountainheads of modern Judaism: Elijah, the Gaon of Vilna, the Baal Shem Tov, and Moses Mendelssohn. Bialik is on much sounder ground when he focuses upon Luzzatto's poetic contribution, the purification and healing of a defiled and sick language, the concrete expression of the soul of the people. Deliberately following Luzzatto, Bialik indulges in bold imagery. Luzzatto is always compared to the light of redemption; just as his disciples saw in him a redeemer and messiah, so Bialik, referring to Hebrew literature, does not hesitate to name Luzzatto "The Redeemer" and "The Messiah"; it was through Luzzatto's genius (always described in popular kabbalistic terms) that the morning light of Hebrew literature burst forth to "a new life, and most importantly, a life different from that which preceded it.[27] The modernity of modern Hebrew literature, for Bialik, begins with the explosive literary creativity of Luzzatto, an explosion repeatedly portrayed in kabbalistic metaphors connected with the purifying light of redemption. (It would be interesting to compare Harold Bloom's recourse to kabbalistic metaphors with that of Bialik.)

No less crucial is Bialik's formulation of the manifold aspects of Luzzatto's personality and creativity, a problem that troubles most critics, even so perceptive a scholar as J. Schirmann, whose essay on Luzzatto's plays is still the point of departure for all studies of this material.[28] Both at the beginning and the end of his essay, Schirmann wonders about the contrast between the "enlightened" poet who writes pastorals in the Italian style and the mystic who heard voices and claimed he was the messiah. (The naïveté of this query is puzzling and exhibits a resistance to a common phenomenon in religion. Luzzatto's combination of mysticism and dramaturgy is no more paradoxical than Joseph Karo's mysticism and rational jurism, as demonstrated by R. J. Z. Werblowsky.)[29] In several well-crafted, almost lyrical passages, Bialik claims that this confluence of seething, seemingly contradictory streams gathered in the pool (*berekha*, the same metaphor for the introspective soul in Bialik's *poema* "HaBerekha"), "which God prepared for their repose in the soul of his chosen one, Luzzatto. From there they emerged, sevenfold pure and cleansed, with a different face, and a totally different appearance."[30]

Though much more responsible to historical fact and sober in his language, Lachower's position on Luzzatto clearly resembles that of Bialik, as do Halkin's and Shapira's.[31] Certainly, there is a dimension to modernity in literature that transcends ideological positions, either traditional Zionist (Klausner) or traditionally religious (Kurzweil). When one approaches the literary text on its own terms and formulates the initial questions in accordance with the peculiar nature of literary language, the line of investigation leads us to different perspectives regarding the meaning of the text or its modernity. If, for instance, scholars studying Luzzatto's plays, all of which have a pastoral element, had spent as much time delving into the assumptions of the genre as in mechanical line-by-line comparisons of Luzzatto with Guarini, they would have asked more interesting questions?[32] For instance, the psychological impulse that generates the pastoral poem is the sense that the world is too much with us, that we must find an escape from the overwhelming present to a past Golden Age of simple innocence and happiness, or forward to an equally tranquil, carefree utopia. From the Hellenistic period on, pastorals are written by urban dwellers about an imaginary landscape free of urban concerns. As P. V. Marinelli puts it succinctly:

> The land of Arcadia is really the landscape of an idea....Arcadia is primarily the paradise of poetry. It is a middle country of the imagination, half-way between a past perfection and present imperfection, a place of Becoming rather than Being, where an individual's potencies for the arts of life and love and poetry are explored and tested. It points two ways, therefore, backward into the past and forward into a possible future.[33]

Speculative and practical mysticism, we are told, does not arise in a void, but rather within the circles of institutionalized religions that the mystic feels no longer satisfy his deepest religious needs. One then creates a Zohar, figuratively speaking, a work of literary speculation about the inner workings of the cosmos or the soul or the Godhead. The literary form may be entirely different, homiletic rather than pastoral drama, but the psychological similarities are too numerous to dismiss. Both the author and his receptive audience obviously find in this literary, mythic world, an escape from the real world in which they are constrained to pass their daily existence. While Luzzatto patently found it necessary to purge the pastoral of pagan or Christian elements, to Judaize it, his choice of the pastoral as a genre of literary composition implied certain assumptions and conventions that are not contradictory with zoharic modes of thought, but actually complementary to them.

The first generation of maskilim also praised Wessely's *Shirei Tiferet*[34] primarily for its poetry and not for its rationalist ideology. One of the poetic aspects admired is the narrative sweep of the biblical tale retold in clear, unencumbered verses, free from convoluted syntax and quantitative metrics. And while this lengthy epic on the life of Moses leading up to the Sinaitic Revelation failed to maintain the readers' interest after the 1880s, we should not overlook the innovation it represented to Hebrew readers and writers between the publication of its first volume in 1789 and the end of the subsequent century. Despite Wessely's enlightenment didacticism and veiled philological pedantry, the poem was the first intentional *epic* treatment in Hebrew of the Exodus and the Revelation at Sinai. For readers intimately acquainted with the biblical original, the epic treatment, in alexandrine sestets, was not only exciting, but revolutionary, precisely because of its narrative line, energized by a sense of the sublimity of subject and hero.

Unlike the satirists like Euchel, Berlin, or Wolfsohn,[35] Wessely was one of the most conservative, pious, and reverent of the writers associated with the Berlin Haskalah. Despite his intention to create a work that would render the sacred teachings of the Torah more accessible to the reader, he actually produced one of the most *modern*, even potentially subversive, works of the period: he departed from the traditional norms of exegesis and homily, and rendered the most theologically central moments of the Pentateuch in a verse form adopted from the German literature of the period. In a sense, this was a literary act far more daring than that of Luzzatto's. Ironically, the dangers of this departure from, hence challenge to, traditional norms of literary expression associated with Scripture were never an issue at the beginning of the nineteenth century. And when Uri Kovner, by no means a defender of the faith, opened his attack on much of Haskalah literature in 1866 by savaging *Shirei Tiferet*, he faulted Wessely for trying to compete with the original biblical text, not because this act was sacrilegious, but because it was aesthetically a failure.[36] *Shirei Tiferet* thus presents us with a *Rezeptiongeschichte* totally different from that of Luzzatto's dramas. Wessely's work found or created its audience upon publication, but lost it within two generations. S. D. Luzzatto, for whom anything written in Hebrew was a source of national pride, found it boring; even Klausner, who posits Wessely as the father of modern Hebrew literature, must strain to describe its virtues.

The first two important literary works we have discussed, Luzzatto's *Layesharim Tehilla* and Wessely's *Shirei Tiferet*, each commonly recognized as a major work in the first generation of what we call modern Hebrew literature, were written by pious Jews. Our third example, *Shivhe HaBesht*,[37] actually a compilation of Hasidic tales edited and published by Dov Ber ben Shmuel in 1815, also took shape in the last decades of the eighteenth century in circles of pious Jews, this time the Hasidim of the Ukraine, who knew nothing of the Italian pastoral or the German epic poem. Our inclusion of Hasidic literature is done with full awareness of the problematics of such inclusion; no history of modern Hebrew literature has, to date, included the Hasidic tale. Zinberg did include the tale (in vol. 9), since he was writing a comprehensive history of Jewish literature, not only Hebrew literature or belles-lettres. Since the Hasidic tale was ordinarily first told and transmitted in Yiddish but then transcribed either in Yiddish or Hebrew, Zinberg's Marxist leanings would naturally lead him to include such popular literature. Sadan, as mentioned above, insists on including the Hasidic tale, though he has never written a history, while Kurzweil dismisses Sadan's suggestion together with his entire holistic theory. Halkin supports Sadan's contention and finds the concomitance of the emergence of modern Hebrew literature in the west and the Hasidic tale in the east not a coincidence, but an historic inevitability.[38]

The justification for this inclusion is complex, but defensible. Though the tale was not the prime genre of Hasidic expression (the homily was), most students of Hasidism concede that the movement did endow the tale with an importance and dignity it had not received previously. The oft-quoted preface to *Shivhe HaBesht* by the printer, Israel Yoffe, corroborates this contention.[39] From it we learn that even in the period of Menahem Mendel of Vitebsk's sojourn in Eretz Yisrael (1777–1788), it was already a custom among Hasidim to substitute pious tales for the customary Torah lesson at the third Sabbath meal late on Saturday afternoon; the tale, that is, had already assumed a quasi-ritual function and could be substituted for a Torah lesson. This, of course, is not the aestheticism we find in Western Europe, an integral part of the maskilic ethos with all its ambiguities. The tradition of storytelling became well entrenched in Hasidic circles and continues till today.

While it is true that maskilim ridiculed Hasidic tales until the 1880s, the enormous popularity of these tales among Hasidim cannot be overlooked unless we choose to restrict modern Hebrew literature to writers directly associated with the Haskalah. One cannot neglect, furthermore, the satires of Perl and Erter, which parody Hasidic tales, since these satires are among the most significant achievements of early modern Hebrew literature (1819 ff.).[40] However negative the portrayal of Hasidism, the Hasidic tale, with its motifs, enters the mainstream of Haskalah literature at that point. As the Haskalah waned in Russia in the late 1870s and the early 1880s, the partial nationalistic turning inwards led secular Hebrew writers to the abundant corpus of Hasidic tales for materials to collect or recast for their own purposes and own audiences. This process has continued for a century and shows no signs of abatement. On the contrary: in the past decade the Hasidic tale has become a subject for serious academic study as literature.[41] Close analysis of the tales included in the two classical collections: *Shivhe HaBesht* and *Sippure Hama'asiyot of Nahman of Bratslav*[42] reveal a surprising literary sophistication that raises many unanswerable questions regarding one provenance of the tale-telling tradition, the nature of the intended audience, the reception by the actual audience.

✿   ✿   ✿

In the light of our discussion of the perspectives on modernity prevalent in the studies of modern Hebrew literature and our examination of the three cardinal cases taken from the eighteenth century, it should be clear that one must constantly approach this problem from several perspectives at once. What is or is not *modern* depends upon the beholder of the phenomenon—as the Latin etymology of the word "modern" *(modo)* denotes: "just now." The etymological sense was very much alive in the seventeenth century debates in France, Italy, and England of the Ancients vs. the Moderns and implies simply "what we believe in, or delight in, now." During the course of these debates, the term became reified, and the original implication lurking beneath the surface, i.e., we, as opposed to the ancients, are bound by no stable truths, was blurred. Specific critics might then identify modern with secularism, or nationalism, or Marxism, all with the inevitability that today's modern is tomorrow's ancient. One can handle these shifting perspectives only by maintaining the clear distinction between what E. D. Hirsch calls interpretation, i.e., the investigation of textual meaning, vs. criticism, i.e., the relevance to the reader of a specific period.[43] "Meaning" in this sense is parallel to Husserl's "inner horizon;" "relevance," to his "outer horizon." Jauss, as we have seen, builds on Husserl and Ingarden to provide us with the conceptual tools for a sound literary history.

The notion of secularism is no less troublesome. While it derives from "of this world" as opposed to the world of faith (originally: of the Church), its Hebrew equivalent, *hol* is by no means as distinct, since traditionally the *hol* was embraced by a world whose coordinates were categorically *kodesh*. Though oblivious to historical research, Kurzweil's distinction between traditional *hulin* and modern *hulin* was valuable. A more precise and fruitful formulation can be found in Luzzatto's contemporary and countryman Giambattista Vico, whose *Scienza Nuova* was unappreciated for at least a century after its initial publication in 1725.[44] Vico's concept of the New Science, the science of human society, involved a universe of discourse in which what man recognizes as true (*verum*) and what he himself has made (*factum*) are identical. In short, the "physics of man" reveals that men have created themselves and their concept of God in their myths. Not only does man create societies and institutions in his own image, but these, in turn, create him. In this process, language, myth, metaphor play a dominant role, since they are the tools by which man shapes the world in his imagination, and which, in turn, shape his perception of the world.

The realization that this is fundamentally a world without God, that God has been a creation of the human imagination, that the ultimate reality is language, is what informs much of the discussion of modernity during the past generation. Bate and Bloom, for instance, refer to this realization and its psychological consequences, as do many other theoreticians of repute. It is therefore crucial that we examine our eighteenth-century texts for signs of this anxiety of modernity.

Kurzweil's claim that the last two decades of the eighteenth century are marked by a radical change in the nature of Hebrew literature would be difficult to substantiate on the basis of the evidence of these central texts. Indeed, if one were to seek undeniable proof of radical secularization, one would have to advance about a century to the 1890s, where the secularization one thinks of in European literature bursts forth in full bloom. One, of course, could find instances in the 1860s, but the attack upon traditional institutions and moeurs that one finds in such abundance in the 1860s refrains from any open denial of divine providence. This unmistakable mark of secularism begins to surface in the 1890s. As for the sense of belatedness that generated anxiety in eighteenth-century English poets, one cannot find it in modern Hebrew literature until the first decade of the twentieth century, when the new, overwhelming standards of literary achievement had been set by Mendele, Bialik, Ahad HaAm, and Tchernichowski.

Modernity thus is a term applicable to modern Hebrew literature, only with the greatest caution. We certainly cannot simply equate it with a vague notion of secularism and go on from there. An analysis of eighteenth-century texts precludes the possibility of this common option. We cannot, furthermore, avoid the difficulties of the problem by facilely attaching the literary problem, which has its own determinants, to general considerations of Haskalah culture (which, incidentally, is fraught with ambiguities) and therefore claim that the literature is *modern* rather than *medieval*, whatever that means. We must ask what works display signs of modernity that we can agree upon. (Perhaps, for instance, *Shirei Tiferet* is the most *modern* eighteenth-century literary work, precisely for the reasons suggested above.) We must ask what were the notions of modernity maintained by the audience of the work in the specific period under study: the 1780s or the 1830s or the 1860s or the 1890s or the 1980s. Perspectives change rapidly, since the very term *modernity* implies unstable norms of perception. We must concede, furthermore, that anyone engaged in the academic study of Judaism is, as Y. H. Yerushalmi notes, "a product of the rupture" in history. "Once aware of this, he is not only bound to accept it; he is liberated to use it."[45] The acceptance and productive use of the rupture is an act that would elicit assent from such disparate figures as Foucault, Bloom, and closer to home, M. Y. Berdyczewski.

It is precisely Berdyczewski who among Hebrew writers was most aware of the ruptures of *modernity* in the sense used today. Though he appeared on the stage of modern Hebrew literature in the last decade of the nineteenth century together with such *strong* (in the Bloomian sense) writers as Ahad HaAm, the late Mendele (of his second Hebrew period), Bialik, Tchernichowski, and Frischmann, he was regarded by them as an *aher* (an "other"), and reveled in this position. Refusing to paper over the cracks in the facade of Jewish existence with verbal formulations of one sort or another, he was sensitive to the crisis of consciousness which motivated his contemporaries, Nietzsche and Freud. If, then, one is to discuss modernity in terms meaningful today, terms compatible with those employed in theoretical discussions in France, Germany, England, and America, one should investigate the problematics of the texts of the 1890s, not those of the eighteenth century. Rather than beginning with Luzzatto or Mendelssohn or even Ahad HaAm, one should begin with Berdyczewski and move from his texts to those of his contemporaries and successors.

NOTES

1. W. Jackson Bate, *The Burden of the Past and the English Poet* (Cambridge, Mass., 1970). "The burden of the past" has, to be sure, Nietzschean overtones. See Hayden N. White. "The Burden of History." *History and Theory* 5 (1966), 111–134.

2. On Hebrew literature in eighteenth-century England, see J. Schirmann, "The First Hebrew Translation from English Literature: the Play *The Mourning Bride* by William Congreve" (Hebrew), in J. Schirmann, *Letoldot hashirah vehadrama ha'ivrit, vol. 2* (Jerusalem, 1919), and articles on Ephraim Luzzatto and Samuel Romanelli in the same volume, 211–301.

3. L. M. Price, *English Literature in Germany* (Berkeley, 1953).

4. The books by Bloom pertinent to this argument are *The Anxiety of Influence* (New York, 1973), *A Map of Misreading* (New York, 1975), *Kabbalah and Criticism* (New York, 1975), *Poetry and Repression* (New Haven, 1976), and *Agon* (New York, 1982).

5. See Hayden N. White's remarks on this subject in the article cited in n. 1.

6. See Y. Friedlander, "The Concept of the Essence of Poetry at the Beginning of the Hebrew Haskalah" (Hebrew); *Bikoret ufarshanut I* (March 1970), 55–60; I. Barzilay. "The Ideology of the Berlin Haskalah," *PAAJR* 29(1956), 1–37; and "The Italian and Berlin Haskalah," *PAAJR* 29 (1960–61), 17–54; A. Altmann, *Moses Mendelssohn* (Philadelphia, 1973), particularly chapters 5 and 8; Azriel Shohet, *Im hilufei hatekufot* (Jerusalem, 1960); Moshe Schwartz, "The Poetics of Sublimity and Solomon Loewisohn's *Melitzat Yeshurun*" (Hebrew) *Moznayim* 17 (September-October 1963), 373–383; Tova Cohen, "Influences upon Solomon Loewisohn's *Melitzat Yeshurun*" (Hebrew), *Bikoret ufarshanut* 6 (December, 1974), 17–28.

7. The histories of literature (and several high school textbooks) have been treated in detail by Avraham Holz in "Prolegomenon to a Literary History of Modern Hebrew Literature," *Literature East and West II,* n.3 (1967), 253–270. I discuss only those writers and aspects relevant to my argument.

8. Leipzig, 1836.

9. *Toldot hasifrut ha'ivit hahadashah* (Tel Aviv, 1928). We shall quote from the 1952 edition. To this one should add Lachower's *'Al gevul hayashan vehehadash* (Jerusalem, 1951), which contains three essays on Luzzatto, 29–95, published some twenty years earlier.

10. *Hahistoriah shel hasifrut ha'ivrit hahadashah* (Jerusalem, 1930; 2 ed., 1952). Klausner had already established his position in brief in his Russian language history of modern Hebrew literature first published in Warsaw in 1900.

11. Kurzweil's many essays of the 1950s on this subject were first collected in *Sifrutenu hahadashah: hemshekh o mahpekhah* (Our Modern Literature: Continuation or Revolt?) (Jerusalem and Tel Aviv, 1959).

12. This pamphlet was published in Berlin at the beginning of 1782 as a reaction to Joseph II's Edict of Toleration, promulgated October 13, 1781.

13. In *Kol kitve H. N. Bialik* (Tel Aviv, 1951). The article on Luzzatto, first published in 1927, appears on 228–229; that "On the Revealed and Hidden in Language," on 191–193.

14. *Mishnat HaZohar.* vol. I (Jerusalem, 1948), vol. 2 (Jerusalem, 1961). Tishby shared with Lachower a lifelong fascination with Luzzato. See Tishby's two definitive

essays on Luzzatto's mysticism in his *Netive ha'emunah vehaminut* (Tel Aviv, 1964) chapters 8 and 9.

15. H. N. Shapira, *Toldot hasifrut ha'ivrit hahadashah* (Kovna, 1939), 1–168.

16. Halkin's position is found in his *Modern Hebrew Literature: Trends and Values* (New York, 1950), chapters. 1–4; *Mavo lasiporet ha'ivrit,* notes taken at Halkin's lectures by Tzophia Hillel (Jerusalem, 1954); and in a much-neglected essay, "History and Historicism in Modern Hebrew Literature" (Hebrew), in his collection of essays *Derakhim utzedadei derakhim basifrut,.* vol. I (Jerusalem, 1969), 155–182. The last essay, written after Kurzweil's savage attacks on Halkin, demonstrates that these attacks had little effect on Halkin's initial position.

17. Dov Sadan's central essay, *Al sifrutenu.* first appeared as a monograph in 1950, Tel Aviv, but was later included in his *Avne bedek* (Tel Aviv, 1962), 9–61, under the title "Masat mavo" ("Introductory Essay").

18. Israel Zinberg's *History of Jewish Literature* has a complicated publication history. Its first volumes were published in Russian in the 1920s, but the entire work, including the incomplete last volume, was issued in Yiddish beginning in the late 1920s in Vilna and ending in 1943 in New York. The six-volume Hebrew edition appeared between 1955 and 1960 in Tel Aviv. A twelve-volume English edition was translated and edited by Bernard Martin (Cincinnati and New York, 1972–78). Zinberg, incidentally, includes Luzzatto among the medieval Hebrew poets.

19. Max Wiener, *Jüdische Religion in Zeitalter der Emanzipation* (Berlin, 1933).

20. Isaac Breuer, *Judenproblem* (Frankfurt-am-Main, 1922).

21. *Jewish Philosophy in Modern Times from Mendelssohn to Rosenzweig* (New York, 1968). Original Hebrew: *Hamahashava hayehudit ba'et hahadashah,* 2 vols. (Tel Aviv, 1945–50). For a summary of Kurzweil's career and ideological stance, see James S. Diamond, *Baruch Kurzweil and Modern Hebrew Literature* (California, 1983).

22. The popularity of the book might reflect a readership beyond maskilic circles. Luzzatto was admired among pious Jews for his ethical tract, *Mesillat Yesharim.* *Layesharim Tehilla* would not offend a pious reader, since it demonstrates the victory of the just (the yesharim: note that the term appears in the title of both books) over the evil and all the "characters" bear the names of virtues or vices.

23. Hans Robert Jauss, "Literary History as a Challenge to Literary Theory." *New Literary History* 2, n. 1 (Autumn 1970), 7–38. Also collected in H. R. Jauss, *Towards an Aesthetics of Reception* (Minneapolis, 1982). Page numbers in text refer to *NLH.*

24. On Wessely, see Klausner, *Hahistoriah shel hasifrut ha'ivrit hahadashah* (Jerusalem, 1952), 138–143. On Luzzatto, see Simon Ginsburg, *The Life and Works of Moses Hayyim Luzzatto* (Philadelphia, 1931), 110, 113–114; Yonah David, *Hamahazot shel Moshe Hayyim. Luzzatto* (Jerusalem, 1972), notes 9, 14, 37, 38, 40, 41, 46.

25. See above, n. 13.

26. M. H. Luzzatto, *Sefer hamahazot* (Tel Aviv, 1927).

27. Bialik, *Kol kitve H. N. Bialik* (Tel Aviv, 1951), 228.

28. J. Schirmann, "The Plays of Moses Hayyim Luzzatto" (Hebrew). in J. Schirmann, *Letoldot hashirah vehadrama ha'ivrit,* vol. 2 (Jerusalem, 1979), 161–175.

29. Joseph Karo, *Lawyer and Mystic* (Oxford, 1962).

30. Bialik, p. 229.

31. *Toldot hasifrut ha'ivrit hahadashah* (Tel Aviv, 1952); xi–xii. Introduction written in 1927 for first (1928) edition.

32. See Sergio J. Sierra, "The Literary Influence of G. B. Guarini's *Pastor Fido* on M. H. Luzzatto's *Migdal Oz*," *Jewish Quarterly Review*, n.s. 50, n. 3 (January 1960), 241-255 and ibid., n. 4 (April 1960), 319-337. Though Yonah David (op. cit.) does discuss the pastoral or allegorical features of the plays, he draws no substantial conclusions. Nomi Tamir-Ghez seems to be moving towards a deeper understanding of the pastoral, but ultimately concentrates on the disjunctive nature of *Migdal Oz* in "On Literary Contacts and the Thematic Structure of *Migdal Oz*" (Hebrew), *Hasifrut*. nos. 30–31 (IX/1-2) (April 1981), 95-100. The literature on the pastoral is vast. See Peter V. Marinelli, *Pastoral* (London, 1971). Bibliography, 83–88. Of particular interest are: William Empson, *Some Versions of the Pastoral* (London, 1950); H. Levin, The *Myth of the Golden Age in the Renaissance* (Bloomington, 1969); and Renato Poggioli, *The Oaten Flute* (Cambridge. Mass., 1975). The concept of the allegory has been radically revised in Angus Fletcher's *Allegory: The Theory of a Symbolic Mode* (Ithaca, 1964).

33. *Pastoral* (London, 1971).

34. Berlin and Prague, 1789–1811. Klausner provides full bibliography on Wessely until 1930 in *Hahistoriah shel hasifrut ha'ivrit hahadashah* (Jerusalem, 1930: 2 ed., 1952), 103–104.

35. Moshe Pelli, "Naphtali Herz Wessely: Moderation in Transition," *Hebrew Studies* 19 (1978); 43–55, and Yehudah Friedlander, *Perakim basatira ha'ivrit beshilhe hame'ah ha-18 beGermania* (Tel Aviv, 1979).

36. Originally in *Heker Davar* (Warsaw, 1876): 41 *ff.* Collected in *Kol Kitve Kovner* (Tel Aviv, 1948), 33-34.

37. 1st edition, Kapust, 1815. The most frequently cited Hebrew edition is that of S. A. Horodetzky (Berlin, 1922: Tel Aviv, 1946). English edition: *In Praise of the Baal Shem Tov*, edited and translated by Dan Ben-Amos and Jerome R. Mintz (Bloomington, 1970).

38. Halkin, "History and Historicism," 175–176. Halkin, like Shapira and Sadan, leans heavily on G. Scholem's "Mitzvah haba'a ba'avera," originally in *Keneset* (Tel Aviv, 1937); English translation, "Redemption Through Sin" by H. Halkin in *The Messianic Idea in Judaism* (New York, 1971).

39. Horodetzky, ed., 33–34.

40. There are many articles on both Joseph Perl and Isaac Erter (see bibliographies in *EJ* and *EI*), but there is no scholarly monograph on the satire in the Galician period of the Haskalah. Perl's *Megalei Temirin* (Vienna. 1819) has elicited some of the best research efforts, since it is one of the most accomplished Hebrew works of the nineteenth century.

41. See Joseph Dan, *Hasippur hahasidi* (Jerusalem, 1975) and Gedalya Nigal, *Hasiporet hahasidit* (Jerusalem, 1981). Also articles by A. Band, J. Elbaum, Y. Elstein.

42. *Sippure hama'asiyot of Nahman of Bratslav*, ed. Nathan Sternhartz (Ostrog, 1815/16).

43. E. D. Hirsch, *Validity in Interpretation* (New Haven, 1967) and *The Aims of Interpretation* (Chicago. 1967). See F. Lentricchia's critique of Hirsch in *After the New Criticism* (Chicago, 1980), 256–280.

44. *La Scienza Nuova* (Naples, 1725). English edition: *The New Science*, trans. Thomas G. Bergin and M. H. Fisch (Ithaca, 1948). Though the studies of Vico are numerous, Isaiah Berlin's *Vico and Herder* (London, 1976) is particularly applicable to our study.

45. Y. Yerushalmi, *Zakhor* (Philadelphia, 1982), 101.

❧ The Ahad Ha-am–Berdyczewski Polarity

Odessa. April 12, 1899

To M.Y. Berdyczewski, Berlin

I am delighted by your report that your articles are finally being collected in one volume. But I would like to advise you—and you certainly will not take offense—that it is essential to entrust your writings (even those which have already been published in daily and weekly periodicals) to someone who knows grammar so that he might correct the many mistakes which disfigure their shape....I would also advise you that you apparently think the term *al em ha-derekh* means *the right road.* But this is a mistake. *Em ha-derekh* is what you call a *Scheideweg* [a crossroad] in German.[1]

A rapid reading of this brief note, one of the shortest in Ahad Ha-Am's six volumes of letters, reveals the characteristically controlled, correct tone of his style, evident even in his letters and autobiographical writings. But there is a strange, discordant note in this brief document. The unified style both mitigates and exacerbates the internally contradictory message: although Ahad Ha-Am congratulates Berdyczewski because his collected articles are to be published as a book, he gently (or slyly?) suggests that he learn Hebrew properly and even calls attention to Berdyczewski's shocking ignorance of the precise meaning of *em ha-derekh,* one of the key words in Hebrew publications of the 1890s. What I mean by this is simple: How do we read this letter? Or, by extension: How do we read anything written under the pen name of Ahad Ha-Am, one of the great masks created in modern Hebrew literature? These questions, for which I have no simple answer, must be asked before we can make any statement about Ahad Ha-Am, let alone about

Berdyczewski, his most dogged opponent. Any document signed either "Asher Ginsberg" or "Ahad Ha-Am" underwent a double self-censorship: Ahad Ha-Am had to avoid the strictures of the Tsarist censor; he also had to protect his historical image. His letters are probably the most self-censored in the long history of Hebrew literature. Briefly: do we really have the documents to write about Ahad Ha-Am or are we writing about a persona Asher Ginsberg created? With this caveat in mind, I return to the brief *congratulatory* note.

Considered in its historical context, this note, which might pass for an incidental, even insignificant, gesture, is truly remarkable. The correspondents, after all, were two of the leading protagonists in the heady ideological debates that took place in the Hebrew press in the formative period between 1881 and 1914. The year was 1899, at the peak of the mass Jewish emigration from Eastern Europe, three years after the dazzling appearance of Herzl on the stage of Jewish public life, and less than a year after Ahad Ha-Am's celebrated attack upon the Nietzscheans among the younger generation who clustered around Berdyczewski and who named their publishing house "Tze'irim"(The Young [Rebels]). Ahad Ha-Am's prestigious editorship of *Ha-Shilo'ah* was in its fourth year while Berdyczewski had already published his article of resignation from the staff of *Ha-Shilo'ah*. Moreover, he had violated Ahad Ha-Am's confidence by publishing his own reply to Ahad Ha-Am's article "Shinui ha-arakhin" (The transvaluation of values) even before it appeared in print.

I cite these items not as an anecdotal prelude to their ideological positions, but rather as emblematic elements in the dynamic relationship between the two men, a relationship that must be kept in view if their ideological positions are to be fully understood. For though Berdyczewski had published some one hundred items of all sorts before his first attack (1892) on Ahad Ha-Am in "Reshut hayahid be'ad ha-rabbim" (The individual and the community) and the latter had published much less since his literary debut (1889) in "Lo zeh ha-derekh" (This is not the way), there is no question that throughout their careers Berdyczewski considered Ahad Ha-Am the more established, authoritative figure. Berdyczewski's attitude can be ascribed not only to Ahad Ha-Am's greater age—he was nine years older than Berdyczewski—but rather by two aspects of the Ahad Ha-Am phenomenon that could not fail to impress any sensitive young man.

When they first met in Odessa in 1890, Ahad Ha-Am was already a respected and forceful political figure in Hovevei Zion circles, a fact that both Ahad Ha-Am and his official biographer, Leon Simon, endeavored to efface; and Ahad Ha-Am had developed a prose style that conveyed self-confidence and authority. Not only was Ahad Ha-Am's style lucid, precise, and unerringly idiomatic, but, in the best English tradition, it was calculated to sweep the reader along from one seemingly well-established point to the next in rather lengthy sentences that always appeared to know where they were going and how to get there. The tone was not the coffeehouse patter of the continental *feuilleton*, but more like the thoughtful, responsible dignity of the editorial column of the London Times or a Foreign Office white paper. The style was the external expression of a personality who realized the manipulative power of language and did not hesitate to employ that power; in brief, it was a formidable polemical—hence political—weapon. The first dozen articles Ahad Ha-Am published in the early 1890s became instant classics; and their author emerged as a public figure who could, and did, take daring stands on sensitive issues, often attacking close colleagues and cherished ideals.

Although negative reactions on the part of pious Jews and the Hovevei Zion could be anticipated because Ahad Ha-Am was an avowed secularist and deplored the feeble, awkward approach of Hibbat Zion, the attack mounted by Berdyczewski was from a more radical quarter and implicitly labelled Ahad Ha-Am as the bourgeois conservative he really was. We should never forget that both men basically began with the same set of assumptions: belief in God is no longer a vital force in Jewish life; and the various substitutes suggested (including Hibbat Zion) for the rejuvenation of Jewish life were hardly adequate. Neither were concerned primarily with the physical plight of the Jews and both, in fact, deplored the mass emigration from Russia. Both rejected the naiveté of the *Haskalah*, the assimilatory tendencies of Western European Jewry, and the redemptionist claims of socialism. Neither considered Herzlian Zionism the galvanizing force it was for many thoughtful Jews at the turn of the century. On the other hand, though this difference is not central to our consideration, Ahad Ha-Am was obsessed by modern antisemitism with its racist overtones, whereas Berdyczewski does not seem to have been unduly exercised by it.

Berdyczewski's attack was so disturbing to Ahad Ha-Am because it was directed against the latter's most crucial and most vulnerable argument. Ahad Ha-Am claimed that the lost, vital religious culture could be replaced by the inherent will of the Jewish people to survive in history. This will, fundamentally nationalist in nature, had been constant in Jewish history and was the foundation stone upon which one could build the rejuvenated structure of Judaism. As early as "Reshut ha-yahid be'ad ha-rabbim" in 1892 and "Liheyot o lahadol" (To be or not to be) in 1894, Berdyczewski challenged significant aspects of Ahad Ha-Am's position. Though his point of view did not emerge fully formed until the end of the decade, Berdyczewski was already busy assaulting the tendency towards the imposition of authority over the individual throughout Jewish history, hailing hitherto neglected personalities in Jewish history such as the Zealots, Shammai, and Jacob Emden, and calling attention to the liberating force of such contemporary writers as Ibsen and Nietzsche.

As the decade progressed, Berdyczewski developed his ideology more fully, though he could never present it with Ahad Ha-Am's clarity. Berdyczewski flatly rejected the notion that Judaism possessed a constant moral characteristic throughout history or any other spiritual continuity for that matter. There simply was no unifying, authoritative element in Jewish life; Judaism, rather, was a conglomeration of constantly diverging groups and contradictory theories. In each period, one particular group dominated and often suppressed others: the prophets suppressed the idol worshippers, the Israelites suppressed the Samaritans, the Pharisees suppressed the Sadducees. But these suppressed groups often surfaced and preserved fragments of their traditions. The victory of one group over the other was not a historical necessity and might even have been a mistake, especially when a more *spiritual* group dominated one with a greater affinity to nature and to beauty. Because there had never been an authoritative strain in Jewish history, there is none now, and no Jew is required to submit to the moral dictates of any branch of Judaism, but rather can choose according to his own reason and personal inclination. Though the term or even the notion of existentialism never appeared, to my knowledge, in Berdyczewski's essays, the tenor of his thought was clearly existentialist, whereas it is equally undeniable that Ahad Ha-Am was constantly referring to essences in Jewish history, secular ones, it is true, but essences nevertheless. The "national will for survival," is just such an essence in Ahad Ha-Am's thinking. For better or for worse, neither ever connected their ideologies with either essentialist or existentialist thinking. Had they done so, they might have both enriched and systematized their often random thoughts and would have anchored them in contemporary European thought.

The short, seemingly courteous note cited at the beginning of this essay assumes extraordinary importance when we realize that by the spring of 1899, not only were the positions of the two men firmly established at opposite sides of several central issues, but that the preceding years had been full of turmoil in both the public sphere and in their personal lives. Upon receiving his doctorate in Berne in 1896, Berdyczewski unleashed a torrent of articles, reviews, and stories (forty-seven items between the fall of 1896 and 1898 alone) many reflecting Nietzschean views. During this same period, Ahad Ha-Am invited Berdyczewski to participate in the new journal, *HaShilo'ah*, which first appeared late in 1896, even offering him a monthly column and some administrative work in Berlin to assist him in making a living. As is well known, it took Berdyczewski only a few months to rebuff his benefactor, again on a matter of principle.

Ahad Ha-Am, both in his famous *Ha-Shilo'ah* manifesto and in his firm editorial policy, made it emphatically clear that the journal's purpose was the clarification of ideas and issues central to Jewish concerns. On the basis of clear, well-formulated thinking, he believed—naively, in my opinion—one could formulate correct public policy, and that was precisely what Judaism needed in the last decade of the century. We should not forget that Herzl's *Judenstaat* was already in wide circulation, and plans for the first Zionist Congress were well-developed. Simultaneously, though of less importance to Ahad Ha-Am, Jewish workers were organizing (the first meeting of the Bund was in 1897), and solutions to the *Jewish problem* were forthcoming weekly. Ever a believer in the supremacy of reason *(Shilton ha-sekhel)*, Ahad Ha-Am was convinced that properly phrased public debate would lead to correct decisions in public policy; the idealized English political model obsessed him. (One often wonders at the tenacity of this belief, given his abundant experience with Jewish political life in Odessa).

For Berdyczewski, public policy debates were inadequate because they avoided the main issue, the personality of the individual Jew stunted by centuries of rabbinic regulations and inhibitions. If, as he assumed, the root of the problem lay in the warped individual, one had to destroy those forces that had done the damage, and then build on a new foundation, on the instincts, passions, and aspirations of the individual. Berdyczewski's program was no more specific in its execution than was Ahad Ha-Am's, but the direction was patently different. *Ha-Shilo'ah*, in Berdyczewski's opinion, should publish not only ideological essays but also stories, poems, and literary criticism not necessarily restricted to the Jewish experience, because these were the literary genres that dealt with the inner life of the individual and were therefore capable of affecting some change in the nature of the individual Jew. How this was to happen was never made clear; at best one gathers from Berdyczewski's essays on the subject that belles-lettres, both Jewish and Gentile, open the individual up to nature, to beauty, to truth. His attack on Ahad Ha-Am's limited editorial goals was part of his repeated insistence that Hebrew literature must expand its boundaries to include the actions and passions of individual heroes and to embrace the entire gamut of human experience.

One seeks, in vain, throughout Berdyczewski's essays for a systematic statement concerning the language of literature, of poetry (in the broad sense of belles-lettres); one does not find in his repeated pleas for an expansion of horizons, anything approaching a defense of poetry. And yet these articles obviously made an impression, for there gathered around Berdyczewski, although usually at distances linked by the mails, a group of younger writers who found his call exciting and liberating. His impulsive style, so discordant when compared to the measured tones of Ahad Ha-Am or Mendele Mokher Seforim was, in itself, a statement of liberation. It is no accident that some ten years later, when asked who the greatest living Hebrew writer was, no less an accomplished literary figure than Yosef Hayyim Brenner could mention Berdyczewski, rather than Hayyim Nahman Bialik or Mendele or Ahad Ha-Am.

Berdyczewski's influence in the late 1890s was forceful enough to induce Ahad Ha-Am to prepare his reply to the "Nietzscheans among us" in the famous article "Shinui ha-arakhin." Characteristically, the argument he advanced seized upon one point in his adversary's position and turned it to his own advantage. We find in the article no sympathy for the yearning of a sizeable group of young writers for greater freedom from the restraints of the past. Ahad Ha-Am shrewdly adopted Nietzsche's concept of the *Übermensch* to the traditional Jewish concept of the chosen people and by substituting *morality* for the *vitality* Nietzsche sought, managed to suggest a possible Judaization of parts of Nietzsche's philosophy. He included Berdyczewski (who was conspicuously unnamed) in his condemnation of all those modern schools of Judaism that adopted foreign ideas without proper internal assimilation and thus abandoned the precious, inviolable tenet: the election of Israel. Taken by itself, his argument was certainly vulnerable; it was more a personal statement of belief, a position paper rather than a tightly reasoned treatise. But what captivated the reader of *Ha-Shilo'ah* in 1898 was less the argument itself than the Olympian tone in which it was conveyed. Even in Leon Simon's English translation, the voice speaking ex cathedra is unmistakable and some of the scorn is manifest.

Amid the confused Babel of voices that are heard in the prevailing chaos of modern Jewry, there is one angry, strident, revolutionary voice which gains the public ear occasionally, and leaves a most extraordinary impression. To most men it is quite unintelligible: they stand amazed for one moment— and go their way. A few there are who understand at least where the voice comes from, and these, because they understand so much, sorrowfully shake their heads and likewise go their way. But the young men, ever on the alert, ever receptive of new ideas, drink in the new gospel which this voice proclaims; they are thrilled by it, attracted by it, without inquiring very deeply what is its ultimate worth, or whether the idea which it contains is really a new truth, worth all this enthusiasm.[2]

In introducing this passage, I have called attention to its Olympian tone, a term readily perceptible to the English reader. My own conclusion, however, is that the tone is not Olympian, but Sinaitic or Mosaic. The confused Israelites are babbling, raucous "kolot shonim u-meshunim" (strange, bizarre voices); there is among them one obstreperous, angry "mashmia hadashot" (promulgator of new ideas); but above them all is the great prophet who, from the summits of his Sinai, perceives the truth and descends to deliver the true *Torah*. His name happens to be Ahad Ha-Am. The Mosaic self-image is evoked not only by the pervasive apodictic Hebrew style or the restricted, select group of activists grouped in the early 1890s under the name "Bnei Moshe" but even more revealingly in that veiled autobiographic essay entitled "Moshe" (1904). The Ahad Ha-Am–Berdyczewski polarity cannot be fully appreciated until we assess their varying attitudes towards the historic figure of Moses, and it is with a comparative assessment of these two images of Moses that we bring this essay to its conclusion.

Ahad Ha-Am, as is well known, depicted a Moses who was in effect the creation of the spirit of the Jewish people as it developed through history. The *archeological* Moses did not interest him. The *historical* Moses was essentially a prophetic figure, obsessed by the truth, extreme in his concept of absolute righteousness, at odds with the people whom it was his destiny to lead. Ahad Ha-Am's modern *midrashic* description of the career of Moses was that of a leader who embodied the spirit of his people who, on their part, could not perceive the justness of his inspiration and were, moreover, not educable. The essay is, interestingly, one of the least controlled of Ahad Ha-Am's creations: though it begins with the customary measured, editorial tone, it shifts in the middle to a rhapsodic portrayal of the prophet's moods, his exultation, and despondency. At one point we learn that the Jewish people were in effect the embodiment of Moses, whereas shortly afterwards we are told that Moses had to die because the people could not possibly fulfill his vision, something he could not endure. Throughout the lyrical effusion of the latter half of the essay—so unusual for him—one senses that the author's identification with his subject undercuts his authorial control; he often sounds like Berdyczewski at his most impulsive. The final passages are revealingly unclear for this master of clarity; at first he dwells upon the prophet's sense of failure; but then, after a striking interlude that refers enigmatically to a recent aberration in Jewish history, the prophet's optimism is restored. The recent antiprophetic aberration seems to have been Herzlian Zionism, never mentioned by name, but pointedly phrased as the desire: "le-hitaneg al hayyei ha-sha'ah, ke-khol ha-amim, u-le-vilti bakkesh min hahayyim yoter mi-mah she-yukhlu la-tet" (to enjoy daily life, like all the nations, and not to ask from life more than it can give).[3] Ahad Ha-Am was clearly talking of prophetic, not *halakhic* leadership, of an inalienable realization that he had been selected by history to show the Jewish people the way to the Promised Land. The historical Moses was very real and lived in Odessa.

Before turning to Berdyczewski's iconoclastic view of Moses, some biographical information is in order. Both Ahad Ha-Am and Berdyczewski were raised in traditional Hasidic homes in the Ukraine in the latter decades of the nineteenth century, though biographers tend to overlook the radical differences between their family backgrounds. Unfortunately, in contemporary popular accounts, all of Eastern Europe turns out to have been one undifferentiated shtetl, and all Hasidim are the same. The Ginsberg family was Hasidic but had no rabbinic pedigree, no yihus (family pedigree). Asher Ginsberg's father was a wealthy factor and businessman, first in Skvira then in a small village (Gopitshitza) until 1886 when as a consequence of the May Laws of 1882, his lease expired. Asher Ginsberg, to be sure, was provided with the finest private teachers available and kept away from secular influences as long as possible; he was also presented with a wife, with whom he lived all his life. Superficially, these were the basic stages in the life of the typical *maskil;* surprising in this case is the absence of a struggle, of the clash of generations one usually finds with Hebrew or Yiddish writers of the period. Amazing, too, is Asher Ginsberg's late development: he lived at home for the first thirty years of his life and could not bring himself to spend any length of time away at one of the major centers of learning. He has also told us next to nothing about his family.

Berdyczewski on the other hand, came from the heartland of Hasidism, from Medzibozh and Uman, and was the first male in thirteen generations of his father's family not to receive rabbinic ordination. His adolescence was marked by the spiritual and personal turbulence of the most radical of *maskilim:* religious reform and the death of God were real issues in his life. He broke with his father and his environment, and spent ten years as a destitute, wandering student in Odessa, Breslau, Berlin, and Berne. In brief, unlike the relative bourgeois stability of Asher Ginsberg, Berdyczewski stormed through the first thirty-five years of his life like a frenetic character from a Dostoyevski novel, hence his attraction for Brenner, who had a similar background. In sum, the Ahad Ha-Am-Berdyczewski polarity was not only a matter of ideology, but perhaps even more one of temperament and background.

Even before his encounter with the writings of Nietzsche, Berdyczewski was reading the most radical and heretical works. Of particular interest to his conception of Moses was a tract he read in the 1880s: *Korot Yisra'el ve-emunato* (The history and faith of Israel) by the *maskil* Shelomoh Hirsh of Tarnopol, which warned the reader on its title page that it was written "lefi shitat ha-minim" (according to the method of the heretics) and presented some of the higher critical theories prevalent then in Germany, asserting that the real revelation to Israel took place at Mount Gerizim and not at Sinai. These antinomian ideas, which surfaced in "Reshut ha-yahid be'ad ha-rabbim" and many other essays, were charged with Berdyczewski's typical pathos, because for him, *halakhic* authority was obviously a crucial issue; it had to be destroyed before one could conceive of building a healthy future. Ahad Ha-Am seems to have liberated himself from the *halakhic* burden before his first essay, "Lo zeh haderekh" and could talk glibly of such matters as "torah she-ba-lev" (The *Torah* of the heart). For Berdyczewski, this remained a burning issue all his life and he devoted much of his creative efforts between 1904 till his death in 1921 to a laborious scholarly attempt at parricide: father Moses had to be killed, in essays, footnotes, and quotations. His *Sinai and Gerizim* was a truly Promethean attempt to prove, from thousands of Jewish sources, that the original revelation was at Mount Gerizim and was marked by a life-giving love of nature, later suffocated by the Sinaitic *Torah* imposed upon the Israelites by Moses and his followers. The first distortion of the original revelation set the pattern for successive, even more drastic distortions, which eventuated in both physical and psychological exile. The great tragedies of Jewish history were not the destruction of the temples but rather the imposition of the myth of Sinai and the crippling moral code that it implied. If one were "to destroy in order to build," a seemingly Nietzschean phrase that appears in Berdyczewski's writings as early as 1892 and perhaps even five years earlier (the Hebrew terms are, incidentally, from Jeremiah), one must destroy the myth of the revelation at Sinai; one must, in effect, depose Moses.[4] For Berdyczewski, secularizing and co-opting Moses was not enough; parricide was required, not a trifling gesture for a Jew of his background and temperament. One can read Berdyczewski's essays, his fiction, and his scholarship as a lifelong struggle between the recognition that the deed must be done, and the recognition that the price to be paid for it in terms of oedipal guilt, was catastrophic.

By the end of the first decade of this century, the Ahad Ha-Am–Berdyczewski controversy was no longer a major issue; so much had happened since the debates of 1897–1899 that their ideological polarity seemed irrelevant, even trivial: Herzl, despite his diplomatic failures, had changed the entire political scene; the pogroms of Kishinev and Bialystok, coupled with the abortive Russian Revolution of 1905, had brought to prominence a new generation of leaders with a heightened sense of urgency; left-wing theoreticians were making their impact upon the most activistic elements. (Ahad Ha-Am published only about a dozen pieces between his move to London in 1907 and his death twenty years later; Berdyczewski continued to publish prodigiously, some two hundred items between 1907 and his death in 1921). By the late twenties, when the entire Hebrew literary establishment had moved to Palestine from Europe, the books of both had already become classics; their collected works were published and became the staple of the average well-stocked library; as abridged editions, they became items in the standard high-school curriculum. Their influence, to be sure, was more extensive and harder to trace. Chaim Weizmann, David Ben Gurion, Berl Katznelson, and Mordecai Kaplan turned to Ahad Ha-Am's writings for ideological support, and generations of high school teachers taught them as models of the essay style. Berdyczewski's impact was more diffuse and subtle, because the range of his creativity was not limited to the essay. He also never settled in or even visited Eretz Yisrael. Because Brenner so admired Berdyczewski, it is not surprising that any writer influenced by Brenner—and that included most serious Hebrew prose writers—found their way to Berdyczewsi's stories, including such disparate writers as S.Y. Agnon and Amos Oz. Furthermore, whenever you encounter an essentially iconoclastic position that seeks, wittingly or unwittingly, to maintain some connection with the Jewish historical experience in all its bewildering variety, look for echoes of Berdyczewski. Here, too, the range is wide: we have the "Canaanites" and Saul

Tchernichowsky on one side, and possibly Gershom Scholem on the other.

Even after our analysis of the historical and personal context of the congratulatory note to Berdyczewski, we still return to it with unanswered questions. Do we really know what Ahad Ha-Am wished to convey to him (to begin with, do we have the original letter or even the entire letter?). What did he really feel about Berdyczewski? One thing, however, is clear: the famous Ahad Ha-Am–Berdyczewski polarity was not merely a difference in ideological positions. Ahad Ha-Am's comment that Berdyczewski seemed to think that *'em haderekh* means "the main road" rather than "crossroad" speaks volumes.

NOTES

1 *Iggerot Ahad Ha'Am*, vol. 2 (Tel Aviv, 1957), 276.

2 The original essay appeared in *Ha-Shilo'ah* in 1889, vol. 4, n. 2, 97. It was called "Li-she'elot ha-yom" (Regarding the questions of the day), a generic title Ahad Ha-Am often employed for editorials. The essay was later renamed "Shinui ha-arakhin"(The transvaluation of values). See *Kol kitvei Ahad Ha-Am* (Jerusalem, 1947), 154. The translation is from *Selected Essays of Ahad Ha-Am,* trans. Leon Simon (Philadelphia, 1912), 217–241.

3 Ibid.

4 The phrase appears several times in the essay "Reshut hayahid…" (The individual and the community), which was first published in *Otzar ha-sifrut,* 4 (1892), 1–40, under the pseudonym "Yeruba'al." When revised for the collected works, the essay was altered drastically and, practically speaking, was not the same article.

✒ The Sacralization of Language in Bialik's Essays

After many centuries of poverty and degradation from without, and faith and hope for the mercy of heaven from within, a new idea with many implications has come into our generation: to bring faith and hope down to us from heaven and make them vital, active forces. To establish our hope on the earth and our faith in the Jewish people.

> Ahad Ha'Am, "Lo zeh aderekh" (This is not the way) 1899

The howl of jackals here and the dance of wild goats there: There is no Hebrew Literature. And meanwhile there have sprouted in our abandoned garden several superb after-growths, fresh talents. Three of them have recently blessed our young poetry with volumes of their poetry in each of which the juice of life bubbles and gushes like new wine in a jug and like blood boiling in live flesh, and each one establishes the sheheyanu blessing for himself.

> Bialik, "Shiratenu hatze'ira (Our young poetry) 1907

For one tutored in the "Great Tradition" of Modern Hebrew Literature, these two passages hardly need identification, for they are two of those rare, reassuring, even triumphal texts that are cultural events. In the case of the often desperate struggle on the part of a small group of passionate believers, they are texts that transcend the merely literary. Both were the first significant published prose statements of their authors—somewhat belatedly, incidentally, in their careers. The first passage resounds with the authority, lucidity, and syntactic balance of Ahad Ha'Am, ever striving to emulate the tone of the editorial column of the *London Times*, the voice of a self-assured empire in his days.

Even the title, "Lo ze haderekh" (This is not the way) speaks authority. The second reflects the lyrical genius of Bialik, with its figural richness, deft manipulation of heavy irony, its linguistic sensuality, so daring, as opposed to the stringent style of his putative mentor, Ahad Ha'Am. I say *putative* since more than a generation has passed since we were disabused of the simplistic notion that Bialik was the poetic incarnation of Ahad Ha'Am's theories of cultural renaissance, though this cliché still appears in popular and even scholarly articles written by scholars foreign to the field of modern Hebrew literature.

Though some contemporary critics hailed Bialik's "Shiratenu hatze'ira" (Our young poetry) as a "hymn to the Hebrew language," Ahad Ha'Am expressed his displeasure: the meaning of the statements, he felt, was obscured by the profusion of figural language. In his criticism, Ahad Ha'Am was being consistent both with his theories on language and the revival of Hebrew culture published in the early 1890s and his editorial policy of *HaShilo'ah*. Bialik had disagreed with him radically, but courteously, on both issues—a disagreement so well known that it needs no rehearsal here. What should be amplified somewhat is Ahad Ha'Am's aversion to figural language, in general, and its implications. And it is no accident that in registering his displeasure with the profusion of "meshalim" (parables/ metaphors) in the article (ostensibly a book review), he added that these "meshalim" might be proper to "derashot," (sermons) but certainly not to the expository essay. One feels in Ahad Ha'Am an instinctual abhorrence of metaphor, of what we in our post-Saussurian terminology would term any loosening of the natural bond between sign and referent or signifier and signified. It is precisely in that threatening area of looseness, of what Bialik calls tellingly "tenuatiut" (mobility) in his essay "Giluy vekhisuy balashon" (Revealing and concealing in language) written a decade later, that the poet felt most comfortable and creative. For him, this "tenuatiut," was the dynamic force of language, the secret of its redemptive power.

The diametrically opposed positions these two writers maintained on language suggest that we should read each in a different way—something rarely done. We should read Ahad Ha'Am primarily for his discursive analysis of problems, point after point, with only occasional digressions to examine his language except, for instance, to note its authoritative tone and abstinence from metaphor. Bialik, on the other hand, should be read through his metaphors and, only after they are examined and comprehended, through the ostensible argument of the essay. The Bialik essay should be read more as poetry than as prose.

The difference with Ahad Ha'Am's concept of language is not the only contextualizing feature of Bialik's essay worth noting here. In the former's statement quoted above, the opening gambit of "Lo zeh haderekh" of 1889, he posited in one sentence the cultural problematics of the generation and thus the agenda for subsequent generations: since we no longer believe in God, we are obliged—and free—to find a substitute matrix for our culture. If this problematic tortures and energizes so much of modern culture, it was particularly crucial in Judaism because of its hyper-valorization of the book and the language, Hebrew, which had been the linguistic vehicle of the religion for centuries. Ahad Ha'Am's substitute matrix was later considered nothing more than a paper bridge over an abyss by Berdyczewski and his colleagues, who relentlessly attacked the former's aristocratic, positivistic posture. Bialik's predicament was severe, as Dov Sadan has remarked: temperamentally a conservative and personally affiliated with Ahad Ha'Am, Bialik was first and foremost a poet, and his development in the late 1890s carried him into intense confrontations with the mysteries of the imagination and the mediation of language which went far beyond Ahad Ha'Am's rationalism.

Upon repeated readings of "Shiratenyu hatze'ira" one is impressed by two dominant features: (1) the rich figural language so much more germane to the genre of poetry than to that of the essay; (2) the obvious absence of Bialik himself from the history of modern Hebrew poetry, which he presents as the background of the three volumes of poetry he is supposedly reviewing, but never really does. Each feature generates a question: (1) What is the implication of this intense figurative language? (2) Where is Bialik, the leading poet of the generation, in this essay? The two questions should be answered together, but we shall address the second question, first. The question, "Where is Bialik?" requires some background. In post-Haskalah poetry or literature in general, Bialik enumerates four generations: (1) Mendele, Peretz, Frischmann; (2) Berdyczewski, Feuerberg; (3) Tchernichowski; (4) Shneour, Kahahn, Steinberg. The last three are, as mentioned, ostensibly the subject of the review and instead of analyzing them, Bialik characteristically sketches them in figural language or, as Werses has demonstrated, embodied allusions to specific lines in the poetry in the very fabric of his essay. Lachower, for one, claims that Bialik included himself in both the first and second group (though chronologically he belongs together with Tchernichowski). It is more plausible, however, that Bialik's seeming absence is really his omnipresence, his appropriation of the entire literary and linguistic experience described as his own and its internalization.

This appropriation is accomplished—wittingly or unwittingly—not only by the synoptic view, but by the pervasive prodigious use of figural language that expresses and evokes a unified, articulated consciousness. Had the essay been written in a more discursive, less figural style—similar to that created by Ahad Ha'Am—our reading of it would be more constricted to the bald communicative, rational level, but what Bialik gives us is actually a prose poem, more confessional than argued, couched in a style that diverts our attention from the declared theme of the essay to the language itself. Hardly a line fails to evoke memories of previous texts usually ingeniously manipulated to generate a tension between the original contextual meaning and that in the essay. In a sense, this persisting, inescapable demonstration of his power to manipulate the past and its texts, is Bialik's way of claiming his centrality in the development of the living idiom of modern Hebrew literature in which past texts are not a burden, but an aesthetic experience or asset. It is this idiom that has enabled the three poets under review, these alleged harbingers of a new age, to write their poetry free of the burden of the past. It is this implicit claim that Ahad Ha'Am obviously understood and resented.

Unlike Ahad Ha'Am, however, Bialik does not maintain the certainty of his opening statement throughout the essay. By the end of the essay, for instance, he questions whether these flowers are those of spring or of autumn, whether this sudden outburst of creative poetic energy will last. He entertains other doubts that are aptly conveyed by the ambiguities of the figural language, but would be either too obvious or even trite in straight discursive prose. While praising these young poets for having such individualistic voices, he seems to evince a wistful awareness that he has been too bound to the past. After two chapters of historical survey (the first taking us from the middle ages through the Haskalah; the second from the Haskalah to his own days) he digresses, as it were, to a consideration of what constitutes "national poetry" (shirah leumit). After characterizing the national poetry as a long, plaintive lament which elicits the most ambivalent emotions—both communal warmth and personal disgust, he justifies the fresh departure of these new poets by asserting: whatever embodies the creative, poetic, force of the nation and its individuals is national poetry, a lame compromise between Ahad Ha'Am and Berdyczewski, at best.

The final chapter of the essay is a hyperbolic paean to these young poets and, despite a faint tone of doubt, hails them as the hope of the future of the national literature who, by their poetic energy, make their predecessors obsolete, antiquated. One must ask at this point: Where does this leave Bialik who, too, felt his poetic energies waning in that year, after a period of intense creativity. Or, more broadly, how does one write Hebrew poetry given the problematic status of the language? The essay, we should never forget, is that not of a theoretician, but of a practicing poet who speaks from and of his experience in shaping this problematic language.

Similarly, *Gilui vekhisuy balashon* (Revealing and concealing in language), Bialik's central essay on language, is not really a theoretical or metaphysical essay as some would have it, but the pained confessions of a seasoned practitioner. The theoretical content is actually slight and derivative. Following the Romantic tradition, he posits language as a mode of expression rather than of communication (probable provenance: Schiller) and a flawed form of expression at that, since its prime function is the concealment from man's consciousness of the void which underlies his existence. Exactly what this void or abyss is is never specified, but given the pervasive Kabbalistic figures and the obsession with Creation, and the Romantic strain in Bialik, one gathers that it is the agonized sense of absence felt by one who no longer believes in an authenticating divinity, a sense of absence which never disturbed Ahad Ha'Am. What is of particular interest is the linguistic plenitude which Bialik exercises to describe or enact this sense of absence and the failure of language to penetrate to this void. The description is studded with phrases from Biblical and Kabbalistic texts, always altered in meaning by contextualization. Language, in addition, is often called a "kamea" (amulet) that man wears to ward off the terror and loneliness of the abyss. The abyss, on the other hand, is as attractive as it is terrifying and man attempts to rend the fabric of language in order to catch a glimpse of the abyss. Even more: the concluding paragraph of the essay asserts that there is a non-verbal language comprised of song, tears, and laughter which open, rather than close the barrier between the abyss and this world; they rise from the abyss and are the rising of the abyss. All creative activity, we are told, must echo these three non-verbal modes of expression. The abyss, then, is not the fecund Kabbalistic Ein-Sof, but it is also not a sterile void.

The key to an understanding of the abyss is to be found in the last chapter where Bialik indulges in an ecstatic description of the power and function of poetry. *"Ba'ale ha'aggadah* (the practitioners of aggadah) introduce into language at every opportunity—never ending mobility (tenuatiut), new combinations and associations….By this process there takes place, in the material of the language, exchanges of posts and locations: one mark, a change in the point of one iota, and the old word shines with a new light….The profane becomes sacred, and the sacred profane….Meanwhile, between the concealing, the void looms. And that is the secret of the great language of poetry." When one reaches this passage, one realizes that Bialik has been preparing us for this powerful statement on metaphor all along—for that is what this is. The poet who had expanded the metaphoric potentialities of the Hebrew language more than any predecessor in centuries, was keenly aware of the process, its enrichment of the human experience and the dangers of indeterminacy or at least, polysemeity.

Language is inadequate, frustrating, a "giluy" (revealing) rather than a "kisuy," (concealing), but it is all that we have to face the otherness of this world and the abyss underlying it. And in the hands of the poet, the master manipulator of figural language, it is the arena of creative activity fraught with ecstasy and danger, the poet's privileged precinct of spirituality. In the case of the Hebrew poet, as we can see so well in the essay, again really a prose poem, the intensely figural language must derive from originally religious texts, and even though certain words or entire phrases have been "secularized," the overall tenor of the linguistic medium, especially in the case of Bialik, resonates unavoidably with religiosity. When Bialik states that in this world of "tenuatiut," of the constant semantic shifting and seething of figural language "hol" (profane) becomes "kodesh," (sacred) and "kodesh, " hol," and that these categories are no longer distinguishable or meaningful, he speaks with the experience of the master of figural language.

The essay "Halakaha ve'Aggada" (Halakha and aggadah) written one year and one half later in 1916, also during the turbulent days of World War I in the last years of Czarist Russia, really betrays an obsession with the same themes, the expressive capacity of language—though many commentators have read it otherwise. The entire essay is a fascinating play between the two terms: the "halakha," the traditional legalistic world, and the "aggadah," the sphere of traditional, but non-legalistic, figurative language. Both the opening and closing passages of the essay are often quoted, but it is the closure which is widely remembered and, in my opinion, misinterpreted. The passage reads:

> Come, impose upon us commandments (mitzvot)!
> May we be given forms into which we pour our fluid and flaccid desire (to make) solid, enduring coins. We are thirsty for the substance of deeds.

Grant us a disposition for action greater than the utterance in life, and the disposition for halakha greater than the aggadah in literature.

We bend our necks. Where is the iron yoke? Why does the "mighty hand and the out-stretched arm" not come?

Now when Bialik declares: "Come, impose upon us commandments!" is he really suggesting that we should return to Volozhin, to the yeshiva world of his youth? Is Bialik a "baal teshuva" (religious repentant) in the normative, not the current debased sense of the word? Does he really call for a regime of halakhic mitzvot? Hardly! True, in a world of chaos— let us not forget the period—one yearns for order, stability, traditional norms. If, I would argue, Bialik simply wanted a return to Volozhin, to the religious life, he would not have been forced to spend most of his essay groping for a tentative definition of "halakha."

In his opening passage, he presents a series of standard definitional antinomies that are the equivalents of the binary opposition between halakha and aggadah, an opposition which he rejects in the next passage. Using technical vocabulary culled from medieval Jewish philosophy, he posits that the two are really two aspects of the same thing or different stages in a process. More interestingly, he equates the relationship of halakha to aggada with that of "the word" to "the thought" or "the event or object to the word." This is very close to the relationship between Sign and Referent or Signifier and Signified. Twice Bialik calls halakha "a symbol," once when talking of "hayim" i.e. human activity, the extra-literary world, and once when discussing literature. In both cases "symbol" means a concrete event or object which either embodies within it or has been endowed by history with meanings which transcend the narrow meaning of the statement or object. To demonstrate his point, he presents a discourse on the Jewish holidays and several Talmudic passages which contain "in kernel" broad concepts. The "halakah" he admires is not traditional religious behavior, but the idea of religious behavior viewed generically, "bikhlal," and imaginatively. When one studies the Mishnah, for instance, one should imagine walking among the ruins of an ancient city where the people whose lives are reflected in the Mishnah once lived.

When one approaches the last pages of the essay, it becomes clear that Bialik has been talking about literature—not religious behavior—all along. He attacks "art for art's sake," deplores the meager achievements of modern Hebrew literature (a tiresomely cliched stance), and the prevalent rejection (obviously by writers and intellectuals) of halakha as a *genre* and the preference of aggadah, a reversal of the traditional preference of pre-Haskala Rabbinical Judaism. This anemic, "non-Halakhic" literature is obviously the reflection of the "ethereal Judaism" that we have today, based on love ("hibah") of land, language, and literature, but lacking in textured substance, the substance from which great literature is made.

To understand Bialik's call for "hovah" (obligation) rather than "hibah" (love) in his closure as he reverts to a discussion of "life" rather than that of "literature" (it is curious to note that while Bialik labors to prove that halakha and aggadah are really not two separate categories, he fails to realize that he conceives of "life" as a text) we must pay close attention to his diction. What he is attacking is the notion of Hebrew, hence Zionist, nationalist activity and discourse. He derides those who speak in the name of "nationalism, revival, literature, creativity, Hebrew education, Hebrew thought, Hebrew labor"—all terms culled from the political discourse of the day. Bialik's thinking is concretized when he resorts to the historical example of the last prophets, Haggai and Zechariah, and following them, Ezra and his class, all halakhists. Like other writers of his time (Brenner, Agnon et al.), Bialik was tired of Zionist cant; he wanted constructive, concrete action. Notice the inevitable juxtaposition in the final passage cited above: Greater, concrete deeds in both life and literature. This statement immediately precedes the famous final cry: "We bend our necks? Where is the iron yoke?" This is not an appeal for a return to Volozhin, but a critique of the over-valorization of aggada, taken broadly, at the expense of halakha, also taken broadly. If language is to develop properly, Bialik argues in his essay "Hevle lashon" (The pangs of language) (1908), an earlier attack on Ahad Ha'am, it must comprehend all facets of life and must draw upon all forms of experience as expressed in the texts of the past. Bialik, who invested so much of his creative efforts in *Sefer HaAggada* and in the texts of medieval poetry, was impelled towards very clear goals. The creation of a new poetic idiom in Hebrew between the years 1898 and 1910, the expansion of the library of available Hebrew belletristic texts in subsequent years, was his "hergel asiya" (disposition for action) and "hergel halakha," (disposition for halakha), the "hova" (obligation) he bore with such contagious devotion. Prattle about the revival of Hebrew, etc. was, for him, cant, but the actual work was a "halakha," a "mitzvah." In his own, idiosyncratic way, the way of an innovative poet constantly working with the language of traditional Hebrew texts, Bialik sacralizes the languages and through it his own literary projects.

Bialik's sacralization of language can be seen most clearly in his brief essay on Moshe Hayyim Luzzatto, "HaBahur miPadova," (The boy from Padua) published upon the publication of S. Ginsburg's edition of Luzzatto's plays in 1927. He attributes, of course, the beginnings of modern Hebrew literature to Luzzatto: "He was the one who began in his days to teach the language itself to speak correctly." He calls him the "hatan bereshit" (the person privileged with the first aliyah in the annual Torah reading cycle) of a mighty period pregnant with the end of days and redemption." (Hatan bereshit shel tekufah kabirah harat aharit ugeulah.) He explains this creative energy by an exposition of Luzzatto's multi-faceted personality, particularly his mystical tendencies. "He, the last mystic among the Jews, was the first vessel for all the contradictions together." (Hu, ish hapardes ha'aharon beyisrael, hayah ha'keli harishon lekhol hahafakhim yahad.) Bialik reaches a pitch of ecstasy in the very middle of the essay by declaring "He was the redeemer and the Messiah!" (Hu hayah hago'el vehamashiah!). One must ask with some skepticism here: "The redeemer and the Messiah" (hago'el vehamashiah) of what? Certainly Bialik did not believe that Luzzatto was really the Messiah who came to redeem the world, but rather the redeemer of the Hebrew language, which, once redeemed and "purified" (he uses the root "thr"), becomes a proper linguistic vehicle for the expression of the inspired poet, a new revelation, for him, the only revelation.

It is difficult to read Bialik's panegyric to Luzzatto, the first *modern* Hebrew poet in a new tradition in which Bialik clearly saw himself as the crowning glory, without sensing his powerful identification with the earlier poet. The language of the essay is much more intensely figural and syntactically rhetorical than any of his essays. This identification suggests comparison with the one essay, "Moshe" (Moses) (1904), in which Ahad Ha'Am truly abandons his traditional, measured style and evokes the image of the biblical Moses, the great historical leader who led his people out of Egyptian bondage, an image with which he identifies so patently. Each writer identified with a redemptive figure in the tradition of Jewish history meaningful to him. With Ahad Ha'Am it was Jewish political leadership; with Bialik, it was Hebrew poetry.

⧟ The Archaeology of Self-Deception: A. B. Yehoshua's *Mar Mani*

Within weeks of its publication in the spring of 1990, A.B. Yehoshua's *Mar Mani* (Mr. Mani) was recognized as a major achievement of modern Hebrew fiction, one that demands and deserves scrupulous critical attention. In an uncanny consonance with its internal structure and thematic system, the book has had a peculiar pre-publication and post-publication life.[1] It had a remarkably privileged career as an embryo in the four years before its birth as a fully-formed book in May, 1990. A few months after its publication, as the wide audience of readers settled into discussions of the book, Iraq invaded Kuwait and the book's readers were distracted by more immediate concerns culminating in the nightmarish weeks in "sealed rooms" during the Scud attacks of January and February, 1991.

The opening paragraph of the novel sets a tone familiar to any adult sitting in a sealed room:

> HAGAR SHILOH: Born in 1962 in Mash'abei Sadeh, a kibbutz thirty kilometers south of Beersheba that was founded in 1949. Her parents, Roni and Ya'el Shiloh, first arrived there in 1956 in the course of their army service. Hagar's father Roni was killed on the last day of the Six Day Was as a reservist on the Golan Heights. As Hagar was five at the time, her claim to have clear memories of her father may well have been correct.[2]

With the exception of the birth date of the first speaker, Hagar Shiloh, time is measured by Israel's frequent wars: 1948, The War of Independence; 1956, the Suez War; 1967, The Six Day War. In the next paragraph we learn that the action of the first sihah (the novel is divided into five sections, each called a "sihah") takes place during the Lebanese War in 1982. In the epilogue of this first sihah, we learn of the Intifadah, 1987. That human time should be measured by violent eruptions that imply death rather than birth, ends rather than beginnings, raises serious questions about the nature and meaning of life lived in Israel, and, by implication, about Western Civilization since the Enlightenment. The statement that Hagar's claims "to have clear memories of her father may well have been correct" alludes to the truth claims of memory in general, both personal, family memory and collective, national memory. These questions have obsessed Yehoshua since the beginning of his career as a writer in 1957. With his felicitous fusion of individual and group behavior, he creates situations that enact the problematics of nationalism and sexuality at the same time. *Mar Mani* is thus the latest— and probably most profound—of the author's meditations on life lived in the new Jewish state. And though the underlying issues that inform the novel are deadly serious, the novelistic execution is a comic tour de force, with often ridiculous characters and hilarious scenes. Clearly, this is a work that will intrigue readers for many years and will raise a host of questions regarding the legitimacy of interpretation.

Precisely because this novel is so polythematic, so cleverly constructed, and its author so obviously enjoys challenging his reader's interpretive talents, the selection of a dominant theme as an opening gambit in the game of reading, can very well shape the interpretation.[3] The goal of this paper, then, is the development of an analysis of what I feel is the dominant, organizing theme of the novel, its obsession with the Sephardic identity.[4] To argue this point, I shall begin my discussion not with the novel itself, but with another document by Yehoshua that sheds light on this novel. Yehoshua has written occasional articles over the years and these have been collected to date in two volumes: *Bizekhut ha-normaliyut* (Between Right and Right) (1980) and *HaKir vehahar* (The Wall and The Mountain) (1989). The first, subtitled "Five Essays on Zionist Questions," constitutes a sustained argument regarding the Holocaust, exile, the neurosis of Judaism, Zionism, Israel. In each case, Yehoshua tries to derive lessons from history, draw distinctions and clarify definitions. (It is instructive to read *Mar Mani* against the rhetorical certainties of *Bizkhut ha-normaliyut*.) The second, a more random collection, bears the subtitle "The Extra-Literary Reality of the Writer in Israel" and treats a variety of political and social topics. Only in the last of these essays does he deal with the "Sephardic problem." The belatedness of this essay in Yehoshua's career—it was written in 1987—is, in itself revelatory, as is its genesis.

In the spring of 1987, Abraham b. Yehoshua wrote an introduction to a posthumous collection of his father's essays and crowned it with the patently cliched Proustean title: "Behipus ahar hazeman haSefaradi ha'avud," (In Search of the Lost Sephardic Time).[5] At first we might wonder why Yehoshua would use such a clichéd title, but as we progress in our reading of the essay, we notice that this title assumes, however retrospectively, a certain ambiguity. Yehoshua clearly knows that too often the Proustean enterprise is misrepresented by others as a superficial exercise in nostalgia, while for Proust—and Yehoshua—it is a struggle to formulate or question one's identity through fiction. The nostalgic recreation of an idyllic past is how his father's writings are characterized in this essay; his own fictions, he suggests, are charged by the Proustian struggle. The tenor of this dedicatory essay is qualified by this awareness, for what purports to be a eulogy on one author, Yaakov Yehoshua, turns out to be the introspective confession of another author, Abraham B. Yehoshua, his son. The eulogy becomes an elegy and the thematic nexus between the two modes of discourse involves writing and Sephardism.

The essay is a rich, revelatory document and deserves attention on its own merit; its becomes all the more compelling when we realize that its author, Abraham B. Yehoshua, wrote it while working on *Mar Mani*. A disjunctive note is struck in the very opening statement of this essay, ostensibly offering bibliographic background: "My father published his first book, *Yaldut Birushalayim* (Childhood in Jerusalem) when he reached his sixtieth year, three years after I published my first collection of stories, *Mot hazaken* (The Death of the Old Man)..."(228). And though this publication competition between father and son is treated in a subsequent paragraph as a family joke, the father-son relationship (or rather: the son-father relationship) is firmly established as the dominant theme that energizes the entire essay. Yehoshua asserts in a variety of ways that he is, but is not his father's son. In a sense, he is actually his father's father, not only the first to publish, but a more sophisticated writer who, unlike his father, comprehends and actualizes in his fictions the true import of Proust's search for time lost. He can actually claim: "in a certain sense I feel that he began writing because I became a writer and gave him the strength and emotional legitimation to search for his lost time" (228). The term "legitimation" is crucial here and appears later in the essay, again in the context of his father's writing about his childhood in the Sephardic community of Jerusalem: "He had to give legitimation to his works by painting the past in sweet colors, precisely because the remnants of that past world stood so poor, miserable, and distinct before his audience" (237). Consequently, while the father indulged in nostalgic, often charming but simplistic and journalistic re-creations, he regarded his son's writing with some "suspicion and distance" (335). What, after all could he make of the dense texture of his son's prose with its frustrated characters, bizarre situations, its webs of analogies, its ironies and satires, and its need to problematize everything. What, furthermore, would the father make of the son's obvious familiarity with a whole panoply of Freudian—and perhaps Lacanian—formulations?[6]

One finds here a revelatory parallel: the father turned from his scholarly preoccupation with the history of the Palestinian Arabs to the Sephardic community of his childhood after his own father's death in 1955; Abraham b. Yehoshua turned more openly in his fiction to Sephardic characters after his father's death in 1982. The original concept of *Mar Mani* seems to date from 1983–84; its third section was written about 1984–85 after which Yehoshua dropped it for two years to write his other "Sephardic" novel, *Molkho*; after that he returned to *Mar Mani*. Though no comparison is drawn in this essay between these two turnings, his father's and his own, it is surprising that Yehoshua, the most perceptive and introspective of Hebrew writers, is not aware of this. The "family romance," after all, is one of the recurring matrices in his fiction. In general, when one reads Yehoshua's fiction, one cannot escape the impression that the author has fully absorbed the basic Freudian structures, themes, and psychic operations. From his first short stories published in the early 1960s through *Mar Mani*, the Freudian modalities in Yehoshua's fiction are inescapable.

Thoroughly steeped in psychoanalytic modes of thinking about sentiments and behavior, he admits that he is using the occasion of the posthumous publication of his father's last volume of essays to deal with his own Sephardism:

> This introduction seems to begin to answer the question which hovers over my head all the time: Where is your Sephardism? And what about your Sephardism? Why is it that in your works one does not find the old Sephardim whom your father describes so well? Why do you look like such a typical Ashkenazi without the het or the 'ayin or the trilled resh? Why doesn't your being radiate nostalgia to your roots? In brief, they see me as a complete assimilator and I think they see in this a moral defect (230).

This impassioned rendition of the accusation motivates the heated protest of the article and shapes its flow. Without apologizing, Yehoshua argues: "I must explain at least to myself what were the reasons that caused me not to identify openly at first with the Sephardic signs of my family" (230). To defend his disinclination to identify, he cites parental influence: his mother, of Moroccan background, spoke French not Ladino, and identified primarily with the secular Zionist culture of the Yishuv, while his father, though a Sephardi, admired mostly the Ashkenazic intelligentsia of Jerusalem, the Jewish officials and Hebrew University professors. Both parents saw to it that he studied not at a Sephardi or religious gymnasia, but at the Hebrew Gymnasia of Rehaviah, the prestigious Ashkenzic High School in Jerusalem. Yehoshua's prime allegiance, therefore, was and is to secular Israeli culture, but he is introspective enough to realize, and honest enough to admit, that his Israelism allowed him an easy solution for the potential identity conflicts generated by the mass immigration of Oriental Jews in the early 1950s. Though he insists that he is a Sephardi, not an Oriental Jew, the dim association with these non-Ashkenazic Jews was problematic.

The self analysis is plausible but deftly avoids any mention of resentment he might harbor for possible slights he might have suffered for being a member of a degraded minority group, i.e. the Sephardim. We might find a convenient transference in his description of his grandfather's Turkish looking garb or his father's humiliation at the hands of the "Yekke" professors of the Hebrew University whom he admired so much. Perhaps the most insightful passage deals with the compartmentalization of his personality as he matured. Note the sustained metaphor of the drawer, the "megerah."

> My Sephardism began to enter a drawer, not too small and surely not locked, but a definite drawer, that you open from time to time, but mostly it is closed. And since then I have a feeling of a certain playing with double drawers which, afterwards, I believe, endowed a certain quality to my works that always sought to maintain a certain multi-drawer character which stimulated and still stimulates many interpretations of my works. That entire 'symbolic' or multilayered aspect derives to a degree from that type of life which had in it a certain element of concealment of a part of one's identity (232).

The central Hebrew phrase is all the more revelatory for in it we find a play of "megerah" with "gerah," i.e. the drawers stimulate not only the interpretations of his works, but the works themselves [ofi rav-megerati asher gera umegareh parshanim rabim shel yestsirotay]. Fully conscious of the unconscious (the closed drawers) and creativity, Yehoshua suggests as a fruitful topic for investigation the concealment of identity in the central Israeli authors, such as his friends and colleagues, Amoz Oz, Yitzhak Orpaz, and David Shütz. What is never clearly articulated in this essay, but should be obvious to the reader, is the fusion of three themes: Yehoshua's relationship to his father; his attitude to his Sephardism; and the type of fiction he produces. The ambivalences of the first and the second inform the multivalences and polyphonies of the third. We thus see in this essay of 1987 some of the same basic structures that shape *Mar Mani*, which was written at about the same time. Significantly, but understandably absent, is any reference to the world of the libido.

We should not be surprised to discover that *Mar Mani* is not a nostalgic, sentimental evocation of the Sephardic past or an embittered tirade against Ashkenazic humiliation of Sephardic or Oriental Jews, the two convenient sub-genres of Hebrew fiction situated in non-Ashkenazic milieux. Rather, it is a dazzlingly comical and agonized fictionalized evocation of the problematics of Israeli existence in the time of its composition, after the Lebanese war and at the beginning of the Intifada. Actual political events of the 1980s such as the Lebanese War, are referred to only in the first of the five sections of the novel, and then only as background to the story that takes place in Jerusalem. Like many other Israeli novels, it is motivated by a well-grounded conviction that something has gone awry in the realization of the Zionist dream.[7] Yehoshua, like other authors of such books, attempts to work out in his fiction the tale of this descent from Eden, which implies a search for the moment of error when things went wrong. The innocent assumption, of course, is that if you can identify the wrong turn, you can return to it and make the right turn. Yehoshua, however, is no innocent, and the best he can hope for as a writer of fiction is that he might gain a purchase on life.

You can detect this awareness of malaise in Yehoshua's early stories of the 1960s, and certainly in his three previous novels: *HaMeahev* (1976), *Gerushim meuharim* (1982), and *Molcho* (1987). In each, the themes of family disintegration, impotence, loss of purpose, and obsessive consumerism are the vehicles that convey this repeated drama of degeneration. In *Mar Mani* the author shifts the arena of his fiction from contemporary Israel backwards to selected moments in Jewish history of the past two centuries. The book, however, is by no means an historical novel; on the contrary, it is an anti-historical novel in that it is an attempt to undo Jewish historiography of the past century. But it is even more than that: it is the author's major challenge to the reader's understanding of himself. For once you think you have a fix on a possible interpretation, the author undermines your confidence in what you might know. (Yehoshua has learned this game well from his reading of Agnon.) Reading *Mar Mani* is thus an enlightening and humbling experience, for understanding the world of human existence is a much more difficult enterprise than you ever thought it was—and this has profound political and moral implications.

The book is patently structured to subvert our assumptions about the history of Zionism and thus about the nature of Israeli life—even more, of Jewish life at the end of this century. To begin with, it does not follow the traditional emplotment of the novel that narrates events in chronological order from past to present. On the contrary, the book shatters any possible sense of continuum by focusing on five moments presented in reverse chronological order, from present to past. Our normative comprehension of meaningful historical sequence is subverted; our reading is actually archaeological since we are led to dig from the present through successive layers to the lowest, initial level.[8] Even more: each of the five sections is written as a "sihah," a conversation between an individual speaker/narrator/confessor and a listener whose response to the speaker's words is not recorded in the text. These truncated dialogues— that are really neither monologue nor dialogue—are contextualized, each in a prologue and epilogue, by the stylistically dry and learned explanation of the putative editor of the volume. The reader is thus confronted in each of the five cases with a relentlessly challenging and engaging interpretive experience, for while you might understand quite clearly what each narrator is saying, you never know what you can believe since none of the five discrete narrators could be characterized as reliable. In each case, you don't have the words of the second person that might help you to establish and stabilize meaning.

Within and through this ebullient confusion of narrative, some order is suggested by a brilliantly wrought network of situations and images that recur, at times subtly transformed, in each "sihah." Still, during the actual reading of the text, no determinate structural meaning is conceivably possible. And this is precisely what the author, Yehoshua, is aiming at: the questioning—or deconstruction—of the myth of history that we have all accepted as a given. It is replaced by a vision of a world in which complex, real individuals with seething passions and bruised egos attempt, and usually fail, to arrive at a degree of personal fulfillment and self-understanding, all within historical circumstances beyond their control or comprehension. While one might hear post-structuralist or post-modernist echoes here, one can easily find a powerful precedent for this in the writings of M.Y. Berdyczewski (1865-1921) (and his "Canaanite" intellectual disciples).[9] It was Berdyczewski who argued that the modern period demands that the received narrative of Jewish history be subverted, that life must be understood and organized on the basis of individual, not collective needs; he also understood the steep human price one pays for doing so, a price that is exacted through man's erotic drives.

Since Yehoshua is not a historian but a novelist, the historiographic structures that he aims to disrupt are more properly understood as received narratives. These narratives, like the myths of less self-conscious generations, underlie and shape our view of the world and hence determine our political behavior. Clearly, if the society we live in is corrupt, one corrects it only by questioning its destructive underlying narratives; this is the moral message of the book—to the extent that it has one. In *Mar Mani*, each "sihah" focuses upon an event in the life of a different member of a putatively typical Sephardic family, the Mani family, beginning with the present and going backwards to the middle of the nineteenth century. Note the list of events and their locales:

1. The Kibbutz Mash'abei Sade in the Negev in 1982, the year of the Lebanese War, where a student, Hagar Shiloh, tells her mother about her strange three-day encounter in Jerusalem with the judge Gavriel Mani, the father of her boy-friend whose child she will bear.

2. Heraclion on the Isle of Crete, occupied by the Germans in 1944. There, a German soldier, Egon Brunner, relates to his adoptive mother his misadventures on the island and his experiences there with the Mani family that he hunts down.

3. Jerusalem, recently occupied by the British army in 1918, In it a young Jewish lawyer, Steven Ivar Hurwitz, serving in the British army, explains to his superior the case of political agitator, Yosef Mani, who is exiled to Crete.

4. Yelleni-Sad in southern Poland (near Oswienczin) in 1899. The young doctor, Ephraim Shapiro, reports to his father his experiences at the Third Zionist Congress and his subsequent trip to Jerusalem with his sister, Linka, who had an affair with a Dr. Moshe Mani, an obstetrician, who subsequently committed suicide in Beirut.

5. Athens, 1848. Avraham Mani reports to his elderly mentor, Rabbi Hananiah-Shabtai Hadayah, the intricate tale of his trip to

Jerusalem and the death there of his young son, (the first) Yosef Mani. To ensure the continuation of the Mani family, Avraham sleeps with his daughter-in-law, his son's young widow, Tamara.

When we roll the film backwards, we get: 1848, 1899, 1918, 1944, 1982. These historical markers are obvious, recognized stages or episodes in the construction of the Zionist narrative: the rise of nationalism in Europe, the Zionist Congresses, the Balfour Declaration, the Holocaust, and the Lebanese War. Significant by its absence is the most crucial date in the rise of modern Jewish nationalism: 1948, the establishment of Israel as a sovereign state, the epochal date without which one cannot conceive of the modern Jewish world—or the world of this novel. These events, however, are often mere echoes, at best, background radiation. The Hebrew reader, coming with his cultural suppositions, seeks some connection with this historical grid, and the author is playing with these suppositions. The problems of reading this novel are phenomenal. The implied author assumes that the implied reader knows a great deal about modern Jewish history. As for the "filling in of gaps" Wolfgang Iser has taught us every reading requires, Yehoshua clearly makes it very hard for us to know how to perform this basic act of reading.[10] On first reading—but only on first reading—what we seem to be given is an alternative history of Zionism, alternative to the Ashkenazic history that has brought the state of Israel to such a state of moral and political disrepair, most pointedly exemplified by the Lebanese War, the first arguably unmotivated Arab-Israeli war.

From Yehoshua's earlier stories and novels one might formulate the development of a coherent ideological position embedded in the literary texts but often more explicit, however fragmentary, in his essays. This hypothetical position can be summarized as follows:

1. Israeli society has failed to achieve the dreams of its Zionist founders and resembles in many ways other Western societies. The most corrosive and urgent problem of Israeli society is the Arab-Israeli conflict, more specifically, the Israeli-Palestinian conflict.
2. Israeli political behavior fails because its mentality is shaped by the Ashkenazic galut experience which made them neurotic, guilt-ridden, and inflexible and because they have adopted a European-styled nationalism, called Zionism, which is not indigenous to the area. The "old man" (in the story "Mot hazaken"), Classical Zionism, is long dead and there is no possibility to resurrect him.

3. Israeli society should therefore free itself from its Ashkenazic-Zionist and Exilic heritage that is no longer appropriate in the present state-oriented situation. Israelis should live a normal life in their state as do other nations. Perhaps an alternative, Sephardic Zionism would be more constructive.

While this ideological matrix can be found in the background of the novel and motivates some of its episodes, there are many episodes that certainly suggest the opposite, i.e. that the world of the Sephardim is not the world of psychic tranquility, not a viable alternative to the Eurocentric, Ashkenazic ethos. These somewhat simplistic ideological formulations are immensely complicated within the fictional situation where the subtlety of Yehoshua's literary imagination cannot tolerate easy solutions to social problems. Yehoshua the novelist is much more complex and interesting than Yehoshua the ideologue; the insights embedded in his fiction are much richer than those in his essays. I shall cite several passages as examples of this assertion.

Late in the novel, in the last "sihah," we learn that Yosef Mani (1826-48) was the first member of his family to settle in Jerusalem, an act of cardinal importance in a novel which attempts to formulate—or reformulate—the historical background to the Zionist state. Young Yosef travelled to Jerusalem from Istanbul in 1846 not out of any sense of religious yearning or nationalism, but simply to marry his young bride, Tamara, to whom he had been betrothed in Beirut the year before. The social picture we are given in that "sihah" is that of a world of Sephardic families residing in the major cities of the Eastern Mediterranean: Salonica, Istanbul, Beirut, Jerusalem, etc., and living out their lives essentially unaffected by the dynamic political winds sweeping Europe. Yosef, for instance, was born in Salonica, spent his youth at the home of his teacher, Rabbi Hananiah Shabtai Hadaya in Istanbul, is betrothed in Beirut to Tamara Valerio from Jerusalem. He is familiar with the streets of Istanbul and Jerusalem; he speaks Ladino, Turkish, French, English, and Arabic; in Jerusalem, he works as a courier and a guide for the British consulate. He is impressed by the similarity between the Arabs and the Jews and develops a theory that the Arabs "are Jews who still don't know they are Jews." In isolation, this statement may sound like a romantic, "Canaanite" manifesto.

To his precocity and seemingly comfortable cosmopolitanism there is, however, a dark side: he is a homosexual, a voyeur, and will not have sex with his wife and will not, therefore, father children. When he is killed, apparently by one of his Arab lovers, his father, Avraham Mani, who came to Jerusalem from Salonica to look into the doings of the young couple, sleeps with his daughter-in-law, Yosef's widow, Tamara, and she bears his child, Moshe, who appears in the fourth "sihah" where he attends the Third Zionist Congress, falls in love with Linka, a young Ashkenazi from Galicia, and commits suicide when he cannot have her. The complications of plot and narrative perspective are, to be sure far richer than this brief sketch would suggest, but it should be clear that if any reader imagines that Yehoshua is portraying a Sephardic world that is more *normal* and relaxed than the Ashkenazic world that created political Zionism and the State of Israel, he is sadly mistaken.

The fifth "sihah" is of particular interest not only because it is the historical point of departure, the bottom archaeological layer, as it were,— and therefore originary—but because only in this "sihah" is the narrator/confessor a member of the Mani family. This Mani, however, not only sleeps with his son's widowed wife, a mere child, but exploits the opportunity of his confession to his elderly, ailing teacher, the Hacham Hadayah and to his wife, Dona Flora, to take revenge against both of them for thwarting his desire. For though he had wanted to marry Dona Flora when she was still single, she spurned him and married the elderly rabbi with whom she would never have sexual relations. The last "sihah" is thus both a confession and an act of vengeance. And since this narrative, which focuses upon how the Mani family settled in Jerusalem, seethes with repeated instances of incest, both latent and manifest, and with abstinence from socially legitimated sexual relations, the reader must conclude that there is something rotten in the house of Mani as it first strikes roots in the sacred soil of Jerusalem in 1847–48.

The house of Mani, in fact, really doesn't exist, for just as Yehoshua reverses and fragments the stages of history to subvert any sense of historical continuity, he takes great pains to frustrate any conclusion that either the Manis or the reader might arrive at regarding family continuity, of that feeling of dynasty, which is one of the hallmarks of the Sephardic myth. The significant lineage in the novel starts with Avraham Mani, who began life in reduced economic circumstances, since his father had lost most of his considerable wealth after the Treaty of Vienna in 1815. We have already seen that his only son, and potential heir, was killed in Jerusalem in 1847 and that he (Avraham) fathered a second son, Moshe with his son Yosef's widow. Moshe, in turn, fathered a son, Yosef, whom he neglected because he devoted his energies to a maternity clinic that would be "open to all nations." Yosef, because of a childhood sexual trauma (which is described in detail), shunned all sexual relationships and his son, Ephraim, is really his step-son, perhaps not even the son of a Jewish father.[11] Ironically, it is this Mani who is killed by the Nazis off the coast of Crete in 1944. His son, the judge Gavriel Mani of the very first "sihah", is returned to Jerusalem as a child by his mother after World War II, but though he identifies freely with the Sephardic community of Jerusalem, he does not point to any noble ancestral lineage, because there simply isn't any. In a variety of ways, the novel is thus a devastating parody of the notion of Sephardic family purity, of the "Sephardi Tahor." In a very profound and personal—for Yehoshua—sense, Sephardic racialism is the prototype of destructive, modern nationalism.

This parody of a central, cherished Sephardic concept is so relentless that it becomes paradigmatic of all other forms of disabusement and deflation proffered in the novel; the self-understanding and the self-deception of the individual regarding his real identity is a powerful leitmotiv throughout. In each case, the author provides a plausible psychological reason for this self-deception, usually a compensation for lack of affection in childhood. Hagar Shiloh, the student narrator of the first "sihah," lost her father in childhood, no longer finds her place in the kibbutz, and has no real interests in her studies and thus seeks kinship with Gavriel Mani, the father of her boyfriend, Efraim, whose son she imagines she is carrying. Egon Brunner, the second narrator/confessor, a soldier in the German army in World War II, was deliberately conceived and reared as a surrogate for a "brother" who was killed in World War I. To compensate for his mediocrity and surrogacy, he manufactures an entire myth about the history of Western Civilization at Minos and the role of the German nation in it. The clumsy contrivances in his self-made ideology/identity/myth are painfully apparent. The first Ephraim Mani, killed off the coast of Crete, imagines that he can "nullify the Jew in him," that he can thus escape history and, perhaps, his death by the Nazis. Brought up without a mother by an adoptive father who shunned the physical presence of women, and perhaps aware that his real father was not a Jew, he believed he could escape his historical identity and destiny.

His father, Yosef, fashioned himself as a political theorist, even in his youth when he tried to persuade the Arabs in 1918 that they, like the Jews, should adopt a modern nationalism. In his old age, when he serves as a tourist guide on Crete, he peddles his amateurish theories about the dawn of civilization at Minos. We are shown, however, that he became a self-styled "homo politicus" as a result of his fear of sexuality and his neglect by his father, the obstetrician. Many more examples of self-deception as compensation for inadequacy, loneliness, or humiliation can be found throughout the novel. Just as individuals often do not understand themselves and the motives for their behavior in personal relationships, they fashion group-identifications (Sephardism, Zionism, Pacifism, Universalism, Nazism, Religion) which, they delude themselves to believe, will solve their problems. The reader is cautioned, not openly but in literary situations, that attempts at self-understanding and self-identity might result in nothing more than self-deception.

The literary genre which envisages human beings as posturers, imposters, or self-deceivers, is what we call comedy and Yehoshua is a quintessentially comic writer. The novel abounds in comic situations such as the meeting of Dr. Moshe Mani, the Levantine obstetrician, with Theodore Herzl at the Third Zionist Congress. The implausibility of the chance meeting and the pedestrian treatment of a high epic moment are the stuff of situational comedy. More pervasive, however, is the repeated parody of discourse in each "sihah." Throughout we are treated to a dazzling array of studied styles which, like all distinct styles, are by definition parodies of themselves. The prologue and epilogue of each "sihah" is rendered in the dry, factual style of an encyclopedia and arrogates to itself the posture of authoritativeness. Each narrator/confessor speaks in a characteristic style that is less a statement of individual personality than a rendering of self as stereotype. The narrators imagine themselves to be original persons, but they are closer to stock types than they would like to believe; here, too, the self-deception of self-imaging is operative. Hagar Shiloh, for instance, talks in the unadorned, breathless language of the average Israeli student recently mustered out of the army. Egon Brunner's diction, a Hebrew representation of his ponderous German, is a mannered, arrogant yet obsequious facade which covers the vacuousness and frustration of his mind. And Avraham Mani's insistent importuning is both fawning and manipulative, a parody of elegant Ladino locutions. The attentive reader, receptive to Yehoshua's parodic cues, cannot help smiling with the author at the unconscious posturing of the narrators; the reader must, in addition, be sensitized by the constant challenge to his interpretive powers, to the acute problematics of understanding what in human speech is true, what is deception—and what is self-deception.

Like other comic writers, Yehoshua can mock and parody his own passionately held positions. He is a Sephardi, but portrays Sephardim not as the idealized nobility of blood lineage, but as the paradigms of the human race with all its libidinous drives and foolish behavior. His *dovish* politician position is well known, but the solution to the Arab-Jewish conflict based on mutual understanding is espoused in the novel by the first Yosef Mani who is killed by an Arab and by the second Yosef Mani whose political theorizing is clearly portrayed by the author as a warped compensation for deep-set psychological problems. The native Israelism of Hagar Shiloh, the typical daughter of the kibbutz whose father was killed in one of Israel's wars, lives in adolescent fantasies, in a film of her own making, as it were. Yehoshua is a serious writer, but the author of *Mar Mani* makes light of the novelist's craft—with a degree of self-mockery—by flaunting his devices such as in the obviously archaeological stratification of the book. At times he seems to wink at us and quip, "You see, I've read Freud, too."

The literal-minded reader who represses the figurality of the text might find *Mar Mani* nihilistic since in it all values and postures are questioned, even ridiculed. This reading of the text, though superficial, is understandable since Yehoshua deals forcefully with such charged subjects as the failure of Zionist utopianism, the emptiness of Sephardic nostalgia, and the pervasiveness of sexual drives and fantasies. But, we should remember, that this author, despite his intense political engagement, is primarily a novelist, that his narratives are infinitely richer than his political pieces; his fiction is deftly controlled, analytically penetrating, and generously comical. The literary-minded reader, finally, should recognize the entailment of the comic genre, that in addition to or through the sheer entertainment of the book we are treated to the comic writer's perennial moral admonition: It is very difficult to distinguish between self-understanding and self-deception. The wise man should therefore approach such matters with both clarity of intellect and humility.

NOTES

1. The reception of *Mar Mani* is one of the most unusual in modern Hebrew literature and is, in itself, a topic worthy of investigation. Several points can be made at present. (1) The book attracted considerable favorable attention even before it was completed since a section of the third sihah was published in *Politika*, 5-6, March 1986 and shortly thereafter Dan Miron wrote a short piece on it in *HaOlam hazeh*. Both journals are essentially political rather than literary. (2) In 1987 Yehoshua published his first *Sephardic* novel, *Molkho*, which was widely reviewed in the press. The hiatus in the writing of *Mar Mani*, during which the author wrote *Molkho*, was duly noticed. (3) In April, 1988, the third sihah was performed as a monologue in the Municipal Theatre of the City of Haifa and was written up in *Bamah*, 2, April 30, 1988. (4) In the winter of 1988, a section of the fourth sihah of *Mar Mani* was published in *Moznayim*. (5) In the seven months after its publication, some thirty articles were published on the novel including Dan Miron's lengthy, seminal article ("Me'ahare kol mahshava mistateret mahshava

aheret," in *Siman Keriah* 21, 139–150) dealing with many of the salient features of the novel, its dazzling array of themes and devices that invite inexhaustible and successive interpretations. Despite the unusual length of the article, Miron was compelled to confess that he was only scratching the surface of this complex work. (6) In December, 1991, Nitzah Ben-Dov published a valuable collection of some 43 items dealing with the reception of the novel (Haifa University; Department of Hebrew and Comparative Literature).

2. *Mr. Mani*, translated by Hillel Halkin, (Doubleday: New York, 1992).

3. The notion of dominant theme is taken from the Russian Formalists and the narratologists who have refined their ideas. Throughout this essay I lean heavily upon M. Bakhtin's *The Dialogic Imagination* (1981): Frederic Jameson's *The Political Unconscious* (1981); Peter Brooks' *Reading for the Plot Design and Intention in Narrative* (1984); and George Mosse's *Nationalism and Sexuality* (1985).

4. The connection of *Mar Mani* with *Molkho* is obvious. Avraham Balaban has treated the relationship between the two books in a study called suggestively: *Mar Molkho* (HaKibbutz Hameuhad: Tel Aviv, 1992).

5. The father's collection of essays is called: *Yerushalayim haYeshanah ba'ayin uvalev* (Old Jerusalem In The Eye And The Heart). The paper was delivered in a somewhat abbreviated form about a year later at Bet Ticho in Jerusalem on the occasion of the actual publication of the volume of essays by Ya'akov Yehoshua. The introduction was later collected in the novelist's second volume of essays, *Hakir vehahar* (The Wall and the Mountain) (Jerusalem, 1989) and in the volume of Yaakov Yehoshua's essays. The citations here are from Avraham Yehoshua's collection of essays.

6. For an excellent treatment of the Freudian sophistication of Yehoshua, see Miron's *Siman Kriah* article, cited above, Malkah Shaked's "Mehomo libidus lehomo politicus," *Iton* 77, 129 (October 1990), 18–20. Avraham Balaban's *Mar Molkho*, and Anne Hoffman's "In the Womb of Culture: Reading A.B. Yehoshua's *Mar Mani*," in *Prooftexts*. Though these critics all point to an awareness of Freudian narrative situations and perceptions, I would push the argument a step further and state that the Freudian traces are so marked in *Mar Mani*—and elsewhere in Yehoshua's fiction—that it is inconceivable that he has not read certain of Freud's essays thoroughly. Yehoshua, furthermore, spent several years in Paris in the mid-1960s precisely when Lacan was a public figure in intellectual circles.

7. This sense of malaise often finds its most powerful expression in the creation of anti-hero types as documented in Gershon Shaked's synoptic article "Or vatzel ahdut veribuy," in *Alpayim* 4 (November 1991), 113–139.

8. Apart from its effectiveness as a narrative device, the archaeological process elicits other comparisons. The psychoanalytic process is often compared to the archaeological stripping away of layer after layer of historical experience in an attempt to uncover the origins of a psychic disorder. Sigmund Freud, furthermore, like many other nineteenth century intellectuals, was entranced by the science of archaeology and amassed during his life an enormous collection of Roman, Greek, and Egyptian artifacts.

9. Yehoshua's "Canaanism" deserves further study. Suffice to say at present that one finds very distinct echoes of "Canaanite" echoes in his essays, especially in *Bizekhut hanormaliyut*, and in *Mar Mani*, e.g. the ruminations of Egon Brunner in the second sihah concerning Minos. See Yaakov Shavit's *Me'ivri 'ad Kenaani* (Tel Aviv, 1984) and James S. Diamond's *Homeland or Holyland* (Bloomington, 1986). See also Anne

Hoffman's anaylsis of the "womb of culture" theme in her article, "The Womb of Culture: The Reading of *Mar Mani*," in *Prooftexts*.

10. Wolfgang Iser, *The Act of Reading*.

11. See Malkah Shaked and Anne Hoffman.

ANTI-SEMITISM AND HOLOCAUST

⮰ Refractions of the Blood Libel in Modern Literature

> The boy Leib felt that the stupid goyim were actuated by an easy and irreverent good nature, which paid less honor to the deity than did his father's solemn mercilessness; thus the concept of piety came to be bound up in his mind with that of cruelty, and the idea of the sacred and the spiritual with the sight and smell of spurting blood.

If this sentence were less intricate and self-conscious, one would readily identify the notions it conveys, especially in the original German, with the May 1, 1934 issue of *Der Stürmer* dedicated to the blood libel. The voice of this passage, however, resonates not with the strident tones of Julius Streicher, but with the carefully modulated syntax of one of this century's great writers whom we ordinarily identify as a bitter opponent of Nazism and the barbarity it implies: Thomas Mann.[1] This famous passage from *The Magic Mountain,* one of the monuments of high modernity, illustrates the intriguing intellectual complexity and the potential threat of the "blood libel" which is not a distant historical phenomenon associated with a few notorious medieval cases such as William of Norwich (1144), or of Hugh of Lincoln (1225), or Simon of Trent (1475). Rather it is one of the sad instances of the modern abuse of history and the manipulation of memory. There have been more instances of the blood libel recorded between 1870 and 1940 than at any other time in history—more, in fact, than all the previous recorded instances put together—enough, surely, to disabuse one of the naive optimism of the Enlightenment. Precisely because we might still be children of the Enlightenment, we find it difficult to imagine that the blood libel is so

317

frequent a phenomenon in post-Enlightenment years. An investigation of refractions of the blood libel in modern literature might provide a salutary corrective to our reluctance to realize that this pernicious accusation and all it implies is not restricted to the Middle Ages.

The quote describing Leib, i.e., Leo Naphta, is a case in point, for though it does not specifically mention the blood libel, though we might initially think that it has nothing to do with it, we are disabused several sentences later when we learn that Leib's father, Elie, a schochet (ritual slaughterer) was connected with "the unexplained death of two gentile boys, a popular uprising, a panic of rage—and Elie had died horribly, nailed crucifix-wise on the door of his burning house" (MM, 441). As Sander Gilman has noted: "the set of associations seems to be complete—the ritual slaughter, the physiognomy and the psyche of the Jew, the Jew who cures using blood, and the blood libel accusation, which ends in the imminent death of the Jew crucified as a Jew."[2]

Though the present essay intends to explore a series of modern literary responses to the blood libel, some prefatory remarks to the blood libel, in general, are in order. In his preface to a collection of essays entitled *The Blood Libel Legend: A Casebook in Anti-Semitic Folklore*, Alan Dundes draws several useful preliminary distinctions: "Ritual murder is a general term referring to any sacrificial killing—of either animal or human victim for some designated reason….Jewish ritual murder, in particular, refers to Jews killing Christians for some alleged religious reason. The blood libel is a subcategory of Jewish ritual murder. Not only is a Christian child killed—usually a small child, typically male—but the child's blood is supposedly utilized in some ritual context, e.g. to mix with the unleavened bread eaten at Passover."[3] (In many of the medieval cases, such as that of William of Norwich, so meticulously examined by Gavin Langmuir, the child was allegedly killed by crucifixion.)[4] The modifiers "allegedly" and "supposedly" bracket the substance of the "blood libel legend" which Dundes treats as a pernicious "legend" circulated by certain Christians from the twelfth century until most recent times. Developing the research of previous scholars, Dundes treats the legend as an example of "projective inversion": Christian accusations against Jews are a mechanism to deflect their guilt for drinking the blood and eating the body of Christ in the Eucharist; they blame the Jews for doing to a Christian child what they, in their ritual, do to Christ who, ironically, was a Jew. The intersection in one matrix of so many charged ideas is rare in history and contributes much to the durablity of the legend, despite the repeated refutation of any truth claims in it; it also explains both its virulence and capability to absorb new ideas, e.g., modern racist theories in the late nineteenth century.[5]

The basic accusation refers, by transference, to the inveterate accusation of deicide, for here the Christian child is a substitute for Christ. The charge of deicide, in turn, involved the passion of Christ and all that it implies for the ideological and emotional content of Christianity; and deicide, a one-time event, is rehearsed repeatedly in the Jews' refusal to embrace Christ as their savior. The utilization of the child's blood for the baking of the matzah invokes the Eucharist—by projective inversion, to use Dundes' phrase—and, on the other hand, Jewish dietary laws connected with both the preparation of meat, specifically kosher slaughtering of animals, and festival customs. The implied antagonism between the two religions engages deep Oedipal feelings in which the son who wishes to replace the father imagines that the father wants to kill him. The libel, argues Dundes, is thus an accusation of Christians against Jews in which the former subscribe to and propagate a myth that is meaningful to them since it was introduced into their collective memory through religious instruction: the crucifixion as celebrated in the Eucharist. For the Jewish victim of the accusation, the myth was puzzling and unintelligible. To begin with, Jews refrain from eating meat even slightly marred with blood, let alone unleavened bread mixed with blood. Indeed, the accusation that Jews killed Jesus while not unfamiliar to some Jews, was certainly not a central component of their faith (e.g., in *Toldot Yeshu*). And while the drinking of blood and the eating of flesh, first as mere symbolic act, but after the Fourth Lateran Council (1215) as transubstantiation, was a prevalent Christian experience, to a Jew it was bizarre and bordered on the cannibalistic.[6]

The generation of this legend, a product, according to Langmuir, of the High Middle Ages, has been well studied for several reasons: first, as it has been the source of considerable woe for Jews, it required refutation; second, modern scholars have been affected by the recurrence of this medieval accusation in their own times, even in their own cities; and, finally, it is an intriguing example of the intricate fashioning of powerful historical myths in which the associative functions of memory are so obvious. In the construction of the myth we find the full array of subconscious activities that Freud and his disciples examined, among them: transference, displacement, repression, and inversion.[7]

We begin our investigation not with a major novel or author, but with one of the most famous Jewish legends, the legend of the golem, most frequently associated with the Great Rabbi Loew of Prague

(c. 1520–1609). In the version most commonly disseminated today, Rabbi Loew, like many other Jews of his time, made a golem (automaton) out of clay to assist him with his housework during the week. Rabbi Loew's golem, however, had a special task: he was ordered by his master to defend the Jews of Prague who were being attacked by a frenzied mob enraged by rumors of a blood libel. The golem successfully defended the Jews from their enemies and peace was restored to the Jews of Prague.

Some thirty-five years ago Gershom Scholem observed in a footnote to his masterful essay on the "Idea of the Golem:"[8]

> This version [that connected with "Great Rabbi Loew" of Prague], in which the golem takes on the entirely new function of combating lies about ritual murder, is a free invention, written about 1909, and published in Hebrew by Judah Rosenberg (the author?), supposedly after an apocryphal "manuscript in the Library of Metz," under the title: *The Miraculous Deeds of Rabbi Loew and the Golem*. Language and content both show it to be the work of a Hasidic author with a kabbalistic education and (something unusual in his circles) novelistic leanings, written after the ritual murder trials of the eighteen-eighties and nineties. Chayim Bloch's book, *Der Prager Golem*, Berlin, 1910, is a German version of the text, whose wholly modern character escaped the deserving, but quite uncritical author.

Scholem's essay traces the idea of the golem from late antiquity until the modern period and demonstrates that until the early modern period the entire focus of attention was devoted to the creation of a golem from clay, a theurgic act paralleling God's creation of Adam. In the early modern period, the notion of the golem as house servant developed and made its way in German folktales, too, as in the collection of Jakob Grimm. In an extensive study of the life of Rabbi Judah (Yudel) Rosenberg (1859–1935) and his literary creations, Eli Yassif corroborates and refines Scholem's argument.[9] Yassif demonstrates that Rosenberg's seemingly pious tales generally reflect the political events and the popular literature of his times. Though a Hasidic rabbi, Rosenberg was obviously exposed to the currents of the modern period as he wandered from one rabbinic post to another, from Lodz to Warsaw, and finally to Canada (Toronto, 1913–1919, and Montreal, 1919–1935).

What makes Rosenberg's fabrication so interesting is that, confronted with the recurrence of blood libels in his days and the attendant pogroms in Eastern Europe, he imagined a narrative solution that combined a miracle, i.e., the fashioning of a golem that always requires prayer and incantation, and physical self-defense, a notion then spreading among the

Jewish masses of Eastern Europe. Prayer for deliverance was not sufficient for this Hasidic rabbi; he had to concoct a superhuman physical
force that would protect his helpless brethren. Ironically, when one visits Prague today, every tour book and guide relates with utter certainty
the wonderful tale of how Rabbi Loew of Prague fashioned a golem to
save the Jews from an attack by gentiles incited by a blood libel.

Upon analysis, Yudel Rosenberg's version of the golem story turns out
to be an enhancement of a traditional folktale so seamless that only a diachronic study of the tale and its versions could reveal that the Rosenberg
version is *modern*. Shifting from Rosenberg's pious tale to a clearly modern play affords us the opportunity of seeing the range of possible refractions of the blood libel in modern literature. Far more complex and
conscious of history is the best-known modern literary response to the
blood libel, Arnold Zweig's play, *Ritualmord in Ungarn* (1914) republished and finally staged in 1918 as *Die Sendung Samaels*, which takes as
its setting the Tisza Eszlar blood libel of 1880. Throughout the play, it is
obvious that Zweig is not interested in historical authenticity. The author
invents scenes in the heavenly court and alters several salient historical
facts: the victim, a young girl, is made five years older than the historical victim, Esther Solymosi, so that she can be a plausible object of the
lustful desires of the fictional murderer, a Hungarian nobleman; the
body, actually found in the river in Tisza Eszlar, is exhumed in the play;
and the protagonist, the young Moritz Scharf, a synagogue sexton's son,
commits suicide, whereas in reality he simply moved with his family to
Budapest after the trial.

The play concentrates not on the blood libel itself, but on the
psychology of the boy, Moritz, who is coerced into bearing false witness
against his father and the entire community. The coercion is painfully
revealing, since after torture and starvation fail to persuade the boy to
testify falsely that he saw a ritual murder in the synagogue, he succumbs
to blandishments, to promises of a comfortable life among the gentiles
after the trial. Zweig thus explores in his play the corrosive effect of
acceptance in gentile society upon the Jewish sense of self-confidence
and solidarity.[10] The boy's psychological struggles are dramatized: at first
he must resist torture, then succumbing to enticement, recite the
planted accusations, step by step, though he obviously doesn't believe
them; after the body is exhumed bearing no signs of a ritual slaughter,
he is accused of lying and, in desperation, commits suicide with the same
knife supposedly used for the ritual murder. Moritz Scharf is therefore

the true victim of the blood libel, ironically killed by his own hand, a new, grotesque twist to a traditional plot.

The play adds to the traditional account a passage reflecting the modern racist motifs of the blood libel, recited by a Hungarian nobleman: the Jews are diseased and infect the healthy gentiles; they are leeches and vampires sucking on good Hungarian blood; they carry a contagious skin infection. As Gilman has noted: "His speech contains quotes from the most infamous (and widely read) tractate on the blood libel, August Rohling's *Der Talmudjude* (1871)."[11] This racist position actually eliminates the possibility of integration in gentile society through conversion, the path suggested to Moritz, since the pollution of Jewish blood cannot be removed through an act of faith. Zweig does not develop this point, which would offer an intriguing complication to the plot.

Though Zweig's play dealt with the Tisza Eszlar affair that took place in 1887, five years before his birth, he wrote it under the impact of a contemporary blood libel, perhaps the most famous of all, the Beilis trial, conducted in Kiev between 1911 and 1913. Echoes of that trial turn up in a variety of literary works throughout the century, most notably, perhaps, in Bernard Malamud's *The Fixer*,[12] which I shall not treat in this essay. It was the Beilis trial that enabled me to solve a problem in Kafka's fiction and originally piqued my curiosity about reflexes to the blood libel in modern literature. Since I have elsewhere discussed the echoes of Beilis in Kafka's works of the period and this nexus is now generally recognized by Kafka scholars, I shall present here only the gist of my discovery and its implications for the theme of this conference.[13] In addition, I shall speculate on how this blood libel case was formative in Kafka's career as a creative writer. While Zweig's use of the historical example was open and programmatic, Kafka's was internalized, even repressed.

Dissatisfied with the standard explanations of Kafka's obsession with trials, judgments, verdicts, and guilt in the seminal stories written between 1912 and 1914, such as "The Judgment," "Metamorphosis," "The Penal Colony," and *The Trial*, I asked a relatively simple question: Was there, in Kafka's experience during this period, a real trial that could have deeply impressed a sensitive writer of Jewish origin, himself a lawyer by profession? The answer was readily available, though hitherto undetected. It was the famous trial of Mendel Beilis, who was imprisoned in Kiev on March 20, 1911, and finally brought to trial after two years on October 25–28, 1913. The Beilis affair was a traditional blood libel: Beilis was accused of killing a Christian child before Passover in order to use his blood in the preparation of matzah for the holiday. This particular blood libel shook the entire Jewish world because the Czarist government, first locally but then nationally, supported the prosecution and took advantage of the incident to fan the flames of anti-Semitism in Russia, resulting in familiar consequences, from scurrilous accusations to pogroms. Such official behavior was unexpected.

As in the Dreyfus affair some fifteen years earlier, echoes of the trial reached all corners of the world. Besides threatening the security of Jewish communities, the Beilis affair implanted in the mind of the observer a basic structure: a powerless man, innocent of any crime, stands alone before an awesome state tribunal whose sole aim is to convict him. For Kafka, the situation was a concrete example of one of his main obsessions: justice was perverted and subordinated to political or private interests that have nothing to do with the defendant, and which he cannot comprehend. The cynical perversion of the truth, the mass hysteria, the eruption of the repressed primitive instincts and fears—all called into question the validity of rational, enlightened consciousness, particularly as it manifested itself in language. The threat to the ideological assumptions and physical wellbeing of the Jewish bourgeoisie, including Kafka and all his friends, evoked both feelings of insecurity and demands by some Jewish leaders, e.g., the editors of the weekly *Selbstwehr,* that an aggressive defense be mounted. A young Jewish writer with Flaubertian artistic ideals would find his moral position severely challenged. A sensitive artist whose relationship with his father and authority in general was one of conflict might suffer a radical exacerbation of these personal tensions.

Was Kafka aware of the Beilis affair or trial? (It was called "Der Beiliss Prozess" in the German language press.) Both direct and indirect evidence attest to Kafka's awareness. Max Brod mentioned that Dora Dymant, Kafka's last love, burned at Kafka's request and before his very eyes several notebooks of works that were never published, including a story on Mendel Beilis. Though this story about Beilis might have been a late composition, it is impossible that Kafka did not read the newspapers or speak to his family or friends who, like the rest of Prague Jews, were obsessed by the Beilis affair. We now know that Kafka identified much more fully with the concerns of Prague Jewry than even Brod had led us to believe; Kafka, in fact, clearly knew much more about Jewish history than most, as attested by his diaries of 1911–1913.

The blood libel against Mendel Beilis was not the only one which affected Jews in Prague during Kafka's lifetime. The Tisza Eszlar affair of

1882–83 and the Hilsner Prozess of 1899–1901 were the most prominent of those which preceded the Beilis trial. One should add to these
the Dreyfus affair (1894–1899) which, though not a blood libel, evoked
both the emotions and rhetoric of the blood libel and was associated by
the editor of *Selbstwehr* with the Beilis affair. No literate Jew brought
up in a central European city at the turn of the century could be indifferent to these repeated threats to his sense of belonging and well-being.

When the Beilis affair erupted, it evoked all the blood libel experiences of Kafka's youth. *Selbstwehr,* the leading weekly journal of
Bohemian Jewry, which Kafka read religiously, was obsessed with the
affair from its very inception. In 1912 alone, twenty-two articles were
devoted to the Beilis trial, and by the end of the summer of 1913, the trial
had become so notorious that the name of the accused, Mendel Beilis,
was often omitted and the trial was simply called "Der Prozess," a generic
term with all the cosmic power of the generic titles of Kafka's stories.

No article in *Selbstwehr* sums up the emotions of the period as pointedly and passionately as the editorial of April 11, 1912, entitled "Kiew."
Close analysis of this impassioned plea—which Kafka certainly read—
reveals much more than the model of an innocent man falsely accused
by a malicious government. From the initial reference to the Dreyfus
affair to the closing mention of *Galut* (Exile), the framework is that of
Jewish alienation in a hostile gentile world; the assumptions and much
of the language are those of classical Zionism, as befits such a newspaper, the organ of Bohemian Zionists. Just as Jewish history is viewed as
a continuum, the Jewish people are assumed to be an indivisible whole
with a common destiny and strong obligations of solidarity. When
Dreyfus or Beilis is accused, all Jews are in the prisoner's dock and,
though some might resist this conclusion, the facts are inescapable. The
editor, Weltsch, calls attention to the perversion of language in the cunning and malicious accusation and to the concomitant threat to all Jews.
When primitive instincts are unleashed, the truth is subverted in the
name of truth. The three words—*verurteilt, Urteil,* and *Prozess*—that
appear together in the second paragraph of the editorial, are key terms
in Kafka's vocabulary; likewise, many of the basic notions are familiar to
any reader of his fiction.

While it would be rash to argue that Kafka would not have written
his trial-and-guilt-ridden stories of 1912–1914 if the Beilis affair had not
occurred, it is highly improbable that he was unaffected by the claims
the trial made upon his allegiance or the moral lesson it suggested. It is
also possible that the prolonged pressures of the Beilis affair served as a

creative crisis which enabled him to universalize and objectify certain emotions which had hitherto seemed private, even solipsistic.

My speculations here are directed at answering two questions: (1) Are elements of the Beilis affair reflected in Kafka's stories? (2) How might these elements fuse with other concerns which obsessed Kafka during this period? Since they overlap, both questions will be answered jointly. Strong support for my contention that the Beilis trial made a definite impression on Kafka can be found in the short story *"Das Urteil"* (The Judgment), written in a single night (September 22–23, 1912); in it, Kafka broke away from the norms of the fragmentary sketch. The story begins with the hero, Georg Bendemann, ruminating about his upcoming marriage to Frieda Brandenfeld, and his hesitation to write about it to his friend who works in St. Petersburg. In the course of the story there is a clash between father and son, and after a violent quarrel the father condemns his son to death by drowning. Bound by this injunction, Georg jumps off the bridge near their apartment.

Despite the various illuminating interpretations of the story, several mysteries remain. Why, for instance, does the friend wander about in Russia, a land described as foreign and hostile? Why was the son sentenced to such an unnatural death by drowning? And what is the implication of the apparently unspecific title *"Das Urteil"*?

In reference to the friend in Russia, it is worth citing a paragraph from the story itself. Georg Bendemann quarrels with his father over several things, but especially over the friend in Russia. At one point the father doubts the very existence of the friend. Georg protests by saying that the friend paid them a visit and in fact recounted several bizarre stories which interested the father: "He used to tell us the most incredible stories of the Russian Revolution. For instance, when he was on a business trip to Kiev and ran into a riot, and saw a priest on a balcony who cut a broad cross in blood on the palm of his hand and held the hand up and appealed to the mob." On various occasions in the story the friend is referred to as the friend from St. Petersburg since that is where he resides. However, in the passage just quoted, the priest's appeal to the mob occurs in Kiev, the city where Beilis was tried. The reference to the revolution (apparently that of 1905) could be a convenient ploy. A page later, when the father intensifies his attack on Georg, the latter conjures up the image of his friend with searing intensity: "His friend in St. Petersburg, whom his father suddenly knew too well, touched his imagination as never before. Lost in the vastness of Russia, he saw him. At the door of an empty, plundered warehouse, he saw him. Among the wreckage of his showcases, the slashed remnants of his wares, the falling gas brackets, he was just standing up. Why did he have to go so far away!" Though these two passages are among the most dramatic in the story, their position in a plot dealing with the relationship between a father and his son is not patently motivated. The motivation becomes clear when Georg's orderly and rational world falls apart, and he is beset by images associated with disintegration and terror: Kiev, blatant religious provocations, pogroms, and the like. It is highly plausible that the image of Beilis, the wretched accused, played a role in the formation of the character of the friend in Russia as well as in the various passages cited above. Since this friend is linked psychologically to the hero, and probably to the author, Franz Kafka, the reference to a barbaric environment across the border cannot be without significance.

It is also plausible that the hero's death by drowning was prompted by the "Who by water" of the *U'netaneh Tokef* prayer of the Jewish High Holy Days. This central prayer declares that between Rosh Hashanah (New Year's Day) and Yom Kippur (The Day of Atonement) the fate of each person is determined. In the list of possible rewards and punishments, e.g., who shall live and who shall die, we find the resounding words: "who [dies] by fire and who by water, who by sword and who by beasts, etc." The passage in the *mahzor* is comprised of the same notions which inform Kafka's *"Das Urteil"*: an omniscient judge; the trembling of the soul; the consciousness of guilt; the recognition of God's eternal judgment (or the father's judgment); man's inability to hide from him, though he might attempt to do so; the begging for forgiveness; every man's sinfulness; and the resounding final word, *Urteil*. In the prayer book commonly used in many German language liberal synagogues of the period that Kafka probably knew, the translation for the Hebrew term, *gezar hadin* (roughly: judgment) is not *Geschick* or *Verhängnis* as in other *Mahzorim*, but *Urteil*.

The noun *Urteil* and the verbs derived from it *(beurteilen, verurteilen)* with all the sundry implications deriving therefrom (such as the sentence, a trial, the judge's relationship to the accused and that of the accused to the judge) comprise the focus of Kafka's thoughts during the decisive years 1912–1915, during which he wrote "The Judgment," "The Metamorphosis," "The Stoker," "The Penal Colony," and *The Trial*. These terms occur in many contexts in all of these works. Years later, when Kafka wrote the *"Brief an den Vater"* (1919), he was still under the influence of this complex of terms and ideas: "But for me as a child everything you called out at me was positively a heavenly commandment

(Himmelsgebot), I never forgot it, it remained for me the most impor- tant means of forming a judgment *(Beurteilung)* of the world, above all of forming a judgment *(Beurteilung)* of you yourself, and there you failed entirely." The father represents God, His reprimands and command- ments; by these commandments the son assessed the world and by this assessment the father failed abjectly. In general, the terms for judgment and guilt recur as leitmotiv throughout the "Letter," and evoke associa- tions with Kafka's obsessions with these terms between 1912 and 1914.

The similarities in terminology and ambiance among the four items we have adduced—the Beilis affair, *"Das Urteil,"* the *U'netaneh Tokef* prayer of the Day of Atonement, and Kafka's description of his relations with his father—yield a structural pattern worth noting. In all these cases, the relationship between the protagonist and the person, God or society he must deal with, is not one of mutuality and fulfillment but of contention, of *Urteil.* The figures are adversaries in the legal sense. This structure, like all structures, is obviously reductionist and simplistic, but it helps us uncover Kafka's unique linguistic and situational strategies. Kafka's use of the trial atmosphere is the opposite of that in the standard detective story. In the latter, the trial scene pulls things together and brings the narrative to a plausible solution. In Kafka, the trial atmosphere tears the fabric of normal existence asunder and offers a solution that is either ambiguous or puzzling. For Kafka, the structural energy of *Urteil* both unifies his fiction and tears it apart.

Identification with the Beilis trial could have provided Kafka with the necessary validation of his own feelings of insecurity and loneliness, an expansion and objectification of his Oedipal torment, corroboration of his doubts about the validity and viability of language, and a moral justification for the bewildering dialectic between self-corrosive guilt and subtle imposture that marks so many of his protagonists. While we have investigated the traces of the Beilis trial in "The Judgment," we have not done so in other stories of the same period. "The Penal Colony," for in- stance, with its setting on an island so reminiscent of Dreyfus's "Devil's Island" invites such study since it focuses upon an avowedly archaic, grotesque process of brutal punishment, the lacerating inscription of the crime on the body of the putative transgressor.

Our first three examples—Rosenberg, Zweig, and Kafka—differ from each other markedly, but they are similar in their limited vision of the blood libel. They consider it the source of contemporary threats to indi- vidual Jews or the Jewish people, but they are not concerned with the historical origins of this repeated accusation, or its implication for the definition of the traditional Jewish position in European society, the position of the other. This otherness has several peculiar characteristics: it is rooted in the ideological stance of Christianity towards Judaism which it is supposed to have superseded; the other, though usually excluded, still lived within the majority Christian culture; too frequently, the tangible results for the other have been disastrous. The last examples that we shall explore, Lamed Shapiro's "Vaise khale" (White Chale) of 1918 and S. Y. Agnon's "HaAdonit veharokhel" (The Lady and the Peddler) of 1943, go beyond the immediate impact of the blood libel—incited pogrom or insecurities to an investigation of the historical origins and entailments of the blood libel. In a profound sense, the two stories are major documents in the series of literary articulations of Jewish responses to historical catastrophes.

The articulation of responses to catastrophe is so well known a genre in Jewish literature of all periods that it needs no introduction or elaboration here. The genre, in its historic manifestations, was described admirably by both Mintz and Roskies, each in his own way.[14] In this essay I do not intend to add another chapter to this story. I will rather argue at this point that the genre reaches its ultimate definition when the author can both thematize and ironize the otherness that animates the hostility that leads to the hatred of the Jew and his final destruction. I will suggest, in the light of these stories, that totalizing destruction—that which we call the Holocaust—is the final solution to a problem created by the sense of otherness inherent in both the situation and the notion of Western Civilization, which since the Middle Ages has been defined as Christian. Both stories are narrative responses to violent and massive destruction of Jewish communities in World War I and World War II, respectively. (And while Roskies has dealt with these two stories among many others in chapter six of his book, *Against the Apocalypse,* my treatment, I believe, takes the argument in a different direction.)

Both stories are built on the assumption that the murderous desires or intentions directed towards the Jews derives from the teachings of the Church: the antagonists in both stories, Shapiro's peasant soldier Vasily and Agnon's Lady, believe that the Jews killed Christ and this is the fundamental discriminator between the characters, the generator of otherness. This theme is, of course, far from exceptional or interesting. And though the thematizing of the passion of Christ or identifying him as a Jew in fiction written by and primarily for Jews was new in the first decade of this century (cf. early Manger and Leivick, or Sholem Asch), it was hardly revolutionary by 1918, let alone 1943, the dates of our two stories.

What is interesting is the narrative exploitation of the Eucharist theme with all its rich possibilities. If the Jewish author can perceive that these accusations are projections of the guilt that the Christian feels for the violence he himself commits—the drinking of Christ's blood and the eating of his flesh—the irony of the transference opens up infinite narrative possibilities. The Christian who accuses the Jew of such heinous acts, which delineate and seal his otherness, is actually indulging in cannibalism: the Christian is eating God and drinking his blood, while blaming the Jew for doing so. And if that very God was, historically, a Jew, the mirroring of ironies can be endless. In the following pages I will demonstrate how these two authors exploit the narrative possibilities of this ironic complex, how they use history to create fiction, and how they use fiction to explain history.

In order to prevent or minimize the slippage in reader's response from an awareness that we are reading fiction, to an easy belief that we are reading history, we should note that both authors were far from the scenes of slaughter, or impending slaughter that they describe. While there is little danger of this slippage in the case of Agnon who endows his story with clear folkloristic markings, it frequently happens in the case of Shapiro whose pogrom stories, especially "Vaise khale," are cited as historical records. Shapiro, living in America (New York, Chicago, Los Angeles) in 1917–18, was as removed from the scene of his story, the Eastern Front in World War I, as was Agnon, living in Jerusalem in 1943, from the events of the Holocaust in Europe.

"Vaise khale" was by no means Shapiro's first pogrom story, but it is the most appropriate for our investigation since in it Shapiro narrates much—but not all—of what goes on from the point of view of the slow-witted gentile peasant-soldier, Vasily. We are asked to perceive reality, partly as Vasily did and partly as the narrator did. The narrator's voice embraces and interprets Vasily's consciousness and also tells us facts about the war that Vasily could not have known or understood. We are, furthermore, told time and again that Vasily was confused and inarticulate; the gap between his consciousness and that of the narrator is designed to constitute a major theme of the story. Shapiro uses this gap both to project how he imagines a Vasily-like person perceives Jews and to concretize the vast difference between Vasily and the Jews he observes.

Woven through the texture of the violence of war and pogrom, a texture that Shapiro fashions with horror mixed with strange fascination, is the Christ-seller theme, a variation of the Christ-killer theme. The narrator first presents Vasily's (Vasya's) perception of Jews in an oft-quoted sentence:

> In the town there were Jews—people who wore strange dress, sat in stores, ate white Chalah, and had sold Christ. This last point was not quite clear: who was Christ, why did the Jews sell him, who bought him, and for what purpose. (p. 325)[15]

In the four-part definition of the Jews, the first two items, the strangeness and the shopkeeping, seem to fit together, but the last two, the white Chalah and the selling of Christ, do not—that is, until the shocking last chapter of the story. Vasily, always portrayed as a being on the threshold between barbarism and humanity, makes these rudimentary associations that will ultimately reveal the narrative goals of the narrator. The otherness of the Jews puzzles Vasily and is usually connected with the selling or killing of Christ:

> There were a few Jews in his regiment—Jews who had sold Christ—but in their army uniforms and without white chalah they looked almost like everybody else. (326)

As the army retreats and blame must be assigned for human failure, Vasily learns of a new attribute of the Jews: "Someone said that all this was the fault of the Jews. Again the Jews! They sold Christ, they eat white Chalah, and on top of it all they are to blame for everything" (328). Vasily is capable of rudimentary associations, but of no analysis or irony. The otherness of the Jew in this military/political situation is one of the few things that is clear to him even though his heroic comrade in arms, Nokhem (Nahum) Rachek, is a Jew. Vasily cannot grasp the irony in Nokhem's sardonic reference to a propaganda leaflet accusing the Jews of treason and which Vasily, of course, cannot read: "It says I'm a traitor, see? Like that German we caught and shot. See?" (328).

The echoes of the Jew as Judas—or as Dreyfus—are clear to the competent reader. And when Rachek is killed, Vasily blames the "Jews...traitors..., sold Christ...traded him away for a song" (329). When civil war breaks out and the Jewish soldiers are sent away—perhaps to be executed—"Everyone felt freer and more comfortable, and although there were several nationalities represented among them, they were all of one mind about it: the alien was no longer in their midst" (330). Though the two warring sides in the civil war are never named, the reader and Vasily know that the other side is identified with "the Jewish Government"—

the Bolsheviks. To rally the anti-revolutionary forces, "the priests with icons and crosses in their hands led processions through villages, devoutly and enthusiastically blessing the people, and the slogan was, 'the Jewish Government'" (331). By the time the reader finishes the first six of the seven chapters of the story, the Jew-Christian dichotomy is firmly fixed in his mind as it is seen dimly by Vasily and lucidly by the narrator.

As Vasily breaks into the Jewish home during a pogrom, the hitherto puzzling association between "eating white Chalah" and selling–or killing—Christ becomes brutally clear. We learn not only the logic of the narrative connection, but that there is a subterranean logic of thematic connections—elective affinities, if you will—beneath the logic of the ordinary discourse of civilized, western society. And it is the logic of this pre-civilized discourse that gives the story its coherence. As Vasily tore off the dress of the young Jewish woman, "His eyes were dazzled, almost blinded. Half a breast, a beautiful shoulder, a full round hip—everything dazzling white and soft like white *chalah*. Damn it—these Jews are *made* of white *chalah*!" (333).

In his confusion of hunger, rage, and lust, Vasily does not merely rape the woman. He disfigures her by tearing her flesh, twisting her nose, seizing and strangling her neck. Maddened by the blood on the white, chalah-like flesh, he bites into it and sucks her blood.

> White chalah has the taste of a firm juicy orange. Warm and hot, and the more one sucks it the more burning the thirst. Sharp and thick, and strangely spiced. (333)

Vasily becomes a vampire or a cannibal and Shapiro has his narrator draw away from him again completely at this point as he moves us slowly towards a mythic closure. "In a circle, in a circle, the juices of life went from body to body, from the first to the second, from the second to the first—in a circle." The violent, primal circulating of the juices of life, of blood and semen, preface a broader scene of devastation composed ironically—or sardonically—of allusions to biblical sacrifice.

> Pillars of smoke and pillars of flame rose to the sky from the entire city. Beautiful was the fire on the great altar. The cries of the victims—long, drawn-out, endless cries—were sweet in the ears of the god as eternal as the Eternal God. And the tender parts, the thighs and the breasts, were the portion of the priest. (333)

The god who is eternal as the Eternal God of the Jewish religion—
or of all monotheistic religions—is the god of violence, of primitive lust
and hatred. Here, too, my reading of the story differs significantly from
that of Roskies and A. Nowersztern who argue that this ending implies
the failure of the Judaeo-Christian tradition.[16] Coming, as it does, after
repeated references to Christian hostility towards the Jews that is based
on a radical otherness, the final passage cannot refer to the failure of the
Judaeo-Christian tradition "to humanize the animal instinct in man," as
Roskies would have it. I would argue that it is Christianity alone "that
stands condemned in this parting tableau of desecration," but not for the
reason that Roskies and Nowersztern give. Roskies contends that "Vasily,
acting on a central article of Christian faith, has inverted the priestly rite
of substituting the Host for the flesh of Christ." But this is a misinterpretation of the Eucharist: the priest transforms the Host into the flesh
of Christ, but completes the act by consuming that Host which is now
the flesh of Christ. Shapiro understands this well. Vasily is not inverting
the role of the priest; he is simply acting it out. He is—in a very literal,
and literary way—realizing it. Shapiro invests this passage, and the whole
story, with an ironic perspective on the Eucharist which, expanded from
its ritual, ecclesiastical situation, becomes the basic behavior pattern of
Christians vis-à-vis the Jews. Again, the irony is compounded because
the Jews are accused of selling Christ, betraying him and the state, political betrayal being a modern version of selling or killing Christ, of drinking the blood of Christ or his children-surrogates, of desecration of the
Host, or the poisoning of wells.

The story is political and religious at once since the political situation
is religiously motivated as far as the Jews are concerned. The alienation
of the Jew from western civilization persisted even after the legal elimi-
nation of the ghetto, because for that civilization, which is predominantly
Christian, the Jew must be "the other" and "the other" must be rejected,
pilloried, and even finally eliminated. The celebration of the passion of
Christ in the Mass is thus not the celebration of transcendent love and
saving grace that it was to Sholem Asch, for instance, but the institution-
alizing arid aestheticizing of primitive bestiality, for Vasily's bestiality in
this story is inseparable from his Christianity. The eternal god of violence
is akin to, if not identical with, the God celebrated in the Eucharist. Finally, while the story is set in a war that was the expression of unbridled
national loyalties, Shapiro presents the passions aroused as deriving ultimately from deep-rooted religious sentiments.

The harsh, expressionistic tones of "White Chalah" give way when we shift to the lulling cadences of Agnon's "HaAdonit veharokhel" (The Lady and the Peddler) of 1943.[17] We leave the epic sweep of battle and pogrom for an intimate tale about a lady and a peddler. But the horror of the situation is no less evident by the time the reader reaches the middle of the story and realizes what the stakes are, in this uneven relationship. While the ambiance and modality of the story are Jewish, the plot is situated in a world ruled by Christians. Again, the deeper meaning of the seemingly simple "Once upon a time" narrative is conveyed by two narrative devices—the disparity between two consciousnesses, here the narrator's and the peddler's; and the latent imagery taken from the blood libel.

The characters, both nameless for the first five pages of this twelve-page story, differ in religion and status. The Jewish peddler making his rounds in a nameless, timeless forest ingratiates himself with a Christian noblewoman who lives alone in what appears to be a hunting lodge. He shrugs off her initial insults ("What do you want, Jew?"), fawns disgustingly, but makes his way into her house and, after some time, into her bed. His naïveté is designed to shock the reader throughout the story: at the first encounter he sells her a hunting knife that we surmise she might use to try to kill him; as the story ends, he sets out again to make his peddler's rounds as if nothing had happened.

The measured pace of the tale quickens as he begins to forget who he was and this manifests itself first in food: he ate meat roasted in butter and fowl she slaughtered with her own hands. Precisely when we are told twice that they begin to forget the differences between them, we learn for the first time that:

> there was one thing that made him wonder: in all these days he never saw her eat or drink. At first he had thought that it was beneath her to eat with him. After he got used to her and forgot that she was a lady and he, a Jew, he wondered more and more. (174)

Here, too, for the first time we learn their names: she is Helene and he is Joseph—names with many hermeneutic possibilities. When he presses her to tell him what she eats she says openly: "Human blood I drink and human flesh I eat." After kissing him, she continues: "I never imagined that the flesh of a Jew is so sweet. Kiss me, my raven. Kiss me, my eagle" (174). As he kissed her he thought: "These are poetical expressions, such as noblewomen are wont to use when they give pleasure to their husbands." At this revelatory juncture the author takes pains to alert us to the difference between literal and figural usages of language that inform the whole story. Her confession about drinking human blood and eating human flesh coupled with her delight at the taste of the flesh of a Jew coalesce to evoke associations with the Eucharist and consequently the blood libel.

After that unsettling scene, we read of the disintegration of their re-lationship. Added to the mystery of her not eating is the fate of her many husbands. When asked where they are, she tells Joseph, the peddler, the literal truth which he fails to understand completely. "She stroked her belly and said: Perhaps some of them are here" (176). As he is struck dumb, she pursues the subject:

> "My darling, do you believe in God?" He sighed and said: "Is it possible not to believe in God?" Said she to him: "Aren't you a Jew?" He sighed and said: "Yes, I am a Jew." Said she: "But the Jews don't believe in God, for if they had believed in him, they would not have killed him." (176)

The juxtaposition of the eating theme with the Christ-killing theme should be familiar to us by now. The peddler, of course, does not make this connection. The Christ-as-Jew theme is evoked as Joseph awakes abruptly from a terrifying dream:

> It seemed to him that a knife had been plunged into his heart—no, not into his heart but into that stone marker,—no, not into that stone marker, but into another marker, made of ice, as the Christians make it by the rivers on their holy day. (178)

As the peddler's terror increased, he moved from the bedroom to a storeroom. He wants to recite the traditional Jewish bedtime prayers, "but as a crucifix was hanging on the wall, he left the house to pray out-side" (179). His walk outside apparently saved his life since, returning to the room, he noticed that his bedclothes "were punctured all over. No doubt these holes were made by somebody, but for what purpose? He looked around and saw a spot of blood" (180). The punctures evoke descriptions of the desecration of the Host or of the ritual murders in blood libels. He found Helene apparently wounded on the ground, the hunting knife he had sold her in her hand. As he lifts her tenderly to the bed,

> She suddenly raised herself up and dug her teeth into his throat and began to bite and suck. Then she pushed him away and cried, "Phew, how cold you are! Your blood is not blood, but ice water. (180)

The reference to the statue of Christ in Joseph's nightmare should be evident. Joseph, the peddler, tried to nurse Helene, but could not help her since she could not eat, "for she had unlearned the art of eating as humans eat" (181). When she died, the frozen earth refused to receive her and he had to bury her coffin under the snow on the roof. But there, too, burial is impossible. In a biblical ending, the birds come, peck at the coffin, break it, and "divide among themselves the corpse of the lady."

Helene dies, but Joseph returns to his peddler's rounds. The narrator leaves us to conclude that the gap between the Jewish peddler and the Christian lady is unbridgeable since their diets are different: he eats the food humans eat, but she eats human flesh and drinks human blood.

Neither Shapiro nor Agnon suggest that Christians generally eat Jewish flesh or suck Jewish blood. Their employment of the blood libel theme is much more profound: they both capture the irony involved in the Christian accusation of the Jews for ritual murder and understand it as the paradigmatic projection of Christianity's guilt and desires, its imaginary construction of those they dominate. The Jew is the other within western Christian civilization who can be blamed for selling goods rather than producing them, lustily eating strange food, betrayal of the state, and pollution of the sources of life. In each of these two stories we find both a keen comprehension of this complex and its subtle, ironic thematization.

The analysis of stories like these reaffirms the creative subjectivity of the author, a species of creative humanity that has been erased from too much literary criticism over the past generation. For what we find in the examples presented above is evidence of the author utilizing history in order to create fiction and, in turn, utilizing fiction in order to comment upon history. The movement from history to fiction and back is dialectical, and we, the readers, are all the richer for it. The blood libel matrix, as we have seen, attracts or even generates a variety of associated themes, and is thus a convenient matrix for literary composition. This matrix can also be transfigured in a variety of protean ways and still maintain its basic characteristics.

We shall conclude, as we began, with a brief example of the transfigurational potential of the matrix. In Philip Roth's most recent book, *Operation Shylock,* the antic narrator recounts a variety of experiences and presents a new ideology known as Diasporism. In one of his hilarious monologues (157), he praises the father of the new Diasporist movement, the song-writer Irving Berlin:[18]

People ask where I got the idea. Well, I got it listening to the radio. The radio was playing "Easter Parade," and I thought, "But this is Jewish genius on a par with the Ten Commandments." God gave Moses the Ten Commandments and then He gave to Irving Berlin "Easter Parade" and "White Christmas." The two holidays that celebrate the divinity of Christ—the divinity that's at the heart of the Jewish rejection of Christianity—and what does Irving Berlin brilliantly do? He de-Christs them both! Easter he turns into a fashion show and Christmas into a holiday about snow. Gone is the gore and the murder of Christ—down with the crucifix and up with the bonnet! *He turns their religion into schlock.* But nicely! Nicely! So nicely the goyim don't even know what hit 'em. They love it. *Everybody* loves it. The Jews especially. Jews loathe Jesus. People always tell me Jesus is Jewish. I never believe them. It's like when people used to tell me that Cary Grant was Jewish. Bullshit. Jews don't want to hear about Jesus. And can you blame them? So—Bing Crosby replaces Jesus as the beloved Son of God, and the Jews, the *Jews*, go around whistling about Easter! And is that so disgraceful a means of defusing the enmity of centuries? Is anyone really dishonored by this? If schlockifled Christianity is Christianity cleansed of Jew hatred, then three cheers for schlock. If supplanting Jesus Christ with snow can enable my people to cozy up to Christmas, then let it snow, let it snow, let it snow! Do you see my point?

Well, we do see his point. In one manic outburst, Roth tangles together several themes: traditional antagonism between the religions; the schlockification of American life—including its religions; the frequently offered accusations against Jews who are so prominent in the entertainment industry for "schlockifying", i.e. de-Christing, i.e. polluting the dominant religion; the natural Jewish desire to ward off the hatred of the gentiles. Beneath the transformed themes and the comic inversions we can detect the clear outlines of the blood libel, which go to prove that in the right hands, even the blood libel can be transformed into hilarious comedy.

NOTES

1. Thomas Mann, *The Magic Mountain*, trans. H. T. Lowe-Porter (New York: Knopf, 1982), 440–441.

2. Sander Gilman, "Kafka Wept," in *Modernity/Modernism* I, no. 1 (1994): 17–37. Gilman is primarily interested in demonstrating that "at the turn of the century the categories of race, illness, and gender were the organizing principles of the construction of the world"—a sweeping thesis, to be sure, but helpful in suggesting that the blood libel is a matrical event or myth, the intersection of several powerful, easily related themes, clustering a set of associations even in the premodern period when it might not have involved the specific categories of race, illness, and gender that intrigue Gilman.

3. Alan Dundes, "The Ritual Murder or Blood Libel Legend: A Case Study of Anti-Semitic Victimization through Projective Inversion," in *The Blood Libel Legend,* ed. Alan Dundes, (Madison: University of Wisconsin Press, 1991).

4. Gavin I. Langmuir, "Thomas of Monmouth: Detector of Ritual Murders," in *The Blood Libel Legend,* ed. Alan Dundes (Madison: University of Wisconsin Press, 1991).

5. New light has been shed on the origins of the blood libel by the article of Israel J. Yuval, "Vengeance and Curse: Blood and Accusation" (Hebrew) *Zion* 8 (1993): 33–90.

6. For a classic medieval source of the Jewish perception of the Eucharist as cannibalism, see David Berger, *The Jewish-Christian Debate in the High Middle Ages* (Philadelphia: Jewish Publication Society, 1979).

7. The two well-known refractions of the blood libel in premodern literature, Chaucer's "The Prioress's Tale" and Shakespeare's *Merchant of Venice,* however interesting, are beyond the scope of this essay, as is Heine's *Rabbi of Bacherach* based on the blood libel at Oberwesel in 1287.

8. Gershon Scholem, *On the Kabbalah and Its Symbolism* (New York: Schocken, 1969), 189 n. i.

9. Eli Yassif, *Yehudah Yudel Rosenberg: The Golem of Prague and Other Tales of Wonder* (Jerusalem: Bialik Institute, 1991).

10. In this sense Zweig takes a position opposed to Ahad Ha'Am's famous essay of 1892, "Small Consolation" *(Hatsi nehama),* which argues that the blood libel has one great advantage for the modern Jew who, bereft of his traditional sense of identity, often believes in the accusations that anti-Semites bring against him: the blood libel is so patently absurd, that even a modern, rootless Jew could not believe that this anti-Semitic canard is true. It is highly likely that Zweig knew this essay either in translation or through Martin Buber, his mentor at this period.

11. Gilman, "Kafka Wept."

12. Bernard Malamud, *The Fixer* (New York: Penguin Press, 1962). Malamud's novel is clearly the most famous fictional treatment of the blood libel and shall be treated at length in a book-length study of this phenomenon. Contemporaneous with the actual trial, the Yiddish writer Shalom Aleichem (Rabinowitz) composed a novel in serials which followed the developments of the trial. The novel, *Der Blutige Shpas,* was published in English as *The Bloody Hoax,* trans. Aliza Shevrin (Bloomington: Indiana University Press, 1991).

13. Arnold J. Band, "Kafka and the Beilis Affair," *Comparative Literature* 32, no. 2. (Spring, 1980), 168–183.

14. Alan Mintz, *Hurban: Responses to Catastrophes in Hebrew Literature* (New York: Columbia University Press, 1984); David Roskies, *Against the Apocalypse* (Cambridge, Mass.: Harvard University Press, 1984).

15. Lamed Shapiro, "White Chale," in *A Treasury of Yiddish Stories,* ed. Irving Howe and Eliezer Greenberg (New York: Holt, Rinehart, and Winston, 1969).

16. Roskies, *Against the Apocalypse*; Abraham Nowersztern, "The Pogrom Theme in the Works of Lamed Shapiro" (Yiddish), *Di goldene keyt* 108 (1981), 112–116, 142–145.

17. S. Y. Agnon, "The Lady and the Peddler," *Twenty-One Stories* (New York: Schocken, 1970).

18. Philip Roth, *Operation Shylock: A Confession* (New York: Simon and Schuster, 1993).

Scholarship as Lamentation: Shalom Spiegel on "The Binding of Isaac"

As we approach the end of this turbulent century, it has become clear that American Jewry had come of age in the decade following World War II. A sense of belonging and confidence was engendered by a variety of factors: massive personal participation in the war effort in which specific Jewish interests, the defeat of Nazism, were roughly congruent with American goals; the prosperity on the home front that ended the Depression; the G.I. Bill after the war. The destruction of European Jewry and the ensuing refugee problem, generated an inchoate, yet palpable consciousness of community primacy and responsibility. The struggle for the creation of Israel, its victories on the battlefield, converted most American Jews to Zionism, producing both pride and problems of identity. All these well-documented currents serve as the context of our investigation of one of the most remarkable and influential intellectual achievements of American Jewish scholarship, Shalom Spiegel's book length essay, first published in Hebrew as "MeAggadot haAkedah," in 1950, then translated by Judah Goldin as *The Last Trial* in 1967.[1]

Though the English edition has gone through several editions (most recently republished in 1993), this essay is far from a household word; while most Jewish Studies scholars and rabbis admire it, relatively few American Jews have ever heard of it. Marginal to the articulated mainstream concerns of American Jewry, it is a foundational text of Jewish Studies in the second half of this century. I will argue, however, that this seminal scholarly work raises a host of intriguing questions about historical consciousness and identity that should occupy any serious student of the American Jewish scene. For in its marginality, it helps define and critique the center. These questions, in turn, affect the discussion of American Jewish culture and its prospects.

I deliberately call Spiegel's magnificent study an essay since it is energized by frequent subjective interventions, usually tactfully embedded in the text that has all the trappings of a scholarly article. It was first published in the Jubilee Volume (Festschrift) celebrating the 70th birthday of Alexander Marx (1878–1953), the historian and bibliographer who, starting in 1903, built the impressive Judaica collection of the Jewish Theological Seminary in New York. Unlike most jubilee volumes that are little more than exercises in academic collegiality, this Festschrift constitutes an eloquent historical document for several reasons. First, this was truly an assemblage of the best scholars of the generation, forty-five in number. Second, this was the first significant Judaica Festschrift to appear after the war in which so many major centers of Jewish life were destroyed.[2] It was a powerful affirmation of historical continuity for it represented a continuation of the modern scholarly effort to recuperate, reconstruct, and *reinvent* the Jewish past. It was published in America, under the joint sponsorship of the Jewish Theological Seminary, the American Academy for Jewish Research, (both in New York) and the Jewish Publication Society (Philadelphia). Third, issued in two hefty volumes, the larger in English, the smaller in Hebrew, it offers a panorama of the world of Jewish scholarship in the decade that I mentioned above. There are, for instance, no participants from the European continent, except for two from Budapest. No one from Berlin, or Breslau, or Warsaw, or Vilna. There were nine contributors from Jerusalem, all except one professors at the Hebrew University. The list is indeed impressive: for example: among the *Ss* in the Hebrew volume we find: Gershom Scholem [the towering scholar of Jewish mysticism], Moshe Shwabe [a classicist, most recently remembered as the teacher of Emmanuel Levinas in Kovno], Isaiah Sonne [the editor of many medieval texts], and Shalom Spiegel.[3]

Since the articles were ordered alphabetically, Spiegel's is the last in the Hebrew volume. One might argue that there is nothing significant in Spiegel's writing his article in Hebrew since of the 23 Hebrew articles, only nine were written by scholars from Jerusalem. And yet, Spiegel's case is different since he really represented something new in the world of Jewish scholarship. Born in Romania (1899), he received most of his education in Vienna at both the University and the

Hebräische Paedagogium. An active member of HaShomer HaTzair, he was strongly influenced by Nietzsche, Freud, and fresh memories of the ravages of World War I. He made aliyah in 1923 and taught in the Reali Gymnasium in Haifa until 1929 when he was invited to teach Medieval Hebrew poetry at the Jewish Theological Seminary in New York. At the Seminary, Spiegel taught Bible, Medieval Poetry, and Midrash, all with a dazzling literary flair. For him, a consummate master of Hebrew texts of all periods, the Hebrew language was not only the Holy Tongue, but the vehicle of Jewish cultural creativity throughout all history. For him, as for Ahad HaAm whose cultural Zionism he embodied, Hebrew was the necessary and inalienable identity marker of the Jew in history.

His first book published in English (1930), significantly, dealt not with medieval poetry or midrashim, but with modern literature. It was a collection of perceptive, elegantly written essays, revealingly entitled: *Hebrew Reborn*, the first (to my knowledge) book in English on modern Hebrew literature. In that volume, it is clear that one of Spiegel's favorite writers is the poet, Saul Tchernichowski, a very *Nietzschean* poet, who wrote in 1902 a lengthy ballad, called "Baruch miMagentza" (Baruch of Mayence), which deals with a Jew who, crazed by suffering in the time of the First Crusade, sets fire to a convent and riots through the streets as the flames spread through his entire city. Tchernichowski obviously found the dynamism of this act of revenge attractive since it heralded the new, modern Jew, freed from the shackles of traditional passivity. Spiegel's admiration for the poem was profound but, by 1930, a bit tempered.

The essay before us is ostensibly a lengthy (66 pages in Hebrew; 135 pages in English) explanatory preface to a hitherto unpublished medieval Hebrew lamentation (104 lines) written by Rabbi Ephraim ben Jacob of Bonn sometime after the Second Crusade of 1146 during which the poet, only thirteen years old, took refuge with his family in the fortress of Wolkenburg that was under the protection of the bishop of Cologne. But this preliminary statement is more than a scholarly introduction. As Judah Goldin, who translated the essay into English says in his superb introduction:

> We may say, then, that by means of his discussion Spiegel is teaching us how to read the poem and by implication any Hebrew poem, how to recover the ensemble of ideas and images inhabiting the poet's consciousness and sub-consciousness as he wrote his lines.(ix)

Goldin suggests, furthermore, that Spiegel is driven not by the poem itself, but by his years of reflection on this great theme, the Binding of

Isaac, the Akedah, which has haunted the Jewish imagination since its first inscription in Genesis 22. The story of the gracious and merciful God who commands his favorite, Abraham, to offer up as a sacrifice his beloved son, Isaac, "is sure to produce not only fear and trembling [as it does in Kierkegaard] but prolonged reflection."(x) The story as a sample of narrative art was chosen by no less a critic than Erich Auerbach when he wanted to find a text to compare with "the genius of the Homeric style" in the first chapter of his monumental study of representation, *Mimesis.*

In the ten chapters of this essay Spiegel examines a variety of themes generated over the centuries by this cardinal narrative in Jewish, Christian, Muslim, and pagan sources. Most of the prooftexts he adduces are from the midrashic literature covering over a millennium, from the second through the thirteenth centuries C.E. One of the episodes that Rabbi Ephraim emphasizes is based on a tradition that Isaac was not only actually slaughtered by Abraham—a tradition which, in itself, counters the literal sense of the Biblical narrative—but that he was slaughtered twice. Spiegel, in fact, spends all of chapter ten on this issue. Goldin uses this issue to present a striking exposition of midrashic method:

> ...the Scriptures are not only a record of the past but a prophecy, a fore-shadowing and foretelling, of what will come to pass. And if that is the case, text and personal experience are not two autonomous domains. On the contrary, they are reciprocally enlightening: even as the immediate event helps make the age-old sacred text intelligible, so in turn the text reveals the fundamental significance of the recent event or experience. (xvi)

Goldin demonstrates how Spiegel's enormous erudition and exquisite literary sensitivity enable him to capture the nuances of this fragmentary literature, to synthesize coherent clusters of ideas, all in a supple Hebrew style that appropriates, in each instance, the peculiar style of the text under scrutiny.

And yet, for all of Goldin's elegant emulation of Spiegel's admirable qualities, he notes, but fails to exploit one of the most interesting aspects of this essay. Goldin is awed by Spiegel's ability to listen to the voices and silences of the midrashic text, especially by his discovery in a text: "...the fury and outcry of historical factuality—a discovery, incidentally, that brings him (and thus us too) to the recognition of a fundamental methodological principle of research." (xxii) Goldin, however, does not apply that very principle to Spiegel's text, he does not ask himself what "fury and outcry of historical factuality" can be discovered in Spiegel's text that has appropriated all the resonances and density of the classical sources. When we treat Spiegel's text as a modern midrash, when we interrogate his text to discover what historical contexts might be embedded in it, we discover new, rich meanings that transcend by far the merely scholarly. In the following pages, with full self-consciousness and proper lack of humility, I am writing a commentary on Goldin's commentary on Spiegel's commentary on the midrashic commentaries on the Scriptural text.

❁   ❁   ❁

From the vast literature on the Akedah and allied themes, Spiegel selected certain central issues in order to fashion a complex, compelling argument in an elegantly penned Hebrew text which, if read sensitively as Spiegel would read a text, forces us to listen to "the fury and outcry of historical reality." Focusing on the figure of Isaac in the exegesis of the Biblical chapter, rather than on Abraham as did Kierkegaard, for instance, Spiegel indicates that he is more interested in the paradigm of the victim than in the patriarch who has to fulfill God's harsh command to sacrifice his son to Him. He assumes that his audience knows the implications of this choice, the identification with a traditional Jewish paradigm prominent in the Middle Ages: Isaac as victim. His Prologue comprises the opening gambit in a bold argument. He raises the central question known to traditional Jewish scholars, but to few others: Where was Isaac when Abraham returned from Mount Moriah? Abraham had sacrificed the ram instead of his son, and as he returns home with his servants, there is no mention of Isaac. In the midrashim Spiegel adduces to answer this question, we learn that Abraham might, indeed, have killed his son and burned his body on the altar, or even, that following his death Isaac spent three years in heaven before he was resurrected. After presenting these ostensibly outrageous explanations, Spiegel asks: "What compelled the faithful of Israel to depart from the clear statement of Scripture...?" (8) What we learn from this essay is that there is a long and rich history of such deviations and it is the goal of the book to study such deviations, to probe their meaning, and to demonstrate that these texts comprise a fascinating history of the figuration of Isaac as victim.

This opening gambit determined the trajectory of the essay's argument and afforded us the insight that this daunting scholarly effort is a profound, troubled meditation on the violence that lurks beneath the surface of civilized society and occasionally erupts devastating, as it had in the Middle Ages, sizeable portions of the Jewish people. If we follow

Spiegel's methodological guidance and identify those contemporary events that inform the spiritual climate of his research just as "the biblical figures were drawn in the light of the actualities of the Crusades, when the saints of Germany and France sanctified the name in droves,"(134) the historical inspiration of this scholarly essay is not hard to find. The study was composed in the middle and late 1940s and is obviously a response to the horrible events of World War II, those events which were *later* called the Holocaust or the Shoah. Our argument that this seminal essay has an added dimension of meaning, that it is—consciously or unconsciously—a lamentation, a very authentic Jewish type of lamentation, does not challenge the validity of the scholarship exhibited in it. It enriches it by considering it an historical document with significance beyond the merely scholarly. It can also serve as a marvelous example of the problematics of historiography.

Spiegel devotes the first three chapters to situating the story in the Jewish imagination from the Hellenistic period through the Crusades, demonstrating how specific generations stressed different aspects of the story: Philo, aware that many Greek myths contained stories of fathers sacrificing children, lauded Abraham as unique in that his test was personal, independent of public needs; the mother in Maccabees II boasts that Abraham lost one son, but she lost seven; a midrash from the time of the Hadrianic persecutions derides Abraham for being only tested, while contemporary Jews were really martyred; the victims of the Crusades felt that their suffering was the greatest in history, and in telling of how fathers killed their entire families and committed suicide, argued that their act of faith, the Sanctification of the Holy Name (Kiddush HaShem), was far greater than Abraham's and their victimhood, far greater than Isaac's. Contemporary with his colleague and neighbor on Morningside Heights, the eminent historian Salo Baron, who vigorously contested "the lachrymose history" of the Jewish people, Spiegel portrayed vividly a history replete with tears, blood, and ashes.

Blood and ashes dominate the central chapters (4–8) of the essay, which assume, for the most part, that Isaac was indeed killed, but that he rose from the dead. In fact, the midrashim cited relate that Isaac's body was burned to ash, was offered to the Lord as "a burnt offering." The Hebrew term throughout is "olah," the technical term for the sacrifice which, in Greek, was translated as "holokau(s)ton" (all-burnt). In English, this is "holocaust." Let me hasten to state that in this I am not relying on a superficial verbal association. The term "Holocaust" referring to the destruction, the cremation, of European Jewry was not current until the late 1950s, even though the word in English is already found in the 17th century referring to a massive destruction.[4] For Spiegel, the word is central to those texts that claim that Isaac's sacrifice, his being offered as an "olah'" a "holocau(s)ton," was considered an atonement whose "zekhut" (merit) might protect the victims of later atrocities, such as the Crusades. The same is true for the ashes and blood of the ram which was sacrificed, according to Scriptures, "instead of" or "after" (in midrashic interpretations of "tahat") Isaac.

The "olah" ("holokau(s)ton" or " burnt offering") becomes the dominant image in the book, the figure that focuses and embraces all other figures, and unifies Spiegel's narrative of Jewish history. Isaac is not only the tentative victim; he *is* the actual burnt offering. The persistence of this theme in midrashic literature proves to Spiegel that even though in Scripture human sacrifice is rejected as a method of worshipping the Lord, and thus the passage constitutes an eloquent statement of the triumph of Israelite monotheism over paganism, in reality, this relic of a darker comprehension of divine forces, was not totally eliminated. Such rites as the offering of the first-born, the blood on doorposts, the blowing of a ram's horn had all been transfigured in Judaism, but they still retained vestiges of the period in which blood, for instance, has a terrorizing yet redemptive potency, and is spilled in an "apotropaic sacrifice of cleansing and protection" (52). Spiegel, of course, was not the first scholar to regard the Akedah in Scripture as a narrative of the triumph over pagan atrocities, or to discover in rabbinic literature echoes of pagan practices, however attenuated and subverted.[5] What strikes me, however, is his obsession with the fact that these forces of violence are so deeply embedded in human consciousness and are never far from the surface of civilized life. The reference to his contemporary world is subtle, but inescapable.

Spiegel, to be sure, is not merely interested in anthropology and folklore. The final direction of his argument becomes clear when, in chapter nine, he turns to Christianity, the dominant religion of Western Civilization, from late antiquity, through the Crusades, down to our times. In introducing the rise of the new faith which "disputed" and "derided" (81) the claims of Judaism, he states, in barely contained anger and scorn:

> It was especially the Cilician disciple, by trade a tentmaker in the city of Tarsus, who assailed the Law and the Commandments with a singular

vehemence. It is he who wove together an entire system of forgiveness of sin without the works of the Law, from a hybrid mixture of Jewish messianic hopes and pagan notions of gods dying and returning to life in recurring cycles.

As counterpart to the *Akedah Story*, Paul placed the Golgotha Event at the heart of the new faith. (81-2)

Note that Spiegel does not compare Golgotha with Sinai, the mountain of the Revelation of the Law which Paul came to displace, but with Moriah, the locus of the Akedah. Spiegel will argue throughout this chapter that the Crucifixion story is an inversion or a counterpoint to the Akedah. He, of course, was not the first to claim that Isaac is the prototype of Jesus. One finds it, he tells us, as early as the Epistle of Barnabas, a contemporary of Paul, and certainly in the Church Fathers. Throughout the chapter he draws parallels based on a host of documents: just as Abraham sacrificed Isaac, the Lord sacrificed Jesus; just as Satan tries to deceive Abraham, he tried to confute Jesus, etc. In each case, he is careful to point out the subtle differences, to explain them in terms of the overall belief structures of the two religions. The unmistakable implication, however, is that Christianity has absorbed from pagan antiquity many of those features which Judaism had struggled so fiercely to eradicate, not always with complete success. Mainstream Judaism, for instance, did succeed in eliminating the belief in the need to sacrifice the first-born or favorite son in order to ensure the welfare or redemption of mankind, a widely attested pagan belief. Yet in Christianity, Jesus dies to redeem the sins of mankind.

This assertion with all its documentation, prepares the grounds for the vivid portrayals of Christian atrocities during the Crusades that end the essay. Focusing on one verse from the Scriptural story of the Akedah, Spiegel weaves an elaborate and powerful thesis of "double dying." In Genesis 22:15 we read: "The angel of the Lord called to Abraham a second time." While a casual reader might read this verse without undue concern, the rabbis were clearly troubled by it. "Why a second time?" they asked. Many explanations are presented: some emphasize the crucial fact that Abraham, in his love for God, was willing to sacrifice his son even though he did not consummate the act; others argue that Abraham failed to perform the commandment and that the act was completed only in the days of Jesus. Spiegel ascribes the latter to the deplorable fact that "the ancient pagan demand for actual sacrifice of children was not uprooted from the world, nor perhaps from the heart either." (129) He has to repeat this point here because he wants to conclude his essay with an introduction to the poem of Rabbi Ephraim of Bonn, which he is publishing for the first time since "there may be something of this spiritual climate" (129) in the poem.

Rabbi Ephraim offers in his poem a new interpretation to the Scriptural passage: Abraham did exactly as he had been commanded, and immediately slew Isaac *one time*; the resurrecting dew fell upon Isaac and revived him; Abraham was about to slay him a *second time*, but the flood of the tears of the celestial angels swept Isaac away, out of reach, to the Garden of Eden. This second slaying puzzles Spiegel for he can find no precedent to the story:

> But this second slaying, which Abraham attempted against Isaac, where did Rabbi Ephraim get it from? "Scripture, bear witness! Well-grounded is the fact: And the Lord called Abraham even a *second time* from Heaven." Was this terrifying thought born only from a meticulous study of the Biblical text? Or is it perhaps an echo out of the historical nightmare of those times? (131)

Spiegel answers his question with a series of gory accounts of "second slayings" taken from medieval chronicles. In 1096—900 years ago— the Mainz community elected to be slain for the Sanctification of the Name (Kiddush HaShem) rather than escape by conversion. We are told that after the Jews were slain, the "uncircumcised ones" came upon them to strip their bodies and hurl them out the window. When they found some Jews still barely alive, they taunted them with offers of baptism. When the Jews refused again, they "proceeded to torture some of them some more, until, *they killed them a second time.*" (132) In the village of Mehr, a certain Jew named Shemariah killed his family and tried to commit suicide. When he failed at this, he was buried alive *twice*. After the first burial, the Christians discovered he was still alive and dug him up offering life in exchange for conversion. When he refused again, they buried him alive *a second time until he finally died.* Spiegel brings somewhat similar stories from Blois and Orleans of Jews being burned alive— all told in great detail. Some six pages (131–137) vibrate with graphic accounts of atrocities, one piled upon another. While these passages might, indeed, prove Spiegel's point that Rabbi Ephraim's notion of a *second slaying* is indeed based on historical fact, they are a fitting climax to the essay: in a crescendo of detailed violence, they realize dramatically the arguments that Spiegel has mustered throughout his study. These brutal accounts, in turn, constitute the immediate introduction to Rabbi Ephraim's poem on the Akedah.

The grisly descriptions of the slaughter of Jews during the Crusades, pale in comparison with the reports of the massacre of millions of Jews during World War II, accounts, pictures, and films of which had been widely published since the liberation of the death camps in May and June of 1945. It is inconceivable that Spiegel, living in New York, and well attuned to the fate of European Jewry, was not aware of them, that they did not affect his writing of this essay. With his profound knowledge of Jewish history and his own personal experience, he clearly saw the savage murder of Jews in World War II as a continuation of a pattern going back to late antiquity. It is even possible that the *second slaying* that obsessed him in his last chapter, refers to World War II conceived as an intensified sequel to World War I in which scores of thousands of Jews were killed, precisely in those areas of Eastern Europe close to where Spiegel lived. Spiegel expressed his sorrow and anger in the genre he knew best, the scholarly essay.

When we recall the chapters he wrote on Saul Tchernichowski and his ballad, "Baruch of Mayence," twenty years earlier in *Hebrew Reborn*, we are struck by his spiritual development. Even in that early book, he asserts that one of the most significant developments in Hebrew literature of the 1920s was the conquest of the language (*kibbush halashon*) by the Hebrew authors, and the conquest of the authors by the language. To the extent that writers mastered their linguistic vehicle, they were, in turn, shaped by its historical semantic structures. To this he credits Tchernichowski's subtle moving away from his early Nietzscheanism with its adulation of untrammeled primal forces, towards a greater appreciation of the traditional moderating values of Judaism. In *The Last Trial (MeAggadot haAkedah)* of 1950, the Nietzschean tones that he had admired in Tchernichowski, are now condemned and considered pernicious. Spiegel certainly understood that other forces had adopted this Nietzschean philosophy to justify and inspire the destruction of European Jewry. The essay thus comprises an angry condemnation of Western Civilization, and his admiration shifts from the avenger, Baruch, to the martyrs. His efforts are invested in a sober attempt to understand the historical roots of the savage hatred that led to the slaughter of so many Jews. As such, his essay should be included among the great laments in the long history of Jewish literature. Once we have reached this conclusion, we should look elsewhere in the scholarly literature of the post-World War II period for other examples of scholarship as lamentation. We shall find, I suggest, more than a few similar examples.

Still, the essay is much more than a lament. There is, in Spiegel's essay, an artful mustering of the details and the scholarly arguments to produce a coherent narrative of Jewish suffering. It is energized and hence somewhat mitigated by the author's relentless exploration of the traditional Jewish responses to past events and by his own formulation of the descent into barbarism that he attributes to the church. The argument's vitality is felt more acutely in the Hebrew than in the English, since the Hebrew is the virtuoso demonstration of the potency of that language as a bearer of Jewish culture in all periods. Ever the cultural Zionist, Spiegel wields Hebrew here as an affirmation of the revival of Jewish creativity in the modern period, the logical vehicle for writing an essay in the cataclysmic days between the liberation of the death camps and the establishment of the State of Israel.

Both lamentation and implied affirmation of restoration, *MeAggadot HaAkedah* is the product of an exquisite talent and a fine training in the reading of texts. For those of us who devote their intellectual energies to the interpretation of texts, the essay suggests another profound message. Just as the midrashic tradition was a legitimate enterprise—a reinterpretation by the rabbis of the scriptural heritage through which they could understand the world in which they lived—so the modern scholarly tradition might also be a legitimate enterprise through which we might understand the world in which we live by recreating the past. For while we strive to recreate what a text might have meant in its historical context, we are saying something about what we mean or who we are in our historical context. Interpretation, as Simon Rawidowicz has taught us in his masterly yet neglected essay on the subject (also written in the United States shortly after the Spiegel essay), has been the emblematic Jewish intellectual activity since the days of Ezra the Scribe in the fifth century B.C.E.[6] Interpretation may take the shape of midrash, a philosophical essay, or a scholarly article. Those who engage in this creative activity should therefore be conscious of their place in history and the responsibilities it entails.

NOTES

1. Shalom Spiegel, *The Last Trial*, trans. Judah Goldin (New York, 1967). All page numbers in this article refer to the 1979 edition. (The most recent edition was published in 1993).

2. *The Louis Ginzberg Jubilee Volume* was published in New York in 1945–1946, but articles in it were submitted by November 28, 1943, when the editorial committee presented Dr. Ginzberg with a preliminary announcement of the volume enumerating

papers, which "with some modification now appear in two volumes, one in English, the other in Hebrew." See the foreword to the English volume.

3. Contributors to the English volume are: W. F. Albright, Elias J. Bickerman, Boaz Cohen, Walter J. Fischel, Aaron Freimann, Harry Friedenwald, H. L. Ginsberg, Robert Gordis, A. S. Halkin, Guido Kisch, Jacob Raider Marcus, Moses Marx, Abraham A. Neumann, Cecil Roth, Alexander Scheiber, Alexander Sperber, E. Taeubler, Charles C. Torrey, H.A. Wolfson, and Solomon Zeitlin. In the Hebrew volume are: Ch Albeck, M. Arzt, S. Assaf, D. Z. Baneth, U. Cassuto, M. Davis, J. N. Epstein, L. Finkelstein, A. Freimann, S. Greenberg, J. Guttman, A. Heschel, M. Higger, S. Krauss, S. Liberman, S. Loewinger, I. Markon, I. Rivkind, G. Scholem, M. Scwabe, I. Sonne, and S. Spiegel.

4. For the history of the usage of the term "holocaust" in reference to the destruction of European Jews in World War II see Z. Garber and B. Zuckerman, "Why Do We Call the Holocaust 'The Holocaust?' An Inquiry into the Psychology of Labels," *Modern Judaism*, 9, no. 2 (May 1989): 197–212.

5. For a recent study of the sacrifice of the first born see Jon D. Levenson, *The Death and Resurrection of the Beloved Son* (New Haven: Yale University Press, 1993)

6. Simon Rawidowicz "On Interpretation," in *Studies in Jewish Thought*, Nahum N. Glatzer, ed. (Philadelphia, 1974), 45-80. First published in *Proceedings of the American Academy for Jewish Research* 26 (1957): 83–126.

JEWISH STUDIES AND THE COMMUNITY

❧ Our "She'ela Nikhbada": Whose Hebrew Is It?

The obvious reference to Eliezer Ben-Yehudah's famous article of 1879 in my title is, of course, a self-referential rhetorical ploy. And yet, precisely because it is so obvious, you must realize that I am not interested in celebrating once again Ben-Yehudah's signal contribution to the revival of Hebrew. His article shall serve as a foil for my remarks, for the situating of the "she'elah" I want to discuss.

Like many other famous articles—more often cited than read—the Ben-Yehudah article does not say what all the text books claim it says. (And I am not the first to make this point; cf. George Mandel, et. al.) It does not propose a program for the revival of spoken Hebrew; it really doesn't focus upon the question of language use or renewal. It is a brief essay on nationalism (called here "le'umut"), replete with ideas mostly culled from Smolenskin, and in it the young author berates contemporary Hebrew authors for failing to deal with and propagate the "she'elot"—let's call them issues—that concern him. Language, to be sure, is one of the aspects of nationalism, but it gets less attention than settling Eretz Yisrael or the cultivation of the soil.

The meager reference to Hebrew is eloquent: Ben-Yehudah didn't have to dwell upon the importance of Hebrew since he was writing in Hebrew to a very specialized, elitist Hebrew-reading audience. The article presumes an indissoluble bonding between language and culture, perhaps even a type of linguistic determinism, a doctrine that Ben-Yehudah probably learned from Herder, or one of his many explicators, and which has found its most articulate expositor in this century in Benjamin Whorf. This doctrine holds that the relationship between

353

language and culture is not only implemental or symbolical, but is actually causal, that languages shape persons and cultures. It maintains that the authentic richness of any culture throughout history can be attributed to the specific language which the classical expositors of the culture used. Ben-Yehudah's article therefore implies that only in the ancestral homeland could the language, the literature, and "hokhmat Yisrael" flourish. This implication obviously troubled Smolenskin who published the article with a personal disclaimer about the aggressive, rash tone of the young ideologue and activist who demanded the clarification of issues and urgent action.

Much, of course, has happened in the world of the Hebrew language during the 111 years since the first publication of this article and it is hard to imagine any century in the long history of the language that has witnessed such exciting development. I will not recount these here. The manifest issues which motivated Ben-Yehudah need not interest us now, but the latent matter of the association of language with culture which we all take for granted, cries for re-examination and, at least, refinement. I will argue that many of our problems in the world of Hebrew in the American university stem from our reluctance to rethink this question. While discussion of methodology is always valuable, it is time that we turned our attention to issues of ideology—and this I intend to do this evening, however briefly.

To focus the issue, I ask the bold and bald question: Whose Hebrew is it? The interrogative "whose"—I hasten to note—does not refer to ownership, to a possessive, chauvinistic hold on the language which excludes somebody else. I mean here not ownership, but cultural association. The questions I ask are those of the socio-linguist: What specific group of users is associated with this language? What are their cultural characteristics which qualify and shape their attitude to the language? An illuminating example is at hand. Today, as in the past, Hebrew is used by a community of pious Jews primarily, but not exclusively, as the holy tongue of Jewish tradition. On the other hand, most of us in this conference hall are not pious Jews and our usage of Hebrew is generated by and entails other associations. Are we really using the same language? Or are we using two dialects of the same language? And what, if anything, happens to the user when he or she shifts from prayer to the reading of an Amichai poem, which often uses the same phraseology for ironic purposes? Are you the same person? Is it the same culture? These are not merely playful, Alice in Wonderland questions; they penetrate to the heart of all of our professional activities and much of our private lives.

To develop this question further, and ever closer to home, we should ask a variety of questions about how Hebrew has been taught and is taught in American universities. Why is Hebrew being taught? What is the putative target audience? What are its expectations? Within what cultural framework is the language being taught? What, if any, ideological views are implicit in the institution's support of this academic enterprise? How closely allied is the study of Hebrew with Jewish Studies and in what sense is the concept of the language shaped by this nexus? When we do ask these questions and review the history of the study and teaching of Hebrew in the university, we begin to observe that a variety of discrete models—seven, in fact—can be identified. These models, like all models, are, to be sure, constructs hopefully useful for organizing, focusing, and giving coherence to an otherwise chaotic flow of information. We make no claim that they are all-embracing; they often overlap as do any models situated within the course of history. They can, nevertheless, shed light on areas beyond the academy. As we review them chronologically from colonial days to the present, we will note that successive models embody and transmute some of the features of earlier models, but can, nonetheless, be identified as discrete. While I have identified and described seven historical models elsewhere, I shall restrict myself to four this evening.

The first model, then, is Protestant, theologically oriented. Since it was situated in the divinity schools of the universities as the latter grew more secular during the founding years of the republic, we shall call it Divinity School Hebrew (DSH). Let me hasten to note that I am not citing the Colonial example, e.g. Judah Monis and Ezra Stiles, as proof of the antiquity—hence the legitimacy—of Hebrew Studies in the university. That embarrassing, apologetic claim to legitimacy has been with us too long and should be laid to rest. I begin with this model both because it was the first, and it forcefully raises the issue of cultural association. The "oracles" of the Old Testament might, indeed, be sacred, as Monis claims they are in his *Dickdook Leshon Gnebreet* of 1735—but to whom? It could not be to the Jews or, for that matter, to the Catholics. And what does sacred really mean in this case? Certainly it carries Protestant, but not Catholic or Jewish connotations. Hebrew conveyed the word of the Lord which was meaningful to contemporary Protestants; the word was spoken to them—and for them. We should not forget how exclusive the established religion was until the early decades of the nineteenth century. The Jews of Boston, for instance, were not allowed to purchase land for a cemetery until 1844, over a century after Monis' *Grammar of the*

Hebrew Language and long after Hebrew had been dropped as a requirement in the university. Hebrew, in Puritan New England, was the original language of the text sacred to Protestants, a text created by a *primitive* people, the Jews, who were of little contemporary relevance except for millenarian groups.

The filiation is easy to trace from the early Protestants in Germany in the sixteenth century; to the Netherlands, England, and Switzerland in the seventeenth century; and then to the colonies in the eighteenth century. The textbooks usually are modifications of the work done in the mid-seventeenth century in Basel by the Buxtorfs, who were amongst the most liberal of these scholars. Despite the contact with Jewish scholars induced by this scholarly work, the underlying purpose was always Protestant. And while the role and positioning of Hebrew studies varied from university to university, and from generation to generation, the Protestant sponsorship must entail profound cultural implications even today, when the more advanced schools teach modern Hebrew, too. We call this model Divinity School Hebrew (DSH) because the Divinity School—or the Religion Department—is the determining environment of this linguistic activity.

During the nineteenth century, as religion was relegated to the divinity schools and Semitic Philology, often associated with Biblical criticism, began to penetrate the major universities, Hebrew was taught within the university proper as an ancient Semitic language along with Aramaic and Arabic. The commanding figure of this nineteenth century model was, to be sure, H. F. W. Gesenius (1786–1842), whose dictionary of 1810–12 and Grammar of 1813, established the norms for more than a century. The dictionary was Anglicized by Brown, Driver, Briggs in 1907 ff. and the Grammar by Cowley in 1910. By the end of the century, Semitic studies in the respected Germanic tradition were firmly established at Harvard, Columbia, the University of Pennsylvania, Johns Hopkins, Chicago, and Berkeley. In some of these universities, Mishnaic and Midrashic texts were studied—as they were by the younger Buxtorf in the seventeenth century.

Since the avowed goal was the study of Hebrew as an ancient Semitic language, I call this second model (SPH), i.e. Semitic Philology Hebrew. The language was still studied as the key to the Old Testamental text and most of the students were, in fact, associated somehow with the Protestant ministry (Davidson's *Hebrew Grammar* was often used by both divinity and philology students), but the more serious and advanced scholars *attempted* to invest their efforts in an interpretation of these texts as documents of an ancient culture, that of the Hebrews, rather than the word of God, which is relevant to the contemporary Christian. I stress "attempted" since it is obvious that the two models often operated simultaneously in each scholar, that the Divinity school model (DSH), affected the Semitic Philology model (SPH). We see this even in so brilliant and open-minded a philologist and archaeologist as William Foxwell Albright, who set a standard for so much of Hebrew and Semitic Studies in the American Academy between 1920 and 1950, a century after Gesenius and his colleagues. It is sobering to realize that the two dominant modes for the study of Hebrew in the university until 1950 were, in effect, (DSH) or (SPH), though there were some important changes in the first half of this century. This was, for all practical purposes, a Hebrew without Jews.

The academic study of Hebrew was usually independent of any significant influence from the Jewish communities that were growing as a result of the successive waves of immigration after the 1840s. The last two decades of the nineteenth century are crucial for the subsequent history of Hebrew in the American university, less because of what was done within the university (the number of students studying Hebrew was negligible), than what happened in the major urban centers, particularly in the Northeast. Between 1880 and 1910 some of the major cultural institutions of American Jewry were established: the three leading rabbinical seminaries; the Jewish Publication Society; and the *Jewish Encyclopedia.* The great waves of immigrants from Eastern Europe brought with them both their knowledge and attitudes towards Hebrew, ranging from traditional religious to secular Zionist. These attitudes, of course, were to change in the process of Americanization of these masses of Jews, confronted for the first time with a relatively open society. Hebrew had to compete with both English and, until World War II, with Yiddish.

Any attempt to describe the status of Hebrew within the university from the beginning of this century on must factor in as a parameter the presence of a growing Jewish community, its experiences and expectations, since Hebrew occupies so central a function in Jewish life, be it in prayer, in study of Torah, or in the evolution of the Zionist enterprise. Even the indifference to these manifestations of Hebrew usage on the part of an academic Hebraist is a statement. Certainly the cultural and socio-linguistic situation of American Jewry at the turn of the century is an indispensable factor in our consideration of the spread of Hebrew studies throughout the universities after the late 1950s, for had there been no aggressive Jewish community in America by that period, there would have been no appreciable growth of Jewish Studies and Hebrew in the last thirty years, Israel or no Israel, Holocaust or no Holocaust. This basic existential fact is always overlooked in our discussions of the development of Jewish and Hebrew Studies in the university. Furthermore, one cannot gauge the import of the study of Hebrew without factoring in the anticipations of the student body that is attracted to these courses; these anticipations are shaped by the pre-university experiences of the students who are, for the most part, Jewish and involved in community activities.

As the American Jewish community with its cultural institutions begins to take shape at the end of the nineteenth century, it becomes evident that the concept of Hebrew espoused by the university differed markedly from that variety of perspectives on Hebrew maintained by the Jews, themselves. While reference to Colonial America is of minor interest for our understanding of Hebrew in the university in the mid-twentieth century, a firm grasp of the American Jewish cultural situation at the beginning of the century is essential.

Since the use of Hebrew entailed a spectrum of specific ideological implications at the turn of the century, from the religious to the secular Zionist, it is important to note how the *Jewish Encylopedia* (1901–1904), the first complete modern Jewish encyclopedia in any language, describes Hebrew. Though fully cognizant of the status of knowledge of Semitic philology of the period, the author, Caspar Levias first tells us where and when the term "Hebrew language" and, later, "The Holy Tongue" were used. From the very beginning of the article, the language is identified with a certain people, their literature and authors. The first half of the article is devoted to the characteristics of the language in its classical form and to its use in the Bible, but the second half deals with post-Biblical periods: Mishnaic; Neo-Hebrew i.e. from Amoraic until the present; Philosophic and Rhetorical; Poetry; and even a brief section on the revival of Hebrew as a spoken language. The final paragraph is remarkably perceptive:

> The national and realistic tendencies of the present generation have inspired many writers to try to enlarge the vocabulary of the language by the coinage of new terms and to revive Hebrew as a spoken language. Throughout Europe circles were formed that had as their object the cultivation of Hebrew conversation. It was in the nature of conditions that in Europe such efforts could meet with no signal success. It was otherwise in Palestine. There the resurrection of Hebrew as the tongue of the home and of the school has been realized to a considerable degree.

The concept of the Hebrew language here is holistic: it embraces the totality of Jewish history and is thus bound to the destiny of the Jewish people. It is more than the language of the sacred oracles of the Old Testament or one of the ancient Semitic Languages. The impact of M.L. Lilienblum, H. Graetz, E. Ben-Yehudah, and Ahad HaAm (Asher Ginzburg) is evident. From this period on, the study of Hebrew is increasingly allied with Jewish Studies.

The *revival* of the language as a viable, modern medium of communication is dimly perceived by this period. Ben-Yehudah's "She'ela Nikhbada"(1879), the founding of Va'ad HaLashon (1889), the feeble attempts of Hoveve Tzion to found schools in Palestine, and the prodigious literary productivity of the modern Hebrew classics after 1885: Mendele (S.Y. Abramowitz), Ahad HaAm, Bialik, Tchernichowsky, Berdyczewski, and Brenner—all contribute to this awareness of language revival. This awareness, though already recorded in the pages of the *Jewish Encylopedia,* did not penetrate the American university for another forty years until the late 1930s. The indifference to the revival of the language in university circles is noteworthy.

Still, there is more than a trace of inhibition in this article as there is in the entire *Jewish Encyclopedia*, which both reflects the knowledge of Judaism prevalent in the most sophisticated scholarly circles and how that information should be presented to the English readers, many of whom were, potentially, non-Jews. Following the tradition of *Wissenschaft des Judentums* as it evolved after over two generations of research, the focus of the *Encyclopedia* is on intellectual history and pre-modern texts or events. Its editors were not fully aware of the implications of the two immigration waves taking place at the time: the massive transfer of populations to America and the re-establishment of a Jewish center in Palestine. Since it was produced before World War I, it obviously could not reflect the upheavals that shape the destiny of Hebrew as we know it today. It was also published in and by a society that referred to many things Jewish as "Hebrew," from the Hebrew Union College to the Hebrew Immigrant Aid Society. Few of its leading contributors were situated in universities since there were few academic positions in either Hebraic or Judaic Studies—the titles often used—either in America or in Europe where many of the contributors still lived. I choose to call the model of Hebrew introduced at that period in scholarly circles "Americanized Wissenschaft Hebrew" (AWH) to distinguish it from a later model. It was the model of Hebrew espoused, however implicitly, by the founders of the American Academy for Jewish Research in 1920.

The advantages of positing the "Americanized Wissenschaft" model become clear when we approach the two leading professors of Jewish Studies who emerged in American universities between the two World Wars and loomed as the authoritative figures until the 1970s: Harry Wolfson at Harvard and Salo Baron at Columbia. While they were imbued with this concept of Judaic Studies and Hebrew, they also imbibed some of the Hebraism associated with the Zionist movement. They actually wrote some of their articles in Hebrew at the beginning of their careers. (Wolfson also wrote Hebrew poetry.) In their academic interests they also represented new departures: Wolfson was a medievalist and Baron, a modernist. In their orientation, then, they represent the third, Wissenschaft, model, with an anticipatory admixture of the fourth: Tarbut Ivrit Hebrew (TIH).

The cumulative effect of the various Hebrew-oriented nationalist impulses and organized movements from the 1860s until World War I generated both a considerable literature of remarkably high quality, centers of activity in Europe, Palestine, and America, and a distinct ideology. This ideology, a variegated, militant Hebraism energized both the Tarbut Ivrit movement in America and its counterparts in Europe at about the same time during World War I. In Eastern and Central Europe this ideology was given state-sponsored legitimacy in the period following World War I as *minorities* were allowed to cultivate their indigenous cultures. The Versailles treaties strongly encouraged the spread of Hebrew language schools, mostly secular, pro-Zionist, and opposed to the Yiddish schools that flourished, abetted by the same treaties. Hebrew in these schools embraced the entire experience of the Jewish people and, being the language of instruction throughout the gymnasium, was greatly enriched by the need to teach all academic subjects. Language was not merely a tool for communication or self-expression; as the dominant discriminator between ethnic groups, it assumed a valorization of its own and formed a culture of its own. Passionate devotion to the niceties of the language particularly in its manifestations in literary texts of all periods was assiduously cultivated. The "holiness" (or "sacredness") of the Hebrew tongue was one of the cardinal, inevitable features of the value system and rhetoric of these schools and youth groups, however irreligious they might have been, e.g. HaShomer HaTzair. We call this cultural model of Hebrew "*Tarbut Ivrit* Hebrew" (TIH).

In Europe, the *Tarbut Ivrit* movement thus had a sociological substance that it never had in America, where it would have died had it not been for the infusion, in the five years after World War I, of immigrants educated in the Eastern European *Tarbut Ivrit* schools. These schools, often associated with the *Tarbut* network, produced a generation of dedicated Hebraists who populated the Hebrew schools and Hebrew colleges in this country—and in Israel—from the middle 1920s through the late 1950s as teachers and educators. The transplanting of these *Tarbut Ivrit* Hebraists could only generate ideological dissonance and frustration since the ideology was shaped by a specific post-World War I sociopolitical situation that did not obtain in America. Later, American born students, in moments of impatience with the uncritical and seemingly naive passions of these transplanted, Americanized *Tarbut Ivrit* Hebraists (TIH), would call them, somewhat pejoratively, "maskilim" without really examining their cultural impulses. Few of them received an American college education, but those who did went on to assume significant positions in a variety of professions in this country. Most, however, lived in ever increasing alienation; trained to think in terms of exclusive ethnic minorities separated by different ideologically-charged languages, they were destined to teach American youngsters living in a relatively open, mono-lingual society.

Most of the Hebrew Colleges were founded or staffed by *Tarbut Ivrit* Hebraists, but within the general (that is, not supported by Jewish funds) academic world, the *Tarbut Ivrit* Hebraist ideology found a home, characteristically, mostly in the New York area. At New York University, Hebrew was situated in the late 1930s only in the School of Education, not in the College of Liberal Arts. Led and partly funded by Abraham I. Katsh, this unit had to struggle for academic recognition for some twenty years. Some of the New York City colleges, Brooklyn and City College of New York, in particular, also introduced Hebrew as did a few public high schools. Though a variety of Hebrew texts were taught in the courses offered, these programs made their reputation by pioneering the university study of modern Hebrew language and literature. The textbook which reflects the crystallization of these efforts is A. Aaroni and R. Wallenrod's *Mavo lalashon ha'ivrit vedikdukah* (1942), which was used in many colleges until the mid-1960s. The implicit norm of Hebrew in this primer was that of a putative Hebrew community residing in New York and since that community really did not exist as a socio-linguistic unit, the norm was a quasi-norm. Note the avowed goal:

> It is mainly the modern idiom and communication of thought that the authors wished to emphasize. The exercises are, therefore largely based upon modern writers and spoken Hebrew, the grammar stresses modern usage, and the literary material has mostly been drawn from the pages of modern writers.

Here, for the first time, we have "modern usage" and "spoken" Hebrew presented as parameters and goals. A comparison of this text with Davidson's *Hebrew Grammar* used for Divinity and Semitic students since the late nineteenth century would provide revelatory documentation of our argument.

The emphasis upon the modern and the contemporary in Jewish life both induced a rethinking of the way Hebrew was to be taught and bridged the gap between the educational goals of the university curriculum and those of the Jewish community. The closest logical academic unit was the modern foreign language departments and one finds repeated reference to them in the many publications of the New York University center. By the outbreak of World War II, then, four models for the study of Hebrew in the American university had been established: the Colonial/Divinity school; the Semitic Philology department; the Americanized Wissenschaft mode; the Modern Language departments.

World War II changed many things in American higher education. The GI Bill made university studies accessible to millions who would not have had this opportunity before the war and also left America the major industrial and educational force in the world. The overall expansion and generation of new ideas opened the university to area studies, among them Near Eastern Languages. The creation of a sovereign, Hebrew speaking state in Israel, obviously contributed measurably to the *normalization* of Hebrew as a language which could thus be taught in the academy—and in public high schools—alongside other *foreign* languages. Ironically, Hebrew, in monolingual America, could become *normal* only when it became *foreign*. (The impact of the Holocaust on the study of Hebrew or Judaism in the universities was negligible until the 1960s or 1970s.) It is no accident, then, that Hebrew or the study of Hebrew texts grew in the 1950s in departments of Near Eastern Languages, some of which had previously been departments of Semitic Studies. It was not difficult to justify the teaching of Hebrew since it was the language of a real country and America, with its world-wide interests, could support Hebrew as well as Arabic, often both at the same time in the same departments. It was also understandable that under the National Defense Acts, funds could be budgeted for the study of Hebrew together with other foreign, especially *exotic* languages.

The model introduced in the 1950s was thus Area Studies (ASH) and Hebrew was *normalized* during that period together with the concept of a Jewish State, though the normalization of the former was by no means dependant upon the normalization of the latter. Federal funds for the study of Hebrew together with all other foreign, especially exotic languages, made the difference. Language, rather than literature or culture, was the focal point of many of these government inspired efforts. This tendency was strengthened by the spread, within the academy, of the structural linguistics of Saussure and, in America, of Leonard Bloomfield that privileged speech and thus undermined the normative authority of written texts.

The growing acceptability of modern Hebrew within the university enabled the formation of the National Association of Professors of Hebrew in 1950. Headed for many years by A.I. Katsh of New York University, it was, from its very inception a hybrid of model four, *Tarbut Hebrew* with an updated version of model one, "Divinity School Hebrew" since most of its members were professors in Protestant Bible colleges. It often conducted surveys for the Modern Language Association of the numbers of students enrolled in Hebrew courses throughout the country, rarely distinguishing between the type of Hebrew taught in these courses. It also organized scholarly tours to Israel and propagated the awareness of the importance of modern Hebrew for the professors of Bible.

During the same period, but for different reasons, some of the same structuralist linguistic notions were beginning to make way in Israel, with the publication of such seminal books as Hayyim Rozen's *HaIvrit shelanu* (Our Hebrew) of 1955. The argument that the norm of Hebrew to be taught is the norm of current speech in a viable Hebrew-language society, i.e. Israel, was revolutionary in its time, as reasonable as it might seem today. It took at least another ten years for the notion to be accepted in Israel, let alone in America even though the prevalent textbooks, designed especially for the instruction of immigrants to Israel, such as Aharon Rozen's *Elef milim* (One thousand words)—later replaced by many other texts—began to find their way into the university curriculum. In general, the massive efforts invested in Israel in the Hebrew language education of hundreds of thousands of new immigrants generated an aura around the *ulpanim* (workshops) where this work was done. The so-called *"ulpan* method" (never really a definable method) was often used for conversation courses in some universities. Inevitably, the norms of structural linguistics backed by the growing presence of Israel made the quasi-norm of New York Hebrew embedded in Aharoni and Wallenrod, or Blumberg and Lewittes' *Ivrit hayya* (Living Hebrew) appear obsolete, even absurd.

By the mid-1960s one can begin to detect the concomitant emergence of two new, discrete models, our sixth and seventh, between which there is no intrinsic causal connection; historically, they happened to develop at the same time, each for its own reason. These are Jewish Studies Hebrew (JSH) and Israeli Hebrew (IH). I will treat Jewish Studies Hebrew first since it was generated by forces indigenous to American society.

The story of the spread of Jewish Studies during the 1960s and 1970s in the American university, and with them, in many places, the introduction of courses in Hebrew to support them, has been told many times and there is no need to rehearse it here. It is, nonetheless, still imperative to argue that this proliferation cannot be attributed to any one cause, and certainly not to the growth of ethnic consciousness in the United States. The growth process was well under way in the early sixties before "ethnicity" became a positive virtue in intellectual circles.

And while ethnicity might have contributed something to the acceptability of Jewish Studies after the late sixties, there were no curricular models in Black, Latino, or Feminist Studies at that time. What we do find is a fusion of several trends that reinforce each other: the further development of area studies which we have noted above, a development which could not suffice with language study alone, but had to embrace the texts written in the language; the acceptance of Israel as the new center of Jewish culture; the emergence, by the late fifties, of a new self-assuredness and aggressiveness in the American Jewish community that slowly realized that with European Jewry annihilated in the Holocaust—consciousness of which was slowly penetrating the American Jewish mind in the late 1950s—it was the center of Jewish Diasporan life and responsibility; and the acceptance of religious studies in general within the university.

In 1990, after thirty crowded years of historic events and drastic changes in the academic world, it is often difficult to recreate the state of the field of Hebrew in 1960. We are talking of a seemingly antediluvian era before Vietnam, the Six Day War, and the campus riots of the sixties. Not only were there relatively few instructors of Hebrew in the liberal arts universities (Hebrew was taught, of course, in many divinity schools), but there was little awareness that a new era with new opportunities had already begun. When I was invited some twenty five years ago to write what was considered a pioneering article for the *American Jewish Yearbook* (1966), I defined "Judaic studies as the discipline which deals with the historical experiences, in the intellectual, religious, and social spheres, of the Jewish people in all centuries and countries." (And this was several years before ethnic studies became a popular item on campus.) It was becoming clear that we were in a new academic situation and my closest colleagues could not relate either to the American Academy for Jewish Research with its *Wissenschaft* orientation or to the National Association for Professors of Hebrew most of whose members at that time were professors in Protestant Bible colleges, though the president and founder was Abraham I. Katsh of New York University. The choice of the term "Judaic," incidentally, was not mine, but the editor's. Several years later, in 1968, when the Association for Jewish Studies was founded, the name was fixed as "Jewish" to reflect the deliberate comprehensiveness of definition: all periods, modern and Biblical as well as medieval or "Rabbinic"; all languages, Yiddish and American fiction as well as Hebrew; all disciplines, sociology and literary criticism as well as philology and philosophy.

The model of Hebrew that would theoretically accompany Jewish Studies so defined, i.e. Jewish Studies Hebrew (JSH) offered a holistic, uninhibited view of the language in all its historical periods from the Biblical through the rapidly developing *modern*. It suggested a preparation for the reading of Hebrew of all types, for speaking and writing, the treatment of Hebrew for what it is: both the language of challenging classical texts and a dynamic contemporary literary culture. It was assumed that one would specialize in a certain genre or period, but would also have an intimate knowledge of the entire range of the language. The possibilities for courses and textbooks were infinite.

Unfortunately, this model turned out to be mainly theoretical. The liberality of the definition welcomed many who had little Hebrew since one could do serious work in many aspects of American Jewish history, or German Jewish history, or Yiddish, or the sociology of the Jews in the modern period with little, if any Hebrew. The amount of Hebrew required was thus determined by the subject to be studied, the availability of translations, and the demands of the instructor. The results varied from school to school, but it is undeniable that the spread of the study of the Hebrew language lagged far behind the proliferation of courses in Jewish Studies, mostly given totally in English. Students came to the university in the seventies and eighties with ever decreasing Hebrew backgrounds, just as American students, in general, come to the university with little foreign language preparation.

Our last model, Israeli Hebrew (IH) generates its own opportunities and challenges. Even the most conservative observer of the cultural scene since the Six Day War, must grant the centrality of Israeli cultural life for Hebrew and Jewish Studies in the entire world. Israel, often imaged as Jerusalem, is the situation of the critical language speaking mass, the major concentration of Judaics scholars, and the historical omphalos of Jewish culture, specifically that which finds its expression in Hebrew. Israel and its language, Hebrew, become more and more accessible both because of the improved communications technology and the frequent interchange between Israeli and American scholars of Jewish Studies. The sophisticated linguistic study of Israeli Hebrew has developed rapidly in the last ten years as evidenced by a cumulative study such as Lewis Glinert's recently published *The Grammar of Modern Hebrew*. (1989). The Hebrew of Israel has, in effect, become the norm in our Hebrew language instruction courses primarily because the overwhelming percentage of Hebrew language instructors in our universities received the major portion of their formal education in Israel. They think in Hebrew, as does any native speaker of the language, not in English, the language of their students. They have taken over the language instruction in many universities primarily because the indigenous American community has failed to produce instructors capable of teaching the basic Hebrew courses on a university level. The norm of language taught is that of contemporary Israel with varying degrees of emphasis on conversation, though the avowed ultimate goal is the reading of modern literary texts and newspapers. As such, this model of college Hebrew instruction can benefit significantly from the Junior Year Abroad programs offered in Israel since the Hebrew norms of those programs are usually those of Israeli Hebrew. Over the past five years, the instructors who espouse this model of Hebrew have formed a special interest group on the methodology and pedagogy in the university teaching of Hebrew language and literature within the National Association of Professors of Hebrew. Many of them, incidentally, have produced their own textbooks for the courses they teach, some still betraying elements of the "*ulpan* method" used for the integration of immigrants into a Hebrew speaking society. The appropriateness of this tendency is questionable.

While there is, to be sure, much overlapping between the last two models, those we have called Jewish Studies Hebrew and Israeli Hebrew, one notices in many universities a striking division of labor. The basic language sequence plus the modern literature course, if there is one, might be taught according to the seventh, the Israeli Hebrew model, while the more advanced "content" courses are taught in the light of the sixth, Jewish Studies, model. Similarly, the instructors in the first series of courses are more likely to be Israelis while those in the second "content" series, including the well-populated courses in Holocaust, Jewish Religion, and Jewish History surveys are more likely to be American born. An analogous division can be found in the non-orthodox elementary and secondary Jewish sponsored schools: the teachers are mostly Israelis; the administrators are usually Americans. The implications of this division of labor should be obvious.

We have offered these seven models as coordinates to map out the field of Hebrew studies in the university both diachronically and synchronically. These are:

1. DSH=Divinity School Hebrew
2. SPH=Semitic Philology Hebrew
3. AWH=Americanized Wissenschaft Hebrew
4. ATH=Americanized Tarbut Hebrew
5. ASH=Area Studies Hebrew
6. JSH=Jewish Studies Hebrew
7. IH=Israeli Hebrew

Clearly, these models do not include the pervasive usage of Hebrew in Jewish prayer or Torah study that have never been considered legitimate goals within the university curriculum. These models are approximations, they might overlap, and even be congruent. Their usefulness, however, becomes evident when we focus upon three issues:

1. Who are the instructors? What are their backgrounds and orientation towards the use of the language? In what language do they think?
2. What is the avowed purpose of the program of studies offered? What is its implicit ideology? What are its goals?
3. What is the target audience? What is its background and in what language does it think?

Addressing these issues in the light of the models we have provided should contribute measurably to the advancement of our thinking on our "She'ela nikhbada." Our question is not whether we should teach Hebrew, but which type of Hebrew and for what purposes. The usefulness of our models for situating the argument can be demonstrated by selecting real situations of potential conflict. Three come to mind.

a. The model of Hebrew in the basic courses is usually IH, while various instructors in more specialized courses expect their students to be able to read literary texts of all periods. How are these two goals reconciled? Is there a clear ideological difference involved, or is it merely a matter of unexamined preferences deriving from the instructor's personal background?

b. In a specifically pointed instance of the first situation, Bible instructors often insist that students study *classical* rather than *modern Hebrew* so that they can read Biblical texts when they enter their classes. Are the two models of Hebrew, i.e. the so-called classical, or in our terms (DSH) (Divinity School Hebrew) or (SPH) (Semitic Philology Hebrew) and the modern, (IH) (Israeli Hebrew) so different that one must budget two beginners courses? Are the motives ideogically determined?

c. Students often come to the more advanced text courses after years of intensive study of rabbinic texts in a religious atmosphere where Hebrew is also used for daily prayer. In their university courses, they are required to be engaged with the Hebrew language as a historical, linguistic artifact with its norms, peculiarities, cognates. Is a psychic dissonance generated or does a subtle synthesis develop?

These concrete examples suggest that two models might be operative in one university program—or even in one person. It is entirely conceivable that we might find in the same person two models: the sixth (JSH) (Jewish Studies) and the seventh (IH)(Israeli Hebrew) or even three: the sixth, the seventh, and the second (SPH) (Semitic Philology Hebrew). In that case, it would be fruitful to compare these different models to registers in speech. Ordinarily, we speak to different persons in different registers, one for instance, for our parents or teachers, one for friends, one for children, one for strangers, and so forth. Our dialogue with a language of such antiquity and variety as Hebrew may very well elicit a variety of registers. The complexity of the problem merely mirrors the richness of the Hebrew language and its historical experience. We should not be daunted by this complexity. By avoiding a serious confrontation with the problems posed by the concomitant existence of several models, we would deprive ourselves and our students of the variety of linguistic experience embedded in every Hebrew utterance. It is a rich language, and we should not beggar it by our sloppiness or our cowardice.

⤫ Jewish Literature in the University

Let us begin with Paul, known among the Pharisees, his teachers, as Saul of Tarsus. For no discussion of any facet of Jewish intellectual history in its relationship to what is commonly called Western Civilization of the past thousand years can be historically oriented or comprehensible without a consideration of the role of the man who gave Christianity its rationale and direction. Western European universities, so central in the development of Western cultural concepts, are the creations of late medieval Christian society. Furthermore, the European world most Jews have lived in was (with the exception of Moslem Spain and Ottoman Turkey) decidedly Christian. And the fact that Jewish writers generally knew little and grasped less of Paul's mission, which affected them so profoundly, only proves that Paul was eminently successful. Paul it was who defined the relationship between Christianity and its mother-religion, Judaism; Paul it was who declared Judaism obsolete, decadent, hypocritical—hence superseded by its more righteous and vibrant daughter; and Paul it was who, therefore, essentially excluded Judaism from the realm of Western intellectual history.

Western Civilization as we know it from the fourth century C.E. is fundamentally a Christian civilization; in spite of its pagan and Judaic origins, its institutions and modes remained Christian. If the Christians adopted the "Old Testament" as a sacred text, it was not the same Bible sacred to Jews. The very name "Old Testament" implies that there is a "New Testament" and that the original book testifies to the authenticity of the advent and crucifixion of Jesus. The Jewish writer, taking his sacred text as a point of departure in his creative ventures, never thought of it in these Christian terms. When I assert that the exclusion of Jewish intellectual history can be traced to Paul, I mean Jewish intellectual history as lived by the writers who made it, men for whom Jesus was either ignored or disdained and Christianity, at first a vexatious heresy, and then, after centuries of persecution, the living symbol of human depravity. Cultures should be understood in the light of their own norms; their achievements should be judged in the light of their own self-image. In that Western Civilization has not accepted Judaism on its own terms, it has excluded it.

The American university is a new departure in the long history of universities going back to Europe at the end of the Middle Ages. Though our universities thrive upon their intellectual freedom from either church or state, even though our wider knowledge of varieties of cultures has broadened our concept of culture, the notion of Western Civilization current in the university is predominantly Christian. Open a standard textbook in history or literature, scan a syllabus and you will see: the Hebrew Bible or Israelite culture is tucked in between Mesopotamia and Egypt, all presented along with Greece and Rome as adumbrations of Christianity; post-Biblical Jewish literature is not mentioned at all. (Islam, incidentally, rarely fares better, and since Islam is slighted, Jewish cultural creativity within the Moslem world also receives the scantiest notice).

The outlook of the American college professor is certainly more enlightened, but still far from adequate. Often his knowledge is arrived at as a fragmentary by-product of his own interests; few universities even today offer courses covering the material. His concept of Jewish intellectual history highlights the Biblical period and some aspects of the past century but leaves the rest in total darkness. Granted that Christianity has been the dominant European and American culture, the picture a university presents still cannot be complete, hence authentic, without an adequate understanding of both Jewish and Moslem intellectual history. In America, it would seem, the time is ripe for an advance toward this greater catholicity of concept. World politics and improved communications have subjected dozens of new modes of thinking and living into our consciousness, and we are obviously on the threshold of a new period of cultural adjustment in which we shall have to reassess the European and American experience in the light of an expanded universe. Perhaps we shall now be more open to the diversity within the Western tradition.

In adding Jewish studies to its curriculum, for instance, a university renders itself a great service and takes an important step towards the achievement of authentic objectivity and perspective, which is one of its prime goals in society. Let us see, then, what the university can learn from Jewish or Hebrew literature. We shall begin with a consideration of several broad aspects of Jewish literature of all periods, and then focus upon modern Hebrew literature.

✿   ✿   ✿

The two terms "Jewish literature" and "Hebrew literature" introduce us to a set of problems unique to these literatures. Historically, Jews have always considered Hebrew their sacred tongue, but also wrote extensively in Aramaic, Greek, Arabic, and Yiddish. Though writing in these secondary languages, they wrote primarily as Jews for a Jewish public and could therefore assume certain conventions of genre, metaphor, and allusion. In this sense, what they wrote is Jewish literature; that which is outside the scope of these conventions is not. With the possible exception of the early Biblical writers, Hebrew or Jewish writers in general have always been bi-lingual, if not trilingual, or quadri-lingual. One can assume the knowledge of Hebrew and Aramaic in most cases and often a vernacular which was spoken when Hebrew or Aramaic were no longer vernaculars. The interplay of linguistic elements in a book or a mind, the fusing of recognized literary convention with different languages in different ways, is an endless source of fascination for the literary scholar.

It is not insignificant that medieval Hebrew writers in Moslem Spain wrote prose in Arabic, but poetry in Hebrew; that Immanuel of Rome, a contemporary of Dante, wrote sonnets both in Hebrew and Italian; that Mendele, in the late nineteenth century, began his career in Hebrew, switched to Yiddish to reach a wider public, but then recast his stories into Hebrew to give them permanence; that for most modern Hebrew writers their medium of expression was an acquired language. Even in the centuries of greatest cultural isolation from the Gentile world—the sixteenth, seventeenth, and eighteenth centuries—no Jewish writer could get along without extensive knowledge of three languages. Certainly this phenomenon and its literary results should recommend themselves as a fascinating area of study to the American student who rarely knows more than his native tongue. Ordinarily, this polylingualism engenders a critical turn of mind and an ability to assimilate many new concepts without undue displacement, since this process in Jewish literature is inherent in its medium. Written in different languages, in different cultural milieus and in different centuries, Jewish literature by itself is a perfect paradigm of comparative literature, by which we mean a concept of literature which evolves from the study of several literatures, each in itself and in comparison with the others. The intellectual community at large is rarely aware of this diversity within Jewish literature and ordinarily call a specialist in the field "a Hebraist," a term more appropriate to the Gentile Renaissance Biblical scholars who were, indeed, Hebraists. When you denominate a man as "Hebraist" everyone assumes that he is a Biblical scholar. Actually, we don't even have a label in English for the specialist in post-Biblical Jewish literature.

The medium of Hebrew literature, in particular the Hebrew language, calls attention to itself in ways unknown to most European languages. Not only is Hebrew the language of the sacred text from which the culture takes its point of departure, but, according to abundant literary tradition, it is the Hebrew word by which the Lord created the world. Reverence for the word was not restricted to circles of mystics but underlies such major genres as commentary and midrash (homiletic discourse), and informs not only medieval poetry but also much of modern Hebrew literature. The art of words, literature, has always been the primary art expression of the Jew; as far as we know, neither the graphic arts nor music reached high degrees of sophistication. (By art, of course, we do not mean the autonomous realm of emotional expression and imagination envisaged by the Romantics.) Even the daily ritual of living was imbued with complex, ennobling meanings by the wealth of legendary and symbolic verbal lore that accompanied each act. It is often implied that without speech, man is no different than the beast; without the word, the world disintegrates into chaos. Literacy, therefore, has always been one of the cherished ideals of the Jewish community. And since the word assumes significance and responsibility far beyond the ordinary function of communication and expression, the independence of art, or aesthetics in general, is a notion foreign to Hebrew literature. Jewish literature as a whole, therefore, has usually included genres that few other literatures would include. Legal and philosophical texts, commentaries and homilies, were included in the same literary continuum with poetry or romance. Since all Jewish writers were subjected to rigorous training in Rabbinic literature, it is not bizarre to find Shmuel Ha-Nagid writing both a treatise on Talmud and lush court poetry, or Yehuda Ha-Levi writing both pious philosophy and erotic love poetry. Significantly, the dichotomy between belles-lettres and the other literary categories becomes pronounced in the modern period.

Reverence for the word is not a matter for the academicians or aestheticians alone. In his book *The House of Intellect* Jacques Barzun traces what he considers the disintegration of the concept of intellect in the past century and demonstrates its manifestation in the disregard for the usage of words. Intellect, he asserts, is a product of social effort and an acquirement which requires conventions of communication. Intellect is social; intelligence, private. Intellect presupposes literacy, schooling, and is built upon the word. Paralleling Barzun's thesis, George Steiner outlined the debasement of the word in many facets of modern intellectual life in a series of articles aptly named "The Retreat from the Word," which appeared in *The Listener* two years ago. He surveys the many art forms and intellectual pursuits which emphasize non-verbal expression in an attempt to seek liberation from convention, from history. Steiner deplores this tendency since it tends to slight the truly great achievements of human intellect and settles for a childish primitivism; it rejects sophistication and complexity of tone for almost inarticulate abstractions. In retreating from the word we retreat from man's finest accomplishments.

Having inherited this reverence for the word, the Hebrew writer has been able to withstand the tendency described by Barzun and Steiner even in our current period of social and ideological flux. The major writers of modern Hebrew literature have excelled not only as literary artists but as imaginative linguists who mediated between the old and the new, between time-honored texts and the impulses of life. They were assisted in this venture by a reading public that was relatively wide and well-educated. (In the Arab world, on the contrary, excessive veneration of the holy word, coupled with mass illiteracy, have resulted in a serious bifurcation of the language into two strata: a literary language that relatively few could read, and many vernaculars that are often mutually unintelligible). The word in Hebrew has rarely been an ornament, a triviality; on the contrary, while linguistic problems are followed quite ardently, change is appreciated if it is necessary and imaginative. The most influential safeguard for sensible linguistic growth is the widely literate public: neither the purist nor the innovator can get away with nonsense. The Hebrew reading public has always been aware of the centrality of its language in human discourse. When, therefore, two writers quarrel, as they often do, over the use of a word, to some this quarrel may seem to be scholastic bickering, but we would suggest that they are actually fulfilling the intellectual's duty: they are doing their bit to prevent the world from slipping back into chaos.

History is ever with the Jewish writer and the Hebrew writer, in particular. His literary conventions, his media of expression go back centuries. In this sense his problem is the opposite of that facing the American writer who is always in search of a usable past, of historical roots and conventions that he can share with his public. When you read the poetry of Ibn Gabirol of the eleventh century, you hear echoes of Biblical verse; when you read the poetry of Bialik in the twentieth century, you hear echoes of both the Bible and Ibn Gabirol. Most writers have exercised their individual talents through the traditional modes, and the very fact that some Israeli writers don't choose to do so is in itself significant.

The historical sense manifests itself both in general orientation and in the texture of a phrase or a sentence. The Jewish writer's historical orientation does not necessarily depend upon his acceptance of divine causality in history; his identification with the experience and destiny of his public gives him his orientation, gives him the *myth* by which he lives as an artist. And when he writes in Hebrew, his desk is surrounded by rows of Hebrew writers from the Biblical Deborah to his own colleagues, all pressing in upon him to advise or censure. A metaphor or turn of phrase that has once been used must be avoided or used in a new context. Historical resonance can be either a curse or a blessing. It is a curse when it dominates a writer and serves as a substitute for literary talent and achievement; it is a blessing in that it gives an author, quite gratuitously, the historical dimension that few authors in other languages can have. It is one of the great joys of the Hebrew reader or literary critic to see how an individual literary talent fights his battle with the angel of literary tradition and wins.

Since the Hebrew word is ordinarily uttered with a consciousness that transcends the merely artistic, and since Hebrew literature is of such long memory, it is what cultural historians would call "an institution." In his essay "Literature as an Institution" Harry Levin states:

> The truth is that literature has always been an institution. Like other institutions, the church or law, it cherishes a unique phase of human experience, and controls a special body of precedents and devices; it tends to incorporate a self-perpetuating discipline, while responding to the main currents of each succeeding period; it is continually accessible to all the impulses of life at large, but it must translate them into its own terms and adapt them to its peculiar forms.

If literature as a whole can be considered an institution, Hebrew literature, considered broadly, was an institution of cardinal importance within its culture. Without real political power in most countries, and without a clearly defined hierarchy of religious authority, Jews lived through their books, by their books, with their books, and at times against their books. Books were not read; they were studied. And since intellect is required to understand and describe the complexities of human existence, intellect became a symbol of esteem and a key to power. When political Zionists claimed that the Zionist movement was "the state in process of becoming," the Hebrew critics punned upon this rhetorical cliché and said that Hebrew literature was "the state in process of becoming," or even a surrogate for a state.

One would be hard pressed to find so vibrant an intellectual tradition so firmly entrenched in a widely literate society. The humanistic tradition in the American university is still a lonely island in a vast sea of technologists and quantifiers, both within the university and without. A society which still considers the egg-head a *square*, and thinks that college graduates and computers are intellectual, obviously has much to learn about intellect and the humanistic tradition.

o   o   o

Modern Hebrew Literature is, in itself, a source of endless fascination and presents to the literary scholar many problems he cannot find elsewhere. Its peculiarities stem from the fact that it corresponds so closely to the peculiar destiny of the Jews in the modern era. Nevertheless, to the literary scholar working in other languages it is unknown territory, if not a mystery. The mystification is often generated by the erroneous notion (which, again, can be understood under the Pauline thesis) that there has been no Hebrew literature since the Bible and that modern Hebrew literature, therefore, came into existence with the State of Israel in 1948. There has been, of course, an unbroken tradition of literary creativity in Hebrew throughout the centuries, and that period that we arbitrarily call *modern* antedates the State of Israel by over one hundred and fifty years. The beginning of modern Hebrew literature is usually placed in the last decades of the 18th century, and its development since then has been well documented.

Mystification aside, the real problems still remain, problems that shed light on the intricacy of the human condition and upon the ingenuity of the human intellect. What, for instance, is *modern* about modern Hebrew literature? Why did these writers select Hebrew and not any other language used by Jews? Which areas of literary activity did it embrace, and which did it exclude? Why did it flourish when and where it flourished? And finally, what does this body of literature mean in relationship to the totality of Jewish literature over the centuries? We shall address ourselves to these questions in order.

Modern Hebrew writers themselves call their work *sifrut hadasha*, which simply means *new* literature, or *recent* literature. A term for *modern* did not exist—at least not for *modern* in the sense in which we understand it today. When late Renaissance Gentile writers in several countries joined the battle of the Moderns versus the Ancients, they referred to the struggle between the current aesthetic concepts of the vernacular literature and the imagined canons of Greek and Latin literature. In the past two centuries, however, *modern* often means something else: the culture that was called *modern* and that writers or intellectuals considered worthy of emulation, was not an ancient culture, but rather a contemporary one, which was considered superior to one's own. Usually the word "modernization" is synonymous with "Westernization," since the cultures, and particularly the literatures, which writers considered worthy of emulation since the 17th century have been in the West: first France, then Germany and England, and finally Russia and America. This is true not only of the Jewish community of Eastern Europe but of certain European nations, e.g., the Germans, the Poles, and the Russians, and, for that matter, the Islamic world, India, Japan, and most recently Africa. For Hebrew writers at the beginning of the modern period, the models were Western—French and German, in particular—and those were, on the whole, enlightened, liberal, cosmopolitan, and erudite. To the scores of individual talents which began to leave the Rabbinical academies to migrate westward, or to the more "westernized" burgeoning cities, the glitter was irresistible. It is at this point that the Jewish intellectual, confronted by the brilliant glow of the West, began to feel inferior to it: he had, after all, come from a cultural community that had been isolated in a rather backward section of Europe for three centuries, and he could not possibly conceive that his own literary training might have humanistic virtues equal or superior to those of Goethe or Schiller. At that period we begin to sense a dichotomy that rises in the hearts of writers between *man*, on the one hand, and *the Jew*, on the other. At that period, for the first time, we begin to find considerable numbers of Jewish intellectuals who accept, often quite unwittingly, the Pauline thesis that Christianity had superseded Judaism, and a few even chose the logical conclusion: voluntary conversion to Christianity.

The appearance of the first samples of modern Hebrew literature in Germany at the end of the 18th century, a period identified with the name of Moses Mendelssohn, was not a historical accident. These writers had two reasons for composing in Hebrew at that period: one consciously and repeatedly verbalized; the other, deeply felt but infrequently mentioned. On the one hand, the writers of Mendelssohn's generation and the one after him hoped to use original essays in Hebrew and translations into Hebrew in order to introduce Western culture to the Jewish public. Ironically, this attempt failed miserably: the natural process of assimilation was so rapid that within a generation there were not enough interested Hebrew readers in Germany to support a Hebrew annual. On the other hand, by pouring his ancestral literary tongue into Western molds, the Hebrew writer tried to find for himself a middle-ground between the two cultures, which would enable him to maintain both his Jewish and modern Western identity. The major poetic achievements of the period—such as N. H. Wessely's *Shirei Tiferet*—are infused with this latent sentiment. The beginning of modern Hebrew literature, then, is a result of this confrontation with the West, a confrontation made possible in the liberal intellectual circles of Berlin and Hamburg and which is charged with the two aspirations that might either merge or oppose each other in the most interesting ways, i.e., assimilation of modern Western norms and modern nationalism. For modern nationalism, taken in its broader, intellectualized sense, is informed by pride in group achievements, in group past, and in group destiny. The line from the early stirrings of this literature to political Zionism and through it to the State of Israel is not too hard to trace. With the increasing disillusionment in the West and its values, which begins in the 1870s and swells toward the end of the century, the nationalist theme becomes more dominant.

Hebrew, then, was the logical choice of these early writers and their successors, not because it was the vernacular (it wasn't; Yiddish was), but because Hebrew had a respectability and historical dignity which Yiddish could never claim. The belated magnificent outburst of Yiddish expression in the past seventy-five years should not blind us to the fact that until the beginning of this century, Yiddish literature, which goes back to the late Middle Ages, was definitely the province of the less educated and bore this stigma. If didactic propaganda had been the only motive for Hebrew literature during the Haskala (the so-called period of "enlightenment" from 1780–1880 roughly), Yiddish would have been the more appropriate vehicle of expression. Hebrew, however, meant reconciliation between the demands of two cultures; Hebrew meant

intellectual respectability. The Bible, the only book in all Jewish literature that had reached the Gentiles and was respected by them, was in
Hebrew. Clearly, French or German or any of the Slavic tongues would
never do.

The Hebrew writer, consequently, lived a split existence: he lived in
Yiddish; he created in Hebrew. In time a certain antagonism grew
between the two languages, exacerbated by the militancy of the
Yiddishists who claimed about the turn of the twentieth century that
Yiddish and not Hebrew should be the national language. This quarrel
of language is reflected in the curious fact that histories of modern
Hebrew literature pretend that Yiddish literature does not exist, and histories of Yiddish literature pretend that Hebrew literature does not exist.
The history of the past twenty years has made this quarrel meaningless,
but we still don't have a history of literature which presents an adequate
statement of the peculiar relationship between the two literatures. After
all, most Hebrew and Yiddish writers between 1860 and 1920 wrote in
both languages, often at the same periods and with equal skill. I know of
no direct parallel to this phenomenon in modern European literature.

In our previous consideration of the basic unique aspects of Jewish
or Hebrew literature, we have included all genres, many of which are
not ordinarily included in histories of literature. The standard texts of
modern Hebrew literature, however, have tended to limit their purview
to belles-lettres alone, with deliberate exclusion of commentary and
homily, of Rabbinic responsa and novellae, and even of the Hasidic folk-
tales. History and philosophy are still considered, albeit tangentially, as
long as they are written in good Hebrew. This dichotomy between the
more traditional and the less traditional modes of literary expression is
almost as artificial as that between Hebrew and Yiddish. While it is true
that in the modern period poets rarely write commentaries or responsa,
the respective publics for these two genres often overlap. All Hebrew literary works written before the First World War, and most of those before
the Second World War, assume, as a literary convention, the fact that the
reading public was conversant with the Bible and Rabbinic literature.
The writer always had to express the new idea or genre. e.g., the novel,
in conventional language; otherwise he would lose both his public and
his historical identity. It is interesting to note how these conventions
begin to disintegrate with great speed after the First World War. Today,
one could actually write a fairly comprehensive history of Israeli belles-
lettres without taking into account what is going on in some traditionally
oriented circles.

Since the canons of modern Hebrew literature were restricted to belles-lettres in Hebrew, they excluded whatever has been written in Ladino, Yiddish, and all the standard European languages. The truth of the matter is that the Sephardic or Oriental Jew is hardly represented in this literature; the bulk of Western European and American Jewish experience is not articulated in it. Obviously, though they claimed to express the historical needs and character of the Jewish people, modern Hebrew writers comprised a determined and talented minority that never commanded a vast audience until the last generation or two. Some of the most important books were published in limited editions of several thousand or several hundred. Even today, one can often sell more reprints of a significant medieval Rabbinical work than a critically successful novel, and certainly more than poetry. We should be aware that the triumph of the Zionist movement in the realization of a national state with Hebrew as its language makes us tend to lose our perspective; if Hebrew literature did exert a force far beyond its circulation figures it is because it reached the right people, the activists in the community, and gave them a new *myth* by which to continue as Jews in a new world.

Modern Hebrew Literature flourished in different parts of Europe at different periods. Starting in Germany in the last decades of the 18th century, it spread to Galicia, the eastern province of the Austro-Hungarian Empire, in the first few decades of the 19th century, and then into the western tier of Russian governmental districts by the second half of the century. By the beginning of this century we witness the establishment of new centers in both Palestine and America. The long history of Jewish literature has shown us that cultural centers have life spans: they are born and they die. Eastern Europe declined precipitously after the First World War and the Bolshevik Revolution, and was annihilated in the Second World War. By then, it is interesting to note in passing, most Hebrew and many Yiddish writers had fled to Palestine or America. Today, I regret to report, America as a center of Hebrew letters hardly exists.

In each case, one can attribute the wax and wane of literary activity either to liberalization of governmental policy or persecution on the one hand, or to the local cultural situation on the other. This phenomenon provides an inexhaustible fund of material for the student of comparative literature according to the French method, which concentrates upon tracing literary influences and relations. The question is not simple, even in the case of the Hebrew writers in Berlin at the end of the 18th century. We would expect to find the obvious traces of Klopstock, Lessing,

Goethe, and Schiller in their works—and we do; but we also find Racine. The problem in Galicia and Russia at the middle of the past century is even more complex since the Hebrew writer, living among hordes of illiterate peasants, had little contact with the native literature, which, incidentally, was beginning to flourish only at that time. It is no accident, then, that the first Hebrew novel, *Ahavat Tzion* by Abraham Mapu (published in Vilna in 1853), manifests the influence of the French popular novel which had penetrated into Russia both in the original and in Hebrew translations. By the turn of the century, the world became an open market for the Hebrew writer: he would translate or assimilate Shakespeare and Homer, Dostoyevsky and Hamsun. Read the poems of young Israeli poets today, and you know that they have read Baudelaire and Rilke, Eliot and Thomas.

The process of assimilation, social as well as literary, is always a gamble: one never knows whether the subject-object relationship will obtain or will be reversed. Individual talents and traditional cultural characteristics dissolve all too readily in a foreign ambience. Hebrew literature, however, has succeeded admirably in assimilating to itself various elements of foreign literatures. The history of prosody (the formal aspects of poetry) is a case in point. From the late 10th century C.E. on, Hebrew poetry, written on Arabic models, was quantitative. This metrical base persisted until the modern period. Since the 18th century, we have had three metrical shifts: to the syllabic in the 18th century (actually much earlier in Italy); to the tonic-syllabic in the mid-19th century; and to what might be called "free verse" after the First World War. It is very rare that a poetic tradition undergoes three radical metrical shifts in less than two hundred years and still continues to yield excellent poetry. Even more than Jewish literature throughout the ages, modern Hebrew literature included all the major components of a body of literature which lends itself to comparative treatment.

In his collection of Hebrew essays, Baruch Kurzweil, one of Israel's leading critics, posed the central question: Is Modern Hebrew Literature a continuation or a revolt (from traditional Jewish values)? Kurzweil's answer: Modern Hebrew literature is a revolt, is not as important as the question itself. The question is based on certain assumptions of interest to the general reader and to the student of literature. To begin with, the question derives from a theory of literature which holds that a book or a poem has a significance far beyond the aesthetic enjoyment of the individual reader; that the individual work of art may be self-contained, but Hebrew literature as a whole is an institution with its historical conventions and social responsibilities; that while literature should not be a tool of a state or a religion, it should not be hermetically sealed from the human condition in each generation. Kurzweil's second major assumption is the historical fact that something radical has happened to Judaism in the past two centuries: that which could be called normative Judaism, having obtained with modifications for twenty centuries, can no longer be called the norm. To these two assumptions Kurzweil adds a third, which is peculiar to him: that all works of art that do not conform to his scheme of orthodox religion are to be damned in varying degrees. The danger in Kurzweil's personal point of view is not in its specific religious bias but in its tendency to prescribe what attitude writers are supposed to have towards Jewish tradition and the human predicament today. The relationship between literature and life is rarely direct, but Kurzweil seems to think that it should be.

Kurzweil aside, the question he posed about modern Hebrew literature remains a central question. Rather than select one particular bias, we would rather say that when viewed historically this literature—with the possible exception of some of its lyrical poetry—documents the unraveling of the fabric of normative Judaism and the passionate intuitive attempt of individual talents to find new values for themselves and their public. These works of art, when studied carefully and judiciously, afford us prime material for the history of ideas in the modern world. With the disintegration of the organic community, its conventions and aspirations, each writer is thrown into a situation which, for lack of a better word, we must call "existential," and each writer must solve his problem in his own way. No writer really escapes this central problem; there are few lyric poets in modern Hebrew literature, for instance, who talk only about themselves with no reference whatsoever to their peculiar position in Jewish history. When I label this ever-present literary theme "nationalism," I do so with reference to nationalism in its broader meaning: I do not refer to the breast-beating chauvinism which portends the death of art and often of simple humanity; I refer rather to the compassionate wisdom emerging from a deep understanding of the interrelations between the individual human situation and the norms of the group that gives him his social identity.

We have already remarked that the first period of modern Hebrew literature, that called the Haskala, is marked by two ostensibly contradictory themes: on the one hand, the assimilation by the Hebrew writer of the values of the West, eventuating, of course, in the bitter criticism of their present life in the light of the ways of the West; and, on the other hand, a nascent feeling of nationalism that motivates the revival and propagation of the ancestral language. Both themes represent an intuitive search for new or renewed values. When the dream of enlightenment and emancipation began to dissipate in the 1870s and 1880s, the nationalist theme became the more dominant and more diversified; writers grew beyond their group inferiority complex. In its more activist turn, it centered about the new national life in Palestine that was envisaged—again intuitively—by writers in their stories and poems not primarily as a home for the homeless but a native soil on which to create a new hero, a new Jew; in its introspective turn, nationalism began to glorify all periods of Jewish history, not only the always respectable Biblical, but even the recent Hasidic and pietistic movements that the Haskala had denounced so violently. In their search for new symbols of identification, writers began to ransack the forgotten niches of history, to reinstate the renegades of Jewish history whom the Rabbinical authorities had bypassed: King Saul, the Hebrews of the desert, the Canaanite cousins, even the ancient Greeks (as long as they spoke Hebrew). The quarrel with Rabbinic Judaism was mollified by keeping it in the family. Since the 1880s, any Hebrew writer could roam at will over the vast expanses of Jewish literary history to select a theme, a posture, or a phrase that suits his purpose; before the demise of the Haskala, few would do this without inhibition: it wasn't proper from an aesthetic and ideological point of view. Generally, a Haskala writer was limited to a rather stilted Biblicized style, more a poor pastiche than an articulation of sensibility; the post-Haskala writer has at his disposal an infinitely wider medium of expression. By the same token, for the literary scholar, questions of style and tone became more complex, hence more difficult, but more fascinating.

After the First World War and the Russian Revolution a pronounced shift in tone is recognizable. It was evident during the forty years preceding 1917, that Hebrew writers entertained little hope for the future of traditional Jewish life; but after these two great upheavals this plaint of gradual decay became a strident cry of doom. This feeling of urgency could be articulated only by the various types of expressionism that swept Europe at the time; if, for the German or Italian writer, expressionism was the articulation of a heightened artistic apprehension of the horrors of the period, for the Hebrew writer it was truly a reflection of reality. By then, there was little left of organic Jewish life in many areas of Eastern Europe. The more talented writers rose to the occasion; in the poems of Uri Zvi Greenberg and some of the stories of Agnon, Hebrew literature reaches apocalyptic vision and provides a fitting prelude for World War Two.

This has indeed been a century of cataclysm, and Hebrew literature records it. Even the poetry and prose written in Palestine under the aegis of the Zionist enterprise was far from euphoric: loneliness, despondency and alienation are rarely absent even from the most optimistic works. This attitude of desperation—so characteristic of Y. H. Brenner—is the soil out of which grows the writer's commitment to the pioneering effort in Palestine, a commitment that generates about it a new set of values, of sancta: self-sacrifice, physical labor, the soil, Biblicism, Hebraism. All these sancta suffice to motivate human action and, consequently, to give coherence to literary form for several decades. In the past decade, however, it has become increasingly apparent that a new generation is pushing its way into literary prominence, a generation for which these ideals are not enough: the state was declared and organized, the war fought and won, and the dreams of their parents and teachers fulfilled. Literature, like life, cannot feed itself upon yesterday's aspirations. With no clear national goals that can form the focus for the individual talent, writers in Israel no longer travel together in one definable direction, but each seems to be searching for new directions that will give substance to his vision.

Returning to Kurzweil's question or to the complementary question often posed by critics: Has Hebrew literature created new values? we would answer that neither question is relevant either to literature in general or Hebrew literature in particular. Interesting as they are, these questions are glaring intellectualizations of the creative process; a person does not write with deliberate intent to contradict a tradition or to revolt against it, nor does he write with an eye to the specific act of creating new human values. He writes to articulate the existential situation in which he lives, to give permanent form to the flux of his life. These questions assume relevance when we realize that a writer's primary intention is to write, and it is the reader or the critic who transfers the writer's intuitions into discursive statement. We ask these questions in retrospect and answer them descriptively; we should not succumb to the inevitable temptation to confuse our situation with that of the writer. We, therefore, use the term "existential" with particular reference to the fact that most modern Hebrew writers have shucked off traditional norms of Jewish life and had to fashion, out of the fragments of a disintegrating structure, an artistic world with a reasonable internal coherence. Writers of the pre-modern era had to mediate between the accepted ideals and laws of their fathers and reality as they lived it; but the modern Hebrew writer began with conventions that were no longer viable to him as they were. His commitment has been to Jewish nationalism comprehended in its widest dimensions: identification with the totality of the Jewish past; participation in the aspirations of the Jewish people for a brighter future, illumined by the humanistic insights of the Bible, refined and sophisticated by centuries of intellectual experience lived in exile. Usually alienated from the religious community that reared them and living, until recently, in the condition of exile known only too well to their ancestors, Hebrew writers, more than any other writers of this century, have felt with their own flesh the agonies and outrages which our times have to offer to man made in the image of God. Only too well have they learned that centuries of painful cultural achievement, of literary creativity can be annihilated in one second and that the guards on the perilous frontier between humanism and barbarism must be mounted daily, since love is not enough. Their prose and poetry, both in their triumphs and failures, assert, however implicitly, that Paul was wrong.

✿   ✿   ✿

Hebrew or Jewish literature is not the only area of cultural importance missing from the curriculum of most American universities, but the exclusion of Jewish literature as described above cannot be attributed either to geographical distance from Europe or the humanistic insignificance of the values embodied in it. But times, perhaps, are changing. A three-cornered exchange on the curriculum of the American university appeared in recent issues of the *Newsletter of the American Council of Learned Societies* and represents a good sample of academic opinion on the subject. Though Hebrew literature is not mentioned specifically, Hebrew certainly fits into the context of the argument as a unique case.

Protesting against the invasion of the college curriculum by Burmese and African studies, Professor Rice of Cornell complains:

> The undoubted practical value and civic usefulness of elementary Burmese should not be allowed to obscure the far greater cultural value of French, nor the vocational knowledge of African cultural patterns the civilizing knowledge of the Italian Renaissance....Even among non-Western subjects the emphasis is significant. We teach Quechua, Urdu, and Malay but no classical Arabic....To teach Urdu but not classical Arabic reveals a confusion of values.

On the other hand, his colleague Professor Smith suggests:

> Those so unfamiliar with the massive accomplishments of [Asian] literatures as to imagine them to represent an achievement secondary to the French, are, I feel, to be urged to look to the insufficiencies of their own educational attainments.

The moderating argument—one which we feel applies, in part, to Jewish literature—was presented by Professor Wickens of Toronto:

> Any civilization, whatever its origins in time and space, is potentially worthy of its first-class citizenship in the humane polity, provided it can satisfy the requirement of having made substantial and available contributions to literature, art, and thought: that we in the West are usually not yet prepared to grant such citizenship (even on a trial basis) reflects, however excusably, only on ourselves.

We would accept Professor Wickens point with one reservation: though he speaks of "first-class citizenship in the humane polity," one gets the feeling that he still refers to academic subjects which might be isolated from the context of human experience. We would broaden his statement by emphatically repeating a point already made: the notion that intellectual pursuits are separable from moral concerns is foreign to the tradition of Jewish or Hebrew literature.

This point is brought out quite clearly in the story of "Shem va-Yefet ba-agala" (Shem and Japheth in the Railroad Coach) (1980) by Mendele (S. Y. Abramovitsh), the man usually considered the great innovator of modern literary style in both Hebrew and Yiddish. A touching satire like much of Mendele's work, the story reflects the confusions of the 1880s: many Jews had again been forced to take to the roads to seek more secure homes, and the ideology of the Haskala, which had formerly given many intellectuals a rationale for their awkward position of exiles in a world of Gentiles, had proved untenable in the face of political realities. The naive Haskala belief that acceptance into the social and intellectual European community was dependent upon the Jew's being less a *Jew* and more a *man* withered painfully, like all naive beliefs when confronted by the facts. Like other Maskilim, Mendele, too, went through a period of disillusionment, which, incidentally, was not as severe as that of his colleagues. Unlike many of the other writers, Mendele never really joined forces with the nationalist activists.

In this particular story, however, we can see an interesting turn of theme. The story takes place in a third-class railroad car filled with Jews on the move, seeking new homes. After the conductor passes, collecting the tickets, a bedraggled character in peasant clothing crawls out from beneath one of the benches, to the astonishment of the narrator of the story who, assumedly, was also traveling in the car. The man turns out to be a Polish peasant, an old friend and neighbor of the Jew who sat opposite the narrator. As the Jew explains to the narrator how he knew the Gentile and why the Gentile was traveling with the Jew and his family, we begin to understand the implication of the story's title and, therefore, of the entire story. According to Biblical tradition, both Shem and Japheth were the sons of Noah; Shem became the progenitor of the Semites, and Japheth of the Indo-Europeans. Mendele's Shem and Japheth are not only expansions of the Jew or Gentile from the individual to the general but a satire of the racist theories spawned in German academic circles in the 1870s.

The two men, the Jew and the Gentile, had for years lived in peace together as neighbors on German territory. With the rise of German nationalism and anti-Semitism, the Jew was hard pressed even by his good Polish neighbor who turned against him. The Jew was forced into exile. As fate would have it, within a few years, the Pole, too, was forced into exile by the Germans who could not tolerate a foreigner on their soil. By coincidence, the two exiles meet again in faraway Galicia. The Jew forgives the Pole and invites him to join his family in their constant search for a tranquil home. As the Jew tells the narrator this story, the Pole dandles the Jew's child and pacifies him. The Jew assures the narrator that the Pole has proved a most receptive disciple, not that he has converted to Judaism—the Lord desires no converts, exclaims Mendele, for he has his hands full with the Jews themselves, but that he has learned the ways of exile. Exile itself, claims Mendele, is far from the good life; but it does teach one the enduring lesson of compassion and inculcates a sense of humanity based on the frailty and tragedy of human existence.

✿   ✿   ✿

POSTSCRIPT: 40 YEARS LATER

When I wrote the article "Jewish Literature in the Universities" in 1962, at the beginning of my teaching career at UCLA, I was struggling with two related curricular facts: there were few, if any, courses offered in America universities on Jewish literature, especially for the modern era; Judaic studies in general were not considered part of the canon of

"Western Civilization," which was tacitly Christian. Jews were the paradigmatic *other* to the Christian world. The article addressed these facts. Since then, the cultural scene in the United States and, consequently, in the American university, has changed radically. The turbulent years of the 1960s undermined many of the basic presuppositions of life in much of the western world. Summarized most forcefully by a writer like Franz Fanon, the others of the world were seen in a different, more favorable light. In response to the demand for the right of many hitherto unheard voices to be part of the American choir, Black Studies, Women's Studies, and Latino Studies were introduced into the curriculum.

By the late 1970s and early 1980s, "cultural studies" infused with a militant "post-colonial" ideology emerged as a dominant force. Multiculturalism became the norm. Ironically, however, within the multi-cultural dynamic Jewish Studies, the study of the paradigmatic *other* of the Western culture, was often no longer included among *the others*. Rather, it was seen as part of the establishment. This paradoxical situation has been analyzed in a variety of articles and books, most preeminently in the anthology *Insider/Outsider: Jews and Multiculturalism*, ed. David Biale (Berkeley, 1998). Jews, who had historically been the *outsiders* slowly became *insiders*—shifted to that position both by the increasing openness of American society and the academy, and by the rising consciousness in both that there were other groups of *others* who were even more *outside* the mainstream than the Jews. In the eyes of some of the newly-conscious *others* Jews were the quintessential *insiders*. Jews were thus both insiders and outsiders, caught between two vectors that drastically complicate both attitudes and analysis. In the light of this tangle of ambiguities, the situation described in the above article of 1962, seems comfortably simple and transparent.

～ Jewish Studies in American Liberal-arts Colleges and Universities

The spread of Jewish studies as an accepted academic discipline in the American liberal-arts colleges and universities since the Second World War is one of the least charted areas of Jewish experience of the past two decades. While there have been any number of brief notices, usually based on the statistics first gathered by Abraham I. Katsh and Judah Lapson, we have but little information on this complex phenomenon and have not yet begun to ask some of the fundamental questions of definition and purpose.

In the process of gathering and analyzing much of the new information presented here, we have been repeatedly impressed by the dazzling variety of programs throughout the country. And because no two schools are alike, constants were difficult to establish, particularly since the source of information was either a questionnaire[1] or the college catalogues rather than detailed personal interviews and a study of the programs as they operate within a wider academic context. And yet, though aware of methodological limitations, we feel that the picture presented here is fuller than any made public to date. It attempts to touch upon the major questions that should concern those interested in this aspect of Jewish cultural life.[2]

In the main, we sought to determine the status and development of Jewish studies in American colleges and universities, the extent to which Jewish students avail themselves of those programs, and the type of faculty they attract. We also had in mind the effect of the growth of Judaic studies on the emergence of Jewish scholarship as a profession, and their potential as an instrument for helping the Jewish community to mature, and for helping its members understand themselves.

PLACE OF HEBREW IN CURRICULUM

Articles on Jewish studies in the American colleges have tended to concentrate on the status of Hebrew in the curriculum.[3] Our interest differs in scope and kind. While Hebrew is obviously one of the central components of Jewish studies, it is not their totality. Hebrew, moreover, is not identical with Jewish studies, since it may be studied by a Christian as background material for theological reasons of his own, or by an orientalist as a tool in the study of one of several closely related ancient Near Eastern cultures. These distinctions become relevant when we consider the structure of the standard article on Hebrew in American colleges. More often than not, the first section of such an article is devoted to the study of Hebrew in the 17th-century colonies. After the citation of the Mathers and the theologically-oriented curricula of Harvard, Yale, and Princeton, which included Hebrew, we usually leap to the end of the 19th century, when oriental studies were introduced into several American universities and, with them, some postbiblical literature usually considered as a branch of Semitics. Then would follow the third period of interest in Hebrew or Judaic studies, which began with the development of programs in various New York colleges in the late 1930s or early 1940s.

The selection of these three periods as peaks—the Colonial, the late nineteenth century, the past generation—is based on certain assumptions which bear examination. It is accurate for the development of the American university. But as a basis for our investigation two questions are important: What did the study of Hebrew mean to the administrators and professors in this discipline? Is the history of the American university the proper context within which a study of this problem should be conducted? The Puritan scholars, for instance, were primarily studying the language of Scripture, which they claimed as their Christian heritage. They did not associate their enthusiasm for the biblical text or Hebrew with contemporary Jews in America or in Europe. Indeed, the Puritans would certainly not have agreed with rabbis of their age, if they had known any, as to who were the legitimate heirs of "Old Testament" inspiration. The Puritan attitude towards Hebrew will, therefore, serve as an example of what we do not mean by Judaic studies, or Hebrew as part of these studies.

JUDAIC STUDIES: DEFINITION

We would rather consider Judaic studies as the discipline that deals with the historical experiences, in the intellectual, religious, and social spheres, of the Jewish people in all centuries and countries. While this definition may generate certain difficulties, particularly in the consideration of Bible studies (where it is difficult to identify a scholar's "Judaics coefficient" because of the subtle differences in emphasis and approach), it will save us from serious confusion. It is, after all, no less reasonable to posit that Judaic studies have to do with the experience of the Jews and its intrinsic shapes and attitudes, than to assume that Chinese studies, for instance, have to do with the historical experience of the Chinese. Every culture has its own structure and the accusation of parochialism leveled at the intrinsic approach is therefore unwarranted.

It is not unreasonable to consider Judaic studies in the university from a broader historic perspective than one limited to the American experience. Our point of departure will then be not Puritan America, but mid-19th century Europe, and Germany in particular. For once Jewish scholarship had been developed as a recognizable discipline by such men as Leopold Zunz, Abraham Geiger, and Heinrich Graetz, who initiated the *Wissenschaft des Judentums*—the substitution of scientific study, based on the principle of historical evolution, for tradition as the foundation of Judaism—it became the fond dream of westernized Jewish scholars that their discipline would be dignified by the establishment of chairs of Judaic studies in the universities. The first published document on this tendency is Abraham Geiger's *Über die Errichtung einer jüdisch-theologisch Facultät* (Wiesbaden, 1838). These dreams were rarely realized, but the cultural situation that generated both these dreams and their frustration must be the frame of reference for understanding the place of Judaic studies in the university ever since.

Emancipation, we know, exacted a high price from those Jews who sought it, and often ended in loss of specific cultural identity; the tensions released by the integration of Jews in the gentile society are still unresolved. Some degree of pluralism, however, is necessary for the creation of a cultural climate in which particularity is accepted both in society and in the academic institutions which that society creates and supports. A study of Colonial American scholarship reveals little, if any, tolerance of Judaic culture except in so far as it relates to Christianity.

Because the academy is a fair reflection of the society which creates it—the notion that the university is an "ivory tower" is a poorly attested cliché—Judaic studies were more often to be found in the university program in the past century than earlier, and in recent times more often in America than in any other country. Between 1886 and 1902, five scholars were appointed to American university posts in Judaic or closely related subjects: Richard Gottheil at Columbia (1886), Cyrus Adler at Johns Hopkins (1888), Morris Jastrow at the University of Pennsylvania (1892), Emil G. Hirsh at Chicago (1892), and William Rosenau at Johns Hopkins (1902). These men are often considered semitists, but they all did some work in rabbinic literature. It is significant that all were Jews, as are most of the professors of Judaic studies today. (A few, like George Foote Moore of Harvard or Herbert Danby in England, were not.) Personal commitment to some aspect of contemporary Jewish life is not a requisite for teaching Judaic studies, but since extensive familiarity with difficult sources is crucial for professional competence, it is only natural that the qualified candidates for posts would be men who had studied these sources before their graduate training, and these are likely to be Jews.

CRITERIA FOR SELECTION OF INSTITUTIONS

The selection of colleges and universities for our study was therefore contingent upon these factors. It would have been useless to poll the 2,000-odd colleges in the United States to determine whether they teach Hebrew, or accept Hebrew as a language for admission or a language requirement toward the BA degree. It would have been just as futile to select such institutions from the *Modern Language List* of schools. We have, instead, restricted our queries to accredited liberal-arts colleges and universities that include Judaic studies and Hebrew in their humanities curricula. Denominational schools and seminaries—both Jewish and Christian—Hebrew teachers' colleges, and Dropsie College were therefore immediately eliminated, leaving two borderline cases: Brandeis University and Yeshiva University. We included the former, and reluctantly excluded the latter. Since our criterion is the pattern of cultural vectors generated by emancipation, the tolerance of the majority group, and the identity-status of the minority group, Brandeis, though Jewish-sponsored, complies to a greater degree with this criterion than Yeshiva, in spite of the latter's liberal-arts program.

The choice between Brandeis and Yeshiva leads us to a question that is basic to this study: What is the power-structure of the university? Who are its administrators, its overseers and trustees, and its alumni? Is it still predominantly "white Protestant" and, if so, how responsive is it to the pressures of other interested groups, i.e., the faculty, the student body (both normally having a sizable Jewish component), and the community at large? This is by no means a theoretical question. It involves the day-to-day life of the university and comprises the real substance of the long-range process we call emancipation. The powers that be have not always been cooperative or magnanimous.[4]

SCOPE OF STUDY

Though our approach to the study was historical, the scope was, of necessity, determined by the raw material we succeeded in gathering and by the realities of the American scene. In this respect, our study differs significantly from that of Ismar Elbogen a generation ago.[5] Then Judaic studies in the universities and seminaries could best be surveyed by a study of Jewish scholars and their scholarship, and the study by Elbogen, which did not set out to review Judaic studies in the American university, reflected the academic realities of the time fairly accurately. In the meantime, however, the situation has altered considerably: as in so many other areas of public life, we must deal with institutions, programs, numbers, and only incidentally with imposing scholars. These are indeed very few and their impact is circumscribed by the organizational structures.

Individuality today is institutional, a fact brought out by the bewildering diversity of programs. Precisely because of this diversity, it is wiser to address ourselves to specific problems than to a profile of each school. We are primarily interested, furthermore, in the broad contours and general problems of our subject, and not in its details.

LISTINGS

The most comprehensive listings of American colleges and universities contain over 2,000, of which about 1,100 are accredited.

The selection of schools for our study was made after a careful consideration of the probability of receiving meaningful information. After collating and comparing lists of institutions offering Judaic studies, derived from several sources,[6] we compiled a list of 54 professors and 34 Hillel directors teaching such courses at 92 American colleges and universities. To them our questionnaire was sent. Forty-eight responded. Wherever possible, information regarding the remaining institutions was gathered from their catalogues.

For a correct evaluation of the various courses in Judaics, it was important to indicate the obvious disparity in quality of instruction at the various institutions. It is true that the most intimate and lasting aspects of the academic educational process cannot be ranked objectively, but it is also universally conceded that there are essential differences, some of which can be measured. Yet the academic community has not really attempted to tabulate even those aspects which can be quantified and there is no one generally accepted list ranking the various schools. A recent attempt, a study by Albert H. Bowker,[7] although far from satisfying, provided some basis for ranking. Using various criteria, including rank lists of graduate schools previously published by Howard Keniston and Bernard Berelson, Bowker arrives at a list of fifty universities with top graduate schools in the social sciences and humanities and twenty undergraduate colleges, most of which belonged to these universities. His list of undergraduate colleges is unfortunately short and favors some of the larger institutions over high-quality small institutions.

For our purposes we have set up two lists of institutions with full-time faculty in Judaics.[8] Table A lists those of Bowker's top graduate and undergraduate schools which offer Judaic studies, plus several small institutions usually regarded highly in academic circles; Table B contains all other schools included in our study. Within list A there are obvious differences in academic standing, but we could establish no objective criteria for subdividing this category. (We would rather err by being too inclusive than too exclusive.) For each of these institutions we have listed the department in which the Judaic studies are offered and shown whether the school is supported and controlled privately or by the state.[9]

Several conclusions can be drawn from these listings:

1. Many of the institutions in which Judaic studies and/or Hebrew are taught are in the top fifty-odd institutions in the country.
2. As far as could be ascertained, no Judaics courses are offered in the following colleges and universities rated high by Bowker: Catholic U.; Connecticut, U. of; Emory U.; Georgetown U.; Illinois, U. of; Mass. Inst. of Tech.; Nebraska, U. of; North Carolina, U. of; Notre Dame U.; Northwestern U.; Ohio State U.; Oregon, U. of; Purdue U.; Reed; Rochester, U. of; Swarthmore; Tulane U.; Virginia, U. of; Washington, U. of; Williams. To these above should be added such smaller colleges as Bryn Mawr, Carleton, and Vassar.
3. In Duke, Stanford, Syracuse, Toronto, and Wellesley—excluded from our lists—Judaic studies are considered as a distinct cultural area and given little attention.

4. Manitoba is the only Canadian university which merits a place on the list.
5. Several of the institutions listed by one or two of our sources as offering Judaics had no such program at the time of polling or listed no Judaics courses in their catalogues.

PLACE OF JUDAIC STUDIES IN HUMANITIES CURRICULUM

When post-biblical Jewish studies were first introduced into the curriculum of American universities at the end of the last century, they were usually placed in the department of Semitics (or oriental languages). This was the logical place for them then, Hebrew being a Semitic language and Semitic studies in those days being almost exclusively philological. Since then both the world and the academic disciplines have become more complex. The very term "Semitics department" is a rarity in the academic language of the mid-twentieth century.

The emergence of America as a world power has forced upon the universities the rather new concept of regional studies, which in turn enhances the academic importance of the modern world. The archaeological and philological advances of the past generation have shown us that this concept is crucial also in the study of the ancient Near East. Near Eastern languages or studies then, is one of the broad disciplines within which one now expects to find much of Hebraic or Judaic studies, particularly since the rise of Israel when a Hebraic-Judaic political enclave became an entity in the real Near Eastern world. And yet, the categorization is not as appropriate as one might think, for so much of post-biblical Jewish creativity is European in provenance and tone, certainly since the tenth century.

The department of religion (or religious studies) is a second logical place in which to offer a program in Judaic studies, and we notice that thirteen of the listed universities do so. We have restricted ourselves, of course, to departments of religion that are included in the general liberal-arts program. (If the university has a divinity school which lists in its catalogue many courses given also in the university's department of religion, our criterion for inclusion has been the apparent independence of Judaic studies from the doctrinal aims of the divinity school.) While in some colleges courses in Jewish religion are primarily service courses offered by the Hillel rabbi on a part-time basis, in other schools we find serious scholars as full-time teachers, e.g., University of California (Santa Barbara), Brown University (often distinguished visitors), Dartmouth, Drew, Iowa, Princeton, Smith, Vanderbilt, Washington University, Yale. That many schools of high academic standing invite specialists to teach Judaic studies in their departments of religion is in itself a sign of our times: religion is studied as a historical phenomenon in these departments and not as a truth to be propagated.

Foreign language departments both modern and ancient, would be the third logical place for courses in Judaics, and Hebrew in particular. Here, too, the study of Hebrew has been encouraged by a more general trend in American higher education—the interest in all foreign languages (stimulated to be sure, by the government for very, practical considerations) and in linguistics *per se.* Hebrew is a "neglected language" (though not on the *critical* list) and funds can be solicited from the government for the study of Hebrew. It is not always easy to deduce why some institutions have put Hebrew with the other languages (and why, among these, some have preferred modern to classical), why for some it is a discipline within regional studies, and why for others it is the language of one of the major western religions. Sometimes the choice is meaningful, but sometimes it is purely accidental, the decision of a dean or a committee at some juncture in the development of the curriculum.

The position of Judaic studies in the humanities curriculum is determined by their complexity. One might rightly expect to find different aspects of Judaic studies in related departments: Jewish history in the history department, Hebrew language in linguistics. At Columbia, for example, Hebrew is in Near and Middle East studies, Jewish history in history, and Yiddish in linguistics; and if we were to include incidental Judaics courses and scholars, they would fall into the departments of religion and classics. This fragmentation is understandable from the point of view of university administration. One could argue the obvious merits and disadvantages of this fragmentation, e.g., the escape from parochialism versus dissipation. One could also argue the merits and disadvantages of concentration, as at Brandeis, a fine example of the concentration of many disciplines in one department.

The fact is that it is often difficult to explain why university x puts Judaic studies in one category, while university y places them elsewhere. The *logical* answer—that is where they belong—proves little, since policy on their position is usually determined on a local and *ad hoc* basis: who sat on what committee when the subject was introduced and what was the forte of the first person to teach Judaics. In universities offering full programs in Judaic studies, the problem of academic disciplines is easily solved by the administrative expedient of cross-listing—a historian may be a member of a department of Near Eastern languages, but his courses are also listed under history.

EVALUATION OF JUDAICS PROGRAMS

Any consideration of the scope of an academic program must inevitably involve the quality of the students and the professional competence of the instructors. It is simply not enough to list the schools offering a Judaics or Hebrew major on the undergraduate level, or where a doctorate can be earned on the graduate level. We must keep in mind both the stature of the university under discussion and the caliber of the faculty. And while a full program demands the presence of several competent specialists, talented, solitary individuals have done remarkable work in several institutions. However, most of the schools on our B list offer no Judaics or Hebrew major, while only few on the A list do not offer such a major (and these, often, because for them the program is quite new), and most plan to have it in the near future or include it in a religion major. A student can gain a fairly adequate undergraduate training in Judaic studies at about 40 accredited colleges in this country, and can acquire substantial information on the subject in at least 25 other institutions offering a variety of courses but no undergraduate major.

On the graduate level the qualitative calculus becomes more crucial. We notice that the list of universities offering graduate programs in some phase of Judaic studies, leading to the Ph.D., is quite long. They are: Brandeis, Berkeley, UCLA, Chicago, Columbia, Cornell, Harvard, Indiana, Iowa, Johns Hopkins, Michigan, New York University, Hunter, Pennsylvania, Princeton, Rutgers, Smith, Texas, Vanderbilt, Wayne, Wisconsin (Madison), Yale. (Hunter, Indiana, Rutgers, and Smith have programs leading to the M.A. only.)

While, on the whole, these rank high among the nation's universities, not all the instructors and directors of these programs have achieved scholarly eminence. The reader can arrive at his own conclusions by considering the quality of the institution, the composition of the department, and the eminence of the scholars in it. It should be pointed out, however, that in many cases the strength of the departments lies in the ancient period, specifically in Semitic philology (and the closeness of the relationship between this discipline and Judaic studies is, as we have noted, open to question). Further, the professor's specialization should be taken into account, particularly in those universities where there is but one instructor at the graduate level who cannot possibly direct doctoral theses in all subjects of Judaic studies.

In general, it should be noted that the existence of a graduate program in universities will ultimately raise the level of their undergraduate studies. These schools naturally have goals that are somewhat different from those ordinarily associated with an undergraduate liberal-arts program. The training of professional scholars and the promotion of research become their professed primary purposes, and their faculties are usually highly qualified to teach on this level.

FACULTY

Since manpower is the major factor in all academic programs, particularly on the graduate level, a listing of full-time, permanent faculty, by universities, together with their field of specialization and the institution where they received their doctorate, will yield much information on the state of Judaic studies in the universities. Our emphasis upon "full-time, permanent" is crucial, for it implies a certain commitment on the part of the university. (Permanent faculty members usually have the rank of assistant professor or higher; there are few instructors now and teaching assistants are far from permanent.) Part-time lecturers were not recorded since it was impossible to determine exactly what their duties are; part-time faculty above the level of teaching assistant would amount to at least twenty scholars of some importance.[10] Because the material elicited by our questionnaires was incomplete, we have supplemented it where necessary and possible from the directories. In certain cases the designation of specialization is based on publications listed in these directories. The list has been restricted as much as possible to Judaics specialists: in the case of scholars competent in Ancient Near East or Old Testament, the inclination to viewing their discipline as part of a historical continuum extending past antiquity, however diffuse and changing, had to be attested in some way; training and competency in post-biblical Jewish texts was requisite for a person to be listed as a "history of religion" specialist.

Even from this incomplete table several important conclusions can be drawn:

1. Over eighty per cent of the professors listed have received their graduate training in the United States. An examination of their biographies reveals that over half were either born here or came here as children. In this crucial area of Jewish life, therefore, the

community is well on the way to providing most of its own university Judaics scholars.

2. The professors who are teaching in the better universities were also trained in fine graduate schools. The contribution of Columbia, often that of Salo W. Baron, is overwhelming. Johns Hopkins, Harvard, Pennsylvania, and Chicago also stand high on this list, as they do on any list of graduate schools in the humanities. Dropsie College, of course, has done its share in training professional scholars.

3. It is almost impossible to tell what a scholar's specialty is unless one reads his publications or his doctoral thesis. The various areas of Jewish scholarship are so often undefined and interrelated that the terms used in academic titles or catalogue descriptions do not convey an exact meaning.

4. An encouraging number of the scholars listed are under forty-five years old—a definite indication that younger scholars consider this academic discipline as one offering a promising future.

5. The general level of professional training is quite high, and interested students in the major colleges and universities, both undergraduate and graduate, can avail themselves of its benefits. For graduate work in a specific area, of course, the student must seek out the scholar under whom he wants to study, and for this he may have to go to another city or to Israel.

GROWTH TREND

In 1945 Judaic studies were to be found in but few universities and colleges in this country. Institutions offering these studies on either the graduate or undergraduate level were the major universities that had had Semitic-languages programs in the previous century (and some of the New York City schools) Berkeley, Chicago, Columbia, Harvard, Iowa (an exceptional case), Johns Hopkins, New York University, Brooklyn College, Hunter, Pennsylvania. The list has grown sevenfold since then and now includes almost every region of the country. The most striking growth in full-time faculty and actual course offerings has taken place in Brandeis, Columbia, California (Berkeley, Los Angeles), Wisconsin (Madison), and Rutgers (see map preceding article).

Doctoral programs in Judaic studies or some aspect of Semitic philology tangential to Judaic studies were offered in Columbia, Harvard, Hopkins, Berkeley, Chicago, and Pennsylvania in 1945. In the past twenty years, doctoral programs have been developed at Brandeis, New York University, University of California (Los Angeles), Wisconsin (Madison), Iowa, and Vanderbilt.

The increase in positions and programs is out of proportion to the increase in college population since 1945–46. As to the causes of this growth, most professors polled mentioned the inspiration of the State of Israel, the impact of the holocaust, the awakening of religious yearnings since World War II, the greater acceptance of Jews and Judaism by the Gentile community, and the response of the Jews to this acceptance. All these factors are operative and no observer of the Jewish scene in America would seriously discount their validity.[11] To these we would add four other explanations for the growth, also reflecting current American realities. (1) The academic intellectual in America is eminently respectable today—not only the scientist whose discoveries have a direct impact on our lives, but even the philologist or literary historian. Judaism is becoming intellectually respectable, a phenomenon that is both a cause and effect of the growth of Judaic studies in the university. (2) Since the war Jews have been invited in unprecedented numbers to occupy university posts in all fields. While in the 1930s and well into the 1940s most departments in major universities were *"judenrein"* (staffed mainly by old-stock Protestants), few are today. (3) Developments in regional studies, in religious studies, and in dissemination of "the neglected languages" have strengthened and legitimized the development of Judaic studies. (4) Fortunately, the needs and desires of the Jewish community run parallel to the educational trends prevalent in the country.

FINANCING

This concurrence of interest becomes most apparent when we study financing. Though our information here is far from full, it is clear that in both private and public colleges at least two-thirds of the funds needed to support Judaic studies come from the general university budget (including grants for language study from the federal government). There can be no more than ten endowed chairs in these studies in the entire country, while there are over 60 professors occupying what may be called fulltime positions.[12] Over the years much has been done in this respect by the Hillel Foundation, which supports three professorial chairs (State University of Iowa, University of Missouri, and Vanderbilt University), not to mention the many Hillel rabbis who give accredited courses; by the Hebrew Culture Foundation, which has initiated many programs and expanded existing ones; by the American Jewish Committee, and by many local groups. Quite often, the university has taken over the financing of the program after an initial period, if there is student interest. This does not mean that the days of the endowed chair are over, but rather that more often than not the financing comes from general university funds. If Judaic studies are considered as an integral part of a well-rounded humanities curriculum, there is no reason why the program should not be part of the regular budget.

STUDENT PARTICIPATION

Aside from its obvious result, the transmission of knowledge to students, the Jewish-studies program has many interesting side-effects which cannot be quantified, but which the respondents to our questionnaire assert are very real. Again and again one encounters in their responses such language as "added self-respect," "intellectual respectability," and "prestige both among Jews and Gentiles." It appears that the very presence of a Judaics scholar on the faculty or a Jewish-literature course in the catalogue has a meaning for students, for faculty, and for the administration. This presence, a sign of emancipation and equality, has its subtle psychological effects, which deserve serious study. Certainly it represents far more than public-relations value.

If we were to talk only in terms of direct student participation in the programs now available, the impact of their spread throughout the country would be negligible. Of the very many thousands of Jewish students in the universities today—Alfred Jospe quotes an estimated 266,000 in 1963 (AJYB, 1964 [Vol. 65], p. 133)—excluding 9,000 in denominational and theological institutions, it would seem that five per cent would be a generous estimate for those taking courses in Judaics. If we were to calculate the percentage on the basis of undergraduate majors, it would, of course, be much lower. The highest absolute figures for undergraduate majors are: Brandeis, 23; Brooklyn, 10; UCLA, 30; Indiana, 13; Hunter, 16; Rutgers, 12; Wisconsin (Madison), 10; and Manitoba, 19. A liberal extrapolation would yield a figure of 500 to 600 undergraduate majors.

The graduate figures are much lower, as one would expect. Aside from Brandeis and Columbia, we have no information of more than ten fulltime Judaics graduate students in any one institution. (On the undergraduate level the number of women equals or exceeds that of men, while the graduate students are overwhelmingly male.)

The survey courses attract larger numbers, but it is impossible to determine how many correspondents arrived at the figures they submitted: is one student taking three courses counted as one student or as three? At any rate, granted that the larger schools are correct in their estimate of 200 to 300 non-majors taking courses at any one time, the national total would not exceed 10,000.[13] Gentile participation is so small as to be negligible.

CAREER AIMS

The reported career aims of students in Judaics are fairly logical: the full-time graduate students aspire to college teaching and research in Judaics; the part-time graduate students—many of whom are practicing rabbis—mention college teaching and research, but add "to continue serving in the rabbinate." Though it is difficult to distinguish between full and part-time graduate students, particularly after the first two years of formal courses, many of the part-time students seem to be rabbis or Hebrew teachers. The career aims of the undergraduate students are usually vague: teaching on various levels, the rabbinate, social work. An undetermined but seemingly large percentage of graduate and undergraduate students are already teaching in afternoon Hebrew schools or are in the rabbinate during their student years.

Indeed, it is only during the past few years, with the availability of substantial financial aid (National Defense Act, National Foundation for Jewish Culture, Danforth fellowships, university grants) that a substantial number of graduate students have been able to pursue their studies without teaching on the side. In Judaic studies, as in other academic disciplines, the graduate student has never before found financial support so available, nor the prospects for advancement so bright. In the 1930s, responsible scholars often tended to dissuade their students from pursuing purely academic careers in Judaic studies, since they knew that positions were scarce; now, however, it is difficult to fill many of the available positions with competent staff. Anyone involved in the search for good faculty cannot escape the fact that we are now in a seller's market for scholars.

PROGRAMS OF STUDY

Hebrew, we have said, is not the totality of Judaic studies. On the other hand, no worthwhile Judaics program is conceivable without the student's preparation in the language in which most of the basic texts were written. All undergraduate programs require Hebrew for a major in some area of Judaic studies. Hebrew may not be required if the Judaics program is a specialty within a religion major, or if it does not lead to a full undergraduate major but is part of a general humanities curriculum or a series of service courses. The approach to the language, however, may vary greatly from school to school.

There are still colleges and universities in which Hebrew is taught only as a classical language, as it has been in American universities since colonial days, but these institutions constitute less than a third of those on our lists. In most cases, the Hebrew taught is what one would describe as standard modern literary Hebrew (which is not the same as colloquial Israeli Hebrew). The inclusion of modern Hebrew in the curriculum is to be expected today and, if taught properly, embraces the basic grammar of classical Hebrew. In some schools, classical and modern Hebrew are taught separately, while in others, one comprehensive course includes both. In several of the larger urban universities, some of the more advanced courses, particularly in modern literature, are conducted in Hebrew, and special conversation courses are offered. At present, Yiddish is taught only at Brandeis, Columbia, City College (N.Y.), and Manitoba. Both Hebrew and Yiddish are often studied by linguists as interesting examples of language structure; hence the housing of Yiddish at Columbia and Hebrew at Texas in the linguistics departments of those universities.

REQUIREMENTS FOR JUDAIC STUDIES

The requirement for the undergraduate major vary greatly.

UNDERGRADUATE MAJOR

We restrict ourselves to the programs of three of the largest undergraduate schools: Brandeis, Hunter, and University of California (Los Angeles).

Brandeis:
Two years, Hebrew.
One year, basic literature.
Two semesters, Biblical studies.
One semester, Jewish history.

One semester, Jewish philosophy, mysticism, or ethics.
One semester, modern Hebrew literature.
Four semesters selected from program offered.

Hunter:
24 units (8 semester courses) in the Hebrew major. A comprehensive
  oral examination in two major fields, e.g., Biblical literature, modern Hebrew literature.

University of California (Los Angeles):
Prerequisites: Four semesters, college Hebrew.
Two semesters, survey of Hebrew literature in English translation.
Requisites: 27 units (approximately 9 or 10 semester courses) including:
Two semesters, Bible
One semester, medieval Hebrew texts.
One semester, modern Hebrew literature.
Two semesters, structural grammar (Hebrew).
Four semesters (1-unit courses), conversation and composition.

Though there is some similarity on paper between these programs,
it would be impossible to compare them because too many unregistered
factors are involved, e.g., the quality of students, the level of instruction,
the pre-college preparation of students, or their experience in Israel.
Most schools responding to this poll indicated that about half their
majors had studied some Hebrew before entering college; in the urban
centers, New York in particular, the percentage is higher. Furthermore,
it is becoming more and more customary for students to spend a year in
Israel before graduation, often in some program connected with the
Hebrew University. These factors make it impossible to answer the obvious question: How much can a student learn in an undergraduate major?

GRADUATE STUDIES

If half the undergraduate students have had some Hebrew before entering college, all applicants for admission to graduate programs should theoretically have had an extensive Judaics background before matriculating.
In most cases, the admission requirements are a B average in a good
undergraduate college and the equivalent of the undergraduate major in
Hebrew or Judaic studies. Departments specializing in the ancient Near
East demand less knowledge of Hebrew than those offering programs in

post-biblical literature. The requirements to be met within the graduate program depend upon the student's specialization and the general requirements of the respective graduate schools. We can detect no uniformity in requirements, and certainly none in the rigor with which these requirements must be fulfilled.

The graduate schools we have listed: Brandeis, California (Berkeley), California (Los Angeles), Chicago, Columbia, Harvard, Hopkins, Iowa, New York University, Pennsylvania, Vanderbilt, and Wisconsin (Madison), offer a variety of areas of specialization within what may be called Judaic studies, though the university may list it as history, Near Eastern studies, or Semitics. However, two crucial factors must be considered: the size and caliber of the faculty and library resources.

While a talented and resourceful graduate student can do excellent work without good direction and good local libraries, it obviously helps to have both. Fine students may not be proof of the eminence of their teachers, but serious young academicians usually select the best professor they can afford to reach. Adequate library resources are not always available. For students who are near the Eastern-seaboard megalopolis (Boston to Washington), library problems are minor; aside from Harvard, Yale, New York Public Library, Jewish Theological Seminary, Yeshiva, Yivo, Dropsie, and the Library of Congress, there are at least six or seven fine smaller libraries (of less than 50,000 volumes). But for those who cross the Alleghenies, library problems become crucial. If they cannot avail themselves of the splendid resources of Hebrew Union College at Cincinnati and of good collections in Semitics at Chicago, Indiana, Minnesota, Wisconsin (Madison), and Berkeley, they have to go to Los Angeles for Judaica—and Los Angeles is not New York City. No statistics on library holdings or course listings, however, will serve as reliable indicators of the quality of professional training offered by any graduate school. For that, one has to study the careers of the products of the graduate school.

COMMUNITY CONTEXT

Were we to study our topic in isolation from the general community of Jewish learning in this country or in the world, we would not be able to understand much of the material presented here. The Judaics courses or programs are but a secular, public sector of a broader educational effort supported primarily by private Jewish funds: the rabbinical seminaries, the Hebrew teachers' colleges, the day schools, the synagogue schools, and dozens of more modest organizational programs. We have noticed that about one-half of the undergraduates had studied Hebrew before entering college, mostly in Jewish schools; most graduate students have had some training in Jewish institutions, and some of the outstanding libraries are supported by rabbinical seminaries or Hebrew teachers' colleges. Many of the leading Judaics scholars in America are on the faculties of Jewish-sponsored institutions that were not included here because of the precisely defined scope of our study, and Judaics in the universities would indeed be orphaned without them. There is considerable faculty exchange, giving full-time professors at one institution the opportunity to offer a course or seminar at a second institution.

By the same token, Israel is an important presence in the intellectual world of the university Judaics professors. This is so not only because American students often study in Israel or an occasional course dealing with Israel is offered in American universities, but also because the greatest concentration of Judaics scholars and publication is in Israel. In the past ten years there has also been significant faculty exchange between American and Israeli institutions. Rare, indeed, is the professor of Judaics who does not have intimate ties with his Israeli colleagues.

From time to time one reads euphoric articles on the renaissance of Jewish learning in America, which cite as a prime example the spread of Judaics studies in the liberal-arts colleges and universities. The material presented here should give us some idea of the extent and limits of this growth. We have seen that relatively few students avail themselves of these courses, and that for most they constitute a vague presence that can imply acceptance in the academic community, intellectual respectability, or a justification for self-acceptance; and the same is true for the thousands of Jewish professors of all subjects who populate American universities. However, since it has finally become abundantly clear that more than two-thirds of American Jews of college age attend some college or university—the estimate for 1963 was between seventy and eighty per cent (AJYB, 1964 (Vol. 65], p. 133)—the campus has become the arena for Jewish organizational activity. The presence of Judaics programs on the campus has therefore attracted the attention of organizations that once hardly noticed them.

The rapid increase in Judaics posts in the universities between 1945 and 1965 from about 12 to over 60 full-time positions has had a profound effect upon the teaching profession. We have not yet seen a major upsurge of Jewish scholarship in this country, but the prospects are encouraging. With two or three new posts created every year, the availability of positions attracts young scholars and enhances the security of more mature scholars. This expansion has provided a broad base for further development. Indeed, the one clear conclusion we arrive at, after examining the fragmentary and complicated welter of facts that emerged from our study, is that we are on the threshold of a new and promising period in Jewish scholarship in America, which merits careful attention and cautious, continual reassessment.

As Weisberg has put it, "Jewish culture in the United States is predominantly what Jews do under the auspices of Jewish organizations,"[14] and these organizations are primarily welfare or service groups. Thus Jews live a surrogate existence, in that their main function is doing things for others. If this is so, then the Judaics studies in the universities and their implications present an added opportunity for an interested minority to learn that philanthropy has not always been the sole purpose of Jewish communal life. We should not exaggerate the potential effect of Judaics programs upon American Jews; nevertheless, they are a significant, though small force, in the slow, silent struggle to give institutional embodiment and communal identification to the essentials of Judaism (a minority tradition) for a meaningful identity within a leveling, permissive society. They might even present a few of the alienated Jewish intellectuals with an alternative to the rejected temple men's club and sisterhood.

NOTES

1. For the questionnaire, the introductory map, and Tables A, B, and C see the original article.

2. In Oscar I. Janowsky, ed., *The American Jew: A Reappraisal* (Philadelphia, 1964), a work of 468 pages, the entire subject is disposed of in one short paragraph (p. 152).

3. The standard works are these: Abraham I. Katsh, *Hebrew in American Higher Education* (New York, 1941); *id.*, *Hebrew Language, Literature and Culture in American Institutions of Higher Learning* (New York, 1950); *id.*, "Hebraic Studies in American Higher, Education," *Jewish Social Studies*, January 1959; Judah Lapson, *Hebrew in Colleges and Universities* (New York, 1958); David Rudavsky, "Hebraic Studies in Colleges and Universities," *Religious Education*, July-August 1964; *id.*, "Hebraic Studies in American Colleges and Universities with Special Reference to New York University" in Israel T. Naamani and David Rudavsky, eds., Doron: *Hebraic Studies* (New York: National Association of Professors of Hebrew in American Institutions of Higher Learning, 1965).

4. The *Study of Jews in College and University Administration* (May 1966), conducted by the American Jewish Committee, found that fewer than one per cent of the presidents and 2.6 per cent of the deans of American nonsectarian colleges and

universities were Jews, in contrast to an estimated 12 per cent ratio of Jews in the student bodies of these institutions.

5. "American Jewish Scholarship," *American Jewish Year Book,* Vol. 45 (1943–1944), 47–65.

6. H. Tierney, G. L. Lund, and M. N. Ball, *Manpower in the Neglected Languages* (New York: Modern Language Association of America, January 1965); D. N. Bigelow and L. H. Legters, *N.D.E.A. Language and Area Centers: A Report on the First Five Years* (Washington, D.C., 1964); Hebrew Culture Foundation list; a list of colleges in which Hillel directors offer accredited courses in Jewish studies; the Katsh and Lapson studies, cited above, both rather old; a list provided by the Society for Religion in Higher Education, and inquiries of colleagues in major universities.

7. "Quality and Quantity in Higher Education," *Journal of the American Statistical Association*, March 1965, 1–31.

8. Lists A, B, and C can be found in the original study.

9. In a depressing number of instances the questionnaire returned was hardly informative. The reader should, therefore, understand the limitations of this study. The information, though fragmentary and, in keeping with our objectives, rather broad in scope, is fairly accurate for winter 1965–1966. (Some universities that do not have a Judaics scholar at present plan to have one soon.) For more specific information, university catalogues should be consulted.

10. More detailed information than we can present here may be obtained in one of the three standard directories: *Directory of American Scholars; Who's Who In World Jewry; Who's Who.* (Note that entries are usually based on material presented by the person listed.)

11. For details on American Jewry since the war see Janowsky, ed., op. cit., especially Harold Weisberg, "Ideologies of American Jews," 339–359.

12. The term "endowed chair" is rather nebulous; some are fully endowed, some partly.

13. Janowsky (op. cit. p. 152) quotes Lapson for a recent figure of 14,000 studying Hebrew alone, which is a bit high. The 1964 report of the Modern Language Association of America records 5,021 for 1962 and 5,347 for 1963. Of these, about one-third are attributed to Yeshiva. Even if we assume that 50 per cent are studying modern Hebrew (most of the other 50 per cent are in Bible colleges), Lapson's figure is still above the M.L.A. figures.

14. Janowsky, ed., op. cit., 348.

POSTSCRIPT: THIRTY-EIGHT YEARS LATER

Since the publication of this article, the field of Jewish Studies has expanded exponentially. The Association for Jewish Studies was founded in 1968, hundreds of new scholars, both men and women, have entered the field, and hundreds of scholarly books on Jewish Studies have been published, primarily by university presses. While the figures in my article are obviously outdated, the basic concepts in it are still quoted frequently.

❧ Popular Fiction and the Shaping of Jewish Identity

The prodigious achievements of American Jews in the area of fiction since World War II are one of the phenomena commonly cited as evidence of the integration of Jews into the mainstream of American life. No account of the historical experience of American Jewry during this period is complete without the evocation of the triumvirate: Bellow, Malamud, and Roth. Just what identifies these writers as specifically Jewish, however, is usually a source of perplexity, even embarrassment, for the critic and historian. I cite the eminence of these writers and the attending problem of definition not to reopen this tired discussion, but rather to identify a problem that has intrigued me for some time.

Contemporaneous with the works of Bellow, Malamud, and Roth, or such authors as Ozick, Doctorow, or Halpern, one finds a group of books of less critical acclaim but of clearer Jewish resolution, books that have enjoyed enormous popularity and have had a significant impact on American Jewish life. Leon Uris's *Exodus* immediately leaps to mind and is, perhaps, archetypical, but there are others of equal significance: *Marjorie Morningstar, Fiddler on the Roof, The Chosen,* and Wiesel's *Night*. While these books differ markedly one from the other—*Fiddler* is a musical, and some of these works have had greater impact as films than as books—I think we could all agree that all these works contributed significantly to the identity articulation and agenda setting of the post World War II American Jewish community. While these are not projects initiated by the organized Jewish community and its variegated institutions, these works evoked responses from both the affiliated and unaffiliated portions of the community. As such, they have been historical events of major import and deserve our serious study. Tentatively, I will call this subgenre "American-Jewish popular fiction," and include in it a wide variety of types, even a musical comedy like *Fiddler on the Roof*, whose popularity and impact are undeniable.

We can examine only a sample at present, and my selection has to be rationalized. As I began to marshal my evidence, a striking pattern began to emerge. Herman Wouk's *Marjorie Morningstar* appeared in 1955; Leon Uris's *Exodus*, in 1958; *Fiddler on the Roof*, a joint composition (Stein, Bock, and Harnick), in 1964. In less than a decade, three of the most significant samples of this genre were issued to great popular acclaim and commercial success. While one can think of other examples from the same period, or from the past two decades, the limited time frame affords us a tight control; the reasonable distance from our vantage point, 1989, allows us the proper perspective.

The commercial success of this genre, its market orientation, has generated much of the negative criticism it has inspired and has surely blinded us to its significance for the formation of the contemporary American Jewish identity. Once we overcome our initial naive impulse to reject as art whatever makes money, a vast territory is opened for exploration as the ground for cultural history. And it is precisely the market orientation that should suggest the proper model for our exploration: the motion picture industry, also a primarily Jewish empire, as Neal Gabler has so cogently argued in his *Empire of Their Own: How the Jews Invented Hollywood* (1988). While the dynamic period of Jewish empire and image-building in Hollywood that Gabler describes ends shortly before the period that concerns us, the operational patterns of the years between 1910 and World War II are still very much with us and suggest ways of understanding the social functions of the three works we will examine here.

Gabler begins his study with a series of paradoxes that enable him to ask the questions leading to his analysis,

> The American film industry...the quintessence of what we mean by "American," was founded and for thirty years operated by Eastern European Jews who themselves seemed to be anything but the quintessence of America...Their dominance became a target for wave after wave of anti-Semites...Ducking from these assaults, the Jews became the phantoms of the film history they had created, haunting it but never really able to inhabit it...What deepened the pathos was that while Hollywood Jews were being assailed by know-nothings for conspiring against traditional American values and the power structure that maintained them, they were desperately

embracing those values and working to enter the power structure. Above all things, they wanted to be regarded as Americans, not Jews; they wanted to reinvent themselves here as men. The movie Jews were acting out what Isaiah Berlin, in a similar context, has described as an "over-intense admiration or indeed worship" for the majority, a reverence that, Berlin also noted, sometimes alternated with a latent resentment too, creating what he called a "neurotic distortion of the facts." Hollywood became both the vehicle for and the product of their distortions. (pp. 1-2)

The Jews also had a special compatibility with the industry, one that gave them certain advantages over their competitors. For one thing, having come primarily from fashion and retail, they understood public taste and were masters at gauging market swings, at merchandising, at pirating away customers and beating the competition. For another, as immigrants themselves, they had a peculiar sensitivity to the dreams and aspirations of other immigrants and working-class families, two overlapping groups that made up a significant portion of the early moviegoing audience. The Jews were their own best appraisers of entertainment. "They were the audience," a producer told me. "They were the same people. They were not too far removed from those primitive feelings and attitudes." (p. 5)

But in order to understand what may have been the chief appeal of the movies to these Jews, one must understand their hunger for assimilation and the way in which the movies could uniquely assimilate that hunger. If the Jews were proscribed from entering the real corridors of gentility and status in America, the movies offered an ingenious option. Within the studios and on the screen, the Jews could simply create a new country—an empire of their own, so to speak—one where they would not only be admitted but would govern as well. They would fabricate themselves in the image of prosperous Americans. It would be an America where fathers were strong., families stable, people attractive, resilient, resourceful, and decent. This was their America, and its invention may be their most enduring legacy. (pp. 5-6)

Though the American Jewish community has changed markedly between the pioneering days of the movie industry and the post-World War II period we are considering, the social and psychological dynamics of the Zukors, the Foxes, the Mayers, and the Warners can serve as a convenient guide to our understanding of those writers who were also seeking to capture a mass, perhaps mostly Jewish, market in the entertainment industry. We should not forget, for instance, that American writers appealing to a large audience must have in mind the possibility of selling their product to Hollywood, where large royalties are available. Precisely because of this market orientation, we can apply reception theory and ask such questions as: For what kind of audience was the author writing? What did he assume about the Jewish cultural background of the audience? What shared values could he take for granted? Was his goal primarily entertainment, or did he have a specific message to convey? What did the audience find appealing in the work: the characters? the plot? some notions about Judaism?

A second set of questions is: Did the work become a cultural event that elicited discussion and perhaps action? Did it modify the reader's notions about a certain aspect of contemporary Jewish life? Did it seek to confirm or subvert certain "Jewish values" held by the audience? Often, we shall discover, these two sets of questions overlap.

The works we have chosen to explore cover a wide range of Jewish concerns: options of behavior in the open society (*Marjorie Morningstar*); the ideals embodied in the creation of a sovereign Jewish state (*Exodus*) and its Holocaust background; nostalgia for the shtetl (*Fiddler on the Roof*). Our study of these particular works should therefore yield interesting information concerning their contribution to the formation of Jewish identity in America over the last few decades.

EXODUS

Leon Uris's *Exodus*, both as book (1958) and as film (1960), clearly ranks as the archetype of the genre under consideration. Its impact on the American Jewish attitude toward Israel since its publication is incalculable. Initially, it projected an image of a country an American Jew might care to visit as a tourist, inspiring tens of thousands to search in the real streets and kibbutzim of Israel for the selfless, dedicated, loyal, intelligent, attractive Ari Ben Canaan of their fantasies. More significantly, it molded and dominated the shared image of Israel that persisted from 1958 probably until the Yom Kippur War in 1973. (It was used in Russian translation, as a consciousness-raising device in the 1960s and 1970s.) As such, it is certainly a major document in modern Jewish history and, once properly treated, can tell us much about the audience which embraced it and was, in turn, shaped by it.

The book and the film gave the American Jew of the period the identity-confirming epic that gave coherence to the turbulent world of the 1950s and 1960s. It presented the emergence of the State of Israel as a saga of drama and success, and rooted it in modern Jewish history, especially in the Holocaust. It thus gave meaning to the Holocaust and allowed for its assimilation in the course of events. Though the story was richly plotted with its tense, exciting moments, and peopled with a varied cast, the message was unambiguous and simple: the line of historical development was envisioned as inevitable and just. Jewish history was portrayed in bold colors as a smashing success, and there is nothing so validating to an American as a sense of being on the winning team. The American Jew, furthermore, discovered in the 1950s that he was a member of' one of the three accepted American religious denominations in Eisenhower's America and could take great pride in his allegiance to this winning team of attractive, air-brushed Hollywood figures, while feeling not the slightest threat to his American loyalties. *Exodus* was conceived as an American epic, a Western set in the Middle East with John Wayne played by Ari Ben Canaan and the bad Indians cast as Arabs, the duplicitous "city folk" as the English led by Bruce Sutherland, a closet Jew.

In commenting on his novel, Leon Uris remarked that "all the cliché Jewish characters were left on the cutting room floor." The cliché characters he referred to were obviously the conflicted individuals, the knights of alienation of Bellow and Malamud, let alone Kafka, who made the Jewish literary hero paradigmatic of the hero of modern fiction. What this has actually given us is a new set of cliché characters, all more acceptable to the middle-brow Jewish audience he was aiming to please. The Ben Canaan family, formerly the Rabinsky family, shook off its exilic characteristics when it settled on the soil of pre-Israel Palestine just as the David Levinskys rid themselves of their "green" East European notions and habits when they settled into their American settings. They are attractive precisely because they are unlike the stereotype of the East European Jew prevalent in the mind of the Jewish audience. Like the children of David Levinsky, Ari and Jordana Ben Canaan maintain, through all adversity, a healthy view of the world and their place in it, unclouded by doubts and ambiguities. They and the kibbutz society they embody and energize comprise a new world that can heal the scars of such survivors as Karen Clement or Dov Landau or even the American Gentile nurse, Kitty Fremont. The latter, the stereotypical shiksa, the fantasy of American Jewish males, learns to understand and even love these determined Jews who make bold to tame the wild west of Mandatory Palestine and build in it a homeland, even a state of their own. *Exodus* thus conforms to the great American tradition of novels of the frontier.

Uris correctly gauged the needs of his intended audience, their desire for an uplifting epic which would validate their sense of themselves as American Jews, predominantly middle-class, appreciative of a fictional world which would allow them to be proud spectators, enthusiastic tourists, but never demand anything of them nor subvert their sense of well-being as Jews who had made it in America. On the other hand, the book coalesced and reinforced the often disparate tendencies that were turning Israel into the "civil religion" of significant portion of American Jews and in the process granting to Israel the moral and political hegemony over world Jewry. Uris's book enhanced those aspects of philanthropy and tourism which characterized American Zionism in the 1950s and 1960s; it probably prepared the way for the next phase, intense political lobbying, which developed in the 1970s.

MARJORIE MORNINGSTAR

In turning from *Exodus* to *Marjorie Morningstar,* we move not only from one writer (Leon Uris) to another (Herman Wouk), but to a significant change in focus. The scope of *Exodus* was epic and distanced. It concentrated on the struggle for the establishment of the State of Israel and, though written for an American, predominantly Jewish, audience, the action and characters never directly involved American Jews. Marjorie Morningstar, her family and friends, her lover, Noel Airman, and the man she finally marries, Milton Schwartz, are emblematically American Jews. Their attitudes and aspirations are those of American Jews of the first post-World War II generation; the book is suffused with the dim realization that these Jews are a new, more self-assured breed, the children or grandchildren of David Levinsky. Poverty and the neighborhoods of initial immigrant settlement are behind them. Their exodus is not from the Egyptian bondage to the Promised Land, or even from the Lower East Side to the Upper West Side, but from Manhattan to Mamaroneck.

This journey, despite its interruptions and divagations, is presented approvingly, even triumphantly, a major cultural statement which differs markedly from the critique of Philip Roth's *Goodbye, Columbus*, published only five years later (1960). The existential dilemma is that of American Jewry; the Jewish dramas being played out in Europe or Palestine are essentially irrelevant to the life of the heroine, Marjorie Morningstar, whose life in the novel spans the crucial years 1933-1954. The question is not how one builds a sovereign state or recovers from the trauma of the Holocaust (the paucity of reference to events outside of America is striking) but rather how one lives as a Jew in an open, affluent society. The process of redefinition, furthermore, is charged with none of the anguish so characteristic of Hebrew or Yiddish fiction of earlier generations; Marjorie Morningstar never feels that in some sense she, too, once fled the Egyptian bondage and stood at Sinai.

As a fictional type, Marjorie relates not to Anne Frank or Hannah Senesh or Golda Meir, but to Emma Bovary and her many literary sisters, daughters of the middle class who fantasize in their adolescence— sometimes a very prolonged adolescence—about a more intriguing world than that of their parents or husbands. And just as Emma attempts to find her escape from the humdrum life of provincial France through the reading of romantic novels, Marjorie aspires to the life of the Broadway stage and the Hollywood screen. Her Hollywood fantasies attract her to Noel Airman, a scriptwriter, more a mediocre fabricator of marketable fantasies than the anguished artist who represents a stance critical of the middle-class culture that Marjorie imagines she yearns to flee. Noel is conventionally, predictably bohemian, as are his sojourn in Paris and his seduction of Marjorie. Their stereotypical bohemianism and romance attest to the domestication of the traditional novelistic topoi within the American Jewish novel. Wouk, nonetheless, cannot let himself go all the way, and hence his success with his suburban Jewish audience. Marjorie initially denies her social background, dreams dangerous dreams, and eats forbidden foods, but finally returns to her people, not on Central Park West, but in its postwar transmogrification, the New York suburb with all its typical assumptions and appurtenances. Marjorie, we should remember, entered the American Jewish consciousness before the emergence of the feminist movement and the figure of the JAP. While we cannot expect her to strive for feminist ideals, we can entertain the possibility that she contributed significantly to the popular and usually invidious image of the JAP.

Unlike Philip Roth, whose polemics with representatives of the American Jewish establishment are well documented, Wouk affirms the practices and values of American Jewish life as he found them in the 1950s. Intrigued by the emergence of a new, self-assured Jewish community in the post-World War II era, he chronicles its rituals and public festivities, thus legitimizing them as a normative aspect of Jewish life. While he does not hide the sumptuary excesses of Jewish weddings and bar mitzvahs (they look worse in the film than in the book) he envelops them in a warm tegument of family togetherness which seems to absorb and atone for all vulgarity. The Hollywoodish names taken by the two principals in their assimilatory process (Morningstar was Morgenstern, Noel Airman was Saul Ehrman) and the professions they choose to catapult them above and beyond their class, both aspects of the entertainment industry, suggest that Neal Gabler's argument regarding the Jews who "invented Hollywood" applies here too. The ideal Jew portrayed in

Marjorie Morningstar is not the rootless intellectual, the stranger within the gates, but the happy citizen at home in Mamaroneck, the Jew living the American dream that he himself invented.

FIDDLER ON THE ROOF

Herman Wouk has his heroine dream of a career on Broadway and in Hollywood, but he could not have imagined her aspiring to star in a musical nostalgically celebrating the life of the shtetl as imagined in *Fiddler on the Roof*. That was not part of her American dream. Ironically, the three authors who collaborated in the composition of *Fiddler* (Joseph Stein: book; Jerry Bock: music; and Sheldon Harnick: lyrics) did conceive of such a musical less than a decade after the publication of *Marjorie Morningstar*, and succeeded in producing not only a Broadway hit but a movie, a record album, and even new materials for Jewish weddings, bar mitzvahs, summer camps, and religious schools. The shtetl and "the world of Sholom Aleichem" as rendered in *Fiddler* is an integral part of the Jewish cultural repertoire in America (and elsewhere), understood by Jews and non-Jews as something authentically Jewish.

Its Jewish "authenticity" is precisely what intrigues us here, since *Fiddler* is obviously a collaborative, commercial production designed to please an audience with beguiling tunes and colorful scenery all carefully calculated to conjure up before an audience that had never seen a shtetl, the image of a shtetl that never existed. The peculiar nexus between vicarious experience and the sense of authenticity commands our attention. To argue that *Fiddler* appealed to Jews merely because of its catchy tunes and modish ethnicity seems to fail to assess the needs and nature of the intended audience. The stated intentions of the playwright, however, can shed some light on the intriguing questions about the audience.

In his introduction to the musical (*Best Plays of 1964–65*, pp. 118 ff.) Joseph Stein offers the standard assertion "that the problem of adaptation was to remain true to the spirit, the feeling of Sholom Aleichem and transmute it for a contemporary audience." The details of this adaptation bear close scrutiny.

> First, the play required the establishment of an overall focus and point of view. Hidden within the stories was the sense of a breakdown of the traditional cultural forms and beliefs of "the shtetl" the village community, under the buffeting of social change and hostile forces, finally leading to

disintegration of that society. We decided to make the crumbling of tradition, illustrated by the daughters' love stories and other developments, the
theme of our play.

Then a fresh story needed to be created, to hold the isolated tales
together. This became the saga of the community within which Tevye and
his family functions: a tightly-knit, rigidly-structured community, surrounded
and constantly under attack, finally breaking up and scattering to different
parts of the globe. Historically, of course, this was accurate. This was the
period of great Russian-Jewish immigration to America...

Tevye himself had to be changed somewhat to make him more effective
in our play. Sholom Aleichem's Tevye, richly amusing and colorful, was a
more humble, more passive character than he is in our play; he was typical
of his community, but certainly not its spokesman. To make him the moving force in our story, it was necessary to give him more strength, while
keeping the shadings of his character intact.

And to give the story a meaning for our times, we brought to the foreground an element implicit in the Tevye tales...the hostility, the violence,
the injustice practiced by a ruling majority against a weak minority. We
wanted in this to point up the internal strength, the dignity, the humor of
that people and, like minorities today, their unique talent for survival.
(p. 119)

The amalgam of cultural rejection and appropriation is fascinating.
We American Jews, we are told, are clearly different from the shtetl
Jews from whom we are descended, since our parents, or even our
grandparents, came to this secure land from that land of "hostility, violence, and injustice." Those people, that Tevye and his daughters, were
a bit peculiar, but they were warm people, sang beautiful tunes, and
danced with genuine joy. Tevye, in fact, is somewhat problematic as a
character: he was a bit too passive, "typical of his community, but certainly not its spokesman. To make him the moving force in our story, it
was necessary to give him more strength." The stereotypical shtetl Jew
we imagine we know was fine in his place and time, but he could never
keep an American musical moving. We American Jews do have this
vitality and initiative, since, after all, we are really no longer a weak
minority "like minorities today," but part of the majority, even quintessential of the majority. We have made it here because of "the internal
strength, the dignity, the humor of that people, and...their unique talent for survival."

The symbol of the musical is, of course, "the fiddler on the roof"
taken from Chagall's paintings, which, it is assumed, is a recognizable
Jewish icon. The surrealistic image of the fiddler hovering above the
straw roof of a shtetl home had appeared as the artist's wry portrait of

himself as shtetl fiddler in Chagall's paintings early in the century, but by the 1960s it was less a charged artistic image than a logo for "the world of Sholom Aleichem." In his first speech addressed to the audience, Tèvye comments on this familiar emblem:

> A fiddler on the roof. Sounds crazy, no? But in our little village of Anatevka, you might say that every one of us is a fiddler on the roof, trying to scratch out a pleasant, simple tune without breaking his neck. It isn't easy. You may ask why do we stay up here if it's so dangerous? We stay because Anatevka is our home. And how do we keep our balance? That I can tell you in a word—tradition!

In one word, we have the secret of Jewish existence throughout the ages: "tradition," sung by the villagers as they enter, filling the stage with their colorful community. As the musical unfolds, we learn that "tradition" is the all-embracing but totally undifferentiated notion for the way all Jews lived "there" as opposed to "here." Because of tradition, "everyone knows who he is and what God expects him to do." We are never really told what this magical practice is, what gives it authority or coherence; we are assured, nevertheless, that it certainly worked "there," and that we "here," in America, obviously don't have it. When you have tradition or "keep the traditions" you are authentic, surely worthy of admiration, if not emulation. And yet, in no way is it suggested that tradition is something we American Jews might care to adopt outside the hall of the musical, or those musical-like occasions of our communal lives like weddings or synagogue socials. *Fiddler on the Roof* thus allows us to have our authenticity and enjoy it vicariously by keeping the areas scrupulously compartmentalized. Again, we are invited to be comfortable, appreciative spectators of a life-style we do not live. Our present mode of existence as middle-class citizens of America is never challenged, but is, rather, fully validated.

Some hundred and fifty years ago, the early proponents of Wissenschaft des Judentums, the first modern scholars of Judaism, realized that the belief in the Sinaitic imperatives which gave both legitimacy and coherence to Jewish life was no longer effective for many Jews confronted with Enlightenment ideals. True to their times, they sought to substitute an awareness of Jewish history, historical self-consciousness, for the eroding faith. Their meticulous research was designed to give the Jews a history like the history the Gentiles had, with personalities, periods, and movements. In brief, they tried to create for the mostly German speaking Jews of the nineteenth century the basis for a new identity, one consonant with "the world as they found it." Whether or not they succeeded or how many people they actually reached are questions still debated by historians.

It might at first seem rash to compare the highly serious efforts of Zunz or Graetz with the seemingly trivial, market-oriented works of Wouk or Uris. But once we ask the basic question, "What shapes the identity (in the sense of self-image) of a Jew in the post-Enlightenment period?", we are compelled to treat *Exodus, Marjorie Morningstar,* and *Fiddler on the Roof*—and dozens of other works of this genre—with the same scholarly seriousness as a truly epic work like Graetz's *History of the Jews,* which reached a popular audience both in its German original and in its translations. Any doubts we might entertain about the significance of these works, particularly in their film versions, should be readily dispelled by our realization of the image-making power of these mass media, as described by Neal Gabler. And while my initial analysis of these works has yielded a picture of American Jewry that is far from flattering. I would argue that the existence and importance of this fictional genre is indisputable.

Printed in the United States
20150LVS00001BA/25-30